Metta Victoria Fuller Victor

The Unionist's Daughter

A Tale of the Rebellion in Tennessee

Metta Victoria Fuller Victor

The Unionist's Daughter
A Tale of the Rebellion in Tennessee

ISBN/EAN: 9783337294571

Printed in Europe, USA, Canada, Australia, Japan

Cover: Foto ©Thomas Meinert / pixelio.de

More available books at **www.hansebooks.com**

THE

UNIONIST'S DAUGHTER:

A TALE OF THE

REBELLION IN TENNESSEE.

BY MRS. M. V. VICTOR,

AUTHOR OF "MAUM GUINEA," "ALICE WILDE," ETC.

BEADLE AND COMPANY,
NEW YORK: 141 WILLIAM STREET.
LONDON: 44 PATERNOSTER ROW.

PRELIMINARY NOTE BY THE AUTHOR.

In the production of the "Unionist's Daughter" slight liberties have been taken with the chronology of events as they actually occurred in Tennessee. Thus, the story assumes the violence toward Unionists to have commenced in the vicinity of Nashville, at a date prior to, and immediately succeeding the Presidential election, in November, 1860 ; whereas the reign of terror really was not inaugurated until after the sale of the State to the Southern Confederacy, May 7th, 1861. The leading incidents of our story are literally "founded upon fact." The violence and suffering which followed rapidly upon the adoption of the "League," and the forced secession of the State, offer material for the novelist as well as for the historian. The world certainly never has witnessed a more infamous use of authority than that which consigned free and loyal Tennessee to the keeping and cruel mercies of the disunionists. Against this infamous *sale* of their liberties and happiness, the Unionists struggled with a patient devotion worthy of remembrance. Suffering, sacrifice, humiliation, death rapidly followed upon their paths ; but a few noble spirits

braved " Confederate " muskets, scorned " Confederate "
dungeons, walked to " Confederate " gallows ; and enough
of them struggled through the weary months up to the
entrance of Buell's forces into Nashville to form the nucleus
of a reorganization of the State under the banners of the
Union.   These few spirits we commemorate ; and if, in the
reading of our story the reader obtains an insight into the
shocking social, as well as political disasters which followed
in the train of treason in Tennessee we shall have accomplished the leading *purpose* of our labors.

M. V. V.

THE

UNIONIST'S DAUGHTER.

CHAPTER I.

THE MIDNIGHT FLIGHT.

" FATHER is late," mused Eleanor Beaufort, as she paced the moonlit piazza; " I hear the village bell striking midnight;" and she paused to listen to the far-away chime, turning her young face so that the moon shone fully upon it, transfusing it with light, and giving it an ethereal loveliness surpassing the sweetness of its day bloom. She did not seem troubled by the lateness of the hour; the happy expression of careless youth was upon her features, and a smile, which some pleasant thought sent rippling up from the depths of her heart, played over them, as she resumed her walk, drawing a crimson scarf a little closer about her shoulders—for the autumn night was cool, not cold—her white garments fluttering about her girlish form.

" The night is too pleasant to be wasted in sleep," and she looked near and afar over a landscape as beautiful as eye could desire—a distant range of low mountains lying like a faint cloud against the horizon ; a valley threaded by a broad belt of silver river ; the steeples of the village visible through groups of trees; magnificent plantations all around ; her own father's farm ; close at hand, the velvet lawn and the clusters of scarlet flowers which trellised the piazza, breaking into splendor on the brilliant atmosphere which fairly flooded the earth with radiance.

The silence was so profound that Eleanor distinctly heard the fall of footsteps on the grass, coming from the orchard, over the lawn and up to the house. Supposing the servants to be all in their quarters—Jim, who took charge of the front door-key, being at that moment snoring on the straw-matting in the hall—she stopped walking, to observe the intruder.

"Is that you, Pomp?" she asked, as a stalwart negro stepped out from under the shadow of a maple, and advanced into the light. The moon made a striking figure of him as he stood there in his striped cotton shirt and trowsers, his straw hat in his hand, his skin black as ebony, his features uncouth and impassive, his great eyes only burning with an inward fire as he raised them respectfully to his mistress. "Why are you out at this hour?"

"Woll, massa tuk me to de village wid him; but he said I need'n stay as de meetin' would keep late. Dar's been very 'citing times to-day—it's 'lection, you know. I hung 'round wherever I could, a kind o' keepin' my eye on massa. I wish he'd come home!"

"Why?" asked the young lady, her curiosity aroused by the slave's manner, but smiling that joyous smile still.

"Woll, I dunno. Only dar's been high times and high words. Massa would'n vote as dey liked—so dey would'n lef him vote at all. Massa's too sperited to stand dat—so dey're talking and argufying ever sence."

"Well done, Pomp; you're quite a politician," laughed the young mistress. "I shall wait till papa comes, and ask him what it all means."

"It means more'n you 'spect," muttered the negro, as he walked down to the gate and stood there. Pomp was a favorite slave with his master, chosen for all those services which required faithfulness or sagacity;—and something of a marvel both for his great physical strength and for having more sense and honesty than most of his class. Although his mental capacity made him valuable, he was not used as a house-servant, his uncouth appearance and superfluous strength unfitting him for such a position ; he was overseer of the sixty or seventy out-door hands.

Presently the approach of a couple of horsemen resounded through the stillness, drawing rapidly nearer, until they paused at the gate.

" Sinclair is with papa," murmured Eleanor, and the scarlet creepers flowing about her were scarcely redder than her cheeks, when the two gentlemen reached the piazza.

" Eleanor," said Mr. Beaufort, scarcely waiting for his companion to greet his daughter, going up to her, and taking her hands in his, " I must leave you—suddenly—this night !"

" Leave me !"

" Yes, my dear child. My life is threatened ; and by those who will not scruple to carry out their purposes."

" What is the meaning of this, father ?"

" It seems that in this country of boasted freedom I am persecuted for political opinion. We have talked of these matters before this, my child. You know my position. But I never thought it would come to violence—I never thought I should hear such plans exposed as I have been asked to give my support, this day. My God, what treason and intrigue ! Nay, Sinclair, I say it, and you must not dispute it. I have no time to tell you all, Eleanor. Sinclair will explain to you more at length, how necessary it is for me to absent myself till this storm blows over. It will blow over—it must ! In the mean time, I leave all in your hands. Pompey is faithful as the day ; he will attend to all the interests of the plantation as if I were at home. To you I leave the charge of the house, my books and papers, and all those matters in which I have already had your assistance. I am sorry to leave you alone, my child ; but I know that you are equal to the emergency.   You are a girl after your father's own heart.   Shed no tears.   You know I am a man to suffer for principle."

"I know it, dear father, and I honor you for it—but it is so sudden—so strange ! I can not—" a sudden sob broke up her words.

"Here, Sinclair, comfort the little one, while I go to my safe for some papers and money.   I must make quick time."

"Where is he going ?" she only thought to ask, when her father had disappeared within the house.

"He wishes to reach Nashville in time to take the early boat ; he will affect to be on a tour of business or pleasure. It is absolutely necessary for him to keep away at present. Our people here have grown furious and unreasonable under long oppression."

"*Our people !*" echoed Eleanor, in sadness and reproach.

"Yes, our people—ridden down, deprived of their rights—I do not hesitate to say that I belong to them fully, heart and soul," and the young man's dark face kindled. "I know your father is wrong, Eleanor—madly, miserably wrong in sticking to an old idea.   But I respect him—and I love you."

The maiden's eyes sunk for a moment under his passionate glance, and again the blush flitted over her tearful face ; the next instant she raised them, saying in a voice as earnest as his own :

"I am like my father—I have never been tried, but *I believe* would die for a principle, if it came to such straits.   Sinclair, my father is *not* wrong.   I love God and the right—most of all earthly things, I love my father.   You must not speak so of him again," and the moon lighted up a face whose lofty expression made youth and beauty strangely powerful.

"And do you not love me ?" he cried, as if that avowal of affection for her parent had given him a selfish pang.

"I answered you that question last week," she replied, raising her eyes with a sweet, serious smile.

"You did—you did, darling Ella," catching her hand and kissing it. "I meant no disrespect to your father. If I had not honored and revered him, despite of our political differences, I should not now be here, aiding him in his escape. I came, Ella, to defend him with my life if necessary, (for your sake,) and to give you what poor comfort I could in the 'assurance that I should work for his benefit in his absence, and keep an eye on the safety and happiness of the one dearest, dearest to me in the world. Yes, *I* will not except *my* father," and he laughed lightly to cover the earnestness of the words.

"Massa Beaufort, dar's hufs of more'n one hoss a-comin," called out Pompey, in an anxious voice. "Dey're comin' from de village. Hurry, massa, *do !*"

"There's a crowd coming this way, Pomp says," echoed Sinclair Le Vert, as Mr. Beaufort came out, buttoning an overcoat about him, and carrying a small valise.

"I shall have to pass through the village to get to Nashville," said he.

"Dey's comin' mighty clus'," Pomp almost groaned.

"Bring in the horses, both of them, quick, to the back of the house," ordered Sinclair. "Mr. Beaufort, you must ride through the lane, take the bridle-path across the plantation, and come out on the road after they have passed. It's probably only a party going home; but if they stop here, I shall be on hand to see that your daughter is not alarmed. Goodby. May we see you back within a fortnight."

Mr. Beaufort released the arms clinging to his neck : "Be brave, Eleanor, all will be right"—the next moment he was riding along the lane, and had barely got into the shadow of the orchard, when the rapid approach of a mounted party became visible along the road. Pomp had concealed their visitor's

horse in the rear of the house; the young couple retired
hastily into the hall, turning the key, and sat down on a cane
settle near at hand—Jim, unawakened by all which had passed,
still snoring on the floor at their feet. A narrow streak of
light from the moon fell across them, showing the lover the
pale face of his betrothed; there were no lights burning, and
when the crowd thundered up to the gate, and drew rein, the
mansion seemed wrapped in the repose proper to that late
hour of the night. Those within could easily distinguish the
forms of some twenty-five or thirty persons; Eleanor observ-
ing, with a pang of wounded pride, that some of them were
neighbors who had been friends—it was not the rabble of the
town, but her associates and equals who had thus set their
faces against her father.

Three groans were given with a will; and then the lovely
quiet of that radiant night was disturbed by shouts and cries
of anger and derision.

"Come out, you —— old abolitionist! we want to see if some
of your own trees won't do to hang you on!"

"Why don't you come out? Daren't you face men of hon-
or?"—sneeringly.

"The abolitionists are all cowards, oho!"

"Why do they call my father an abolitionist? They know,
and you know, Sinclair, that there is no truth in the assertion.
I will go out and shame them by *my* presence. I will tell
them that *I* am not afraid, and that my father, if he were
here, would not submit to their words."

"You must do nothing of the kind, my Ella. Those men
are drunk with excitement and rage as well as liquor. They
call your father an abolitionist because it is the hatefulest term
they can conjure up—they know he is not one. They are
angry with him, because he does not seem to take a proper
interest in the welfare of his own State and of Southern

principles. There were schemes advanced in secret caucus to-
day in which every Southerner *ought* to take a vital part—glorious, promising schemes, Eleanor, which made *my* heart beat
faster with exultation. But your father opposed them, warmly,
bitterly. He did not even hesitate to call some of our most
honored leaders traitors and selfish intriguers. If he had not
been a Southerner born, a life-long friend and neighbor, he
would have been shot on the spot. He must use more caution. Dear Ella, I beg of you to use *your* influence, when he
returns, to persuade him to keep silent, at least, since he
refuses his country his aid in her hour of need."

In the mean time the clamor at the gate had increased.
Pompey came round to the front of the house, rubbing his
eyes and staring at the crowd as if just awoke.

"Hallo, boy, where's your master?"

"Massa not come home yit. Leastwise his hoss hain't, for
I ain't put him in de stable yit. He's in town to polickital
meetin', gemmen. Didn' you see 'um?"

"Oh, yes, we saw him. We liked his sentiments so much
we thought we'd come out and give him a serenade," cried
one, with an ironical laugh.

"Sorry massa not got back, gemmen. You'se berry perlite."

"Yes, we are that. S'pose your master wouldn't object to
a dance on the tight rope to our music—ha?"

"Woll, I dunno ef massa dances. You're berry kind,
gemman."

"Just give him our compliments, boy, and tell him we'll
call again, *soon*—perhaps to-morrow. Come, friends, we may
meet him on our way back to the village, if he hain't returned
yet. Come, give him a parting cheer, and we'll back."

Three more hideous groans profaned the night; the party
turned and galloped away; hardly had Eleanor recovered a

little breath and color, before she heard a loud shout, followed by many more, and the discharge of revolvers.

" They have discovered my father !" she cried.

" I fear they have. Do not be frightened, Ella. Bolt the door after me, sit here, and I will return and put you out of suspense as quickly as possible."

He went out, mounted his horse, and galloped after the mob.

For a half-hour, which seemed to her like a half-day, Eleanor Beaufort paced the hall, pausing to listen to every sound ; then she heard again the approach of horses, and a party of about half the former number passed the gate on their way home. Among these she detected her lover ; he allowed his horse to fall behind the others, waved his handkerchief an in- stant, and galloped on with the rest.

She understood that it was not proper for him to stop at that time ; but she suffered none the less keenly the anguish of suspense. It seemed to her that the air of the house would stifle her. She unclosed the door and stepped out ; the moon had set, a faint flush began to tinge the horizon ; some one was sitting on the piazza steps. It was Pompey.

" Massa got cl'ar. I've been way down de road and I'm suah he got 'way. I listened in de corner of de fence and heerd de men say so, w'en dey was ridin' by."

" Oh, Pompey, I hope you heard true."

" Woll, I did, suah. Nebber see such doins, missus, neb- ber ! T'ink dey's callin' massa Beaufort an abolishioner ! a poor, mean abolishioner ! when eberybody knows he's one de richest, bestus old families in de State. Gorry, t'ings is gwine cur'us 'bout here."

" It's very ridiculous, isn't it, Pompey," remarked Miss Beaufort, and for the life of her, she couldn't keep back one of those girlish smiles of hers at the idea of the slave's insulted dignity in having his master called an abolitionist. Just then the gate swung open, and Sinclair Le Vert came up the walk.

"Your father is safe, Eleanor. They discovered him as he emerged into the road some distance ahead of them, and gave chase, even firing their revolvers at him; but his good animal made extra time and soon left them in the lurch. I rode up and joined them, pretending to be ignorant of what was going on; and so, when they separated, I was obliged to keep with those going my way until we reached my own home, when I only waited for the others to get out of sight before I hastened back to tell you. They're very bitter against your father. I suppose I must leave you, darling, much as I dislike to tear myself from you. Go to your bed, and get a little sleep. Try and sleep as sweetly as if this ugly occurrence had been only a passing dream. I will see you often, and keep you advised of all that happens."

Their hands lingered in a parting clasp.

"Tell no one the true reason of your master's absence," said Miss Beaufort to Pompey, as the gate closed on Sinclair, "except that business called him suddenly away."

"Trus' me for dat," responded the negro. "I'se know bettah dan Massa hisself, what's good for him. I only wish dat young Massa Le Vert was half so kerful as dis poor niggah—or half as true to missus," he muttered, to himself.

Wearily Eleanor went up the stairs which she had descended the previous evening with so light a bound. The crimson flowers she had twisted in her black hair were withered; she shivered with cold and fatigue as she pulled them out and threw them away in the ghostly light of the coming dawn.

A blight seemed suddenly to have fallen over the old homestead—it was so lonely with no one but herself and the servants. It was so strange to have the neighbors seeking her father's life. She could not realize the events of the last few hours, and dropping to sleep, with the groans of the midnight mob in her ears, she slept the carelessness of her almost childish girlhood away forever.

CHAPTER II.

THE LOVERS.

It was late in the forenoon, when Eleanor, having drank the coffee brought to the room by her maid, was putting the last graceful touch to her simple toilet. She was too young and too beautiful to allow the care which oppressed her to overcome all regard for appearances. Her lover might call at any hour; as she thought this, her heart beat faster, she broke off a half-blown rose from a cluster blooming in the window, while the dark, proud eyes which looked back at hers, out of the mirror, softened from their troubled expression into a smile.

"Miss Ellen, Massa Le Vert sends his complemen's, and would like to see you a few minutes in de parler, please," said her maid Caroline, thrusting her head in at the door. "Not *young* Massa Le Vert, not by no means—so you needn't be a wasting of dem pinks in yer cheeks, missus."

"Hush, Caroline, you talk too freely," said the young lady, trying to subdue the warm blushes which she was too conscious had rushed to her face. Her disappointment aided her in this, for she had really, as her sharp-eyed maid detected, supposed it to be Sinclair.

"Oh! now, missus, you don't s'pose I've 'tended you from

a baby, and not know wat's goin' on. I see'd it de berry
mornin' after you was 'gaged. Go 'long, honey, you'se lookin'
sweetly. Massa Le Vert oughter be proud of his new
daughter."

Despite this comforting assurance, Eleanor went down the
stairs slowly; there was something of maidenly diffidence in
meeting the father of her affianced for the first time since
the engagement; and the events of the preceding night lay
with a new and oppressive weight upon her mind.

As she entered the parlor, she recovered all the rare dignity in which she resembled her father, for she became immediately aware of a slight coldness in the manner of her guest,
which the circumstances made painful. There was an excess
of courtesy, which betrayed the want of real feeling.

"I came over to get you to use your influence with your
father, to persuade him from the course he is taking. I tell
you, as a friend, Miss Beaufort, that it will ruin him—politically, financially, socially, every way! He is wrong, and
standing out against the interests of his own rank. As soon
as you learn his address, I beg of you to write to him; ask
him to come back, and prove his fidelity to our cause, by
giving it the support he now refuses. I can not bear to see
an old neighbor, an honored associate, a personal friend,
making the fatal mistake he is making."

"I do not understand this sudden rise of popular fury
against my father," replied Eleanor. "I can hardly attempt
to persuade him out of it, until I know what wrong he has
committed. He is known to be a consistent and conscientious
slaveholder; he is a Southerner by birth and feeling; his
interests are all here; he loves his country. Why is he
branded as an abolitionist, assaulted by his own neighbors in
the disgraceful manner of last night?" cheek and eye kindling as she asked the question.

"I will tell you, my dear young lady," answered the
gentleman, lowering his voice to tones of persuasiveness,
"there are new questions involved in the present state of affairs.
It is altogether likely that the North has elected an abolition
President. If this be so, the South, to her eternal glory be
it said, has resolved to throw off the galling, the disgraceful
yoke; she will own no sisterhood to the craven North. She
will sever herself at once from the United States, and asserting a supremacy to which she is entitled, will form a new
and powerful Confederacy. Steps are already taken—the
country we despise has been made to help us. We have
weapons from their arsenals, money from their mints, officers
from their service. All is prepared. But of course this
splendid empire cannot be founded without cost. There
may be a bloody struggle; though it is not likely that the
hirelings of the North will do much fighting. Be that as it
may, we must be ready for emergencies. Our hands, hearts
and means should be freely given. All true Southern men
feel it. But strangely enough, a few stand out for the old
Union. They are willing to exist in the old oppressive way,
instead of having their ambition fired by the magnificent
promise of a Southern empire. Prominent among these is
your father. We feel that his wealth and social standing
give him an influence which ought, at this moment of trial,
to be thrown on our side. There are too many, still, who
tremble at the chance of asserting our independence. Each
must be put down. They *will not be permitted* to peril our
cause at such a time. If they do not give willingly of their
means, they will be compelled. Ruin awaits those false to the
South at this critical moment. Glory will cover those who are
first and foremost in achieving her empire. There is no
telling what brilliant place your beauty and position may
achieve for *you* in those elegant courts which *are to be.* Write

to your father, my dear Miss Beaufort, and place these things in their proper light. You have great influence with him."

Eleanor arose to her feet.

"If I have influence with my father, rest assured I shall never use it for the purpose you propose. I am not surprised, now that I know the facts, that he refused, even at the peril of his life, to turn traitor to his country. It is like my father. The Beauforts of revolutionary days were true as steel, though Tories would have tempted them, with brilliant promises, to play false to a seemingly failing cause. I do not approve of your scheme, Monsieur Le Vert. Even my girlish judgment condemns it. It will never succeed; and I love my own dear native South too well to see her covered with misery. Our kin of the North have done us no injury that we should steal weapons from their generous hands to plunge into their own hearts. It is dastardly!"

"Beware!" said the visitor, also rising, "the time is coming, if it has not already come, when it will be dangerous even for a woman to insult us with such words. I hope soon to hear of a change of sentiment on your part, Miss Beaufort; for, however much I should otherwise regret it, it would be impossible for me to allow any connection of my family with that of one branded with the disgrace which will befall yours. In the mean time, think better of it. You must see that *all your interests* point to a friendly alliance with the new Confederacy."

All the pride of all the Beauforts stilled the throbbing pulse of Eleanor, as she bowed slightly in return for the polished and smiling adieus of Mr. Le Vert. He could not but admire her air of queenly coldness, however much he hated the cause of it, and he said to himself, as he mounted his horse and rode off:

"She's a splendid girl, by Juno! I don't wonder Sinclair

is infatuated with her.   If we had her spirit and bravery
active on our side, it would be capital.   I'm afraid I was a
little too severe this morning.   Severity won't do with people
of her stamp—she resented it.   But she made me angry with
her impertinence.   I'll forgive her, and instruct Sinclair to
try more persuasive means for her conversion."

In the mean time, Eleanor's burst of pride ended in a burst
of tears, as feminine passion is wont to do.   While her cheeks
burned at the recollection of her visitor's parting threat,
resentment alone could not quiet the thrill of pain which
shot through her heart at the possibility, nay, the probability,
of its execution.

Wandering from room to room of the great mansion, feeling all the desolation of her situation, she pictured to herself
her wretchedness in case of a quarrel with her lover—how
soon her joyous dreams had been broken ; could she live
without him ? could she consent ever to an alliance with his
family after the taunt of the morning ? would Sinclair be
influenced by his father, by a mere political prejudice, to break
vows which she had accepted as binding ?

She passed the piano in the back parlor.   Yesterday she
was so happy ; she had played and sung the whole afternoon,
like a bird, out of excess of life and joy.   Now she sat down
to the instrument to try to forget herself; her hands wandered over the keys like melancholy echoes of her thoughts.

"Dinnah is ready an' waitin'," said Caroline, standing
quite near before she observed her.   " Is missus gwine to
starve herself done out ? she habn't eat a moufful to-day."

"I'd forgotten all about breakfast," said Eleanor, smiling
faintly.

"Lize didn' forgi' what you lub," continued Lina.

"What I love ?" queried the young girl.

"Yis, what you lub—stewed chicken and puff puddin'."

"Oh!" said Eleanor, coming down to the reality of dinner and the affection which had prepared it, "I'm much obliged to Liza for thinking of my favorite dishes."

"She t'ought mebbe you mought not be berry hungry, kase you was so lonesome; so she took 'ticklar pains."

"She is very kind," and tears sprung to the eyes of the mistress. In this time of her distress and solitude, the active, honest affection of her dependents touched her.

It remained for her to test their fidelity much more before the trials should culminate, of which this was but the beginning.

She found the dinner prepared with more than ordinary care, but the swelling in her throat, when she thought of her absent parent, promised poorly for her appetite.

"Massa's cha'r do look awful lonesome," said Jim, the waiter, as he flew about in his extra anxiety to serve his mistress. "But dar comes somebody to fill it, I bet a cookee," and surely enough, the next moment Sinclair appeared at the dining-room door, with a bouquet of such autumn flowers as still bloomed in the open air.

"My father sent you these, Miss Beaufort, and begs you to forget some hasty words which he spoke this morning. He regrets them, and wishes them blotted out of your memory."

The hopeful expression of her lover's face, which the formality enforced by the presence of the waiter could not subdue, had a cheering effect upon the young girl; she felt the full power of an apology from so courteous a gentleman as Monsieur Le Vert. Who that have been young, and lovers, and affianced, will not believe that she was delighted with learning that the messenger bearing the brilliant bouquet, had not been to dinner, or that he was equally pleased with being able to make the statement?

Mr. Beaufort's chair was immediately filled, and the chances for having justice done Liza's skill visibly appreciated.

When Jim went out for the dessert, Sinclair informed his hostess that his father had sent especially, not only to apologize sincerely to her personally, but to tell her to write to her father, so soon as she heard from him, that he was free to return at any moment, and that he, (Mr. Le Vert,) and other of his personal friends, would pledge their honor that he should remain unmolested so long as he did not openly and pointedly oppose their political party.

"Now you look like my own Ella again," continued the young man, leaning back in his chair contentedly—"the sparkle has come back to your face. Do you know what I have been thinking of? I have been thinking how charming it will be when we take dinner together every day. I could almost imagine that you were already—"

"Hush! please be still!" implored Eleanor.

"Already my own sweet, beautiful, loving *wife !*"

Jim's return prevented any more such delightfully embarrassing allusions. His twinkling eyes rolled from the master's triumphant face to the mistress's eloquent blushes, and drew their own inferences, which were duly communicated to the kitchen department in less than five minutes.

"Laws, don't think you're tellin' news," said Caroline, tossing her head disdainfully at the admiring Jim, "I'se know'd all about it long sence 'fore it happened. I could see, 'fore dat bressed chile herself did, w'at was takin' place. An' Jim, you hold your tongue. Don't you be 'traying family 'fairs 'less you're told to. If you do, I'll come home from meetin' wid you know who, the nex' chance I git."

"Pump-handles couldn' git it out of me, to nobody but you and Lize," said Jim, earnestly.

"Glad to hear you say so," responded the maid, distrustfully.

While this little side-play was going on in the kitchen, the young gentleman was sipping his coffee in the dining-room.

"Queer taste this coffee has," he remarked, after trying for some time to find it delicious. Lize can't make coffee equal to Aunt Sallie's."

"I thought it was unusually nice," said the young lady. "I'm sorry you don't like it, Sinclair. What's the matter with it?"

"I hardly know. It has a peculiar flavor. Your cook does not add cinnamon to it, does she? I prefer the pure Java."

"Why, no, the *cook* doesn't," cried the hostess, bursting into a merry laugh, "but I think, I believe I must have given you sugar from the dessert-bowl, well-seasoned with nutmeg and cinnamon for the puff pudding. If you hadn't confused me so—you see it was just when you were making such teasing allusions, and to punish you, I've half a mind not to give you another cup."

".I'd go without coffee a week to see you blush so prettily again," and for this he got a fresh cup.

And so it is quite likely when the young couple strayed back into the parlor they found it full of afternoon sunshine, and that they paid not the least attention to the "little cloud, no bigger than a man's hand," which had arisen in the heaven of their future.

•

CHAPTER III.

TURKEY DAN.

SINCE the election excitement which had aroused the fury of the neighborhood against Mr. Beaufort, many weeks had passed. Assured of the protection of his personal friends, he had returned within a fortnight after his flight, and resumed his usual occupations. Affairs within the Beaufort mansion went on with their accustomed pleasant quiet. Friends came and went; and although some who formerly visited there now stayed away, and others, in jest or earnest, warned and argued with the stout-hearted proprietor, no violent expression of public hatred had again taken place. Eleanor had avocations which caused the days to glide swiftly away; although the wedding-day had not been fixed by the lovers, she had begun some of those preparations with which girls while away the time of their betrothal—embroidering the fancies and dreams of a maiden's soul into the intricate tracery of needle-work which beguiled the hours with play-work. Marcia Le Vert, the sister of her affianced, a tall, dashing girl a year or two older than herself, came often to see her, lounging in her chamber, rubbing her teeth with cigarettes, and frequently wishing that she was situated as delightfully as her sister-to-be.

"But even if I were engaged, I don't think I should bother myself with embroidery, Ella. Why don't you let Lina do all that kind of thing? It's so stupid to sew. Heigho! I wish I knew what to do with myself. I'm tired to death. I wonder if Captain Maurice is ever coming back. He was a splendid fellow, don't you think so? Ella, gracious, I should think you'd die off, reading and sewing. *I* never do either," —and Eleanor would smile to herself; she had "the secret of a happy dream she did not care to tell"—she knew that reading and embroidery were far from being as wearisome as absolute and vacant idleness—that the hardest of all work was to do nothing, mentally and physically, as was constantly being proved by the restless, yawning, grumbling, *ennuied* Marcia. But she would hardly dare to say this to the magnificently indolent sister-in-law, whose only idea of labor was that it made a slave of a human being. So she let Marcia rub her teeth with cigarettes, while they and her complexion grew yellow together, and wonder at her freshness and animation.

During these eventful weeks a great event had transpired. South Carolina had taken the initiatory step in the direction laid out and understood by leading Southern politicians—she had seceded from the United States. The undercurrent so long stealthily drifting had come up to the surface, bearing along on its turbulent bosom the wrecks of past prosperity, drawing into the stream every thing against which its waves beat. Many who at first struggled with more or less energy, succumbed to its despotic influence—the few who braced themselves to resist it did so at deadly peril.

It is not for this brief history of the struggle of a single family to attempt a detail of those times. Tennessee had not as yet openly taken her stand; but she was ripe for revolt against constitutional authority; that is, the most of her politicians and wealthy classes were ready and eager for the proposed change. Yet in this State, more generally than in any other of those who finally seceded, was a party of the middle classes, mountaineers and small farmers, with many of the more intelligent planters, who refused to acknowledge that their State was in any way oppressed or injured by the parent Government, and who clung to the Union as children cling to a tender parent.

One day, a little past the middle of December, Marcia came over to spend the day with Eleanor.

"Jim tells me that your father has gone to the village to be gone all day. I'm glad of it, for I've got plenty of gossip. What do you think, oh, Eleanor, what do you think? Papa has promised me a Christmas ball! I'm to get the invitations out right away, for fear some one else will be before me. And oh, Eleanor, you write so much prettier than I do, and spell better, too, I wish you'd help me with the notes. They must be written, as we can't wait to send to Nashville to get them printed, and there's no one in the village can do it. Sinclair has promised to write half of them this evening, so, Ella, I'm sure you'll do the rest for me to-day. I've brought half the list. Do you know, your name and your father's aren't down on it? Papa says, positively, that unless your father changes his politics before Christmas, it'll never do to have you at the ball. But I *will* have you, I don't care what he says! Isn't it horrid, all this quarreling? And they say, like as not there'll be war. But it will be splendid to have a Southern Capital and President, and all that. Of course, no person of spirit, no Southern gentleman, wants to be ruled by a Northern boor. They do say Lincoln has split wood with his own hands; *mon ami*, just think what his wife must be!"

The languid belle threw herself upon the sofa, rattling on in her foolish way, without noticing the fiery color which mounted to her friend's brow as she spoke of her father's prohibition.

"Yes, Ella, and I heard papa tell Sinclair it was no use—he'd got to give you up—he was getting out of patience waiting for Mr. Beaufort to come round—that he's about resigned all hopes of him; and if he was known to be so intimate with him, it would damage papa's prospects when the new Legislature is chosen. Brother begun to t'ar 'round and sw'ar, but papa just told him he'd got to choose between the two

—if Mr. Beaufort didn't come over within ten days he should break all terms with him. So, thar', isn't it *too* bad? I felt like crying. Sinclair's wandering 'round like a ghost. You must coax your papa this very night to come over to our side. If he don't there won't be any wedding, after all, and I shan't dare to ask you to the ball. So Mr. Beaufort *must* —you'll coax him, won't you, Ella?"

"Not very hard," answered Eleanor, trying to smile. "Let us dismiss the unpleasant subject now, and talk about your ball. Give me the list, and I'll write the notes for you. What dress are you going to wear?"

"Laws, I don't know. If I could get the stuff in time I'd have a light-blue silk;" and thus diverted to her favorite subject, Marcia continued to talk, while Eleanor was glad of the work in hand, which gave her an excuse for not answering all the trifling questions put to her.

Her heart was full; she was longing to be alone, or to have night come and bring her father. A presentiment of some impending evil oppressed her; yet she wrote on rapidly, in a neat, elegant style, the notes and envelopes, until the task was completed which Marcia had had the coolness to exact of her.

"Thank you, Ella. They're as handsome as print. Somehow I never had any taste for writing. I believe I'll go home right off, and send Pete out with them. Do now, *do* coax your papa, for I shan't enjoy my party if you can't come;" and Marcia tied on her black velvet riding-cap, and a long linen riding-skirt over her everyday dress, and ordering Lina to tell Jim to have her horse brought around to the step, she sailed out upon the porch.

It was a relief to Eleanor to bid her good-by, and see her gallop away along the pleasant road. Marcia had a fine figure and rode with elegance; riding was the only exercise she ever deigned to take.

While she yet stood on the piazza, watching the retreating form of her friend, a man came through the gate and made his way up the avenue toward her. He presented a singular appearance, and Eleanor thought at first that she would withdraw and send Jim to learn his errand; but, as we have said, she was naturally brave, and finally concluded to stand her ground.

There was nothing to alarm her. She saw, as he came nearer, that he was one of the "poor white trash" who occasionally came around with something to sell. He was tall and rather thin, but sinewy, with long arms and legs, long, neglected hair of a sunburnt black, small eyes deep set, and thin lips, at present set together with the close look of a man meditating a sharp bargain. His bear-skin cap was of home manufacture, and ornamented by a "brush," which hung to one side; a blue hunting-shirt and leather belt, a pair of buckskin breeches, and of boots which were "odd," if nothing more, completed his costume. A rifle was slung over his shoulder, and depending therefrom was a brace of wild turkeys, and a half-dozen of birds.

"Would you like to buy a turkey or two, miss?"

"Well, I presume the cook would be glad of them," said Eleanor, smiling. "She will be a better judge of the price and quality than I. Take them 'round to the kitchen."

"I reckon she *would* be glad of 'em, miss; but I don't reckon I'm goin' to give any nigger the chance. Them fowl were caught by bein' up 'arly in the mornin', miss, and I've brought 'em forty mile."

"How is that?"

"Woll, I come to town to see what was goin' on, and I fotched along some traps to pay my way. I think some of 'listing, if they get up a company."

"I am sorry."

"You be? Woll, I reckon the man that put a shot through that turkey's head at a couple o' hunderd yards would be good for a few of them Northern trash;" and he gave a quick look at his listener, and then swung his gun to the ground, and began taking off the fowl.

"Have they ever wronged you, those Northern people?"

"No; nuther has these turkeys. I hunt 'em for the fun of it."

"How much do you want for them?" asked Eleanor, coldly.

"They mought be worth a dollar apiece. They weigh twenty pound each. But seein' they're bought and paid for, we won't be partikeler. Your fayther sent 'em with his complements, and word that he wouldn't be hum to-night."

"What has happened? Why didn't you tell me sooner?"

"When I've any thing a little private on hand I allus talk turkey," answered the hunter, with a slight quirk of the mouth. "Did you ever heer them birds a-talking out in the woods, 'arly in the mornin', miss," and the small eyes were fixed coolly on the anxious face of the young lady. "This is the style in which they carry on their conversation," and to her equal surprise and amusement, the low, clear, far-heard "chug-a-lug-gee" cry of the graceful and cunning wild-fowl seemed coming that moment from the dead throat of one of those he had thrown on the steps.

"Why is my father detained?" she asked, again returning to the announcement which troubled her.

"Woll, that's it. *Why* is he? It mought puzzle the judge himself to tell."

At this moment, Pomp, Jim, and several other colored people, came rushing around the corner of the house excitedly, and when they saw the stranger and the game they stopped short, rolling their eyes around and scratching their heads.

"We's heerd a wild turkey, suah," cried Jim.

"Is them alive?" asked Pompey, cautiously.

"Yes, and kickin'," answered the stranger.   "Caught 'em with a lasso."

"Hi!" cried the group, in chorus.   .

"Are you Pomp?" asked the stranger, eyeing that individual from head to foot.

"Dat's my prognostick," was the reserved and lofty reply.

Pomp was an overseer, and the hunter was evidently only a poor white.

"Your master wants to see you at the village, right off."

"W'at you know 'bout dat?" was the doubting question.

"Your master has sent him; saddle Prince and go without delay," spoke Eleanor.   "Where will he find him?"

"In jail," was the low answer.   .   .

She suppressed the cry that arose to her lips.

"What for?"

"I reckon he don't know no more than you, miss.   Decent folks don't seem to have any thing better to do nowadays than to be takin' each other up.   I offered to let you know, and to send Pomp down.   Your fayther said not to mind it, miss.   It would be all right."

"You are so kind to come."

"I come to leave them fowl, I reckon.   And don't forget to look out for a friend if you should ever hear turkey about."

And with this rather mysterious parting injunction, the hunter flung his rifle over his shoulder, and set off on the road toward the village.

"Pomp, take back Prince, and bring out the carriage.   I must go with you to the village."

"Suffin' done happened," commented the negro, as he hastened to obey the energetic command.

When he came to the front door with the carriage, Miss Beaufort stood on the steps, waiting; she sprung in, and nothing was said until the two miles to the village were sped over, when she drew her vail over her face, and said:

"Drive to the jail."

"To de jail, missus?"

"Yes, your master has been arrested."

"Dey oughter be 'shamed of derselves. I knows w'at he's took up fur, missus."

"What do *you* know, Pompey?"

The slave made no reply. A kind of defiant pride settled over his face, and he drove the handsome establishment of the Beauforts through the main street with a dash, and style which eclipsed even its ordinary glory, drawing rein before the two-story hewn-log jail with a curve of the wheels and prance of the horses, as if he were driving the chariot of a queen—holding the door open for his mistress to descend, with the extremest and most palpable deference.

The street, Eleanor had observed, was full of loungers, and there was a disagreeable crowd about the entrance to the building. It was a trial for her to face these staring men, but she walked up to the door, and those nearest made a little way for her; half a year ago, they would have been extremely eager for the chance of testifying respect for the only daughter and heir of "Square" Beaufort. Not knowing the jailer by sight, and seeing Mr. Le Vert among others on the steps, she went to him and asked him if her father was really under arrest, as she had been told.

"He is, Miss Beaufort," was the chilling reply.

One would have thought, had the prisoner been a murderer or guilty of any crime, that a gentleman, seeing the troubled look and shrinking attitude of the young lady in this uncongenial crowd, would have pitied her, and given her feminine delicacy the protection of his gentlest, most courteous attention; but the chivalry of this "friend of the family" did not reach so fine a point; he gazed at the pale face and half-quivering lip as coldly as if he had never seen them before. This unmerited conduct nerved Eleanor to rely upon herself; she had been just on the point of bursting into tears, but instead of tears a bright flash came to her eyes; disdaining to ask *him* any question again, she looked about and inquired if any one would point out the jailer to her.

That personage, vulgar, and of course self-important, swaggered up to her, put his hands in his pockets, eyed her from head to foot, asking her what she wanted. Just then, Eleanor's eye caught Pompey's; he was fairly grinding his teeth, and she was afraid that he would seize the ill-bred officer and annihilate him. His air was that of a savage and powerful Newfoundland who is about to shake to pieces some insignificant whiffet. Pomp's chivalry was certainly of a more refined order than that of the " lords of the manor" at present critically regarding the beautiful woman who was once their social star.

" I want to see my father, Mr. Beaufort."

" Can't do it, ma'am—'tisn't allowed."

" Why not ?"

" Thar's special orders—solitary confinement."

" Will you not tell me the reason for this ?" cried Eleanor, losing her self-reliance in the painful suspense.

" Orders from Nashville, ma'am ; that's all I know about it. Can't say what he's done, but I reckon it's enough. Incinderary language, p'raps ; you're pop hasn't kept shut so clus as he oughter."

He received the lightning flash of indignation on his tough perception as an elephant receives a bullet on his hide. For a moment Eleanor was silent, trying to subdue her anger, for the anxiety to see her father enabled her to brave any insult; then she pleaded :

" Can not I see him once, a few moments, to obtain his orders with regard to his business ?"

" I reckon other folks will save him the trouble of 'tending to his affairs, after this. When a man speaks agen his own Government, his property ain't his own," put in a voice from one of the lower elements of the crowd.

Completely bewildered by such sudden surroundings, the troubled girl clasped her hands together.

" Oh ! do let me see my father a few moments !"

" Can't do it ; not at present, ma'am ; mebbe I can git a permit in a day or so. Call agin, and I'll let you know."

She was obliged to retire more anxious than she came. After Pompey had placed her in the carriage, he asked a fellow-slave who was standing near to take care of his horses a moment, and going into the hall, asked :

" W'ich room you got massa in ?"

" In that six-by-four, thar, in the corner, if it'll do yer any good to know," laughed the jailer.

Pomp strode up and applied his mouth to the keyhole :

" I'se bin here, massa, and so's Missa Beaufort ; dey wouldn't lef her see you ; dey oughter be 'shamed of derselves. Nebber you mind, massa, I'll take care o' things, 'specially of de missus. Has you any thing yer'd like to let us know ?"

Before there came an answer he was pulled away ; he could easily have held at bay a half-dozen men like the jailer, but slaves are too accustomed to submission to rebel except on great occasions.

" Yer won't hev the privilege of talkin' through the keyhole, Pomp, next time you come round ; yer master'll be below stairs, in a nice little place I'm a-fixin'."

" Gorry ; I let massa know we hadn' forgotten him,"

chuckled Pompey, as he drove rapidly away frcm the
place.

Distressed as she was, his mistress smiled at the bold
attack of her faithful servant—a woe-begone smile, that
vanished into a deep reverie, from which she was only
aroused by the stopping of the carriage at home.

Lina stood in the door; a vague rumor had reached
her of something having happened.

" Wot is it, honey?" she asked, almost carrying her
young mistress up-stairs, taking off her bonnet, making
her sit down in the corner of the lounge, and now looking ready to cry for sympathy.

The necessity for self-control which had restrained her
being over, Eleanor could not bear even the tender attentions of her maid; she broke down, in trying to answer
her, and sobbed hysterically.

To the ignorant mind of the mulatto, the simple fact that
her master was in jail was an alarming and marvelous
thing, looked at in the same light as if she had heard he was
in the regions of fire and brimstone.   So she made but a poor
comforter, with her interjections and gesticulations, though
Eleanor felt bitterly that she could not afford to give up her
grotesque compassion ; she was too poor in friends to spare
the humblest—at least, so it had all of a sudden appeared,
though hitherto she had been rich in gallant admirers of one
sex, and flattering imitators of the other.

Trying to think it over calmly in her chamber, she was
still in utter darkness as to the reason for her father's arrest.
The previous menace upon his life had been made by a few
excited fellow-citizens, and had subsided like many village
storms ; but this appeared to be an act cf military or Govern-
mental authority, emanating from the capital of the State and
for it she could see not the shadow of a reason.

The desolating storm which ravaged the State in the following spring had then scarcely begun to gather a cloud; it was not until the future shed light upon the past that she was enabled to understand her father's situation that winter.

In that part of middle Tennessee where the Beauforts resided were many very excellent cotton plantations, where the short-staple upland cotton was raised. Mr. Beaufort's was such a plantation. Among this class of farmers of course the secession element prevailed; but there was a decided Union sentiment amid a large class of the people; they stood midway between the hot-headed secessionists of the western border and the sturdy Unionists of the eastern mountains.

As it afterward appeared when the vote for secession was taken in February, (and which resulted in a Union majority) there had been great anxiety to suppress so wealthy and influential a Unionist as Mr. Beaufort before that election should take place; not only to prevent the public speeches and personal persuasions which he might make, but to inspire others with wholesome awe of the danger of supporting such a cause. Further east, so bold a step at so early a date might not have been permitted; but in this cotton-growing section the act was consummated, and met with general approbation. But of all these schemes the people had as yet heard but little; and Eleanor would hardly have been more astonished if her father had been arrested by a deputation from France for high treason against the Napoleonic throne.

While she was pondering the matter, word came that Sinclair Le Vert was waiting in the parlor to see her. In her distress about her father, Eleanor had hardly dwelt upon all that was implied by the cutting manner of the senior Mr. Le Vert; now it rushed back upon her—the words of Marcia, too—the full loss she was called upon to sustain.

"If *he*, too, can approve of his father's course," she murmured—and the curl of the rich, red lips threatened withering sorrow to the recreant lover.

But when she entered the parlor, he was standing in the
center of the room, pale, his face full of love and pity; he
held out his arms, and she sprung to them, happy to feel,
poor child, not so forsaken, not so desolate.

"They are trying to make me perfectly wretched, at
home," he exclaimed, after he had led her to the sofa, "and
I want you to end the matter at once, Ella. Because your
father is unpopular, they want to break off the match. It's
absurd, impossible! I'll give up my life before I'll give you
up, my Ella. They can not tear us apart."

"I knew *you* could not do as they have done. Oh, Sinclair, your father was very cruel to me to-day. He let me
face all those rude men, as if he had never known me—me,
Eleanor Beaufort, the betrothed wife of his son!"

The lover looked down at the beautiful, proud face.

"If he was not my own father, I'd challenge him."

"It was very ungenerous, Sinclair."

"It was. But what can I do? He says our engagement
must be broken off. It shall not be. Eleanor, I want you to
marry me now—immediately. You have no protector, and
will not have, perhaps, for months. If I take you home as
my wife, there can be no more said ; you will be one of us."

"And my father?"

"He will do as he has always done, I suppose, no matter
who he makes unhappy. It can not better *his* fortunes for
you to remain here alone ; when he is released he can do as
he thinks right. Surely, Ella, you would not hesitate
between your lover and a political quibble?"

"Are you going to do nothing to secure his release?"

"I would, gladly; but I am too young a man to have

much influence, especially as I can not get my father to abet me. I have begged of him to do something, but he refuses. Oh, Ella, let me, at least, protect you, and leave it to the future to see what I can do for your father."

"I should have very little self-respect, or honor for my dear father, if I would go under your family-roof under such circumstances. I will not marry you, Sinclair, to receive support, protection or advice from your family; and I will not marry, at all events, while my father is in prison. You ought to see that it is wrong for you to ask it. 'Alone!' I know it; sadly alone, Sinclair, in the time of trial. But as long as I have God for my friend, and a pair of revolvers for my defenders, I shall not quail."

"You are foolish, or mad, Eleanor."

"Neither, Sinclair."

She had left his side, and was walking up and down the room. It was no wonder that he felt as if he could sacrifice much before he could give up the hand and heart pledged to him by the spirited girl.

She never looked so well, as when her father's soul shone in her face as now—then the smooth brow, the bright, dark eye, the arched lip, were something more than beautiful; while the crown of a queen seemed added to the stature of the slender but superb form.

"Do not talk and look so, Eleanor. I am anxious and willing to serve your parent for your sake. What can I do? Tell me, and I will do it. I will do *any thing* for you, Ella."

"Will you become a Union man? Will you promise to stand true to your country—to defend my father, me, this property, as far as is in your power? Will you marry me to come *here*, as a Unionist, instead of requiring me to go to your home, flying to Secessionist protection, while my father languishes in prison? Will you take the risks? If you will, I will marry you this night."

There was a long silence.

"Why should you require me to give up my family and my principles, when you refuse to give up yours, Eleanor."

"Because, honestly and sincerely, I do not believe your conscience is involved. Mine is. You refuse for social and mercenary reasons—I am ready to sacrifice all things for my country—even your love, Sinclair."

"Eleanor!"

"I speak calmly. And now, since it only unfits me for the many duties I have to perform, to pass through such scenes as these, I must ask you to leave me. Farewell. Whenever you can come to me, loyal to me, my father, and our glorious country, you may come—not before. I shall always be the same."

She waved her hand as she said farewell, and he felt compelled to rise.

"Farewell, Ella, for to-night. My hope and prayer is that these unhappy differences will soon be settled, and we be happy again. Will you not give me one kiss?" for she had not taken his proffered hand.

"Not one kiss, as lover or wife, Sinclair Le Vert, will I give it under the shadow of the dear old national flag."

CHAPTER IV.

BITTEN.

A MOTLEY group were gathered about the bar of a second-class hotel in Nashville; officers, soldiers, ill-clad idlers—all seemed united in two bonds of fraternity : the love of whisky and hate of the Union. The soldiers, gathered from the rough, untutored lower white classes, and clothed in nondescript uniform, were a curious collection of brutal-featured and more brutal-mannered men. The officers were of good appearance and military bearing; among them was one, young and fine-looking, wearing a Lieutenant's uniform. Occasionally a breath of spring air would wander through the place, instantly lost in odors of tobacco and " cobblers."

The three officers were standing a little apart, conversing together; one of them held a letter in his hand.

" They are going to resist the League in East Tennessee," he said ; " they voted against secession in February, and now they swear they will resist the League. Whipping and hanging a few of the ringleaders doesn't appear to have done any good. They are more rampant than ever. H—— writes me here that they want a good spy in his vicinity to search out those who are secretly working against us. He says if we have a good detective in Nashville, and will send him on, there will be plenty of work for him to do. Do you think of any one, Le Vert, who will answer our purpose ?"

" I don't know that I do," answered the Lieutenant, musingly.

A chorus of welcome from a dozen rough voices caused the officers to look aside ; the soldiers had received an addition to their number. One of their comrades, a tall, singular-

looking man, wearing just enough insignia on his hunter's
frock to mark him as a Confederate volunteer, had just come
in, leaning his rifle against the bar while he accepted the
proffered drink.

" *There !*" said the third officer, with emphasis, " there is
the man for our purpose. If we'd have looked three weeks,
we couldn't have found as good a man as Turkey Dan."

" What are his especial qualifications ?"

" In the first place he's an East Tennessean, and a mount-
aineer by birth ; he knows every nook and corner where the
—— renegades will be apt to hide.   Then he can easily pre-
tend to be a Unionist, and go from house to house of the
leading planters with his trash to sell.   He's a hunter by
profession—belongs to our sharpshooters now.   A fish, a
bird, or a leg of venison will be excuse for him to worm himself into the secrets of a family.   He's sharp as steel—I know
him."

" Can he be relied on ?"

" I should rather think so ! What do you suppose brought
him 'way down to Nashville to volunteer, if he wasn't sound
on the goose ? Just ask him, if you'd like to hear his reasons.   Here, Dan, this way.   How's game ?"

" Thick as blackberries in July.   But I tell you what it is,
Captain, I j'ined the ranks as a sharpshooter, not as a nigger-
driver.   They wanted me to help administer a thrashin' to a
gang of Unioners we caught out here about five mile ; I
wouldn't do it, and they threatened to report me.   Now, Captain, I'll be thrashed myself before I'll do that kind of work.
I never sot a bait for a b'ar, nor built a pen for a turkey yit ;
all I ask is a fair shot.   Jus' give me a fair glimpse of a
Unioner's feather in a fair field, and I'll make 'em fly.   I'll
be danged if I do the thrashin'."

" You shan't be asked to," was the Captain's laughing

reply. " There's plenty of worse men for that work, while I reckon you hain't your equal with the rifle—eh, Dan ?"

" Ask the b'ars up thar in the mountains their idea."

" Lots of your old friends and neighbors haven't come over to the new flag, I suppose ?"

" They're mostly a set of fools, I'm afeard, Captain."

" How about the rich farmers over beyond Knoxville and thereabout ?"

" The cussedest set of varmints the world ever see. They hug the old Union as clus as a b'ar hugs his paw in winter."

" I suppose if we'd send you over there—privately, you know—you might peddle a few traps about the country, and find out some of the most prominent ?"

" Blaze every rotten-hearted Northern tree in the woods, Captain, give me time to go through."

" You're the one we want, then, my friend. You'll get a rich reward if you do your work satisfactorily. In particular, find out if there's a young man named Beverly Bell, son of a —— old Methodist parson, playing an active part in Jefferson county. He's Captain of a company; they say he's the doose to fight. There was a price set on his head yesterday—two hundred dollars—to whoever captures or kills him. There's a chance for your sharp-shooting, Dan."

Dan's deep-set eyes twinkled.

" Two hundred dollars ! silver, mind, it must be, if I git it. A man's head is easier hit than a turkey's, and I'd have to hit two hundred turkeys, and sell 'em arter, to bag as many of Uncle Sam's eagles as that. Yer hain't repudiated the eagles, I s'pose, hey ?"

" No," said the Lieutenant, with a mocking smile ; " we've repudiated our Northern debts, but the good old solid bird, yellow or white, is as dear to us as ever."

"Percisely," said the hunter, with a chuckle. "That's usin' common sense and proper sperit, too. A very judicious combination, as the feller said of the brandy and peppermint in his joolep. What d'ye say that high-priced rinegade's name mought be?"

"Beverly Bell. Can you mind?"

"Bev-er-ly Bell; b'longs to a Methodist parson? Woll, I reckon if he knew that Turkey Dan was after him, he would give two hundred dollars for his own head. When shall I start off on my little hunting frolic, Captain?"

"To-night, if you're ready;" and then followed instructions to report names and facts, as discovered, to a certain citizen of Knoxville. Dan's pocket was primed with a ten-dollar gold piece, and he was given written leave of absence from his company for thirty days.

Five days later, the light of the setting sun shone on the tall figure of Turkey Dan, as he stood a few moments on a projecting rock, jutting out of a remote and lonely mountain in the Cumberland range. Below him were forests and grassy sweeps of emerald hills, with farm-houses and cultivated fields gleaming out here and there; for the mountains, down their sunny slopes, presented much good farm-land, and some of the finest grazing pastures in the world. The country which he saw beneath him was very lovely; the air which fanned his sun-burned face was cool and soft—the air of Paradise.

Immediately about him the scene was more wild and rugged; the soil was stony; the evergreens stood in mournful clusters; the broken surface of the ground with the abrupt rocks, making many a shadowy ravine, and lonely lurking-place for wild animals, not yet wholly exterminated from this region; a little to the left the tracery of a rough road was discernible winding down from height to lesser height.

tracking out the most feasible ways. After reconnoitering a few moments, the hunter, rifle in hand, found a narrow path around the base of the rock which led him to a little ravine, thickly shadowed with evergreen, the stony surfaces of the ground carpeted with moss, and the whole place filled with the pleasant dash of a little spring which leaped from the rock and hid itself in the fallen leaves.

In this secluded spot, unsuspected of existence, were a dozen tents or huts, constructed mostly of stray rails, saplings and branches of trees ; a drift of sunshine through a cleft of the hills lighted up the faces of fifty men, as they lounged upon the ground, eating crackers and drinking water from the spring, the most of them with their guns glittering by their sides. Protected by the rock, Dan paused a moment, eyeing the scene, while the peculiar cry of the wild-turkey gurgled on the air, causing the men to look at each other.

" There's a wild-turkey," almost whispered one. " I wish I could sight him ; he would make a welcome addition to our fare, at present."

" If you should kill *that* bird, you'd do the cause a bad turn," said a young man, springing to his feet, and going toward the sound. " Ha, Dan, I'm glad enough to see you here. What's the news ?"

" Woll, fustly, there's two hundred dollars been sot on your head, Bell, and I've come to 'arn it. I've promised it to Jeff in less 'n a fortnight, suah."

" It's flattering to find that even my enemies rate it worth so much," answered the youth, with a light laugh, shaking back his thick brown hair from a face of noble and manly promise,—a face with the softness and color of twenty-one, but the firmness and will of a leader's. " Set a price on my head ?" And who else is deemed worthy of such an honor ? Not my father, I hope."

" I heern nothin' special about him. But it's onsafe to say
who mought be taken and who not, now-a-days. I've seen
things in the last ten days that I'll have revenge fur,—may
I be covered with pitch and sot fire to, if I ever quit till I
do," and forgetting himself in his wrath, the hunter brought
the stock of his rifle down on the rock with a clang that
resounded from the hills.

" Are things getting worse ?" was the anxious inquiry.

" There's been twenty men hung to my sartain knowledge
within a week,—quiet, peaceable men, who spoke agen the
League ten days ago,—there's hundreds been whipped, and
the jails is getting so crowded, they has to empty them by
way of the gallus. I stood by, myself, the day 'fore I started
to find you, and saw five men tied to logs and their backs laid
bar' with switches,—I was in for't, and I couldn't help 'em.
I knew I could do more good, in the end, by playin' out my
part,—but I'll be dod blasted, Captain Bell, if the blood
didn't go a streaking it up and down me like red-hot iron ;
my heart stood stock still ; I gripped my rifle with both
hands, for fear I should let her fly in the faces of the infarnu
varmints. I just made up my mind I couldn't play spy in
that region no longer ; and you may bet I wan't no ways put
out when the Captain chose me, that very night, to come over
here and hunt you up. He sot me to pickin' out the Union
men in the vicinity ; and I reckon he couldn't have found
anybody that knew more about 'em." The low chuckle that
finished up the sentence would have been very exasperating
to the Confederate officers who had dispatched the sagacious
spy, if they could only have heard it.

Many of the men had gathered about the new-comer, anxious for the news he might have brought with him. They
were persons of quiet exterior, ordinary in their dress, and of
respectable appearance—sturdy farmers, more slender denizens

of village offices and stores, and a few hardy, half-civilized mountaineers. It must have been a powerful motive which had driven such a class from their homes, and herded them here in the open air, each man armed with such weapons as he had found ready to his hand.

"Oh! just God, how long shall the wicked prevail?" cried the young man, lifting up his head. "Men! I feel as if we ought not to pause here a day or an hour waiting for further reinforcements. Let us do what we can. Let us show ourselves, with the hope that thousands will follow, who are waiting now in silent dread. Let us do what little we can—if it is only to give fifty lives for our country."

"They're sending their bloodhounds everywhere. They expect a rising over here, and they're sending force enough to keep us down. They're afraid of us here; but whar I've been, Union men are gettin' to be scarce as ha'rs on the inside of a man's hand. They've hunted down purty much all there wur. How ye off for fodder?"

"Well, we've some beans for to-morrow."

"Thar's one o' my tribe is comin' along to-night with a lot of dried meat, and a beef he's going to kill, after he's druv it up. Thar's one thing sartain, boys, the women and chil'ren will be glad to see ye, for their lives are scart out of 'em by the thieving panthers. Start out with fifty, and you'll be five hundred, 'fore you've gone fifty miles. An' I tell you, Bell, ef you ever come face to face with Captain Smalley or Lieutenant Le Vert in a squabble, jus' give 'em Turkey Dan's grizzliest respecks."

"Keep 'em and give 'em yourself. Yer rifle will speak for you, Dan," said one of the mountaineers.

"Yer ain't a-going to leave us, agin, are ye?" asked another.

"Not jist yet. Sence they've started the fight, we'll give 'em more'n they ask fur. I've been some on b'ar and other

wild animals, and I mean to be some on those murderin'
usurpers. They can't put their foot on *my* neck."

" We wan't made to be druv like the poor niggers," added
another, looking along the barrel of his gun, as if he saw a
rebel within hitting distance.

" I'm goin' with ye till ye get a fair start," continued Dan,
" and then I've private business to 'tend to, over beyond
Nashville agen. When I git back, it will be to do the hardest
summer work I ever done."

" Where's your wife and little ones now, Dan ?" asked
Captain Bell.

" They're in the cabin, I reckon. They're used to gitting
along without me. The old woman's got a double-barrel shot-
gun and a fishin'-rod—she'll do without me. Come, friends,
havn't you a bit of grub ye'd offer a man that had traveled a
hundred miles to see you ?" and he rested his rifle against a
tree, and threw himself on the moss at its foot.

" We've three crackers left," answered the commissary,
after a general search of the quarters. " We're going to set
some beans to bake to-night."

" I reckon I'll make out on the crackers, till Black gets
along with the provision-train. But I trust yer not out of
whisky, hey, boys ? because thar *mought* be rattlesnakes, and
if you should get bitten any of yer, whisky is all that'll save
you. The pesky sarpints are as thick here, as Seceshers down
to Memphis. I've been bit six or seven times myself, but I
allus fill up with whisky, so the pizon has no room to work.
Snakes and painters ! I b'lieve I've got another bite ! Did
you hear his rattle ? Thar he goes, now, the infarnal South
Car'lina sarpint !" and springing up, he dashed the butt of
his gun down on the head of an enormous rattlesnake.
" Thar, I guess you'll never sarve another gentleman as you
have me," and he severed the head with the bowie-knife from

his belt. " Lord, Lord, boys, bring the whisky. I *had* hoped
to be spar'd to fight suthin' wuss 'an snakes. Oh ! Lord, thar,
a pint 'll answer to begin on."

He sat down on the ground, writhing and making contortions which drew forth looks of consternation from the company. To lose Turkey Dan was an evil they had not counted
on. Having swallowed a pint of whisky without stopping,
he now rolled up the left leg of his breeches, found a small
red spot, over which he clapped a handful of earth wet with
the spring water.

" Do you feel it much yet ?" inquired Captain Bell, earnestly.

" It's beginnin' to spread. Don't be scart, boys, take it cool ;
I've been bit before. If you've got whisky enough, I'm safe."

Every man of the fifty who had a drop of the precious
liquid, contributed it; there was only a quart more in the
camp.

" I reckon it'll do, I *hope* so," murmured Dan, looking at
the aggregated result, and shaking his head; " if it shouldn't,
give my love to Sallie and the young'uns."

For the next half-hour, he continued to take frequent
draughts, until the supply was exhausted.

" How is it now ?" was again the Captain's eager question.

" Cured, completely," said Dan, rising to his feet, and shaking himself. " The fact is, Captain, I don't believe the infarnal
reptile teched me, after all. He was a-goin' to, when I sot
my gun on him. But thar's no harm. An ounce of pre-
ventive's worth a pound of cure, and if I *should* be bit when
I get to sleep, I'll be all right."

" The whisky ought to kill you, if the snake didn't," half
laughed, half-growled the young man.

CHAPTER V.

CONFISCATED COTTON.

FOUR dreary months had rolled away since Eleanor Beaufort bade her lover farewell—months of such solicitude as had paled the rich rose of her cheek and left shadows under the eyes which wept oftener than they smiled.

In all that long period she had seen her father but once. About a week after his arrest she had been permitted a brief interview with him, previous to his removal to one of the prisons of Nashville. The parting had been almost like that of death, for she had learned to fear the reign of this new and reckless authority; if it could snatch her father from her in this relentless manner, it might go a little further and take life as well as liberty.

When she returned from that sad parting, she had no loving breast upon which to fling herself and sob out her grief, except the ignorant, pitying heart of her maid, Lina. Of all the friends of her prosperity, not any presented themselves; for secession was rank in this cotton-growing vicinity; and those who secretly condemned did not dare to speak out.

Marcia had made her a visit or two, in disobedience of her father's commands, to tell how angry she was because her papa was in jail, and how sorry she was she could not come to the ball—it was going to be splendid—and how like a mope brother was behaving himself—it was too bad! it would half spoil the ball! etc., etc. But these visits were more afflictive than soothing, and Eleanor was not sorry when they ceased entirely.

Her forebodings had been very much lightened by receiving

a letter from her father shortly after his arrival at his new abode—a letter which gave her the instruction she needed with regard to the affairs of the plantation, and which, moreover, overflowed with expressions of cheerful tenderness. Thenceforth she received one of these welcome missives once a fortnight. Not a word was in them of political opinion, of why he was confined and when he hoped to be liberated, for they were written under the eye of a censor; but they were full of love, and they told her all the minutiæ of his prison-life—his room, the furniture, the food, and such few incidents as served to enliven the monotony of confinement. It was some comfort to be told that his room was light and not unhealthy; that he had three companions, intelligent, pleasant men, imprisoned like himself for reasons of state; that the food was wholesome, though by no means superfluously rich or varied.

The Christmas festivities had been few on the Beaufort plantation. Not that Eleanor wished to lessen the pleasure of her dependents because of her own troubles—she gave the cook *carte blanche*, and the fullest liberty of the season to all; but Mr. Beaufort had been too generous a master for his household to forget him in the day of his affliction. The out-door hands did hold a frolic or two, a barbecue and dance; but the house servants betrayed little of their usual jollity.

When the Christmas dinner came on the table, and Eleanor was called to partake of it in solitude, memories of the former times overcame her—she tried to eat, to please the anxious cook; the effort was a miserable failure, and after swallowing more tears than food, she retired to her room to pass the long evening in weeping.

"Poor chile! poor chile!" said Liza, coming in and surveying the untasted dinner, "I don' feel s'prised she hasn't tasted a bit. I should done choke, ef I should try to swallow roas' turkey and plum puddin', and massa way off dar shot up, widout nuffin' but bread and water fer *his* feas'."

" I don' feel no appertite, nudder," said Lina, wiping away a stray tear; " ef it wan't fer der cranberry-sass and pickles I don' b'lieve I could eat anyt'ing at all.   Dey sort of keeps up my appertite."

" Woll, I'se gwine to put away a nice bit fer missa by-and-by, and den you and Jim pitch in, if yer hungry.   *I* can't taste a bit."

" Hi, maumy, *I'se* feel drefful too," snuffled Jim, eyeing the turkey, " but what's de use?   Ef we let our strenf all run down, starbing ourselfs, we can't do massa's work as it oughter be done."

" Jes' as your feelin' 'lows," answered Liza, with mingled reproach and dignity.

" Mine 'lows me to keep up under 'flictions, maumy.   Come, Miss Car'lina, shall I help to a bit of de breas'—a small bit of de breas'?   It's wery nice—and 'tickerly approbrious to dose under trouble—tain't wery hearty."

" Yis, Jim, you may give me a *small* piece," answered Lina, with a deep sigh, " wid a bit of de stuffin', and a leg.   I don' feel like eating much."

" I'se cooked a great lot o' goodies fer de fiel' hands, jes' to pass away de time.   No comp'ny to cook fer, now, oh, my! I never t'ought to see sech a Chris'mas on dis plantation," continued Liza.   " And Miss Eleanor just growed up, and so han'some.   She ought to have dis house chock full of beaux. Now I tell you, Jim, don't you nebber 'base yerself and dis family to speak to one massa Le Vert's niggers agin.   Ef you do, I'll nebber speak to you.   Dar's young massa done gone give Missa Eleanor de mitten; and dar's dat great humbly Marshy, she's guv a ball to-night and hain't even asked her ole frien'.   It's a burnin' shame."

" 'Tis that !" echoed Lina, indignantly.

" I had a berry perlite invertation from der coachman to come ober to-night and hear der music, and take a little shin-dig in de kitchen," said Jim, doubtingly.

" Ef you go, I'll nebber cook anudder 'possum fer you, so long as you lib, Jim."

" Nor I won't nebber set de day," added Lina, giving the butler a flash of her black eyes that made him smile like a sun in July.

" Oh, gorry ! can't stand *dat*, nohow.   Der ladies at home may be suah of my company dis evenin'."

While the other two were taking their dinner, Liza filled a basket with the best on the table, saying :

" I'm gwine to Pompey's cabin wid dese.   I don' b'lieve he's pervided much of a feas', he's so down-sperited.   Mebbe I shall set awhile wid his wife.   You jes' see to dem two lazy gals in de kitchen, Lina, dat dey wash up and cl'ar 'way nice, 'fore I get back."

Lina promised, and the cook set out on her visit to Pomp's cabin, which was quite a decent house of two rooms and a loft, at the head of the lane overlooking the negro-quarters. She found the family about sitting down to a plain meal—a dish of fried chicken alone showing it to be Christmas.

" I know'd you wouldn't have heart to cook much," said their visitor, " so I brought 'long some trash fer de pickaninnies.   *Dey're* troubles come soon 'nuff—let em laugh w'ile dey can," and she placed the niceties on the table, leaving three or four pairs of bright eyes to roll around, and as many sets of white teeth to display themselves, until the pickaninnies, catching from each other the contagion of joy, burst out into repressed giggles which caused their father to threaten to box their ears if they didn't behave derselves 'fore company.

" 'Bliged to ye.   Don't crowd yerselves.   I'll jes' take a

cup o' coffee here in my lap," continued Liza. "I couldn't
eat Christmas dinner to-day, wid massa dar in Nashville.
Dese are great times we's coming on, Pompey;" her voice
lowered itself, and her eyes studied the dark features of the
man with a penetrating look.

"Yes, bigger times dan massa himself dreams on," said the
overseer, in equally low tones. De Souf get a-fightin' de
Norf—den comes *our* time of deliverance; hi, Liza?"

"De time spoken of in de Scriptur'," added Liza.

"Which our prophets has foretold—which has been whispered 'round, and held us up, when de lash cut, and de
chil'ren was sold. De time of our deliverance is at hand,
bless de Lord."

"Oh, Pompey, how you talk!" half-whispered his wife,
looking frightened and glancing around; she was a small,
slender woman, a bright-eyed mulatto.

"It'll not do us much good," went on Pompey; "likely
we'll lose our lives, w'en de struggle comes, but our chil'ren
will be the gainers; yes, Kate, I'm looking fer these pickaninnies of ours *to be free!*" and he laid each of his great,
uncouth hands on the heads of the two nearest him, while a
light like lightning out of a storm-cloud leaped out of his face.

"De Lord grant it," added Liza; "not that *our* massa isn't
a good and Christian man, and we better off dan de most. I
love massa; and I should stick by him, ef I wur free."

"I love and honor my massa," said Pompey, bringing his
fist down on the table. "I shall stick to him as long as he is
in trouble. We isn' so mean as his w'ite frien's—no, sar!
I'll stick to Massa Beaufort, and I'll gib my life for Missa
Beaufort, if it comes to dat. And, Lize, I shouldn' wonder
if it come to dat, 'fore long. Dese wolves prowling 'round,
'seeking whom dey may devour,' will be after our lamb, I'se
afraid."

"Lord bress us, Pomp, you don't t'ink dey would hurt a poor, pretty chile like dat?"

"Dey're a drunken set; dar's no telling what dey'll do. I'm more'n half s'pecting dey'll be 'round to rob de house, or mebbe steal de cotton 'way. Dey'll find *me* ready, any how. Look yere, Lize!" he went up the ladder leading into the loft, and took down a double-barreled gun, and a long knife ground to a sharp point. "I shan't let massa's property be 'stroyed widout doing w'at I can."

"I'm glad you've got the spunk," said Liza. "Whar'd. you git that gun?"

"Oh, I found it," laughed Pompey.

"Yer ain't no better prepared den young missa herself," continued the cook. "Lina says she goes to bed ebery night wid a pair of rewolvers under her piller. She's bin a-shooting at a mark ebery day, lately."

"Yis; I learned her to load and fire. She's a splendiferous girl, Missa Beaufort is. Yer ought to see how cool she handles 'em, and how her eyes shine. Ef it was dat Marshy Le Vert, she'd screech like a night-owl ef a gun went off widin a mile."

"Ho! Marshy can't hol' a candle to our young lady. An' 'tween you and me, Pomp, I'se glad dat match broke off. Der family ain't good enough for *our* missa."

Much more these slaves talked together that Christmas day, than their beloved mistress would have credited was in their hearts or heads. But she had every reason to feel that they *were friends* who might be relied upon in an emergency; and the feeling did much to make her isolation tolerable to her.

Pompey was too discreet to alarm his mistress with his own fears; he contented himself by keeping his own eyes open; and as week after week went by without any demonstration, he was glad that he had not disturbed his mistress by unnecessary fears.

Thus, in that monotony of suspense which is so wearing to the mind and body, had the four months dragged themselves away, and now, on this lovely May day, the 9th of the month, she stood at her window, breathing the sweet air, whose freshness was kindling anew the roses in her cheeks.

·It was not the spring air alone which had brought that sudden bloom to her cheeks. No; an hour previously, the road had been filled by a company of Confederate cavalry; and, as she looked at them from behind the shelter of the muslin window-curtains, she saw among the officers Sinclair Le Vert. She had heard that the company was under marching orders. This was the first glimpse she had had of him since their parting; the sun glittered on his uniform; she heard the tramping of steeds and the clanging of swords, saw the turbulent vision sweep by, and *he*, as he rode, turn his head with a long look, as if he hoped for some signal, kiss his hand, spur his steed, and dash forward till the flash of gilded trappings was hidden by the trees. Then she had uttered a faint cry, and sat down pale and powerless. She felt that she loved him yet.

Then, as the long winter passed in review before her—what she had suffered—how unworthily he had acted—pride and reason had fought against the return of the old passion; until now, she stood up again, with kindling eye and glowing cheek, vowing in her heart that the man who had deserted his betrothed in an hour of oppression, and who was going forth to battle against his own country and kin, should be no more to her than a dream of the past. Yet oh, how desolate she felt.

"I can endure this no longer," she murmured, as she stood there, looking off toward the distant city which held that which was dearest to her on earth. "To-morrow I shall start for Nashville. I will at least see my father, hear him speak, if only for fifteen minutes. I will beseech the authorities myself, personally—I will bribe the jailer. I *must* see my father!"

Mr. Beaufort had left between two and three hundred dollars in gold in his library-safe, when he was taken away; this still remained, as the small expenses of the household had been defrayed by the sale of some beef-cattle, which the planter had directed, but it was not added to. The last year's crop of cotton was still unsold; it had been ginned by the negroes, through the winter, and was now stored in the large building built for that purpose, ready for market.

Full of her present resolution, Eleanor turned to look up and pack a few articles, resolved to take the early train for Nashville the next morning. One of the boys could drive her to the village dépôt; the journey would be brief by rail; and she hoped, within thirty hours, to clasp her father's hand.

While thus employed, an unusual tumult in the yard attracted her to the window. She grew pale with apprehension as she saw a party of the ruff-scuffs from the village trampling the lawn, led by a soldier or two in uniform, and heard a loud knocking at the front door.

"What do they want now?" was Eleanor's silent question. The next moment, Jim came to her door.

"Dar's a man down dar says he wants Miss Beaufort to give him the key to de cotton-house."

"What does he want of the key?"

"I can't perceive."

"Tell him my father is not at home, and I am not at liberty to give him the key."

She said this in a calm, clear voice, which was heard by the deputy waiting in the hall below, who immediately came half-way up the stairs, till he caught sight of the young lady, when he began :

"We know right well your father ain't to home—hain't been lately, I reckon. That's jest why we're after the cotton. Citizens that is doing their duty is all giving freely to the good cause. Our soldiers have to be fed, and clothed, and armed; them as won't give willingly, must give by means of 'sessments. You've been 'sessed twenty-five bales of cotton, and I reckon we'll have it. We've come fur it."

"Not with my aid or consent," said Eleanor, stepping to the head of the stairs. "In my judgment, it will be treason. He or she who gives aid or comfort to the enemy is guilty of treason. To give any thing to support a wicked raid against the best Government in the world would be to sin against my own conscience. I will not give it."

"I'll be bust if she don't go on like a reg'lar abolitionist!" muttered the man.

"No, I am no abolitionist," responded the girl, "but *I am* for the Union—the whole Union, one and inseparable, now and forever. And may God bless and protect it from the assaults of its enemies."

"Well, I allow, you're a regular brick," said the deputy, looking up in surprise at the brave young lady who dared to utter words he had not heard in half a year. "I'd advise you to lie low, and shut up that kind of talk 'bout here; 'tain't safe, even for wimmen. I don't want to harm you, young lady, but we're after the cotton, and if you don't hand over the key, we'll make short work of the doors, that's all. And a piece of advice—for I'm sorry for yer purty face, miss —you'd better hang out the Stars and Bars from your ruf, if you want to be saved further visits. This is the only house in the county that don't show its colors."

"I shall never display the Stars and Bars, sir."

"Ho! you'll have to come to it. Are you going to give us the key, miss? We'll take twenty-five bales—no more."

"You are generous! No, sir, I shall not give you the key."

"Good-by, then. We shan't stint ourselves—we'll take all we can get."

He lumbered down the stairs and went out, shutting the door with a clang. She bade Jim lock it, and all the other entrances of the mansion; then she went to a back window which gave a view of the cotton-house and looked out.

"Good for Pompey!" she cried, as she saw what was going on. He stood in front of the locked door of the building, with his double-barreled gun leveled at the deputy, who headed the crowd of marauders; around him were grouped some twenty of the field-hands, armed with cudgels and knives, and two or three of them with pistols and guns.

The intruding party were not entirely destitute of arms; knives were in tolerable profusion, and the half-dozen soldiers had muskets; but the defenders were rather in preponderance, and no one exactly liked the looks of the huge negro, as he stood like a black Hercules, a club at his feet, a knife in his belt, and the gun in his hands, his face full of fire and fury.

"Dis yere massa's property. He lef' it in my charge; it's my duty to see to it, and I'm *gwine* to. Cl'ar out, or I won't be 'sponsible fer who gits a hole in him!"

Eleanor could hear his fierce tones where she stood.

"Why don't some of you soldiers put a bullet through him?" asked the leader, looking back at those heroes.

"'Kase de fust one levels his piece gits a hole tru' him 'fore he knows it," answered Pompey. "Look out sharp, boys— fire on de first rascal luf's his piece."

"If *I* had a weapon *I'd* use it," shouted the deputy, backing out slowly before the stern eye of the negro. "Cuss it, why don't some of you do something?"

"Here's my gun," said a soldier, holding it toward him, muzzle down, so as to draw no danger on himself.

"Oh, blast it, I don't know how to manage that thing," refusing to accept the proffered kindness. "Come, men, make a charge!" and he took three steps backward.

"I propose that we go back for reinforcements," said one.

"I'm afraid we'll have to," consented the leader; "and look here, you infernal black rascal, next time we come we'll have the cotton, and you, too. We'll whip you to death, you infernal sassy nigger!"

"Ef you gits a chance, sar," answered Pomp, coolly.

"We'll have it within six hours," was the threat with which the marauders ignominiously withdrew.

As they passed the mansion, on their way to the road, they amused themselves hurling brickbats at the windows, trampling the flowers in the garden, and defacing the shrubbery of the lawn as much as possible. As soon as they were at a safe distance, Pompey came to the house, and gave a graphic account of the affair to his mistress.

"Gorry! I mos' got over bein' mad w'en I see dat bellwether turn tail," he chuckled.

"Do you think they will really be back?"

"I'se afraid dey may, missus. We'se going to barrelcade de door, and fight 'em from de inside. We'll get all de knives and guns dar is, and a lot o' dormicks; and den if dey try us, we'll fight."

"If it really comes to that, Pompey, I'd rather you'd capitulate," said Eleanor. "You'll get the worst of it, in the end. They will kill you, perhaps; and they'll have the cotton anyhow; they can set fire to the building, if they get angry, and burn the cotton up, and you too. You'd better

get out the horses, and all hands go to work and tote the
twenty-five bales out to the road, and let them take it when
they come."

" I'd rather fight," answered Pompey.

" It is hard to be robbed in this way by such unrighteous
thieves; but we must make the best of a bad case. I should
have no one to protect me, if they should kill you or drag
you off, Pompey. You know I rely upon you."

" 'Bliged to you, missus," pulling his wool. "Missus can
rely on Pomp long as a drop of blood in his body."

" I believe you. If you should shut yourselves up in the
out-houses to defend the cotton, they might become enraged
and plunder the house, perhaps set fire to it. I should rather
you would be on hand to protect the house, and let the cotton
take its chance." .

" Berry well, missus, if dat's your judgment. But it goes
agen the grain awfully, to see 'em tote away dat cotton.
We'se had busy times picking and ginning dat, missus;
it's half we've got, pretty nigh. Dar ain't but seventy
bales."

" They will have it all, before they are through," sighed
Eleanor. " Oh, dear! I can not see the end of trouble."

" Why don't you holler for de Bars and Stars ?" asked the
negro, with a quick glance.

" If my dear father will not turn traitor, even for the sake
of liberty, perhaps life, I hope I shall have courage not to
falter. I will do what I can to defend what he has left in
my charge; but I shall act as I know he would approve, if
he were here. Pompey," she asked, with a sudden curiosity,
" do you hurrah for the Stars and Bars ?"

"No, missus," was the prompt answer. " We'se know
bettah—niggers do. Missus," he added, after a moment's
hesitation, " is Massa Linkum ra'ly a black man ?"

"Not at all," answered Miss Beaufort. "What put that idea in your head?"

"Kase de 'Federates all swear he is—a great big culled man, big as me. Dey say he's a cannibal, missus—eats chil'ren briled, for breakfast."

"Oh, you silly boy! I thought *you* had more sense!"

"So I has, missus," with that sly twinkle of the eye again; "but that's what they swears to."

"Never mind what they swear to, now, Pomp. Put a bar across the front and back hall doors. Fasten all the shutters. Here is the key. But no, they have threatened you with a whipping. I will give them the day myself when they come. You bring two or three of the trustiest fellows in the house, and let the rest go about their work, as usual."

"Is them revolvers loaded?" asked the negro.

"They are all right, Pompey. Get things in order, quickly."

Miss Beaufort was as cool and prompt as if she had been a business man, giving orders for the day.

The first demonstration had been made at about three in the afternoon, and not long after sunset, a fife and drum were heard in the distance, and soon a mob of two hundred persons came marching up to the gate to the tune of Dixie. True to her principles, not to give aid and comfort to the enemy, Eleanor had reconsidered her plan of depositing the cotton in the road—if they would like it, they took it, free from any aid from her. But when she saw the savages trampling down her beautiful flowers and desecrating the ground, she almost repented of giving them the excuse for entering the gates. A brave array of soldiers, with muskets presented, led the advance, while the rabble hooted and yelled at their will. A goodly number of darkeys and drays accompanied the mob to convey away the confiscated cotton. The Captain of the squad called "halt!" in front of the mansion; and at that instant, Miss Beaufort came out on the piazza entirely alone. She had a faithful band of armed dependents in the hall; but she would not allow them to excite the vengeance of the crowd by appearing. She feared no personal harm; and her courage was equal to facing a brutal and violent rabble. As she came out on the piazza, the last rays of the declining sunset gilded her hair and lighted up her young, resolute face, so fair, so girlish, it might have touched the coarsest to respect. Three hideous groans greeted her appearance; they did not even change the color in her cheek; but when they had subsided, her clear voice rung out like silver:

"Sons of chivalry! I surrender to your unlawful hands the cotton which you demand—twenty-five bales, remember, no more upon your *honor*. Here is the key. I have a well-armed body of faithful servants, who would make this robbery cost you dear; they were anxious to defend their absent master's property; but I was not willing to sacrifice even one life, in defense of a few cotton-bales."

She flung the key on the ground and retired within the mansion; the iron bar was dropped across the door, and she went to her look-out in the upper story to reconnoiter.

With turbulent cries, laughter and oaths, music of drum and fife and hoarse voices, the bales were tumbled out and hoisted on to carts; while, from afar off, the frightened women and children of the negro-quarters gazed tremblingly upon the scene.

"They've taken the whole crop, missus. I counted seventy odd," cried Pompey, from the hall; he too had found a window for observation.

"We will have to submit," answered Miss Beaufort. "Pomp! Pomp! what is this? They have fired the buildings!"

A red glare of light pierced through the partially open

shutters; soon tongues of fire rose up from the windows and
roof of the store-house; the dry wooden structure was soon
enveloped in flames, casting an appropriate lurid hue over the
rejoicing faces of the mob, who had lighted this glorious
bonfire, in exultation over their spoil.

"It's a mercy the wind is not in this direction," murmured
Eleanor, now trembling for the first time; there is something
in the wild terror and sweeping wrath of fire, that will
unnerve those stronger than this young, gentle girl, gazing at
the grim destroyer with a pale face.

"'Tis a mercy," said Liza, who, with Lina and others, had
been weeping and wringing her hands, "but thar's no telling
how long it may last; the wind may shift any minit. Like
as not they'll set the house afire before they quit;" here the
whole colored chorus moaned and groaned.

"Be still your noise!" said Pompey, sternly; "don't yer
see yer upsetting the missus, takin' on so. Cl'ar out, if yer
can't be quiet!"

This reproof quieted them down considerably. The roof
of the store-house tumbled in, with a great crash; the cotton-
gin, near by, was also in flames; the crowd grew more
boisterous as the fire progressed; it was indeed a scene of
unhappy excitement to be endured by the lonely girl. Not
until the glare of the incendiary fire had ceased to illuminate
their exploits, did the murderers think of return. They had
come out for some fun, and they had had it. With a terror
she could not entirely conceal, Eleanor listened and waited
for their exit. A heavy thumping at the door warned her
that they were not going without further mischief. Voices
cried out for the—

"Devilish darkey! they wanted the nigger, who'd threatened 'em. They wasn't going home without seein' him
thrashed within an inch of his life!"

No response being made to this pleasant demand, they threatened to fire the mansion; this being received in absolute silence, they finally concluded to retire. When she heard them actually shuffling away, and made sure by reconnoitering at all points that they had left; when the fife and drum grew faint in the distance, and silence succeeded the brutal clamor, her long-tried courage gave way, and she sunk upon the bed so exhausted, that Lina's utmost efforts were required to revive her.

CHAPTER VI.

THE NASHVILLE PRISON.

EARLY the next morning, Eleanor was at the village dépôt awaiting the train. Her head ached intolerably with the excitement of the previous evening, but only absolute illness would have kept her from her purpose; she must see her father, tell him what had happened, and get his advice.

Pompey drove her to the dépôt in the carriage; he always performed that service now-a-days, for he would not trust his young mistress out from under his protecting eye. He had at first begged to go to Nashville with her; but upon her representation that he was needed at home to take care of the property in her absence, he acknowledged the necessity. He remained near at hand until the train arrived. The early hour prevented them from being the objects of much remark; but as it was, some passing taunts greeted the appearance of the Beaufort establishment.

"Take car' yourself, missa," said the faithful negro, earnestly, as the whistle announced the approach of the cars.

'I shall, Pompey; don't worry about me; and *you* take
of yourself; you've made enemies."

One of her pair of revolvers was concealed upon her person,
and the other she had loaned him during her absence, for she
thought it not improbable that he might need it.

Plainly dressed, with a thick green vail drawn over her
face, as she entered the cars, carrying a good-sized market-
basket, she would hardly have been suspected as the Miss
Beaufort, of Beaufort Place. She had borrowed a pair of
Lina's gloves and drawn them over her own, to conceal the
tell-tale elegance of her hands. In the basket were some
small articles of her father's toilette, and some of the choicest
specimens of Lina's culinary skill, which she had kept up
half the night to manufacture for massa.

The sweet air of a most delicious May morning, blowing in
at the open window, and the exhilarating motion of the cars,
dispelled much of her oppressive headache, so that when the
cars reached the city, she felt a great deal of her native courage
return. Not knowing to whom to apply for permission to
visit Mr. Beaufort, she went first to the prison itself, and there
ascertained from the military guard to what officers to apply.
Leaving her basket with one of these, she went across the
street to the office designated, taking off her gloves and vail
before she entered, that she might appeal in her own proper
character for the priceless favor. She was peremptorily
refused.

"Old Beaufort is a hard old case. He ought to have been
in better business. Have orders from head-quarters to be very
strict with him."

"But what harm can it possibly do for me to see him a
little while? It is four months since I have spoken with my
father—and he is all the near relative I have in the world.
Oh, sir, I *must* see him! I can not go back without seeing my

father !"—but the red-faced official kept a newspaper before his face, so that the clasped hands, the eyes streaming with tears, had no effect upon him.

"It's a narrow chance if you ever see him again, miss," he at last said, gruffly; " we're hanging them off, fast, now—three this morning. There's no telling when *his* orders may come !"

Eleanor gazed at him in a stupor of astonishment:

"Do you mean what you say ?"

"You'll find out, if you wait long enough," was the coarse answer.

She sunk down in a chair near at hand; she had not been asked to sit, but the shock had deprived her of her strength, and she sat to prevent fainting. Her eyes, no longer weeping, but with a fixed sort of terror in them, wandered over to the grated windows opposite.

"Will you tell me if he occupies a front room ?" she asked, after a while.

"Really, don't remember."

She arose and went out on the walk. Many persons of all classes, and especially evil-eyed, low-born soldiers, were passing continually ; but she never gave a thought to these—she saw not their glances, she heard not their words, as, *with her bonnet off*, that he might recognize her, and give her some signal of having done so, she searched those cruel windows over and over again.

"My God ! Eleanor, is this you ?"

The sharp, surprised tones startled her back to things about her ; she looked down and saw Sinclair Le Vert, handsome and tall in his glittering uniform, arrested in his passing walk, appearing distressed enough—his cavalry company had been riding nearly all night ; and had reached Nashville a few hours previously.

"Yes, Sinclair," she answered, too unhappy to feel any pride, "it is me, standing here in the streets of Nashville, in the hope of catching one glance of my dear father's face, which the officers have denied me. What have we done that we should be treated thus? Sinclair, I beg of you, go with me to this office, and see if *you* have not influence enough to obtain me permission to visit my father."

"I will do any thing to save you such trials," he answered, much agitated. "Put on your bonnet, Eleanor; you are too beautiful for these people to stare at."

"I had forgotten," she said, replacing it.

The influence of the name of Le Vert seemed to be sufficient to procure the coveted boon; after a brief interview between the Lieutenant and the officer, he returned to her with a written permission to visit Mr. Beaufort for half an hour. He walked across the street with her; he seemed to wish to say something, but her feelings were all engrossed by the coming interview; she did indeed thank him earnestly for the great favor he had conferred, but it seemed to him only the gratitude a stranger would have earned.

Eleanor was taken into a vacant apartment, and searched, by a woman employed for that purpose; the basket also underwent a thorough probing; and nothing "contraband" having been found, the door was unlocked—she was permitted to pass into the small, close apartment, where four true lovers of their country were suffering the penalty of their faithfulness. A dear face, which had grown thin and pale since she saw it last, turned, unwitting of the joy in store:

"My child!"

"Dear father!" and the daughter lay upon his breast.

For a moment all was dark; she feared she was about to faint; but a swift thought of the few precious moments that were her's to remain, drove back the oblivion that would have seized upon her. His noble-hearted friends, for such they had become, wept as they looked upon the meeting.

After the first emotion was mastered, she recounted to him in as few words as possible the state of affairs at home.

" I hardly know what advice to give you," he said. " If I should make my escape, by any chance, from confinement, it will probably be necessary for us to fly to some State which is under the protection of the old flag. But I will not conceal from you, my child, that such a chance is extremely improbable. It is much more likely that I shall go from this room to the gallows. Others, who have sinned no more than I, go daily. What do you think are our amusements here, my child?—to hear the groans wrung from white men by the lash; to see citizens disgraced by the whip and the razor; to look out of our narrow window, only to see the rough coffins prepared for the yet living victims."

" Oh, father, you did not tell me these things."

" I tried to encourage you while there was hope ; but now, perhaps it is better for you to prepare for the worst. Ella darling, if I die, you had better marry Sinclair, and have the protection of those who are able to save you from the perils which will beset you. You will be poor and friendless—for my property will be confiscated."

" Never, father !" something in her face proved that she meant what she said ; " Mr. Le Vert will seem to me like your murderer."

" He is a K. G. C., Ella ; a Knight of the Golden Circle ;— he was acting out the principles of his order when he denounced me to them. Alas, then I see no way to assure your safety, so that I may feel, in leaving this world, that you are provided for."

" I wish no better fate than yours, father. If they murder you, they may murder me if they will."

" Poor, foolish child !"

" But, father, do not think I am so witless as to make not
one effort to save you," she whispered. " I must be quick, or
my half hour will be up"—she cast a shy glance at the three
strangers, then, with a half-smile, asked her father to make a
curtain of the blanket on the bed. A small penknife which
she had brought in her glove did good service, for in less than
two minutes, the revolver, brought to light from some mysterious complication of crinoline, was in Mr. Beaufort's hand, and
as much more time revealed sufficient material for charging
it ; Eleanor was too artful for the woman who conducted the
search ; her cunning stitch and her persuasive manners had
achieved the triumph.

" My friends," said Mr. Beaufort, turning to his companions,
while a gleam lighted up his worn face, " this will assist us
much in our plan," and he slipped it out of sight in the straw
of his mattress. " And now, Eleanor, I have to tell you in
the three minutes left us, that we have friends, outside, in the
Confederate guard.   There is _a chance_ that we may escape
within the next thirty-six hours.   Go home—gather my
papers and valuables, and fasten them upon your person.   If
I escape, if I can with any prudence, I will make a flying
visit home.   If I escape, and do not dare attempt it, friends
will watch over you ; if you are in any great peril, they will
endeavor to protect you.   You may remain, and try to keep
the estate together, unless you receive warning to fly.   The
time is up ; they are at the door, Eleanor ; if the worst happens
be brave and good.   God bless you !"

The rude summons of the guard caused her father to
lead her to the door ; she could not speak ; grief clutched
at her throat and choked her words ; a rough hand drew
her into the hall ; the key grated as only prison keys can
grate.

" Don't be standin' thar' like a goose on one leg," said the guard, slapping her across the back with his musket,

The lookers-on laughed at the joke—while Eleanor, aroused from her trance by the word and blow, flashed a glance at the soldier's face which might have withered it. Something she saw there made her look again—she had seen the man before, she did⁻not remember where, but that was not what caused her sudden interest,

" You're hard on the young woman, Dan," laughed one of his fellow-soldiers.

" Oh, that's only turkey-talk," responded Dan. " I reckon the young lady never heard no turkey-talk before ; but she's likely to, 'fore long, if she don't change her politics."

It was the expression of his face, more than what he said, which recalled to her vividly the queer visitor who had been first to inform her of her father's arrest ; he had told her, then, that he thought of volunteering, which, it now appeared, he had done. Eleanor was bewildered. The coarse jest and blow (which had been light enough) gave the lie to the friendly spirit he had then shown ; she had no time to consider, and her mind was in too much confusion ; but when she had once more taken her seat in the afternoon-train for home, and sat thinking over what her father had said about having kind friends in the guard, a glimmer of the truth dawned upon her perception.

CHAPTER VII.

KNIGHTS OF THE GOLDEN CIRCLE.

THE evening of the destruction of the store-house on the Beaufort plantation, the attention of Mr. Le Vert. had been attracted to the conflagration, and he had mounted his horse and ridden over to see what was going on. Perceiving the nature of the case, he made no attempt to interfere, but continued his ride to the village, where he called at the post-office, and received, among other things, a sealed circular, reading much in this wise:

"DEAR SIR—It has been decided by a vote of the members of the different castles of the K. G. C.'s of the city of Nashville, to have a general Convention meet in this city on May —, 1861, for purposes of business of importance. It is, therefore, our earnest desire, that you should lay the subject before your castle immediately, that you may meet with us; and we request that as many meet as possible, as the growth and success of our order in future depends greatly upon its numbers and appearance on that occasion. You will please notify all your castles within your county and reach, and be very cautious that outsiders do not find out what we are doing. And if you are not particular about your place of stopping, we would suggest that —— House, on —— street, would be a suitable place.

"NASHVILLE, May —."

In consequence of receiving this circular, Mr. Le Vert was in Nashville the day after Eleanor's visit to that city; and that night, in a certain large hall of a certain hotel, with locked doors, among a great amount of other business transacted, the immediate execution of Mr. Beaufort and one of his companions was decided upon ; and that night, the order was received at the prison for their death, by hanging, at nine o'clock the next morning. It was likewise decided that a large share of the confiscated estates of his old neighbor should fall to Le Vert in reward of his zeal and ability as a leading Knight of the Golden Circle.

But the next morning the news spread rapidly that the whole four occupants of room No. 18 had taken flight, the two condemned ones, of course, making half the party.

Late on the previous evening, while all was quiet at the prison, one of the two guards in that hall into which the door of room No. 18 opened, was summoned to the door by knocking, and when he demanded what was wanted, one of the prisoners had begged for some water—his nose was bleeding excessively. When he unlocked the door to give him the basin, he, the guard, received a blow between the eyes which made the fire fly—in fact, he knew no more of what occurred. When he recovered himself, he found his companion gagged and tied, and the whole building alarmed. The sentry at the outer door had been shot dead ; every thing was in confusion. The police were immediately notified, and the whole force of detectives was at once at work throughout the city and every avenue leading out of it.

It seems that the guard, who had been gagged and tied, was the one who had spoken so coarsely to Eleanor Beaufort on the previous day. His kickings and contortions, until he was released, and the gag taken from his mouth, were wonderful to behold ; and his rage, when he regained his feet, was equally so.

" Dod blast the varmints, what did they stuff thar corn-cobs in my mouth fur?" spitting and sputtering ; " springin' on a man like a painter out of a tree, when he wasn't a-lookin' for 'em—cuss the deceitful Union abolishioners ! If ever I set eyes on *them* agen, you'd better believe I'll cram a gag down their throats so fur they'll never git it out. It was mean enough to tie a pusson's hands; but when it comes to splitting his mouth with a wedge, as if his head was a log of wood—blast 'em, I say, all I want is a chance to return the joke."

. "Thought you was a match for any four, Dan," said one of the crowd, jeeringly.

"So I am, in a fair fight. Dang it, if they'd come back here, now, I'd thrash the whole of 'em at a time. But when a pusson's surprised from behind [cough]—ugh! I'll never git the taste of that kind o' vittals out o' my mouth, till I've stuffed some of the same kind down thur's. I allus had an idee my mouth was big enough, without being operated on. My maum used to say it scart her when vittals wasn't plenty. If anybody had told me Turkey Dan would be fed on corn-cobs by a jail-bird, I'd 'ave thrashed 'im fer lyin'."

Here he walked up and down, too excited to contain himself. Some who had envied him his reputation for being a match against any odds, were disposed to rejoice over his ill-fortune.

"Don't, Captain, *don't* say a word," he implored, as the Captain of the guard came up; "I'm disgraced, and I know it. I shan't hold up my head in these parts agin. I feel like a b'ar that's lost his paw in a trap—'shamed and mad! All I ask is this—jest get me put on their track! I've been in the p'lice business not very far since—I'll hole 'em, if I have to burrow cl'ar down to a warmer climate. And when they're caught, I'll take it as a special favor to be allowed to pull the drop."

The result of Dan's rage and mortification was, that he was given furlough to look up the missing prisoners; if nothing was heard of them within a week, he was to report himself

He had been on guard only three days, since his return from his secret service in East Tennessee, and had only filled that position while waiting further orders. However, the case in hand seemed one peculiarly appropriate to his talents, and his officers were almost disposed to forgive his want of vigilance in allowing their escape, in the great hope they had that he would ferret out the fugitives.

In the mean time, it was a mystery how they had been supplied with the means of escape. That one or more of them had been armed was evident from the fact that the sentry was not shot with his own weapons—it was a pistol-shot wound, two reports of a pistol having also been heard by those who rushed to the spot. The fact of Miss Beaufort having been admitted to the room was recalled; the woman who had searched her person was subjected to severe examination; but she persisted, in tears and under oath, that she had instituted the most careful search, and had found nothing whatever suspicious about her. The basket of dainties had also been most carefully investigated, and nothing more injurious than minced-pie had been contained in it.

It is doubtful if Mr. Le Vert heard of the escape of Mr. Beaufort with as much pleasure as his son Sinclair, whom the vision of Eleanor, as he had seen her on that day, had not elevated in spirits already somewhat depressed by the orders to leave for a distant State, to engage in a war which his heart and conscience in vain endeavored to approve. If it seems unnatural that Mr. Le Vert could have thus aided and abetted the ruin and death of his old friend, then this war of prejudice and ambition has filled the Southern States with just such monsters, thick as leaves in Vallambrosa. He took pains himself to see Turkey Dan, and to offer him privately a double gold eagle as a stimulus to active exertion.

"I don't need nuthin' more'n the taste o' them corn-cobs to

make me savage as a mad alligator," said Dan, as he took the glittering offering. "Howsomever, Judge, seein' it's you, I won't hurt your feelin's by refusin' it. I'll have my paws around their necks in less'n six and thirty hours, or I'll deliver myself up to be hanged in their place. Dead or alive, I s'pose, Judge?"

"Dead or alive," was the terse reply.

"Jest as you say, squire. I've tracked turkeys all my life, now I'll try my luck at a brace of jail-birds."

The result, by-the-by, of Dan's detective mission in East Tennessee had been that he had reported Beverly Bell to be intrenched with a force of men, at a point so far distant from the real spot, or from any Union district, as he dared to put it; and that a large band of armed guerrillas had consequently been dispatched on a wild-goose chase into the midst of a people after their own hearts.

"Bless you, Captain," he said, as he was telling the story, "I slept in his own camp all night; I eat their last hoe-cake, and drunk their last drop o' whisky. I could have cut off Bell's head with my bowie-knife, and brought it to you, without any trouble; but I thought it would be better to make sure of the hull herd. I was willin' to give up the prize, ruther than alarm the coveys, and see 'em all take to flight. They're thar, now—you can trap every one of the infested three hundred, if you're quick enough about it. I was so clus' to the bird I could have put salt on its tail. Mind, now, when they're nabbed I'm to have them two hundred we talked about."

"Never doubt that, my friend," was the cheerful reply of the gratified officer, whom the prospect of securing three hundred of the ringleaders had filled with a *promising* and liberal exuberance of generosity.

CHAPTER VIII.

PUNISHING A WOMAN.

THE third evening after her return from Nashville, Eleanor sat in the library, leaning her head on her hand, lost in reverie. She had obeyed her father's command to collect the most valuable of his papers, and some small articles of peculiar value to him, amid which were her lost mother's jewels; these she had stitched into her garments, and had slept with them about her person the last two nights. Her own watch, a present from her father, she wore, with some other of her most prized ornaments, and in her pocket she carried a purse with a moderate supply of gold.

As she sat in the lonely, dimly-lighted room, strange thoughts filled her heart to overflowing. Would her father escape? *had* he escaped? would they ever meet again? If she got away with the small part of their possessions secured upon her person, where was she to go, how to live, what to do? If her father should be murdered, what would she, a penniless orphan, driven out of her home and country, do? Oh, she would die! Death would be welcome, rather than the troubles she saw in store. Her eyes wandered over the bindings of the dear old books, over the familiar pictures, over the portrait of her mother which hung above her father's writing-desk, and ever grew larger and more troubled as they gazed, while the wan look about the temples from which she had pushed away the hair showed how busy care had been with the young brain. Deep as was her reverie, her face had yet the look of one listening. Her ear had been on the strain for forty-eight hours to detect the slightest signal, if perchance her father should return; even in sleep she had

listened, starting from her slumber at the faintest sound.
Now, as the clock was on the stroke of nine, she sprung to
her feet, standing eager and motionless, gazing toward the
closed door. She had heard the careful click of the gate, and
the fall of many feet, soft feet, treading lightly—so lightly
that no one not listening, as she had been, would have noticed
it. The blood beat in her ears, her breath came fast. There
were a few moments of mysterious movement about the lawn,
and then came a loud knock at the hall-door. Ah! it was
not *them!* they would have been less noisy—but it *might* be!
She sprung into the hall, as Jim came from the dining-room.

"Ask who it is," she said.

"Who's dar?"

"A friend," was the whispered reply.

"Open the door," was the mistress' command, which was
obeyed, and the light of the hall-lamp flashed over the sword
and epaulets of a Confederate officer, backed by a *posse* of
soldiers. The same treachery which has distinguished their
cause from the beginning, was betrayed in this lying appeal—
a treachery which has culminated in flags of truce and Stars
and Stripes, appealing to the friendship of our too generous
men in battle, to their own destruction at the hands of cowards
too mean, and liars too base, for Lucifer himself to own
fellowship with them.

"Is Walter Beaufort on these premises?"

"He is not."

"It is useless to say so, if he is here. There is a double
guard at every door and window of this house; and if he
gives himself up without further words, it will save us the
unpleasant necessity of searching the place."

"Has he escaped?" the eager, joyful voice in which the
question was put, was evidence of its sincerity.

The officer gave her a sharp glance, answering:

"Was you not aware of it?"

"Thank God!" was the young girl's only reply, clasping her hands together.

"We're not going to be taken in by that kind of gammon," continued the officer. "He may be in this house, spite of your pretty prayers, miss. We will see."

"Search! search!" cried Eleanor, almost cheerfully; then in her silent heart she prayed that her father might not be tempted to try and see her, now that it had proved so dangerous. Into every nook and cranny of the large mansion, attic, cellar, closets, wardrobes, into the young lady's chamber, tearing up the nice beds spread in the spare bed-rooms, ripping up mattresses with their swords, pulling down draperies, regardless of the wreck they left behind them, went a dozen or more of lawless soldiers, led by their officers. If Liza, who was a tall, stalwart woman, more soldierly in her bearing than the men who were now making bandits of themselves in the Beaufort mansion, had not followed them up with vigilant eyes, there would have been nothing left many hours after the search was over, as they twice carelessly set fire to curtains and clothing, and did not trouble themselves to extinguish the flames. The soul of the faithful slave burned with wrath, as she heard the crash of mirrors wantonly broken, and saw the splendors of that old, aristocratic mansion, her pride and glory, wantonly desecrated. As for Eleanor, she sat on the hall settee, remonstrating with no word or tear, against any amount of destruction—her heart was full of her father's fate; she was insensible to any other fear than the absorbing terror of his getting back into hands so false and savage.

Although they found no fugitives secreted in the cellar, the soldiers found wine there in profusion, and they helped themselves accordingly. Choice vintages, which had done honor to the Beauforts' hospitable board, were poured down whisky-hardened throats, and even upon the more worthy ground.

The guards at the windows and doors, the gates and all the outposts, were liberally supplied; and to this the officers made no objections; but when the search was over, and the two had betaken themselves to the library to carry on there a private search for such papers, etc., as they might find, they politely requested the lady of the mansion to order in refreshments, with a bottle or two of their best old Madeira, as they had ridden some distance since dinner, and were famished and thirsty in consequence.

"Since you have taken possession, you will order what you please," said Eleanor. "I shall order nothing. With your permission, I will retire to my room, with the single request, that you will not needlessly destroy papers of no importance to you."

She would have preferred remaining during this examination of the library; but the carousal of the soldiers was getting too boisterous for her ears, and as she had every thing upon her person which she had really hoped to preserve, she thought it prudent to shut herself in her room. She had already dispatched word to Pompey to choose two or three more of the servants, who were to take up their quarters for the night on the upper hall floor; with these, and her revolver, she had no especial fear for herself.

"We're going as soon as we have our supper," replied one of the officers. "We shall leave a guard over the premises, so long as there is any likelihood of Mr. Beaufort's trying to return here; and shall be obliged to order that your cook supply them with rations. Invading armies must be maintained by the enemy, you know, madam, ha! ha! By the way, Miss Beaufort, there's some talking of arresting *you*. It's very singular that weapons should have been supplied to the fugitives, the day of your visit, probably."

"If your cause is in such straits as to make it necessary to arrest women, I trust your chivalric instincts will not stand in the way," retorted the young lady. "For my part, I am very willing to take my father's place."

"We may have you and him too, as for that. We have too many on his track to favor the idea of his escape. Should he be retaken, his time will be short; orders came for his execution the very night of his escape."

"For what crime?" asked Eleanor.

"For several crimes of the blackest dye: for living in opposition to the Jeff. Davis Government; for refusing to vote in favor of the Military League; for refusing to vote for secession; for refusing to volunteer in the time of his country's danger. Every such traitorous, d——d rascal ought to swing, and will, madam, you may rest assured."

"Yes," continued his companion, "we will be rid of every such d——d dangerous red-republican; we will destroy them, root and branch; so that when this Confederacy is reorganized as it ought to be, there will not remain the smallest fiber of the poisonous tree to take root again. The time has passed when republican sentiments can live at the South; we will be gentlemen and aristocrats, and rule our slaves as we please."

"I am pleased to hear that you are going to be gentlemen," said Eleanor, as she turned away and passed up stairs.

"Her tongue's a little too sharp for us, Captain," said one of them, laughing. "By George, I'd like to see that girl Presidentess of the Confederacy. She's got as much pluck as she has beauty, and that's saying a good deal."

"You'd better try your influence at converting her," said the Captain, testily. "Come, let's see about that supper, and get through with this."

Jim, not having the courage of Liza, who flatly refused to wait on them, brought in the best he could find.

"This is rare," said the Captain; as he sipped the wine, "let us put a bottle or two in our knapsacks for lunch to-morrow."

Finally, at about midnight, with much clamor, the squad departed, having detailed a portion of their force to remain as guard, and to keep a sharp look-out for the fugitives. The guards, on whom their deep potations began to tell, soon grew silent; and Eleanor, who had paced her room, unable to sleep or rest, at last threw herself on the bed, knowing well that she would be in poor plight to meet difficulties yet to come, if she did not snatch some repose.

As she lay on her bed, with half-closed eyes, trying vainly to still the rapid whirling of her brain, her door, which she had purposely left unlocked, with Pompey barricading it on the outside, softly unclosed, and the figure of the cook, Liza, entered and approached her.

"What do you want, Liza? you'd better go to bed," she spoke, without rising from her pillow.

"Eleanor!"

She sprung to the floor with a bound.

"At my own peril, I could not help coming to say farewell, perhaps forever."

"Father!"

The disguise was very perfect; Liza, as we have said, was tall and masculine in her appearance, and a complete suit of her garments worn over his own apparel, a deep, slouched sun-bonnet, and a little burnt cork, made a figure very passable, in the night, at least.

"Oh, I am so sorry you are here!"

"Don't fear for me. The guard are all dead drunk and asleep. I have good plans of escape. I have changed my dress, hair and complexion; and there are those who will help us into East Tennessee, if we don't get outwitted. Have you those papers with you, Ella?"

"They are here."

"Well, perhaps they are safe with you. Can you keep them about you, without discomfort?"

"Yes, father."

"If you have any money with you, share it with me. I am destitute. And now, to what I want most to say. Start on the early train to-morrow for Nashville; if you go quietly to the dépôt, without the carriage, I think you can get off; when you arrive at Nashville, take the cars on the Nashville and Chatanooga road, down to the Junction in Alabama, where you must take the Eastern and Virginia road for Knox-ville. If asked any questions, you are going to see friends in that place. When you arrive there, go to No. —— in —— street, ask for Clay Putnam, give your name, and you will be welcomed by friends who will take care of you. There wait, until you hear from me. I shall be longer in making my journey than you will yours; but God willing, I shall greet you there within ten days. From thence we must make our escape northward, or to the mountains, as best we can. You have given me pretty much all your money, I see. Your journey will be long and tiresome, and cost you something. If you have not enough, you must borrow of Pompey; he has money, I know, and he can repay himself out of the place. Poor Pomp, if they confiscate him, he will have a hard time. He knows it, and he is bound to escape, if he can. I have told him to do so, since I never expect to get my property together again. And now, darling, be brave and prudent, and I hope you will soon be out of this."

"I dread to let you go, father, and I dread worse to have you stay. I feel sick at heart."

"Don't give up, *now*, my daughter—now, when there is so much to hope. Good-by; I must be far from this before daylight. I shall leave Liza's clothes in Pomp's cabin; but if you were to see me in my new suit, even you wouldn't know me ! I've turned bushwacker, Ella."

He kissed her, and was gone.

It seemed to Eleanor as if she had dropped into a troubled sleep when Pompey aroused her, by whispering within the door :

" It's time to be gittin' ready fer de cars, missus."

She arose and dressed in the early dawn, gave one look around the beloved chamber which had been her's since infancy, took up her traveling basket, kissed Lina, weeping in the hall, and descended to the door, only to be repulsed by the sword of the soldier standing guard.

" I've orders to keep the lady within doors. You're a pris'ner, miss, in your own house."

" Oh, why was I so foolish as not to foresee this, and to steal away before daybreak," she murmured to herself. " I shall be delayed twenty-four hours at least. My only hope is to escape from some of the windows, to-night."

" I wished to go to a friend's. It's not very pleasant for me to remain here under the circumstances."

" 'Spect not ; but can't help it, mum."

So she went back to her chamber, laid aside her bonnet, flung herself on the bed, and cried herself into a deep sleep.

When she awoke, the sun was shining high in the heavens ; it took her some time to recall late events, and to realize that the bright flush of this June morning could bring no happiness to her. The roses, clambering up the portico, swung themselves in at her window, sparkling and blushing, unconscious of impending doom—the world had never been more lovely than on that cloudless day.

" I'se brought your breakfas' here," said Lina, seeing her mistress awake, " so's you needn' meet dem sassy soljers. It's all ready 'cept de eggs and coffee. I'se goin' down fer dem.

Say, missus," she whispered, " Liza says she's got rat-powder enough to pizen the hull of 'em, ef you'll let her."

" Ah, no !" cried Eleanor, shuddering, " I could not consent to such a thing—it would be horrible."

" You could git away, you know, missus."

" Yes, I know, Lina ; but I shall only kill another in actual defense of my own life and honor—no, no ! tell Liza to ' bottle her wrath,' and do the best she can."

Eleanor had not finished her breakfast, before the noise of marching men drew Lina to the window.

" Oh, missus, dey'll never have done wid dis poor house," cried the maid, " dey're stoppin' here."

Miss Beaufort looked out, and such a set of faces as met her eyes she had never imagined before. There were perhaps two hundred men, mounted and armed, dressed in all conceivable styles, with all kinds of weapons. And such desperate, repulsive faces ! She grew white at the first glance of them.

" They are not-regular soldiers. They are the guerrillas I have been reading about," she cried. " Oh, what do they want here !"

The Stars and Bars floated in the air over the villainous array. Some half-dozen of their number rode in the gate ; and shortly after, Pompey came up to inform his mistress that they had made a demand for breakfast.

" Give them every thing they ask," said Eleanor, more terrified than she had been on any previous occasion. " Tell Liza to make coffee—don't make them angry."

Most of the men dismounted, fastened their horses and threw themselves on the grass of the lawn and on the piazza, and a dozen negroes were soon busy watering and feeding the animals, encouraged by the oaths and kicks of the intruders.

All kinds of coarse speeches and cries floated up to the young girl's window, tainting the pure summer air with their grossness.

"Hang out the Stars and Bars!" " —— old renegade, wait till *we* get hold of him!" "We'll tar and feather him!" "We'll roast him by a slow fire, when we catch him!" "Help yourselves, friends, to the best thar' is!" "Where's the gal?" "Helped get him off, did she?" etc., etc.

Eleanor felt almost forsaken of God and man as she heard the frightful rabble—not a friend near, save the few dependents—oh, then how the happy period, this June a year ago, rushed back over her mind, only to make her present danger more appalling. She carefully examined her revolver, and placed it in her bosom. She could use it to defend herself against insult, if she were obliged to turn it against her own heart.

For a while the clamor was changed to the sound of eating and drinking, as all the women on the place were pressed into service to cook for and wait on the unwelcome visitors. But the coffee with which they were supplied was not sufficient for their thirst; a half-drunken guard initiated them into the mysteries of the wine-cellar, and the effect was soon apparent in their increased turbulence.

"Go and tell your mistress we've got a thing or two to ask her," said one of the leaders of the band to Pompey.

"Please 'scuse her, sir," said the slave, deprecatingly.

"Can't, on no account—want to know how t'was she got that revolver to her father. Blast her, she's got to show herself."

"She ain't berry well, missus ain't—she's sick a-bed—" stammered Pompey.

"Oh, is she!" derisively; "then we'll go and take her out. Come on, boys—hurrah!"

"Oh, don't," cried the slave, "I'll fotch her. I'll fotch her right away."

"Do it then, double-quick. Now, boys, we'll have some fun catechizing this Union female."

The whole group gathered about the piazza to "see the fun." In the mean time Pomp ran up to Miss Beaufort's room and gave her the alarm.

"Jes' you steal down back stairs, put on Liza's bonnet and cut over to my wife's cabin—you can hide in de loft, missa."

She lost no time in endeavoring to profit by his suggestion; but the guard at the back entrance detected and stopped her.

"For God's sake, let me go," she pleaded in agony, "I will come back, I promise you I will, when these desperadoes are gone."

He hesitated. The pleading face of the young girl moved him to pity, and he was about to let her pass; but he was too late; a few of the guerrillas, impatient at the delay, were looking for her on their own account, and now seized her and pushed her through the hall on to the front piazza.

"Here's the she abolitioner!" they cried, pulling off her bonnet.

"Don't touch me," she said, to those who were holding her, "I will stand to be looked at as long as you like, if you will keep a little further off."

She folded her arms, and her dauntless glance answered back the hundreds of wolfish eyes which glared at her; she was pale, but she gave no evidence of fear.

Groans, cheers and yells greeted the statue-like girl. In the front ranks, chafing like a caged tiger, his hands tied by a piece of rope, and held by a number of men, Pompey looked on, helpless, while his young mistress faced down with heroic composure the insults of the mob.

"What do you think you deserve for helpin them four scoundrels out o' prison?"

No answer.

"Did you convey to 'em the pistol by means of which a sentry was shot?"

"You dasn't answer. Of course not. You ought to be shot to make up fer that ar' sentry. What dy'e say, feller citizens, had'nt she oughter be shot?"

"Yes, or horse-whipped."

"You may shoot me, as soon as you please. I wish you would."

The clear young voice, sweet and calm, had just the faintest tremble in it as she said she coveted death. If this had been a mob from her own village she would have had more hope; but they were all strangers, brutal, sullen, sunk in savageness to less than the wild beasts, lawless, roaming the country for just such raids as these.

"Oh, ho! shootin's too good fer you. I think a dozen lashes would be about the thing. What say?"

"Go in—I'll give her one!"

"Here's a hoss-whip, purty well seasoned. It's been most used up in such bizness already."

Half a dozen brutes advanced while their comrades pressed closer, jeering and approving.

With a quick movement Eleanor drew the revolver from her bosom. She glanced behind her—alas! she was surrounded. If she could have stood with her back to the wall of the house, she would have kept them at bay, or been shot where she stood; but those who had dragged her there were behind her.

"Keep off!" she cried, leveling the weapon at the one nearest; but her arms were seized by those in the rear, and her last defense taken from her.

"Thirteen lashes on the bare back for that," yelled one.

Their sacrilegious hands had scarcely touched her, before with a roar like the gorillas in their native forest, Pompey snapped the rope which bound his wrists as if it had been thread, dashed through all opposition, leveling every thing near him; snatched Eleanor from her tormentors, swung her like a babe across his shoulder, and with his giant right arm for a buckler, sprung through the band into the hall, shut and bound the door, ran through, upsetting the guard at the opposite end, and darted down the lane which led off the other side the orchard. The marauders lost a moment in pounding at the door, before any of them thought of surrounding the house; and by the time they had recalled their wits and were making their appearance in the rear, he had almost gained the shelter of the trees and fence. With shouts and yells they pursued, pouring a rain of shot after the fugitives. A rifle-ball went through the noble fellow's arm, but he slackened not his speed. They saw that pursuit on foot would be useless, and many returned to mount their horses. At this critical moment, Pomp turned from the alley into the same road which his master had once pursued on his midnight flight. The trees here gave him protection against the shower of bullets, and he pressed on, so desperately that he did not perceive a horseman coming toward him, till a peculiar cry arrested him, and he looked up, to see, and say :

" Take her, Dan, and ride for her life."

" Hand her up," said Dan, " and you, jump into that ravine, and crouch down in the grass and bushes."

As the mounted man dashed into the tree-shadowed lane, afar down the vista the pursuers perceived a horse and two riders, the fluttering garments of a woman proving one of them to be their intended victim.

" Blast the nigger! how did he get a horse ?"

It was useless to pursue, for the long leaps of the animal in advance of them showed him of superior fleetness; so they returned, sullenly, to revenge themselves by such desecration of the old mansion as best gratified their malice. Books and papers strewed the winds, pictures were defaced, draperies cut and slashed, vases were dashed to atoms, the plate stolen, and every vine and flower cut down, sashes and doors broken in, and the ruined mansion left, like a skeleton on a gibbet, a warning to Union sinners. But of such warning there was no further need in this vicinity. The last and only family of any mark was driven out, and henceforth their history was mixed up with that of many others, in a part of the State where secession had not as yet so fully flowered.

CHAPTER IX.

FLEEING FOR LIFE.

THE hot sun of a June afternoon shone down into a lonely valley, lying high amid the Cumberland hills—a valley so secluded that it seemed as if the deep grass had never been trodden by mortal footstep; yet along the bed of a small stream babbling through it might be traced not only the track of human feet, but the deeper pressure of horses' hoofs and of wagon-wheels. Along the almost obliterated marks of former journeyings were fresh traces of recent travelers. And now there came into it, through a narrow defile at its western extremity, a stout wagon of the type used by farmers, well-filled by women and children, and surrounded by an escort of forty-three armed men on horseback. They came along rather slowly, for the sun was scorching, and the road not very closely defined, lying mostly in the bed of the shallow creek.

"How do you stand it, Ella?" asked one of the riders, coming up beside the wagon.

"Oh, father, don't ask *me ;* I am young and well. Poor Mrs. Bostwick has almost given out."

"No, not so bad as that," replied a pale young woman, lying in the bottom of the wagon, with a folded blanket under her head, making a miserable effort to smile. "Miss Beaufort is so kind, she has made me lie down a while. Poor baby, how does she look now?"

"She is sleeping nicely," responded Eleanor, looking down into the wee, pinched face of a three-weeks-old infant she was holding. "Why no ; she is not sleeping — she is—father, look here !"

"Blessed babe," said Mr. Beaufort, speaking very soothingly and low, for he feared the shock upon the weakened nerves of the mother—"blessed, happy babe, its little troubles are soon over. It is better off than we are, Mrs. Bostwick."

"What do you mean?" she cried, raising herself with a wild look. "Ah, Carrie, my baby, my baby !" and she snatched the tiny corpse from the arms of her friend, pressing it to her bosom as if she could restore life to it from the fountains of her own heart. The three children in the wagon pressed up to the sides of their mothers, looking awed at they knew not what ; for a moment or two there was silence, save the moans of the young mother.

"It is a grief to you, dear lady, but it is better for the child," said Mr. Beaufort, presently.

"Perhaps so," she said, meekly, "but it is *our first,* our dear little daughter. Tell Henry."

The gentleman rode forward to one of the persons in advance, a fine, energetic-looking young man, who dropped back

beside the wagon to see his sick wife weeping over their dead
child, till scalding tears ran down his own sun-browned
cheeks.

A bitterness worked in his blood which faith nor patience
could longer sweeten; his delicate wife jeopardizing health
and life, enduring untold privations; his first-born dead of
exposure; their home, the fruit of his best labors, in the hands
of a reckless rabble ! He did not weep for the lost home nor
the lost infant; these things embittered his blood ; but the
great tears were wrung out, drop by drop, at the sight of his
gentle Annie, wasted and worn, looking up at him distress-
fully and holding the little corpse to her bosom. When such
men weep there is meaning in their tears ; it was more painful to see him than the mother.

A strange company was that gathered together in the wagon.
A common cause and common persecution had made friends
and allies of those but a few days ago strangers to each other.
Eleanor Beaufort had been the most luxuriously reared of any
in that little band; but all were women of intelligence, accustomed to rather more than the comforts of life. One of them,
the mother of two little boys of six and seven, was the wife
of a printer in Knoxville; she had left him behind, in prison,
with hardly a hope of ever beholding his face again ; but they
had burned her house, turned her and her little ones into the
street, giving her twenty-four hours to leave that part of the
country, or run the risk of being publicly whipped, and having her head shaved. The other was the wife of a well-to-do
farmer, whose corn had been confiscated, whose barns burned,
and who was now in the company, armed to the teeth, eager
to return, when the women were in a place of safety, and give
fight to the rascals who had destroyed his property. They
had with them a little girl.

Mr. Bostwick was a merchant in a small village not fa.

removed from Knoxville ; his vine-covered cottage—a bower of roses, where only the year before he had borne his bride, and where, three weeks since, a blue-eyed babe had opened its eyes in a shadowed and flower-perfumed room—was in ruins —the guerrillas had helped themselves freely to the contents of his store, and he and his sick wife were flying for life.

Every suffering heart in that company wept with the afflicted parents—it was a band of sisters and brothers.

" Halt !" cried the leader of the party ; " fall back !"

The horsemen closed around the wagon, which came to a stand.

" Don't like the looks o' them bushes," said the sharp, peculiar voice of Turkey Dan, who, sitting his horse as well as he bore his rifle, was the one who had given the order. " I'm gwine to beat the bush, 'fore I let the women-folks any nearer."

Three or four hundred yards ahead, a thick growth of tall hazel-bushes fringed a slight rise in the bank of the stream.

" I wan't lookin' for the devils in this vicinity, no more'n I'd look in a squirrel-hole for a b'ar ; but I'll be chawed up fer bait, ef that ain't the track of a bushwhacker thar in the mud —an' they've tuk to the grass to conceal it," he remarked, casting a keen glance at the tall grass rippling in the breeze, which to an inexperienced eye betrayed no signs of having lately been disturbed. " Wish we had a few trees or a bit of hill to cover the wagon ; but thar ain't such a thing on hand, and we can't stop to make 'em. Have your rifles ready, boys, and stay whar you ar', till Joe and I find out whether thar's anything wuss'n blue-birds in them bushes."

He and his companion rode slowly forward until within about two hundred yards of the suspected ambush, and then began to perform a circuit. Suddenly the sharp crack of two rifles rung on the air, and the thin blue smoke curled up from behind the hazels. The two men instantly wheeled, riding toward their company, and shouting:

"Forward, boys; but don't come within gunshot. Make 'em come out. We're not such fools as to run our head agin a wall—then 'tain't called for. Ef they want to fight, let 'em show their dirty faces. Ho! couldn't hit a full-sized man at a couple o' hundred yards! They ain't much. Let 'em come out. Wimmen-folks, lie low, when you see the shot a-flyin'."

They formed in line and rode a little forward. Bostwick placed himself in the front rank, with a deadly glitter in his eyes, from which the tears had washed all dimness; Mr. Beaufort was by his side—he, though not overly skillful with the rifle, was one of the few of the South's really chivalric sons—one not to lag behind in time of danger; and he knew the use of the revolver in his pocket—the same weapon that had assisted in his release from a Nashville prison. An old sword hung by his side which had done service in the Revolution—a Union matron had brought it forth from the chest in the attic of a farm-house, where it had long lain rusting.

They had to wait some moments for the expected attack. It was probable that the party in ambush, not being mounted, were unwilling to come out on a fair field; it seemed a lack of prudence in them to have betrayed their existence by their fire, as they had; but the conjecture was that they had recognized Turkey Dan, and had resolved to win that prize, if it should be at the expense of the escape of all the rest.

As they waited, just outside of rifle-range, the simultaneous crack of fifty rifles startled the quiet—the guerrillas had relied upon their splendid weapons for carrying a longer distance than they would, or the peculiar state of the atmosphere, sultry and promising showers, had made the Union men appear nearer than they really were—not a shot took effect.

"At 'em!" yelled Dan, swinging his weapon around over his head, "don't give 'em a chance to load,"—and the cavalry dashed forward up to the ambush, pouring their fire into the thicket and plunging into it pell-mell. They were met at the onset with a reserve fire of at least twenty. Mr. Beaufort's horse staggered and fell, his rider just missing being crushed under him; two were wounded; the others pressed on, firing, and cutting into the bushes with their knives. Turkey Dan rode up to the shelter of a thick clump, and deliberately picked off three or four of the enemy, as they rose from their hiding-places—discharging his rifle and all the barrels of his revolver, then pausing to load for a second charge. Mr. Beaufort, dismounted, protected himself by lying alongside his dying horse, and had the satisfaction of seeing one savage drop beneath his fire.

The bushwhackers, though double in number, and concealed, were taken at a disadvantage. They probably had not expected so well-armed and resolute a foe.

"At 'em, boys," screamed Dan, ready for another onset. "Three cheers for the good old flag, and no quarter!"

The men did not stand upon the order of their fighting. The past and future was in their thoughts, as well as the present with its wagon-load of trembling women near at hand.

At the second charge, the enemy broke cover and fled, hoping to intrench themselves behind a low ridge lying a short distance to the right, whence to obtain a chance for deliberate aim; but the cavalry were too much for them; many fell, rode down and bayoneted; and the remainder scattered to such shelter as they could find, worming themselves through the grass like the serpents they were. There was no further attempt at the offensive, and the travelers having routed the bushwhackers utterly, returned to the women, watching the scene with blanched faces—they had none of them obeyed the injunction to " lie low "—they had too great an interest in the struggle.

And now came a sad addition to the number in the wagon. The two men wounded at the first fire, bleeding and begging for water, were conveyed to the vehicle, where Mr. Beaufort, as the most skillful of the party, dressed their wounds as well as circumstances permitted. One was shot in the shoulder ; the other had his left hand dreadfully lacerated.

Then came a still more mournful duty. One of their number, a young man, barely twenty, full of hope and strength, had fallen, shot through the heart. They must bury him. They dared not remain where they were through the coming night; the one vehicle was already overcrowded ; there was nothing to do but to hide in a hasty grave the noble form two hours ago breathing life and animation as flowers breathe perfume. Silently, with swords, and an ax with which one of the company was armed, they chopped out a grave.

Blind with tears, Eleanor wrapped the shawl about the corpse, whose face wore that smile which some who die suddenly, have; they laid him in the hollow bed; then Mrs. Bostwick came forward, kissed her little babe softly, and laid it down herself on the young man's breast; the shawl was their only coffin ; a prayer was said by an old man of their number, the earth was replaced.

The sun set as the earth closed over the grave; a burst of thunder shook the sky, from a ragged cloud flying up from the south-west. Mr. Beaufort had taken a smooth board from a box in the wagon, and marked thereon with a sharp stone :

HIRAM ARNOLD, aged 20 years.

CAROLINE BOSTWICK, aged 3 weeks.

Victims of Tennessee Tyranny.

JUNE 21st, 1861.

This he lingered behind to set up as a head-stone, while Dan hurried the company onward.

"It'll be pitch dark in half an hour, ef them clouds don't lie. We'll never get to Sallie's to-night. That's done gone up. It's goin' to rain pitchforks and blow harrycanes. It's onsafe to stay here; might be s'prised by bushwhackers agin. Thar's a place, about three miles ahead, if we can reach it 'fore the storm busts, we'll be all right. It's a cave, a little off the wood. Rain and wind won't opset us thar, only thar's a power of snakes, 'specially rattles. But we'll build a fire, and whip 'em out."

He dashed ahead, and the others followed. The horsemen could readily have made the three miles, but were compelled to wait the slower movements of the heavily-loaded vehicle, the jolts and jars of which over the rude way were painful to the wounded men.

As Mr. Beaufort's horse had been killed, he mounted the one left riderless by the unfortunate young Arnold, and which had come up, trembling and whining, to his owner's grave. Eleanor, the wagon being now so crowded, proposed to ride behind him; and the cavalcade sped forward, out of the valley, up on to a steep, winding road, along which the vehicle made but slow progress. Eleanor had given one shuddering glance at the face of a dead bushwhacker whom they passed, as they went—a dark, repulsive, ferocious, sullen face, savage and sly, even in death; she had seen that type of countenance before, when the guerrillas had stormed her home, and dragged her out to be the object of their malice, and the very memory it recalled made her sick and faint.

Hardly had they passed out of the valley, and begun the ascent of the difficult road, before a sudden darkness dropped down, and a stillness which was ominous seized upon the air; not a bird trilled, not a leaf stirred in the trees which lined the way. The heat was oppressive, the atmosphere dead; nearer and more near rolled the solemn peals of thunder, sounding more grandly for the hills which echoed them, while the lightning darted its fiery tongues through the mass of vicious-looking cloud sweeping up from the south-west. The strange twilight cast an unnatural hue upon the anxious faces of the travelers.

"Put her through," shouted the leader, riding back beside the wagon, as if he could hurry it up with his voice. "Wall, I reckon it's too late. That storm 'll bust in less'n five minutes. It's no use going into the woods; there's a terrible blow in that whitish-lookin' cloud; it's as ragged as my last year's breeches. Yes-sir-ee! there's mischief in that feller. Miss Beaufort, you'll be blowed into the Gulf of Mexico. Get inter the wagon quick, and down with you. Look out!"

They heard a rushing noise, accompanied by sharper sounds, as of the cracking off of trees; saw a cloud of dust and leaves, sticks and stones; and then they could distinguish nothing, for a deafening tumult and a bewildering darkness encompassed them. Wind, thunder, lightning and rain commingled; it seemed as if the wagon must surely be overthrown, or lifted up bodily; the men could only cling to their horses and shield themselves a little behind them, to prevent being carried from their feet; while, perhaps, the greatest danger was in the constant falling all about them of forest-trees, which, on this slope of the mountain, grew thickly and large.

In a few minutes, the greatest violence of the tornado had swept past, and then began a rain which seemed determined not to be a whit behind the wind in its marvelous show of power. Great sheets of water poured down, while the wind waved them about like wet curtains, dashing them in the unresisting faces of the travelers.

That was a strange night passed in the mountains! Thick

darkness, which permitted no step forward to be made, settled down and lifted not until the dawn drove it away; heavy rain fell incessantly, and a chilly blast blew in fitful gusts all night. Not unfrequently a tree, weakened by the first shock of the tornado, would give way under some lesser pressure, and crash down through the darkness about the alarmed ears of the beleaguered party. There was constant apprehension that they might fall across and crush the wagon, which was half full of water, in which the wounded men, and the sick, delicate women were taking an unwilling foot-bath, in conjunction with a cold shower-bath eight hours in duration.

Even a night as dreary and as pitiless as that, came to a close at last; with the first dawn of morning the rain ceased; and the drenched and wretched company took up their march. Twice, in the six miles they had to travel, they were obliged to chop away fallen trees from the track, before the wagon could pass.

At about nine o'clock, they turned aside through a by-road, leading through an underbrush of junipers, in a wild and secluded part of the Cumberlands, and, after a few moments, came out on a small plateau, where, with the garden-like level in front, and a huge rock to back it, stood the log shanty which Turkey Dan called his. The world beneath them was glittering in sunlight and jeweled drops, as if a storm had never disturbed it since the days of the deluge; a thousand birds warbled and whistled; the day was as full of glory as the night had been of terror. Six or eight urchins, more or less, all half-naked, and only a shade less dark than mulattoes, gathered about the door of the cabin, with their fingers in their mouths, staring at the strangers; and a quiet, strapping woman, in bare feet and a flannel frock, knocked them right and left as she came out to see what was going on.

"Wall, Sallie," said Dan, good-humoredly, "I've brought

yer a leetle comp'ny. Folks down thar is taking a mighty
fancy, this year, to ruskitate in the mountains. How many
first-class boarders do yer think yer might accommodate?"

"Yer wan't out last night in that harrycane?" was her
reply.

"Don't say we wan't when ye know better. We're a
little wet, and a little hungry, and a little tired; and here's
some women, and a couple of us as had bullets put through
'em yesterday, that won't mind how quick ye get 'em to
rights."

"Dan and Enos," said the hostess to the two oldest, "pick
up some brush, and make a big fire, quick; d'ye hear?" One
would have thought she was frightfully angry at the trouble
she had to take, to judge by her sharp, jerking tones. She
marched up, and lifted Mrs. Bostwick from the wagon, as if
she had been a baby. "Tote them others in," she ordered,
carrying her in and laying her down on a corn-shuck bed on
the floor of the cabin. "Thar, honey, jes' wait till I warm a
little whisky."

The man wounded in the shoulder was suffering from it a
good deal, and was "luffed" down on a bunk opposite; the
other, though his wound was very painful, threw himself in
the corner, leaned against the wall, and tried to make light
of his sufferings.

"Now, Sall, if yer havn't guzzled it all yerself, give us a
little red-eye the *first* thing?"

The hostess took a tin bucket, put in it some brown sugar,
filled it half with whisky, and the other half with boiling
water from the kettle in the corner of the great fireplace,
stirred it up and passed it round, giving the feeblest the first
chance. We will not conceal that Eleanor Beaufort raised
the bucket to her lips and took a draught, like her companions; for the first time in her life she made the acquaintance

of a whisky-punch; and to its unwonted stimulus she owed her escape from the ague which beset her. The brush, heaped on the hearth, crackled and glowed; men and women were obliged to dry their clothing upon them, for they carried no extra baggage in their improvised flight; save the farmers wife, had put a few changes of linen in a carpet-bag, which at present was as dripping as the rest.

"How many can you feed, Sallie?"

"Thar's the chicken-coop, Dan."

"Save 'em for supper. Can't wait to pick chickens."

"Thar's a side o' meat, and plenty o' meal."

"Go ahead, old woman. Sallie's great on dodgers."

Liza, professional cook to the Beaufort establishment, would have gazed with pity and astonishment upon her fair and fastidious young mistress, if she could have seen through space, into that log-cabin, and beheld her, sitting on a chunk of wood, holding in one hand a piece of fat, fried bacon, and in the other a corn-dodger, partaking of each with impartiality and immense relish. It took some time for Mrs. Sallie, with her limited supply of frying-pan, to satiate the appetites of her guests; it was not till the meal-sack was emptied and the last rasher gone from the side of bacon, that she ceased her labor, and then:

"Massy! *what'll* we do next time?"

"Go out, and git track of a deer, Sallie, or even a b'ar, ef you can't do no better;" and the woman shouldered a double-barreled gun, and went off into the woods lying up beyond the cabin.

"That's a woman worth havin'," said Dan, confidentially to Eleanor, seeing the perplexed, curious gaze with which the young lady had followed the motions of his wife. "She can shoot a b'ar, skin a deer, clean a rifle, kill a pig, or jerk off a snake's head, nigh about as handy as I can myself.

She's able to keep the cabin in purvisions; she plants the corn and 'taters, and keeps us in meat. I expect she could mend the young'uns clothes if she had a needle and thread. She's good-tempered, too. We never fight, unless she gits a leetle too much whisky, which ain't often. I tell you, she's a great woman!" with considerable pride in his tone.

"She must be," Eleanor replied, in astonishment, overwhelmed at this list of feminine accomplishments.

"Great woman, Sallie is! reckon I couldn' get along without her," and he chewed his tobacco reflectively.

CHAPTER X.

IN THE MOUNTAINS.

THE worn-out travelers were resting wherever they could find a pretense for a pillow, out-of-doors and in the house, on carpet-bags, corn-husks, on the grass, stretched out in the noon-day sun, making some amends for the fatigues of the previous night; their hostess was still absent, performing the duties of hospitality by roaming the woods for the material for supper.

Eleanor Beaufort had fallen into a light slumber; but the moans of the poor fellow on the bed near by soon awakened her. She went softly to him, bathed his face, gave him water, helped him change his position to an easier one; then, seeing every other soul wrapped in slumber, she stole out into the fresh air, and, wandering to the edge of the little plateau, looked away with yearning eyes to the distant land where her home *had been*. Leaning against the trunk of an evergreen, the bare, white arm, from which the flowing sleeve had fallen

back, clasping its slender circle, she stood there a long, long
while, utterly oblivious of every thing but the past and far-
away. A sigh, so soft and near that it startled her more than
the loudest clamor, made her look suddenly out of cloud-land,
and her eyes met the full, fixed gaze of another pair, which
had apparently been riveted to her countenance so long that
they could not turn quickly enough. When they did drop, it
was not without some color rising to the fine, frank features
of the young man, who, climbing a narrow path along the
edge of the bluff, had been arrested by this unexpected vision
in his way.

Have we ever described Eleanor to you? " No ?"—and we
shall not attempt it. Suffice it that her beauty was of that
perfection—so faultless in feature, complexion and form, so
fresh in youth and health, so high-toned in cultivation, and so
charming in expression—that no circumstance of dress or
place could disparage it. So that the fact that her traveling
attire was crumpled, showing the effects of dust and water
combined, and that she had not seen a mirror for a week, was
not sufficient to discredit our statement of the manner in
which she had beamed upon the young gentleman. One part
of her toilet, indeed, was in a state to give her great confusion ;
but the young man would have affirmed, had he been asked,
that all the dressing-maids in the world could have effected
nothing so beautiful. Her hair, very heavy and long, had
been so thoroughly drenched by the eight hours' rain, that,
when she came out to the tree, she had taken that opportunity
of drying it. She had taken it down and shaken it out, and
there it rippled about her, the moisture causing it to break
into a thousand little rings and waves the most charming
conceivable. •

He had traced the veins in the fair hand clasping the
rugged tree, he had seen the trembling lip, and the eyes filling

with tears, and so absorbed had his soul become in the vision that the sigh of pleasure had betrayed him.

The look of admiration on a face of such earnest and serious power would have been an apology to any woman. Eleanor was not the least angry; she slightly colored and slightly smiled as she stepped aside to let him pass. And such was the manner in which Beverly Bell, the young hero of East Tennessee, first made the acquaintance of Eleanor Beaufort— a maiden, suffering hardships in the same cause wtih himself, who appealed at once to all the chivalry and romance of his nature. He hardly needed all her beauty and spirit to make the conquest of his heart and imagination which she did; for to him, it was truly a case of love at first sight.

An angel need not have blushed at the pity and worship he yielded the beautiful young girl. Men of his nature, whc battle for the right, who live purely and aspire nobly, have an exalted ideal of womanhood; and when they are twenty-one, and have never had a love-affair, and are on the look-out for their ideal, and are so fortunate as to meet a woman like Eleanor Beaufort, they plunge into the sea of glory with an enthusiasm that leaves prudence unheeded on the shore. If he had been told any time during those first two days which followed on this meeting that she loved another, that she was betrothed to another, it would hardly have given him a pang; he had not yet aspired to a return of his passion or possession of its object—sufficient for the day was the fullness of his own love.

"So Daniel Drew has returned," he said, by way of intro-duction, looking over to the grass-plot where the host was stretched out amid his guests, his long legs lying at ease, and a log for a pillow. "I am glad of it."

"And brought us with him," added Eleanor.

"Why are *you* here?" he could not help asking. "Are you a sufferer in the good cause?"

"We have lost all but our lives," she said.

"You could bear martyrdom rather than deny your faith," he continued, looking at her curiously.

"I don't know, but I think my father could. I am only a girl, and not so very brave;" and despite herself, the quick tears rushed to her eyes as she thought of the old homestead, of Lina, and Liza, and devoted Pompey abandoned to their fate, of the trampled flower-beds, the portrait of her mother, of the rough experience of the last fortnight, and of the unpromising future.

"Women have a heroism of their own," went on the stranger. "Theirs is as much in endurance as ours in action. I think they shame us men—even girls." His voice dropped down to the most touching tenderness as he said, "even girls;" then he smiled, shook back his hair with a boyish motion peculiar to him, adding, in a different manner: "Daniel Drew is waking up."

A profound yawn, and a stretching of the long arms, and then of the legs, a lifting of the head, followed by a series of stretches, and after a while the hunter was on his feet.

"It takes time for a feller six feet three to git awake all over; I allus 'low five minits for my legs," he remarked to a neighbor also arousing himself. "Wonder if Sallie's got back with some ven'son yet. Ef I could only teach Sallie to hunt turkeys, she'd be the greatest woman out; but females can't keep their tongues still enough for that kind o' game. Turkey takes—hallo, Bell!"

"Hallo yourself, Daniel Drew."

In a moment the whole camp was stirring; every man was on the alert to talk over the tragic business which had brought them together. The most of them had never seen young Bell before, but all had heard of him—his bravery, his wit and energy, his skill in emergencies, his uncompromising

hatred of the tyrannous traitors overrunning Tennessee, the
perfect fearlessness with which he risked life in the good
cause, had already made his name a whispered word by the
terror-stricken firesides of his native State. He had called
together, as we have seen before, men who were willing to
fight; and, while making their head-quarters in some fastness
of the mountains, they sallied out whenever they could get
word of the guerrillas, to protect helpless families and villages,
or to attack*the enemy wherever found. Many a sharp
skirmish and a few pitched battles he had already led,
and victory so invariably waited on his banners, that
there began to be superstitions about him among the enemy,
until the mere fact that he was present in any company
gained him half the battle beforehand.

He had come, by appointment, to find out what reinforcements Turkey Dan had brought him, and all the information
obtained by the acute and double-sided spy since they parted.
The two went apart for a half-hour's conference.

"The partik'ler bizness that called me so fur away this
time, I've finished up, all right. And now, I don't intend to
play spy much longer. They'll begin to smell a rat when
they find I don't report myself. You see, Cap'n, what took
me down south o' Nashville was this—do you see that young
lady thar?" and he jerked his finger in the direction of
Eleanor, who now stood by her father in front of the cabin.

"Yes," was the quiet answer.

Dan was sharp-sighted, but he didn't see the light flash
out beneath the eyelids of the young man, nor the pulse leap
along his veins.

"I reckon you mought not think she was worth so much
trouble. But I seen her once, and I took an interest in her
She's as handsome as an oriole—don't you think so?"

"She looks well enough."

" Well, 'twan't her looks did the job alone ; she's got more
sperit than half the Ginerals in the land ; she's game, that
girl is, and one of your real highflyers too. They'd chocked
her father in prison ; and I couldn' bar to know what 'ud
happen to her, all alone on her plantation—you see she
refused to fly the Stars and Bars, come what would, so I
took it inter my head to git her father out, which I did in
the nick of time, I tell you, Captain—they'd a had a choker
on him in the mornin', and I got her cl'ar from a hell-hearted
gang of thieving rebels that was jest about to have a little
sport a-horse-whipping the daughter of a gentleman—"

" You did right to go," murmured his listener, turning as
white as marble.

" I thought it was worth a-doing," went on Dan.   " Ef a
slave of her father's, a perfect giant of a fellow, hadn't broke
and run with her, I'd been too late as it was.   Poor Pomp !
he got shot in saving his mistress.   I'd like to l'arn how he's
getting along.   Wall, I made out to get father and daughter
along to Knoxville; by night travelin' and one way another,
and thar we was jined by others in the same fix; and we've
got some of the women off safe.   And the men have got the
devil in 'em—they'll fight as long as they can pull a trigger,
and when they're dead and buried their ghosts will go 'round
stirring up the natives."

" What's the name of the gentleman and his daughter from
below Nashville ?"

" Beaufort ; one of the reg'lar improved breed.   But they've
got the true grit in 'em, for all that."

" Beaufort!   Is it possible ?   I have often heard of the
family."

" Thar comes Sall, lugging in a hull ven'son.   That woman
ought to be a Colonel, at least.   Ef ever we're short of men,
we'll take her along;" and Dan started off to help his wife

over the rock, with a young doe, which she had shot and dragged down unassisted through a couple of miles of thick forest.

The company, being rested from their fatigue by the noon-day *siesta*, were all now anxious to assist their stern and imposing hostess, who moved about with a vigor that was really awful. When she spoke, it was in short sentences, discharging her words like bullets, though they never harmed any one ; and it was soon evident that her intentions were as kind as her manner was threatening — the green flannel encased a heart that was like the silken down inside the prickly frock of the thistle.

It is said that "no man is a hero to his own valet," and it became apparent that the redoubtable hunter whose fame spread far and wide beyond the precincts of his own cabin was under pretty good petticoat-government at home. Whatever Sallie told Dan to do, that he did without hesitation ; his obedience, however, seemed rather the result of unbounded admiration for his wife's abilities than wholesome fear of her physical equality.

The feeling of comparative security which settled upon the long-persecuted little party now betrayed itself in the rising of spirits, the laughter and jest with which all the difficulties of the present were met. That there was no bread or potatoes with the meat, no knives, forks or plates, no blankets or beds for the coming night, was the subject of mirth rather than depression. For a few hours, all who could threw care to the winds, forgetting the past and ignoring the future.

The wife of the printer immured in a Knoxville prison, could not forget that perhaps at that moment she was a widow ; the young mother could not shut out the vision of her babe sleeping in the arms of the young martyr beneath the grass of the valley. These two sat together on a bench

outside the door, looking on the scene with faces which
mocked their poor attempts to smile. A fire was kindled out
of doors, in a sheltered nook, protected by a spur of rock
from any eyes in distant valleys which might be scanning the
face of the mountain ; the deer was prepared and put to roast
whole, excepting a few tender bits which Eleanor obtained to
make broth for the sick men, the most seriously wounded of
the two being now suffering from the setting in of fever.

While the venison was roasting, watched by a score of
eager volunteers, Mrs. Sallie sent her boys off, with a bucket,
to find and milk the cow, while she prepared a large iron
kettle full of coffee—that is, of a mixture of parched corn and
rye, which made a tolerable substitute.

The supper which followed, eaten in the glow of the
setting sun, was not famous for the variety of dishes or elegance of appointment; but it was a better meal than one-half
which followed for months after this beginning of fugitive
experience. Salt was the only relish to the delicious venison,
if we except the wit and merriment, which were as good as
pepper and currant-jelly, perhaps. Those who liked had
some crisp young onions from Mrs. Sallie's little garden ; and
the coffee, rich with milk boiled in, was nourishing to the
body and pleasant to the taste. Men cut off their portions
of the feast with their knives, and drank from a common
cup.

Captain Bell, with a grace as if the scene were a ball at
the Capital instead of a barbecue on the mountains, furnished
the ladies with beautiful white plates of clean, new chips, and
individual salt-cellars of glossy leaves. Never, in the palmiest
days of her youthful triumphs, had Eleanor been more
devotedly served, or listened to more arch and piquant small-
talk. Beverly Bell was transfigured even beyond his usual
self on that eventful occasion—eventful to him, who had

stepped suddenly out of the wrath and misery of war into a
Paradise of delight. Men looked at the laughing face, the
light toss of the handsome head, the slender figure—heard the
boyish laugh and the soft voice—and wondered if this were
he whose name struck terror into savage bands, and under
whose leadership they were to marshal their older heads and
sturdier arms.

But when supper was over, and, in the red gleam of twilight, he stood in their midst, all gayety put aside, and spoke
to them as their officer, telling what had been done and what
was to do, every heart took fire, every face glowed responsive
to his own. It became apparent that he had the peculiar
power of one born to be a leader; not the gravest head or
boldest arm could refuse obedience to the resistless will of
such a mind.

Eleanor, from her seat on a mossy log, heard every word
of his brilliant harangue, and her expressive face betrayed the
enthusiasm he kindled.

"Ah, if Sinclair could have thought and acted thus!" she
sighed; and unconsciously she drew the comparison between
this ardent, heroic spirit, and the negative, easily-bent temper
of the man upon whom she had wasted so much high feeling.

After the speech was over, and the company had broken
into little groups, Mr. Beaufort and his daughter discussed the
uncertain future. They had escaped with their lives, but,
save the few articles of value, including her mother's jewels,
which she had brought away upon her person, there was
nothing remaining of all their possessions to them. It was
dangerous to attempt, at present, an escape to the North, impossible to return home; and to remain concealed in these
wild mountains till deliverance came, seemed the only thing
to be done.

"I shall join Bell, with the others, and do my share of the

fighting," said Mr. Beaufort. " I cannot sit idle with the memory of Nashville prison burning into my brain."

" But, father, you are no longer young nor strong," pleaded Eleanor. " We shall need some one to care for us here—why not you ?"

" This place is so secluded, we shall hardly fear to leave you women alone. If any marauders should chance upon it, I think they would pass over Sallie's cabin and pig-pen, and you could conceal yourselves."

" And must we all live and sleep with the family ?" asked Eleanor, half-laughing, half-crying, for the prospect of being herded in that one dirty room, with those children, on those beds, was more terrible than she cared to own.

" Only for a night, I hope. I have spoken with Dan and Captain Bell ; they are willing to delay starting out for a day, in order to put up another cabin for you and the three other ladies. It will be a rough affair, but it will be new and clean ; and there are some corn-husks for beds, and—"

" And it will not be half so bad as a prison, dear father, where you lived four months without complaining. We will have plenty of sunshine and fresh air, at least."

The next was a busy day. Dan himself was obliged to take a horse and go for meal for the family use ; the horses had been compelled to shift for themselves, feeding upon the rich grass of the plateau. All who could muster tools to work with, were busy upon the new cabin. There were three axes and a saw, which were plied energetically, while others drew the prepared logs and laid them up. The timber chosen was small, so as not to be difficult to fell and haul ; and, as there were over thirty men engaged, they made rapid progress. By sundown, a small structure, twelve by fourteen, had arisen beside the cabin of the hunter. It was floored with small saplings laid side by side, and covered over, for

the present, with hemlock boughs. It was the intention to
fill the chinks with mud as soon as convenient, for the double
purpose of keeping the floor dryer and of shutting out inquisitive rattlesnakes and other reptiles. The roof was of the
same fashion. Two small square openings, sawed from the
walls, served for windows. Over these Eleanor insisted upon
having some slats nailed, for the fact that she was in a region
where, occasionally, a catamount or bear had been known to
make his appearance, weighed upon her mind heavily. A
few boards, gathered together at various times by the provident Sallie, furnished a door, with leather straps for hinges,
and a couple of pegs for fastenings. Captain Bell had made
free use, through the day, of the hammer and nails, as well as
the forks of trees, and any material ready to hand; and the
result of his skill and industry was evident in the shape of
two very decent beds—the elastic bark with which he had
interwoven the bottoms making a spring mattress excelling
some more expensive affairs. A coating of clean split corn-
husks, and a blanket spread over, completed their furnishing.

No chimney had been supplied to the shanty, the weather
being so warm, and the arrangement being to share Mrs.
Drew's fire for purposes of cooking.

"Ladies, we welcome you to your new home," said Captain
Bell, standing in the door when all was done. "If Rome was
not built in a day, some lesser things have been. Welcome
home! for you must make a home of this, so long as the dark
shadow of the usurper rests on the valleys below. Look at
them now, bathed in the darkness of twilight, while upon the
mountain-top the sun still shines. This hill is crowned with
burning radiance—God's smile lingers upon it. It is meet
that we have fled to the mountains. They have been the
cradle of Liberty—their air is life to freedom. The exulting
Swiss who climb their native Alps sing hymns to God and

Liberty. The immortal Tell, whose unflinching hand not even a tyrant's mandate could make tremble, though striving to unnerve it with a father's fear—that hand which drove the unerring arrow through the apple on his own child's head—"

"Sho!" broke in Turkey Dan, who had come around the rock with his horse laden down with the meal-bags, "that wan't much of a trick. I could do it myself, any day. Here, you, Enos, take that pertater and stand off over thar by the pig-pen and put it on your head. Stand stiddy, for I'm goin' to shoot it off."

"Oh, don't!" "you are mad!" "foolish!" remonstrated the company.

"Surely you will not consent?" cried Eleanor to Mrs. Drew, who was watching the proceedings with an indifferent eye.

"If the boy don't mind, I don't," was the answer. "Dan 'll hit it—don't you skeer yourself."

The boy walked to the spot designated, put the potato on his shaggy black locks, facing his father with a smile. The hunter lowered his rifle from his shoulder, took deliberate aim, fired, and when the shuddering spectators dared to look, there stood the child, erect, and the potato was missing.

"That's a great boy," said the father, proudly; "he didn't even wink when the fire flashed. Here, sonny, here's a bit fer you," tossing him a piece of silver as he came running up. "I've been ten mile for that fodder, and walked all the way back, to accomodate my hoss. It'll last till we get back agin, I reckon, friends. I count three women equal to one child in the eatin' line."

Having been confined to meat exclusively the last three meals, the corn-dodgers that evening had a fine relish even for the delicate women whose appetites Dan ridiculed. After supper, Captain Bell said a prayer, and as many of the party

as were familar with such music sung a hymn—the sweet
voices of Mrs. Bostwick and Eleanor thrilling with a solemn
fullness upon the air, until even Turkey Dan felt strangely
subdued and reflective, and his little ones, who had never
heard a hymn, nor even of God or heaven, looked vaguely up
into the sky, as if with an instinct, looking for angels which
they knew not how to name.   To the young Captain, whose
powerful undertones sustained the airy flights of Eleanor's
voice, it seemed as if she were leading him on and up to a
faith and rapture he had never experienced. In the new
light of his flaming passion, which burned like tapers of incense before an altar, he saw the interests of his country in a
yet purer view, and felt strengthened to fight for her liberties,
for her hopes, which were so closely bound to all that promises honor and happiness to the human race.   Long after his
companions were sleeping on their couches of hemlock
boughs around him, he gazed up at the spangled curtains of
his mountain bed, the great stars flashing and glowing in the
summer sky, his heart beating too high with passion and
aspiration to allow him to slumber.

CHAPTER XI.

FOURTH OF JULY.

By that band of suffering patriots, hiding in the mountains
from the vengeance of their enemies, it was resolved to " keep
the Fourth of July."   Since the closing of our last chapter,
the men had been away a week affording protection to a village threatened by guerrillas, and had finally frightened them,
for the present, from an afflicted country. They had returned,

on the evening of the 2d of July, to attend to the welfare of their own little colony, and very much dispirited by the constant news of the cruelty and outrage to which the Unionists of the State were everywhere being subjected. Their hearts were sick and sore on the subject. It seemed to them impossible to rest for a day from their labors, small as they were, for averting the public calamities; yet, as they were detained by the necessity of providing food for the women, as also to complete some plans for future action, they decided to celebrate the great national holiday in such manner as their means would permit, with a view to the encouragement of their souls as well as the rest of their bodies.

All day of the third they were busy with preparations. Dan, with several others, went off in search of game. Upon his success in finding it depended the feast.

Captain Bell took upon himself the preparation of the grounds. A pleasant spot, shaded with trees, not too thickly, and with a level stretch of greensward, was selected; and he begged the assistance of Eleanor in completing what Nature had left undone. It was joy enough for him to be near her; to watch the kindling of her eye, the flushing of her cheek, as she became engaged in pleasant tasks—binding garlands of evergreen about rugged trunks, with here and there a knot of violets looking out like soft blue eyes, and wild pink roses swinging from their briery sprays.

"I wish this day would never come to a close," said the young Captain, half under his breath, as he helped her tie the end of a wreath to a pendent bough.

"Then we should never have the Fourth of July," laughed Miss Beaufort, "and with it sweet potatoes and roast partridges." But, as she looked up, his eyes were burning into her face with a look which she could not have misunderstood if she would.

Had she blushed then, had she smiled, and looked deliciously embarrassed, the story of his love would quickly have been told; but her face expressed only pain and a slight reserve which sealed his lips and made his heart sink.

"She is an aristocrat," he muttered to his dejected spirit; "her father is a cotton-planter, and mine only a Methodist parson. If she were in her own home, I could not even speak with her as an equal. Now, in her misfortunes she tolerates me."

Perhaps it would have been an alleviation to his wounded pride if he had known that she was suffering from an unhappy love, a broken engagement, which gave her scarcely less pain from her suspicion that it was ill-chosen from the beginning. The young, secluded girl was learning many lessons from her present eventful experience. The character of Marcia Le Vert, in its indolence and selfishness and want of any fixed principle, showed more hollow than ever in the light of the brave and loyal women who now surrounded her. And Sinclair—could she fail to draw the line between him and some of these admirable men, so true and firm in the hour of peril?—between him and this young Captain whose courage and wit and wonderful power over others was a constant marvel to her? She began to look upon life as something besides a midsummer day's dream, to be lounged away in graceful idleness, with a lover to pay compliments. So, although her face expressed pain, there was nothing either haughty or repelling in it.

"Must we always be after the loaves and fishes?" asked her companion, bitterly. "Yes, that is the height of our desire. Worldly enjoyment, worldly splendor, social position, no matter what—only there is never any union of congenial souls, any simple, pure life of the spirit."

"Speaking of the loaves and fishes reminds me by what almost a miracle the multitudes in these mountains have been fed," said Eleanor, sweetly. " Surely, Captain Bell, you can hardly accuse yourself or any of us of being attracted hither by the prospect of luxury, or—" with a girlish laugh, " high social position."

He recalled the never-failing serenity with which she had borne the privations, the actual hardships, of her new condition, and for what cause she suffered them, and his conscience accused him of injustice.

" I'm a fool to make such a remark to *you*, Miss Beaufort. Really, one ought to be willing to confess that fried bacon and corn-cake, with the Drew family for society, are not any very magnificent luxuries—however, these are for a time only. You'll shake off all your acquaintances here, along with the bacon and corn-cake, I suppose."

" They have all been my friends—none kinder or better than Daniel and Sallie Drew. I hope never to forget them."

" Daniel and Sallie Drew, and Beverly Bell—don't forget him, either."

And then the young lady laughed mischievously, for she saw he was determined to be cross anyhow, and she let him have his way. As he was not contradicted, he grew tired of saying spiteful things; and when their work was completed to their mutual satisfaction, they betook themselves back to the cabin in very good humor. Here they found the hunting party returned with a rich abundance of game; also two fishermen who had ventured to a brook further down the mountain and had caught a few trout to reward them. The promise for a holiday was good, weather-signs included.

As the sun rolled up over the Cumberlands on the following morning, he was greeted by a discharge from Dan's double-barreled gun :

" Take that, and be thankful, old feller," he muttered. " The hull company wanted to salute you, but 'twan't safe,

d'ye see ?   Some pesky rebel might be within ear-shot.   It's
a dod-blasted shame when an honest citizen can't holler as
loud as he pleases for the Fourth of July."

"I guess we can venture to give a good, rousing hurrah,"
said Captain Bell, coming out of his hemlock-bough tent.

"Ef *you* think so, it's all right—come, men, spit on your
hands and make ready—now for't—hurrah for the Fourth of
July."

Three thundering cheers rung hoarse against the echoing
rocks.   At this moment the door of the new cabin opened,
and the four ladies and three children who occupied it, stepped
out, Eleanor foremost, unfurling the American flag.   This
flag was to be a surprise to the party.   For several days, herself and Mrs. Bostwick had been employed upon it, when they
could do so unobserved.   The secrets of the manufactory of
that banner might not properly be exposed, perhaps—yet we
shall not hesitate to say that the white stripes were torn from
a lady's petticoat, and the red from a long-cherished, tenderly
preserved merino shawl belonging to the farmer's wife.   Mrs.
Drew had contributed Dan's best blue silk handkerchief, and
the printer's wife a needle-book and skein of thread which
chanced among the contents of a basket of hers.   A rake-
handle made a standard ; and thus it was complete, with
every one of the thirty-four stars on the azure field.   An im-
pulsive cheer burst forth at the inspiriting sight.   Nothing
had so thoroughly aroused the hopes and energies of this
lovely band of refugees, since their exile from home, as this
unrolling of their country's flag to wave over the festivities
of the day.   To them it was no longer a bright banner to
adorn a ball-room or flutter over the heads of a dress-parade
military—it was a signal and a beacon—the token of that liberty in whose cause they suffered, the incarnation of the spirit
of their institutions.

Eleanor's face glowed like the morning. Captain Bell's eyes dropped from the starry banner to the countenance of the maiden who upheld it, and his own expression reflected hers. But over the face of the printer's wife from Knoxville came a shadow. Her face was always sad, for hers was the gnawing anguish of uncertainty, sharper than almost any other pang. Mrs. Bostwick had laid her baby in the bosom of the valley, but her husband was in the crowd, and she was looking to him with pride and love ; Eleanor's glance sought her father's ; but she—ah, they were going to be so merry to-day ! Would to God she knew whether her husband's eyes yet lived to see the light !—and to stifle back the cry, she stooped and kissed her two children.

" Let us continue the exercises by singing the Star-Spangled Banner," said Mr. Beaufort.

It was sung, with the voice and the heart also. As many thousand times as it had rung forth, within the last year, in crowded halls or on the open field, vibrating with the heroic passion of the popular heart, it never thrilled more profoundly, was never uttered with a more perfect abandon of mingled joy and pathos, than swelled up to the listening heavens from this mountain fastness. They sang it with a solemn exultation, as if they were taking a vow to be true to their country in life and death. And they meant what they expressed.

As the last verse rose up into the smiling sky, Dan's quick eye detected a pale face peering eagerly from behind the rock which fortified their retreat—a pale face, worn with sickness, thin and sallow, but lighted up just now as if the sunlight was all being absorbed by it. As he saw that the hunter had detected him, he rose up, waving a white handkerchief, and then a woman shrieked two or three shrieks of joy so sharp and sudden that it was almost like pain, and two little children were flung away, and the printer's wife darted across the plateau, and flung herself, speechless and swooning, into her husband's arms.

This was a good beginning ; it gave an increased relish to the rye-coffee, fried trout, and corn-cake served up for break-fast. The new-comer was the hero of the hour. All were eager to hear his account of the land from which they had fled ; but their joy at his escape was shadowed by the melan-choly, the horrible story he had to tell of continued and increasing persecution.

" How long are these things to be ?" " How long will it be before our good President sends an army to the relief of his true and faithful, his tortured and dying people in Tennessee ?" cried one and another. Alas ! could they have foreseen how long that terrible as Spanish Inquisition was to keep its fear-ful machinery in operation before ever its power was checked, their brave spirits would have been broken at once. This escaped prisoner, by some unexpected leniency, had at length been released from confinement, received fifty lashes at the Union men's whipping-post, and been warned to leave the State within twenty-four hours. Having received from parties in Knoxville, who were able to give it, a pretty tangible clue to the whereabouts of his wife and a party of Union friends, he had started on the track, and by good-fortune and great tact, had finally made his way to the rendezvous.

The luxurious breakfast—rye coffee and fried trout were the luxuries—being over, the party marched in regular order, a standard-bearer with the colors amid them, to the spot selected for the pic-nic. This was but a short distance in the rear of the cabins, where Dan's two elder boys were left as a guard, who were to fire a gun in case of alarm—their deprivation of festivities being made up to them by liberal allowances of the delicacies of the season, and a stray package of fire-crackers.

The only holiday attire with which Eleanor could do honor

to the occasion, was a wreath of forest-flowers crowning her
hair ; the dark traveling-dress in which she had attired herself to fly from her home one morning, weeks ago, was still
doing service for morning and evening wear, and now for this
fête champêtre. Her complexion had attained a tint of brown
not natural to it, from living so almost entirely in the open
air; but that same open air had deepened her roses and
heightened the luster of her eyes, while her health had in
nowise suffered from the homely fare and bracing atmosphere
of the mountains. She grew beautiful by this rough usage,
like a diamond under the hand of a polisher.

To-day, for the first time since being wounded, the man who
had received a bullet through his shoulder, was borne out ·
of the close cabin and bolstered up comfortably with blankets
and pillows, against a friendly tree, where he could join in
the general gayety. The other wounded one, his arm in a
sling, was around, the merriest of the merry. _

Captain Bell recited the Declaration of Independence, which
chanced to be stamped upon that retentive memory of his ;
there were speeches and songs many and good, with the old
flag flaming over the speaker's stand, which was found ready
for the occasion in the shape of a serviceable stump. And
mixed with the eloquence and patriotism so profuse, was a
matter-of-fact attention to the progress of the dinner, toward
the completion of which nearly every one lent his aid. Not
upon Sallie Drew alone fell the glory of that repast. Most
delicate and dainty birds, wrapped in shrouds of glossy leaves,
were laid in hot ashes, where they slowly baked, without one
hint of their sweetness being lost in the process. There were
rabbits and squirrels stewing with a seasoning of young
onions; a noble venison lacked not for turning and basting
as he swung from a cross-stick before an ample fire. Down
among the embers of that fire were roasting a bushel of sweet

potatoes, the first from Sallie's garden; as for that stately
matron, her green frock hovered about a distant cauldron,
wherein was simmering the crowning excellence of the feast;
a mingling of green-corn, cut from the cob, and young beans,
known to lovers of that succulent dish as succotash.

Finally, dinner was served in a novel style, minus dishes
and tables. Yet, by some happy instinct of nature, there were
none but contrived to find and appropriate their portion.
What prettier dish in which to serve up a little round quail
to a lady, than a snowy chip, garnished with glossy green
leaves ?

Some of the men had amused themselves odd hours carving
wooden spoons with their knives, so that there was a tolerable
assortment of these wherewith to do justice to the succotash,
which was not one of those dishes designed for fingers alone.

Rye-coffee was the drink supplied; though some of the
rougher of the men resorted secretly to that universal necessity
of a Southern merry-making, the whisky-jug. That Daniel
Drew was among the guilty number became apparent, in the
course of the day. That Dan loved whisky, none of his most
ardent friends denied; he could drink a quart or more of old
Kentucky, without the slightest apparent effect; it was seldom
that he betrayed any traces of his devotion; but to-day,
whether he indulged more freely than he intended, or whether
unwonted elation of spirits made quicker work with his wits,
deponent saith not. It was observable that he grew good-
natured to an extent that was absolutely irresistible. For
instance, when Sallie boxed his ears for offering Mrs. Bostwick
succotash on the end of a sharpened stick, he thanked her so
tenderly, and praised her so highly for her courage in daring
to box Turkey Dan's ears—a deed which most *men* would
not care to perform, he remarked—that she had not the heart
to repeat the chastisement.

"You're makin' a great fool of yerself, Dan," said Sallie, scornfully.

"You're mad because you're afraid we ain't saving any for you, wife. Don't you be skeered. I've put away a small jugful in a holler log, fer you; only you'd better make sure of it before long, or some of my friends will be drinkin' it up."

"Where is it?" asked Sallie; it was hard to tell whether she wished to try the contents of the hidden jug, or whether she thought to secure her husband from further excesses that day.

"It's over thar, in that log beyond the kettles," said Dan.

She went to the spot, drew out a small half-gallon jug, shook it, and then her head.

"Dan, this 'ere's empty!"

"Is it possible, wife? thunder and lightnin', so it is! I was afraid somebody'd steal it, and so I emptied it—into—a bar'l."

"Into a hogshead, I reckon," retorted Sallie, in disgust.

"Now, wife, you ain't getting out o' temper on the Fourth o' July, are you?" pleaded Dan, coaxingly. "Don't you remember what the minister told our boys when they scratched and fit so? that time to camp-meetin'?

"'Let b'ars and lions growl and fight,
You were not made to scratch and bite.'

"It's jest so about the Fourth—the glorious Fourth, as the Captain said, it wan't made to get mad in. The Fourth," continued Dan, warming with the subject, and mounting the stump left vacant since dinner, "is a—a—decided rip-snorter. It can't be beat. It never has been beat. Christmas is some, but Fourth o' July is always summer. Ef thar was no other reason on yearth for cussin' and t'aring round 'bout this rebellion, it would be enough to think of its upsetting the

Fourth of July. For, in course, rascals that wipe their feet
on the good old flag, won't keep Independence Day. No-
sir-ee! they'd tar and feather the stature of liberty if they
came across her, and pluck the feathers from the great
American spread-eagle to do it with. I won't say whar they
get the pitch—the place is too far down in a hot climate.
Feller-citizens! them lyin', stealin', treacherous, devil-helped
office-seekers down to Nashville, tell us this State is out of the
Union! They're a pesky set; they drink whisky. Whatever is our fault, *that's* not one of 'em. I'm afraid they was
drunk when they did it. Out of the Union! Tennessee out
of the Union! they can't do it; they hain't done it. Put salt
on the tail of a wild-turkey, catch a weasel asleep, skin a live
painter, hitch up an old mule, tackle it to this mountain, and
set it to hauling it away, or coax my old rifle to miss fire.
You can't any more get Tennessee out—no-sir-ee! no mor'n
you can get Sallie Drew away from that pan of succotash.
She'll stick to it till she busts. 'What did I say?' I said
Tennessee'd stick to the Union till she busts, Sallie. Don't
you think so? I knew you would. We're one on politics,
and on licker, too. I say if this State don't behave herself,
we'll lick her; and, speaking of it, makes me most infernally
dry. I wish we could liquor, right away. I ain't used to
public speakin', and it sort of sticks in my throat.

"Feller-citizens, as I was sayin', this is the glorious Fourth,
and anybody as says it isn't, ought to be horse-whipped. *I
say it is!* It's made me feel so chock full of hail-Columby
I'll go off like a bundle of fire-crackers ef anybody tech fire
to me. I'd like to wind up these exercises by a pitched battle,
single-handed, with about a hundred gorillas, dod blast their
women-scarin', house-burnin', corn-stealin', horse-thieving
souls! They ought to be tied to the backs of live alligators
and swum up and down the Mississippi river for a thousand

years, while the banks was lined with sharpshooters riddlin'
them like an old siv'. I'd volunteer for that service, mighty
quick. They oughter all be turned into rattlesnakes and be
everlastingly walloped with white-ash switches. I'd be willing to be transmogrified into an ash tree and cut up into
switches for that purpose. What you lookin' at me so for,
Sallie? you know I would. 'I'm secesh all over—to the mar-
row of my bones—no, thunder, I mean I'm *Secesh* all over—
that's it; no, no, I mean—well, never mind. I'm all right on
the goose—ain't I Sally? Why, my old rifle's so chock full
of it, it would kick me over and blow me up quicker'n a
wink, if I should turn round and go over to Jeff. You've
seen us mountaineers, when the snakes get too thick; we
build a fire down to the bottom of the hill, and thrash the
reptiles down into it. That's the way we're goin' to serve the
human reptiles: we'll whip 'em down into a hotter fire than
they ever built to cook us by. I propose three cheers for the
glorious old Fourth! It's the Fourth of July, ain't it Sally?
You see the hail-Columby has got into my head so strong, I
jest get a little confused. Didn't I hear somebody a saying,
a spell ago, that this was the glorious Fourth? and if I did, it
must be so. Yes, feller-citizens, this is the Anna Domino
of our Independence, as you've all heard. Anybody as tries
to upset it ought to be compelled to never see no money but
Jeff. Davis's shinplasters, and never have any thing but Mississippi mud to drink on this great day. They oughter be
obliged to drink Mrs. Davis's health in a tumbler of river water
stirred up with a tad-pole. Yes, they had. They're a mean,
sneakin', toad-hoppin', snake-crawlin', house-settin'-on-fire lot;
they're a—"

How much longer the stream of Dan's eloquence would
have overflowed its proper boundaries is uncertain; the sharp
report of the alarm-gun from the cabin summoned the men

in haste to the plateau. Each man caught his loaded rifle; even the orator was not so lost in eloquence and whisky as to be dead to the meaning of the warning; he sprung for his rifle, and ran with the rest.

"What is it?" queried one and another of the frightened boys, who, though a little pale and startled, stood their ground like true sons of their father, the double-barrel pointed to the path around the rock.

"I dunno, sartain," said Daniel, junior; "I guess it was a nigger."

"Yes," added Enos, eagerly, "I seen him. He stuck his head around thar and dodged it back when we fired."

"Only one nigger," said Dan, in disgust. "Why didn't you take car' of him yerselves, boys. Don't ye know ye shouldn' interrupt yer father when he's speakin'?"

"We didn' know how many more thar mought be."

"Of course not, boys; you did right," said Captain Bell. "He may have been a spy, or, more likely, only a poor fugitive. Who goes there?" he called out, loudly.

"Oh, massa, you needn' shoot Pomp Beaufort," sung out a bold voice, and the giant figure of the negro emerged from behind the rock. "Dem b'ys wouldn' give me a chance to send up my card. Hi, Missa Beaufort, hi! massa, here I. is! hi! hi!" The faithful slave rushed forward; all the usual gravity, even dignity, of his deportment vanished in the joy he felt at beholding his master and mistress alive and well.

Truly this had been an eventful day. Pompey, tired and famished, was furnished with a liberal supper from the remains of the feast. As soon as he had thus recruited himself, he gave the father and daughter all the information he possessed about the old plantation. The guerrillas had left it in a wretched plight; but Liza and Lina had done what they could to restore and protect the mansion. They lived in the kitchen, and took what care they could of the rooms. Jim had been impressed into the rebel service as the valet of an officer. Many of the slaves had been stolen, some had gone to town and hired out, a few remained upon the place. Pompey's own wife and children remained in their cabin, supporting themselves by raising vegetables for the market.

"Dey was dar, now," the black man said, "but de Lord knows how long dey'll be permitted to remain. Colonel Le Vert, he wanted my wife to come and cook for dem; he offered a good home to de chil'un, and I tol' her maybe she'd better go, 'cause den she wouldn' be stole away, and w'en I come for her, I'd know whar to find her. 'Kase, Massa Beaufort, I'se gwine to stick to you, in dese troubles; an' if you nebber go home agin, I'll try and find my way North, and take my wife and babies wid me, de Lord willin'."

He said that Lina was much cast down by Jim's absence, and still more so by the troubles of her dear young lady, and that Liza wasn't herself any more. He related the manner of his escape from the enraged "gorillas;" how he crawled through the fence, into the ravine, as Dan had told him, and had lain there hidden in the grass, while numbers went by, cursing and swearing at Miss Eleanor's escape; how his arm bled, until he was so faint he feared he might die, but that he did not dare come out until the band had deserted the place; how he crawled home, and his wife laughed and cried over him, and bound up his arm; how he lay sick with it two weeks; but that, as soon as he could rely upon his strength at all to help him, he had set out at night, following the directions of Dan, as near as he was able, and had crawled from Nashville to the Cumberland mountains, by night-marches, lying in woods' and fields through the day, and sometimes almost famishing.

"Now, bless de Lord, massa, I see your face agin, and my dear, sweet young lady's. I'll do what I can to serve you. Poor Miss Eleanor ain't used to waitin' on herself, poor chile!" and he threw a curious, sorrowful glance at the log-cabins and their surroundings.

Then the story being finished, the company stood up in the lights and shadows of a forest sunset, and sung a few patriotic songs; Captain Bell prayed for the blessing of God upon their uncertain fortunes; the remnants of the feast were gathered up, and with the banner gleaming in the front rank, they marched back to the lawn in front of the cabins, and dismissed the meeting.

It was throughout a day of hope and pleasant events; a beam of light across a dark and stormy sky, all the brighter, all the dearer, for the ominous clouds which accompanied it— for the lightning-flash of disaster which not long thereafter overwhelmed the spot with ruin.

CHAPTER XII.

GUERRILLA WARFARE.

IT was on a hot afternoon in August that Captain Bell, at the head of his company, approached the old familiar rendezvous at Turkey Dan's cabin. They rode wearily, for they had been in battle the previous day, and had scarcely rested or tasted food since. They had formed themselves a volunteer guard over a little village so strongly Union in its proclivities as to have provoked the wrath and covetousness of the guerrillas; this village had been threatened by hovering bands, and had joyfully accepted the protection of the brave young Captain. Children once more went to sleep in peace, and maidens ceased to tremble at a sound, now that their town was guarded by sixty armed men, led by an officer so admired and trusted as Bell. But the rapacious hordes, ascertaining the number of his company, and hoping not only to sack the place but to secure the dreaded Union hero, banded together into a little army of three or four hundred, and swooped down upon the nest one day at early dawn, when it expected to find the eagles sleeping. Turkey Dan was up and moving, though—he always slept with one eye open—and when the marauders rushed suddenly into the village, they were met at the very onset by a sharp, cool fire, directed from behind cover. This was the only advantage of the immensely inferior Union force; it was well bestowed, and fought from chosen positions. Whenever the guerrillas made an attack in force on any conspicuous building, they were repulsed from within, and a galling fire fell on them also from the window of many a private house, where some heroic matron or girl, when not the father of the family, handled the weapons, beforehand provided, with surprising courage.

Their losses made them outrageous. They were determined to "hole" the hated Bell; and being repulsed from the hotel and the three or four stores of the place, they set fire to some minor buildings, every old stable or dilapidated dwelling scorched by the summer suns, and ready to kindle at a touch, being soon in a blaze, which a light wind, rising with the day, fanned into swift destruction. No attempt could be made to put down the fire, because of the presence of the enemy; and as the flames spread down the long main street, women and children were driven from their homes, to face the brutal jests and blows of the ruffians, and some of them were even maliciously shot down. The sight of this was more than Captain Bell could endure. It was not enough to stand upon the defensive; he formed his men into a solid body, and ordered them to "charge." And they did charge, with such resistless fury, that in twenty minutes not a live guerrilla remained within the precincts of that village. But this victory was not gained without melancholy loss. A dozen of his brave men never knew the result of the skirmish which cost them their lives; as many more were wounded. A bullet-wound, tearing open his cheek, a sword-cut across his arm, and two or three shot-holes through his clothing, gave proof that the gallant leader had shirked none of the danger. These were the first wounds he had received in his many battles; he had grown to be looked upon as invincible and unkillable. He did not stay now to dress these injuries; leaving the inhabitants to extinguish the fire, and his disabled men in the care of the women, he pushed forward with the remainder of his force after the flying enemy. It was his hope, now, to "hole" them; and this he did, after a brisk chase of eight miles through an open country, on into a wooded and hilly district, where the guerrillas took refuge in a cave which had been their head-quarters for some time past. Here, with the prospect of being starved out unless they did so, they surrendered, delivered up their arms, swore to behave themselves (!), and were allowed to depart. Alas! what else could the Captain do? He had not the support of an army or a State to back him; he could not hold them as prisoners in a country where the best he or his could do was to act on the defensive. He, however, retained three of the ringleaders, conveyed them back to the village, had them tried by court-martial, for murder, and hung that same evening in the town they had desolated.

That night they buried their dead in the little churchyard,

and the bodies of the banditti in a field outside, consigned the badly wounded to the care of the grateful villagers, whom they furnished plentifully with the captured arms, and started for their rendezvous in the mountains. Captain Bell gave little attention to his wounds, trusting to fine health and the vigor of youth to do the work of healing The cut across his arm had been so arrested by his own saber as to be shallow ; none of the cords were severed ; " That arm," he said, " was good for many another fight."

Shall we confess one weakness of our hero ? Brave as the bravest, scorning pain and danger, shall we confess that he dreaded to enter into that little Paradise away up on the mountain-top, because his face was scarred and disfigured by an ugly wound ? He was afraid that beautiful young girl would look upon him with less favor—perhaps with dislike. Foolish, unwise youth ! unknowing of the womanly heart, that glories in nothing so much as the token and proof of the beloved one's bravery. Not that Captain Bell could be called one of Eleanor's beloved ones. He was not—at least he did not know, or she did not, if he was ; but nothing would have put the question home to her heart so powerfully as the sight of that bandaged face.

Wearily the company rode in the hot August sun, refreshing themselves with the thought of food and rest soon to be obtained on that cool, secluded plateau, where women would welcome and wait upon them. Foremost rode those who had kindred with the little band of refugees hiding in this bird's-nest of an eyrie. Captain Bell had other friends hidden away in other mountain-nooks, but none to whom he turned as he did to these. Mr. Bostwick, Mr. Beaufort, Captain Bell and Dan were the first who drew rein upon the plateau. Great God ! what a scene of ruin and devastation met their gaze ! No wonder their hands dropped paralyzed, and a groan of horror which rent Mr. Beaufort's breast was echoed by the others. A terror which no fate for themselves could have inspired seized upon them, as they thought of the possible tortures and outrages to which their women might have been subjected. The garden was trampled, the lawn defaced, and Dan's cabin was a smoking ruin. The other, though standing almost so as to touch it, had been built of such green material as to refuse to burn readily; it. was charred upon one side, but still stood. At first, no living being was visible; the dead bodies of two desperate-looking ruffians lay stretched upon the grass, showing that some defense had been made by the assailed.

Pompey, who had been left in charge of affairs, was nowhere to be seen. He was so faithful, so apt, and so tremendously strong, that a much greater feeling of security had prevailed since his willing enlistment to watch and wait upon his mistress and her friend. The door of the cabin still standing was closed; but upon one of the party calling out, it. was unfastened, and Sallie Drew, her children, and the two other women with theirs, made their appearance.

" Got back a lectle too late," she said, sententiously.

" Where's my wife?" asked Mr. Bostwick.

" Where's Eleanor ?" cried Mr. Beaufort.

" Carried off," replied Sallie; and then she broke down; covering her eyes with the sleeve of her frock, she sobbed aloud.

" What's the matter with *you*, wife?" asked Dan, scrutinizing her from head to foot with a burning eye.

" They thrashed me—licked me half to death. But I don't car' for that, ef I could see them girls home again."

Dan's face was at a white heat, as he went around and around his wife, looking at her naked back, bleeding, cut to the bone, her torn dress, her swelled, purple countenance

There was death to a hundred bushwhackers in his look.
Mr. Beaufort and Captain Bell stood silent. Neither of them
spoke or stirred. It is doubtful if the father felt a fiercer
pang than the young man who had hoped—ha! there was no
time to think of hopes now. His face was pale as ashes, but
his heart was like a live coal underneath, scorching his breast
unbearably.

"How long have they been gone? Which way?" he
shouted, recovering himself, but in a voice so changed that
even Mr. Beaufort looked around at him.

"They've been gone an hour at least; they went off quick,
for fear you'd surprise 'em. We don't know which way they
went, after they got 'round the rock on the west side."

"The west side? Then they were not on horseback?"

"No. They struck off, 'round the hill, thar."

"Come, men, who will go with me? We must go on foot,
for there is not even a path."

Captain Bell started off, without even waiting for a drink
of cold water. Every man followed him, stopping only to
quench his thirst; some who were very hungry snatched at
the ears of trampled corn, and ate them raw as they ran. For
a mile or two the course of the retreating banditti was obvious
to every eye; then it became less easy to trace; the party
pressed on in the very madness of despair, for night was
approaching, and if they did not overtake the enemy before
the darkness closed in, every thing was lost. Turkey Dan
knew every part of that region—he was allowed to lead.

"After we get through this bit of wood, about three mile
beyond, we come out on quite an open road," he said; "it
crosses the mountains here; they may go up or down it; we
must reach it 'fore dark, so's to have their tracks."

Silently they pushed forward; the red light of the setting
sun sifted through the branches overhead; they could no

longer trace the exact path of the banditti; so they chose the directest course to the road spoken of. When they emerged into it, it was deep twilight.

Dan's keen eye pierced the gathering gloom.

"They left their horses here," he said, at last, "and pushed across; then came back, mounted again, and now they're off in good airnest, the devil alone can tell whar, for part has took one way, and part another, and which one of 'em has the women there's no way of guessin'. I wish I had my horse."

Mr. Beaufort, who had kept up with long-legged Dan and the fierce young Captain with an energy beyond his years and strength, gave way before the utter hopelessness of the case. His previously overtasked mind and body could endure no more; crying piteously—"Eleanor! my child!" he sunk down upon the path in a momentary stupor.

"Take him back with you—he is unfit to go further," said Bell to some of the men who came up. "He can do no good, and perhaps so many of you are not needed. As for me, Dan, I had rather die than give up."

"Blast it, so'd I, Captain! I *won't* give up!"

Mr. Bostwick's clenched teeth spoke for him.

Dan picked out a dozen of the best men.

"I'll take half, and go over the hill," said he, "for I know it better'n you do, Captain. You and Bostwick take the others and go down. You'll find a plain road, and you're sharp enough to look out for by-tracks, ef it is dark. If you come across a horse, take it—I shall."

The friends gripped hands and parted. There was little to hope for; but, as they said and felt, they could die easier than they could turn back and leave those women to their fate.

Two days passed away. Mr. Beaufort, too ill to be out of

bed, would yet drag himself to the cabin-door to look out
with that pitiful, anxious face for the return of some one with
tidings of his daughter. Late on this second day, Dan
returned, with his men, and some sad tidings. By tramping
all night that first night, he had come up with the party who
had taken the direction over the mountain; they had stopped
at a little tavern, tied their horses, and were taking a few
hours rest. Leaving his men hidden in a wood, Dan had got
access to the inn, before the travelers were up, had "camped
down" on the bar-room floor, along with several others, with
ears wide open and eyes that saw every thing. As the
travelers awoke and gathered together in the morning, he
saw that none of them probably knew him; and with his
wonderful genius for changing his voice, manner and features,
he scarcely feared detection any how. By dint of dreadful
swearing at the Union "varmints," and a warmly expressed
wish to join some "fust-rate set of fellers bound on a hunt
after Unioners," he got up a good state of feeling toward himself; he treated the whole gang to whisky before breakfast
and whisky after breakfast; and in the course of an hour or
two had found out that the captured ladies were *not* in their
keeping, and that they were in the hands of their Captain,
who was taking them off to his camp in another county.
The name of this leader was that of one of the most dare-devil,
courageous, and formidable of the guerrilla chiefs—a reckless
adventurer who had been one of Walker's right-hand men in
his unlawful invasions, and who had taken advantage of the
distracted condition of Tennessee to continue his old pursuits.
Dan's heart sunk when he heard this desperado's name.

By dint of a series of cross-questions which would have
made a lawyer famous, he succeeded in ascertaining the exact
position of this freebooter's camp and the number of his
followers; as soon as this was done, he was eager to be off,

but was obliged to bide his time, for fear of awakening suspicion. When the band finally departed, at nearly noon, he
had promised to join them at their rendezvous as soon as he
could provide himself with a horse and some other fixtures.

"I'll meet 'em thar," he reiterated, setting his teeth, when
they finally rode out of the yard, "I'll meet 'em, no doubt, in
a manner they don't expect."

It was necessary to provide food for his men, who had
tramped all night with nothing since the morning of yesterday; so he coaxed the fierce rebel woman who presided over
the inn-kitchen to bake some biscuits and fry some ham for
some of Horton's men, as he expressed it; and to be quick
about it, for they were after a couple of Unionists like a hog
after a rattlesnake. The amiable creature did her best in so
good a cause; he called in his party, made a hurried meal,
and turned homeward.

Back that weary way they trudged, resting a part of the
night on the bare ground, out of sheer inability to keep up,
no rest having been taken since that brisk fight at the village
days ago, except what they had stolen during Dan's visit to
the tavern. On the afternoon of the next day they were
home again, where, for the first time, Dan stopped to inquire
of his wife the particulars of the raid upon their little place.

It seems that, on the day when it occurred, they had sent
Pompey off into the woods to find something for supper.
They expected the return of their friends, and meant to provide a substantial meal to the fatigued and, probably, half-
famished men. As if impressed with a foreboding of danger,
the negro had been very reluctant to leave them; but they
had laughed at his fears; they had been undisturbed for two
months, and had begun to lose that sense of constant danger
which had at first oppressed them. Miss Beaufort, in particular, had been in unusually fine spirits; she had woven a

wreath of the wild-brier rosebuds, and wore it in honor of her father's expected coming (she had *said* her father, whoever else she may have been thinking of,) and was sitting in the door, singing, when suddenly a tall, dark-looking man, well-armed, dashed around the bridle-path on a fine horse, rode up to her, bowed very low, asking her politely if he could have dinner for himself and men. She turned a little pale, but repressing other symptoms of fear, said she did not know, she would ask Mrs. Drew, who was the owner of the place. He was followed by about twenty men, on foot, all armed.

"You had better give them the best you have : do not make them angry," she whispered to Sallie, who had come from her cabin to see what was the matter. But the men did not wait for compliments. It was probably only the dashing beauty of Miss Beaufort which had secured this momentary politeness from their leader. She offered to help Mrs. Drew wait upon the unwelcome visitors, but that person said to her sharply :

"Go inter yer own room, and, shet yerself up ; don't mind *me*—I can take car' of myself."

Taking alarm from this, Eleanor retired inside, and herself and Mrs. Bostwick placed the wooden-pegs to hold the door ; the other two ladies were in the woods with their children, gathering blackberries.

The men pulled down the corn, killed the pig, to have some fresh meat, they said, and committed all the harm they well could ; all of which Sally bore patiently, frying some ham-and-eggs and making some coffee for the leader. But when he tried to frighten her into giving some account of her husband and Captain Bell, she was silent under a torrent of oaths and threats; except when he asked how soon she expected them there, when she quickly told him she expected at least sixty of their friends that very day.

This information, which he partly suspected was given to
carry him off, caused him to finish his repast quickly; he
then went to the door of the other cabin, knocked, and told
the ladies they were his prisoners. They remained silent, refusing to open the door, when he summoned his force and
easily broke it down. They were met by Eleanor with the
revolver, which she had kept loaded always in her room; she
said she would shoot the first man who came inside; but the
Captain was reckless, and dashed in, followed by his men.
She fired three times before the weapon was wrested from her
grasp—one shot took effect in the neck and face of the leader,
but he sprung forward doubly furious, catching her up as if
she were a thistle-down in the power of a whirlwind; the
other two shots, Sallie thought, did no injury. Calling upon
the rest to drag away the other lady, they were making off
with their prisoners, when Sallie, too desperate to think of
her own peril, took down her double-barreled gun, and deliberately shot two of the villains, who fell dead on the lawn.
This so enraged the others, that they turned upon her, tied
her, despite some most furious scratching and biting on her
part, to the little tree in front of the cabin, stripped her frock
from her shoulders, and scourged her with green switches, till
they grew tired of the amusement, or their Captain grew tired
of waiting for them. Then they set fire to the cabin, and departed, whooping like Indians, and giving her their parting
blessing in the assurance that she would roast beautifully
when the house got well a-fire. And so she probably would,
if the other two ladies had not returned from their black-
berrying in time to cut her down.

As for Pompey, he came home that night with a good supply of game.

"I felt it in my bones—I felt it in my bones, suthin' would
happen," he groaned, when he heard the miserable story; and

then he wept because he had not returned in season to go with the others in search of the lost ones.

Dan related to the anxious hearers what he had learned :

" I give those who were with us from now till nine o'clock to eat and sleep," he said, " and then we'll start agin.   We can reach that Horton's camp about this time to-morrow ; we can keep shady till 'long 'bout dusk, and then we'll pitch into 'em.   This 'ere thing we can do, ef we can't do no better : we can kill him and all his band.   I sw'ar, by the God that made me, to have the life of that rascal, ef he's harmed a ha'r of Miss Beaufort's head—onless I get killed fust myself.   So, Sallie, mebbe you'll be a widow to-morrer night."

" I wish *I* could go along," was her reply.

" Thunder and lightnin' ! what do you want to go fer ?"

" To fight," said Sallie, shortly.

" I don't see nothing to purvent—except the young ones. You're equal to two men, wife, any day."

" Dan'l can take car' of the young ones."

And so it was settled that Sallie should have a chance to revenge herself for what she had suffered.

" I wish Bell was back, to go with us.   Howsomever, I hope to come across him on the way."

That night, at nine o'clock, they started, on horseback, with two days' rations of cold pork and corn-cake. ; A small guard was left at home to protect the women and children ; while Pomp and Mrs. Drew (the latter in an old suit of her husband's, looking as soldierly as any in that party) made an important addition to the expedition.   Mr. Beaufort, buoyed up by hope and hate, insisted upon being one of its number.

CHAPTER XIII.

THE GUERRILLA CAMP.

IN a little valley completely shut in by a lower range of the Smoky Mountains, except at its westerly end, where an opening in the hills let the waters of Little river flow out, the crimson light of sunset, pouring through this opening, shone athwart the stream, and tinged the convex tents of a guerrilla camp with the red hue they ought always to have worn. Far away from the common channels of travel, and utterly secluded by its wall of mountains, it was a spot so little exposed to discovery, that the band had thrown off the restraints of war; they had no pickets out; their horses wandered at will in the rich grass; the fires for cooking the evening meal burned palely in the brighter glow of sunset. Around these, some were busy with wooden forks and tin saucepans; others lounged upon the grass in front of their tents, playing cards; a few were enjoying games of quoits, and some waded in the shallow stream, cooling their feet after the heat of the day.

Crawling down among the bushes of a hill which jutted out into the valley, until he was so near that he could almost hear their words, and could easily count their numbers and mark every trifle of the camp, came Turkey Dan, reconnoitering the unconscious enemy.

"A pretty lookin' set of cut-throats," he muttered, "from Alabama and Mississap, the most of 'em. Tennessee, hard up as she is, never turned out such a set of devils. Eighty of 'em, about, I reckon. That must be Horton's tent down by the creek. I'll make for *that*, you may bet your life, when we come a t'aring down. Captain Bell wants me to leave that part of the business to him, but I reckon we'll all have a hand in it. Them devils will fight like wounded b'ars; but we'll have the start of 'em, ef we get down the hill 'fore they set eyes on us."

Having observed things to his satisfaction, he crept back over the hill, into a little clump of evergreens, so far from the camp, that the neighing of horses could not be heard by those below. Here he reported to the others the state of affairs. Since setting out, he had been reinforced by Bell, whom he was so fortunate as to meet. It was concluded wisest to leave the horses where they were, and to crawl down the hill in the twilight, creep up as close as possible, and take the camp in the surprise of the first charge.

" No quarter !" said Captain Bell, under his teeth ; and the fierce cry was echoed by every heart who thought of the two prisoners probably held in that camp. They were not going to meet an honorable enemy in open warfare, but to seize and punish a gang of thieves and murderers of the worst character.

" Isn't it time to move ?" asked Mr. Bostwick, chafing under the enforced delay like a caged panther.

" Not for a full half-hour," was Dan's cool reply. " Don't lose half the victory by being in too big a hurry. Rest yourselves, friends ; eat your corn-cake, and be ready for work."

The most of them obeyed the injunction, catching a brief sleep while they waited for orders ; but some three or four of that company could neither eat nor sleep. Obscured in its own shadow, the mountain-side was soon enveloped in darkness ; but over against it the hills were bathed in the soft luster of the full harvest-moon rising, large and luminous, in the east.

A more favorable hour for the attacking party could not have been desired. They were enabled to steal down into the very camp of the enemy, a portion of which was also still wrapped in the shadow of the mountain. Silent and fierce as the tiger whose young had been stolen from her, they pressed up to the very tent-doors.

"Who goes there?" cried out suddenly a sharp-eared bandit.

His answer was a bullet through the heart. Of the whole camp which sprung to find the cause of the alarm, twenty bit the dust at the first fire. The men, surprised, and some of them at a distance from their arms, could hardly distinguish, in the moonlight, friend from foe ; but the enemy had marked *them*, and bore them down resistlessly. The lawless band merited their name for reckless daring ; they fought desperately ; those who could not get to their rifles, drew their knives, with which they made sharp resistance. On toward the tent which, by the little dark flag flying near it, and its superior size, was marked as that of the Captain, pressed half-a-dozen men. Coming to the door, rifle in hand, and sword in belt, to look out for the cause of the *melée*, the moon shone full upon his lithe figure and dark face—it was Horton, one of the worst of the guerrilla chiefs. One flash of those glowing eyes told him how matters stood ; he made a leap, powerful as the spring of a wild animal, clear past the confronting avengers, turned, fired his rifle, and ran, not straight forward, but in circles and doubles to escape the aim of his enemies ; but he was the object of too righteous a wrath to escape the onset of the resolute men who pressed upon him. He fell, pierced by half-a-dozen bullets. Rising to his elbow, he drew his revolver upon the nearest foe, and the chance shot of his dying hand pierced the left lung of Mr. Beaufort, who staggered and dropped to the earth.

"Take that, you sneaking, prowling wolf," yelled Turkey Dan, in the ear of the expiring guerrilla—"*that* fer stealing

into my brood and carrying off my chickens," and he plunged
his bowie-knife through the body.

"I've kept my oath, Sallie," he said, as his wife came up
and looked upon the dead chief.

"I had my revenge on one of them that tied me up," she
said, "and I let him know who done it."

The remainder of the band, seeing the fall of their leader,
took to flight, catching their horses where they could, and
making for the west pass; some hid in the grass and crept
along into the shadow.

It was not until they turned from the corpse of Horton,
that the friends discovered Mr. Beaufort's condition; their
hearts had been so wild with one purpose that they had
hardly marked his fall. Now Captain Bell attempted to raise
him, but he begged to be laid down again, as he felt faint.

"I am afraid I am dying," he murmured. "Where's Eleanor?
Oh, bring Eleanor to me."

They tried to staunch his wound, but he was bleeding inwardly. Mrs. Drew held his head, and another brought water
from the stream, while Dan, Bostwick and Captain Bell rushed
into the tent, where they expected to find the captive women.
They were not there. In vain they rushed into every tent in
the valley. Not a trace of either could be found. Had they
been misinformed? Was this not the band responsible for
the outrage?—that could not be, for Sallie recognized the chief
and some of his men. Then, what had they done with those
helpless prisoners? Murdered them? The brain of the young
man swam, while Bostwick grew cold and trembling—his
teeth chattered—Dan only retained his presence of mind.

"Let us catch some of the infernal scoundrels, and torture
them, till they out with the truth," said he.

The Captain caught at the idea. The guerrillas were flying,
chased by his men to the inlet of the valley; the leaders

followed ; two of them caught stray horses and dashed forward.

"Halt !" they cried, as they neared a bandit stealing on foot along the base of the mountain.

He had nothing better to do than comply—they rode up, took his knife from him, tied his hands behind him, and marched him back to camp.

Mr. Beaufort, fast failing, rallied to hear tidings of his child.

"What was done with the two ladies taken prisoners by your Captain four days ago?" asked Mr. Bostwick.

"Answer truly, all that you know, or you will be instantly shot," said Bell; "if you tell a straight story, so that we detect you in no lie, you will be permitted to go free."

"And if we catch you lyin' or holdin' back, we'll lick you to death by inches, punch you with knives, and leave you to die of hot weather and starvation," added Dan.

"I shan't tell no lies," was the man's sullen. answer. "I'd as lief tell the whole thing as not. Only give me your word of honor you'll let me off."

"We give you our word of honor," said Bell.

"Wall, them women got away tharselves, and that's all we know about it. Captain Horton didn' no more'n that. He was awfully used up about it, too—he felt as streaked as a zebra. You see when we got to our horses, we rode as fast as we could till about eight in the evening—we was off on a by-road in the woods, then, full ten miles from where we left the wagon-track—thar was a stoppin' place there, where we often took a stray meal—the landlord was one of us. It was a one-story shanty, with a sizable loft, divided into sleepin' rooms. We were all hungry, not having had much except what we stole from the ole woman. Captain Horton chucked the ladies into one of the rooms up stairs, and locked 'em in —there was a padlock on that door, cause we often had occasion to use it. The women was so quiet and kind of took down, the Captain just tied their hands behind, and left 'em in there, while he took his supper. He had a little business talk with the landlord, and then he said he guessed he'd take the ladies something to eat, and he had a hot brandy sling and some biscuits and chicken carried up; but when he unlocked the door, and went in very perlite, there was nobody there; he came down tearing mad; the landlord went back with him, they searched all about; the little window wasn't much too big for a cat; they couldn't have gone through that; the Captain swore somebody had let 'em out—and just then they found out a hole in the roof—it was low, and the shingles was old and loose—they'd got their hands untied—s'pect they chawed the strings apart, got up on the bed, pulled away a dozen or two of shingles, and crawled out. They was smart, I tell you. Wall, we run out and looked on the roof—they wan't there—kill or cure, they'd slid down and sloped. Captain Horton was took down. He'd taken an uncommon fancy to the youngest one; I don't know as he'd have harmed her, if she hadn't run away; anyways he didn't like the notion of her stayin' out in the woods all night, where wolves and panthers were not unbeknown. He sot us all to searching; we lighted pine-knots and looked till we was beat out. It wan't no use, and we had to give up. The next day he stayed around as long as he could; nothing was seen or heard and we come off. The Captain was cross as a bear—and that's all I know about it."

Mr. Beaufort had roused himself to listen; now he sunk again. Captain Bell bent over him.

"I'm going, Bell," he whispered, "I leave my daughter to you. Promise me you will find her and protect her."

"Life will not be worth living to me, if I do not," answered the young man. "I love her, as purely, as deeply, as you do.

Ah, Mr. Beaufort, do not give up. If you can rally, to be carried back to the old cabin, perhaps we will find the fugitives returned in safety."

"God grant it," answered the dying man. "Eleanor, Ella darling, where are you? Give me your hand—it is so dark."

These were the last words of Mr. Beaufort. The noble man, driven from home and property, imprisoned, persecuted, enduring hardships to which habit had not inured him, suffering for the Government he loved, refusing the right of a self-elected tyranny to rule him and his, hoping for the time when the Government he upheld would hold out its strong hand to its wretched, unprotected people, perished in the midst of the struggle, by the hand of a murderous outlaw.

Oh, hearts cry aloud, and hands are raised to a just Heaven, when we know that the heroic, faithful, long-suffering people of distracted Tennessee are just as much exposed to such peril to-day as they were last year. Not a home is sacred, not a hearth is safe, not a wife, or mother, or maiden, but shivers with dread of what may impend over her own head or that of the true man in whose life her own welfare is wrapped. Had the call been made, surely gratitude for those who suffer so much for their country would have urged fifty thousand eager hearts to rush to the relief of their brothers and sisters in Tennessee. No draft need have been made from the hosts at Corinth or before Richmond—another army, vast as either, would have sprung to rescue from the rope and whip, the torch and prison, the bullet and gallows, the most heroic, the most immortal patriots, the Union men of Tennessee—bearing a martyrdom which nothing in history excels, since the Christians hid in the catacombs of Rome to hold the faith which heathens denied them.

That night, the victors rested in the camp of the vanquished; at early dawn they departed, bearing with them the corpse of Mr. Beaufort and one other of their number slain. Owing to the great advantage of the surprise and the darkness, no others had been seriously injured.

Sad as the presence of their dead made the company, they yet were cheered with a hope of finding the two ladies at home; as they had made their escape only about eighteen miles from the place of their seizure, it was not impossible that they might find their way back.

Captain Bell was troubled between hope of meeting Eleanor, and fear of the overwhelming grief into which the murder of her father would plunge her; for he, and all others, knew that her father was the light of her eyes. With less speed than they came, they traveled back to their mountain rendezvous. The lost ones had not returned. Pomp threw himself, frantic with sorrow, upon the body of his master.

"Oh, dat I should live to see dis day; dat I should live to see massa dead and gone—murdered, and Missa Eleanor lost, de Lord knows whar—not eben to see his face 'fore he's put away forever. I can't b'ar it! I can't!" and it seemed as if indeed his strong frame would be shattered by the fast-crowding emotions.

They waited two days; and then the bodies were committed to the earth—Eleanor, were she alive, would never see that worshiped form again.

Feeling that their present haunt, having been discovered and attacked, was no longer a place of safety for the women and children, the men had now to select a new place of refuge, to erect temporary shelter, and to abandon all the little improvements which had given a home-feeling to this pleasant nook. In distress and mourning, the band of Union refugees, men, women and children, turned from the spot, leaving the ruined cabins, the defaced garden, and the new groves.

Over them the grass is growing now the second time; the

sun shines down upon that solitary plateau, lying high up in the Cumberlands, beneath the eye of God, holding its buried martyrs.   And every day the grass is starting over more such groves in Tennessee.

CHAPTER XIV.

THE RESCUE.

THERE was one of that band of refugees who went with them to their new retreat with the purpose of learning its locality in case of future need, but who returned immediately to the old place, there to dwell in the solitude of his sorrow, watching by his master's grave, and holding this spot as the nucleus of a circle of carefully-conducted .expeditions in search of that master's child.   It may be thought strange that Pompey would not improve this opportunity to make his way back to the Beaufort plantation to inquire after the welfare of his own family; but so long as there was one gleam of hope that he could find the missing young lady, his was the nature to turn to it with patient watchfulness.

In the mean time he had a plan, if Miss Beaufort's fate could be discovered, to bring his family, freed by death from their rightful owners, to this mountain retreat, here to make a home, where they could take care of themselves, and cherish and attend upon Mr. Beaufort's grave.   With a view to this, he built a stick-chimney to the new cabin, repaired it with some of the wrecks of the old, cleared off the rubbish, and occupied such of his days as he spent there, in putting things into something of their old order.   He was well armed, and feared nothing for himself, not considering himself worth much fighting for. His gun procured him meat, and he contrived to supply himself with other necessaries.

What he most feared was robbery. He had some valuable and very precious things to take care of. It will be remembered that when Eleanor escaped from her own father's house, she took with her her mother's jewelry, her own watch and other ornaments, and that Mr. Beaufort secured some of the most important of his papers. These things had been left in a little rude wooden box, under Eleanor's pillow; this box he had taken possession of, in her name; and to prevent its being stolen in case of the cabin being entered in his frequent absences, he dug a hole under the door-step, buried it, and replaced the stone.

Week after week went by, until scarcely a foot of ground within a semicircle of thirty miles, embracing the country lying below his retreat, but had passed under the vigilant observation of the slave; night after night he roamed the land, hovering around farm-houses, exploring forests and cautiously investigating villages. Twice he had been accompanied by Mr. Bostwick in these expeditions, who was fast becoming a desperate, almost deranged man, body and mind breaking down beneath the suspense and worse than sorrow of his bereavement.

A dozen times he had been to the wretched little forest tavern from which the ladies had made their escape, and from that, as a center, had worked out miles in every direction, so carefully, that had they fallen the prey of wild animals, even, he might have discovered some fragment of their clothing, but no trace, however slight, had thus far encouraged him.

One day, late in September, while wandering again in this seemingly aimless search, and being, as he judged, about eight miles from the tavern, in a direction opposite his cabin, he sat down upon a fallen tree to the luncheon of cold corn bread which he drew from his pocket. As he ate, he saw on a bush in front of him a few blackberries lingering, ready to drop from over-ripeness. As he stooped forward to gather them, he perceived, amid the tangled vines running along the ground, a lady's shoe. He knew it, the instant his eye rested upon it. That worn, dilapidated little gaiter belonged to Eleanor Beaufort. Poor child! since the day she fled from her home, she had had no shoes but the frail pair she had worn away, and these had seen hard service amid mountain rocks and woods. In vain had she mended and patched, as long as there was thread to borrow; the trim little kid bootees had grown shabby in spite of care, and there had been prospects of her being reduced to a pair of moccasins which Dan had promised to make her out of deer-skin. When torn away so rudely by the dreaded guerrillas, it could easily be guessed that the long flight through these forest-wilds, made in the darkness of night, had completed the ruin of the shoes, until one at least had dropped from the poor, tired feet, and the rest of that wretched journey must have been made in a condition frightful to think of. As Pomp looked at the worn-out tell-tale, and then at the cruel briers and sharp stones besetting the earth, he groaned aloud at the thought of his young missa's sufferings.

However, here was a clue. If it led only to the certainty of death, it would at least put hope at rest. He had been over this ground before, and he knew that not far from here, the forest opened into cultivated fields, the property of a wealthy secessionist, whose dwelling occupied a prominent position on a pleasant rise of ground about a mile beyond the verge of the wood. This mansion must of course first attract the eyes of the wanderers, had they gotten safely through the forest. To the residents they had probably applied for aid and protection. It would not do to go openly and inquire;

for if they had been favorably received at that house, tidings
would have reached their friends long ago. From the well-.
known savagely Confederate politics of the family, it was
probable that the ladies had been repulsed, had they told their
story there. What Pompey desired now to learn was, if any
such persons had called at that place, and trace, if possible,
their fate from there. The farm, which was partly devoted
to stock-raising and partly to wheat, was worked by slaves,
with one or two of whom Pompey had spoken when inspect-
ing the premises upon a previous occasion. Slaves were not
very numerous in that part of the State, and he did not like
to be observed by the owner or overseer, for fear of being
arrested as a runaway, or as one engaged in enticing away
others. He spent the afternoon in close search after other
tokens of the fugitives, but the precious old shoe was the only
relic which the most minute scrutiny could obtain. When
the eagerly-wished for twilight darkened the red of a September sunset into a faint glow along the horizon, Pomp quitted
the shelter of the woods and struck across the fields, the
shortest path to the mansion. Except a surly dog, whose
threatening growls he soon coaxed into good-nature, he
encountered no living thing, till he halted in the shadow of
the farm, from whence he had a view of the house, now
lighted up for the evening. He could see the family at supper through the window of the dining-room, whose curtains
were not yet drawn. He saw a colored girl come in with a
waiter; place food thereon, and go out; he traced her up into
the hall, by the lamp she carried, and thence up to a dormer-
window in the wide, sloping roof of the old-fashioned mansion, through which the light now flashed. As the inner
door was opened, and the lamp flashed suddenly into the
room, the intent negro saw a woman standing at that window,
her head resting against the casement, looking up, as if in

some sad reverie, at the kindly stars. Of course he saw but the outline, but his heart jumped into his throat; he had recognized, as surely as if he had seen her in broad daylight, Eleanor Beaufort. The peculiar turn of the graceful head, the droop of the hair, the slender neck were hers—he could swear to that. He had but a moment's glance, for she turned as the lamp came in, and disappeared in the room—the high window having only revealed her head and shoulders as she stood. In vain he watched for a reappearance of the vision; it came no more, and in about an hour, the light was extinguished or withdrawn. In the mean time, the sleepy-headed chattels were going to bed in the two or three little houses clustered about the main dwelling. It was high time for Pompey to try his luck with some of them. He stole cautiously to the door of a cabin into which he had seen a colored man enter, with whom he had spoken on a former occasion, and to whom his sagacious mind pointed as a man likely to be induced to give any information he might have. His low knock was answered by a mulatto woman, who asked him in, without hesitation. He accepted her invitation, saying that he was tired and hungry; he had been out in the woods hunting, and had got lost. His gun and game-bag seconded his assertion. The husband of the woman sat by the little wood fire, eating his supper; he extended the hospitalities of his house to the stranger, who accepted a share of his bacon and hoe-cake, talking all the time on subjects far removed from that which pressed upon his mind. His entertainers wanted to know his news, and that of his master, where he came from and where he was going to, to all of which he returned discreet answers. Finally, like their superiors, their conversation turned upon war and politics. However crude may have been their conception of the great subjects involved, however ludicrous or ignorant many of their ideas, one thing

was soon apparent: these slaves sympathized with the old
Union, and felt as if, in some inexplicable way, their own
fortunes were wrapped up in its welfare—as if the triumphant
close of the struggle would bring to them some marvelous
millennium, long foretold by their sable prophets. Having
felt about for the direction of their sympathies, Pomp no
longer hesitated to avow his own; the emphasis of this
avowal drew them out still more completely.

"Massa t'inks we're all mad-dog 'sessionists," said the
man, with a sly laugh. "He t'inks we fight for 'em like de
debbil, if he ask us. He's tole us ole Abe Linkum will bite all
our heads done gone off, ef he gets a chance. We'se willin' to
run the resks, hi! Wish he had a chance, right away. Hi,
wouldn' he spit de wool out, w'en he'd bit one off, and tell
de rest, ' cl'ar out and take car' darselves?' yah, yah, yah!"

"Missus she feels round ebery little while; t'inks de
women can't keep *der* mouths shut, as she 'quires about how
our husbands like de new state of 'fairs, and so on. She's
sharp, missus is, sharper 'n massa. She *t'inks* she can see
through a grin'stone; but laws bless us, don't we lay it on to
her thick! We lies to her awfully. It's wicked to lie, our
preacher said to camp-meetin'; but, laws, if we didn' lie
'bout dis war, we'd be whipped, and watched, and have no
peace of our lives. I don't 'zac'ly see how we can get cl'ar
of lyin'," she added, reflectively.

"Any body sick to the master's?" inquired their visitor;
"I saw a girl carryin' tea up-stairs to somebody,"—carelessly.

". They maybe sick or they maybe not; *we* never sot eyes
on 'em," said the woman.

"Oh, visitors, then, I s'pose?"

"Cur'us kind o' visitors," remarked the man.

"Missus 'ud take my head off if she knew I'd tell it," said
the woman, whispering; "She don't know I know it; but

Kitty told me. She told Kitty to say nothing. She's got a couple o' fine ladies locked up in the garret-chamber, 'cause they're Unioners. She said they were spies and ought to be locked up; she calls 'em prisoners of war. But she makes 'em sew mor'n 'nuff to pay their board. She half starves 'em, and they're doin' all her fall sewing, beautifully, too, I'se seen some of it."

Pompey had hard work to control his indignation.

" What kind of looking ladies are they? Do you know?"

" Kitty says they're both awful handsome, specially the youngest, but their dress ain't much. Kitty's got better herself. That's cuz their clo'es was all torn off 'em, getting 'way from the 'sessionists, I reckon; one of 'em hadn't a shoe to her foot. One of 'em's been sick considerable; they're low sperited. Kitty wants to let 'em out, but she's 'feared of her life to do it. Missus 'd s'pect her, right away."

" How long they been here?"

" Oh, five, six weeks, I reckon; good while."

" My frien's," said Pompey, speaking very low, hitching his chair closer to the couple, " dem ladies is just what I'm after. I've been a-lookin' for 'em ever sence they was stole. I belongs to dat youngest lady. She's a born lady, owns twice as much property as dis yer vulgar 'sessionist. It makes me awful mad to hear 'bout Missa Eleanor a sewing and a bein' starved. I can't set still!"

A chorus of interjections followed upon this revelation. Getting up and turning the button which secured the door, and drawing the little check curtain across the window, Pompey reseated himself, and almost under his breath, gave the couple as much of the story of his master, mistress and himself as he thought expedient. The result was their promise to keep him that night, secrete him next day, and get Kitty to convey information to the prisoners of his being here, and that he should attempt to rescue them the following night.

Having sat around the fire until the last ember expired, the host showed his guest to a straw bed in the loft overhead; the next morning his breakfast was handed up to him, and he was requested to "keep dark,"—a thing, by the way, which Pompey had never failed to do.

That day was long, beyond counting, to the impatient fellow. From a hole in the scantling of the garret he could overlook the mansion; he got the bearings of the place fixed in his mind. The high house and steep roof offered not very much encouragement to his plan of rescuing the ladies from the window; but whispering through the floor to Mrs. Dinah below, he learned that there was a long ladder lying behind the barn; and he noticed that strips of wood for staying the feet of persons obliged to go upon the roof were nailed upon the shingles at regular intervals from the window down.

Kitty was consulted by Mrs. Dinah, and avowed her joy at being able to do something for the "poor, pretty ladies;" and not long after she had carried their dinner to them, Pompey saw the face of Eleanor at her window, grown pale and thin, but lighted now with a gleam of hope. She gazed around, as if longing to see his face, and then took an observation of the roof. Mrs. Bostwick also came and looked out; her countenance betrayed recent severe illness.

When Kitty went up to the attic with their supper, she conveyed the final arrangements to the prisoners, which were, to prepare themselves to leave as soon after the family had retired for the night as it was safe to attempt it. They were to listen for the signal from the outside, which Pompey would give when he had placed the ladder and mounted it. If they could climb outside the window, he would see to the rest.

It required courage and care to attempt a descent of the

roof in the darkness of night; certain death would be the
result of a misstep. The prisoners shuddered as they thought
of it; but Eleanor, with her usual determination, cheered her
weaker friend, and set her nerves to the accomplishment of
the task.

It seemed, that evening, to the impatient Pomp, as if sleep
would never descend upon the mansion; as if all the dogs in
the county were barking, and every negro on the estate had
an excuse for hovering around the house. At last, all became
quiet. He and his host dragged the ladder from behind the
barn, and fixed it noiselessly in its place. Off across a wheat-
field, where a private lane led into the main road, a little two-
wheeled cart which stood there, neglected, had been greased
in the axles, strengthened by leather thongs, and a harness
borrowed from the stable, while a horse was borrowed from
half-a-dozen grazing in the pasture. This had been the work
of the slave who was aiding Pomp in his enterprise. Now
he stood at the foot of the ladder, bracing it, while Pomp
ascended, climbed upon the roof, and gave the firm grasp of
his powerful hand to steady the poor lady, who trembled and
clung to it, and never would have succeeded in her dangerous
venture, without its aid.

"Now you just hold tight to me, and I'll tote you down
like a feader," whispered the huge negro—and he did.

In three minutes, bewildered and fluttering, Mrs. Bostwick
stood upon *terra firma.* Eleanor performed the thrilling
journey in the same safe way.

"You jis' run across de garden, and stoop down by de
fence, till we put dis ladder back, all right. Somebody might
be comin' round and see it, and git on our track 'fore we
wanted."

The ladder was restored to its former position, the two men
hurried their charge across the field, they were seated in the

bottom of the dilapidated cart, the men shook hands with
Pomp, wished the ladies God speed, spoke softly to the horse,
and they were off.

Kitty contrived to have it very late before she was ready
to carry up the breakfast to the prisoners, the following morning. When she did get up with it, did unlock the door, and
did find the prisoners gone, great was her astonishment and
consternation! She rolled up her eyes and held up her hands
and "took on so," that her angry mistress sent her off to the
wash-house—she did not want sympathy.

The most innocent of all puzzled and surprised people were
Kitty and the inmates of the cabin where Pomp had found
shelter—"'twas a most extrowdinary piece of business—never
saw the like! must have flied straight out der winder, sure!"

"If dey was dem wicked Unioners," said the man, shaking
his head, "'twas quite likely der fadder, de debbil, help 'em
off. Oh, gorry, glad I wasn' out last night—I'd been scart to
death, ef I'd a-seen his horns and tail—oh gorry!"—and his
owner laughed in his sleeve at the slave's stupidity.

In the mean time, through the night, the old cart traveled
tediously up the mountain, Pomp walking beside it, carrying
his gun, whenever the hill was steep ; and occasionally resting
himself and making better progress, by riding when a level
stretch in the road gave him an opportunity, without overbur-
dening the horse. A waning moon arose about twelve o'clock,
giving light, so that they could keep the way without much
difficulty. Stout as was Pompey's heart and arm, the women
shrunk down in the vehicle, oppressed with dread, as they
threaded narrow roads, overhung with rocks, or so shaded by
pines that the light scarcely cast a glimmer through the gloom.
What armed and heartless outlaws might be lurking in these
shadows, who could tell? Their escort knew the danger, as
well as they ; and knew that his single arm could do small

service against the hidden attacks of a numerous enemy. He scarcely thought of his own peril; but prayed inwardly for the protection of those he was seeking to lead to a place of safety.

The fugitives remembered another awful night they had passed on this very road—a night of tempest, when the windows of heaven were opened, and the artillery of the skies thundered at the rocky fortress of the mountain.

Pompey's soul was sad within him that night. The joy he felt at finding his young lady, in comparative health and safety, was chastened not only by still impending danger, but most and heaviest, by the tidings of her father's death which he should be obliged to communicate before many hours.

Twice and thrice Eleanor had inquired earnestly after her father; and he had answered evasively. The poor fellow was seeking courage for the bitter moment. Once, when with the irrepressible buoyancy of youth, she laughed out at some awkward stumble of the horse, her laughter pierced his heart like a wound—he felt how all that lightness of spirit would be crushed out by the disastrous blow so soon to descend.

The long night rolled behind them; the sun arose, the scenery became familiar; Pomp encouraged the lagging animal and kept up a constant conversation about trifles—anything to keep the mind of the young girl from the fatal subject. Now that the daylight was on it, he could see that her face had lost much of its bloom; but with the animation of the expected meeting, color and light began to come.

"See, Mrs. Bostwick, I know this spot; we are only two miles from the plateau, now. Oh, dear, I almost hear Sallie now, and see my dear father flying to meet me. He is there now, is he not, and Mr. Bostwick?—I mustn't forget who you are looking for, Annie," and she smiled brightly at her friend, who, weary as she was with the uncomfortable ride, sat up erect, and looked forward, flushed and hopeful.

"Didn' I tell you we'se all left the plateau, now ?" said Pompey. "We'se 'fraid to stay dar, after dem gorillas found us out. We went off to a new place. Only I'se staid here, to hunt you up. Mr. Bostwick, he was over, a-helpin' me hunt, last week, but he's gone back now. I'll take you on to the new place to-morrow."

A little shadow came over the expectant faces.

"And where is papa, Pomp ? Is he there too ?"

"Oh, missa, don't ask me ?" cried the negro, and all of a sudden his long repressed trouble burst forth ; he dropped the reins and flung himself down by the roadside in a convulsion of sobs.

Eleanor sprung from the cart ; she took hold of his arm and shook it :

"Is my father dead ?"

"Oh, missa, I wish I was dead myself 'fore I have to done gone break your heart so."

It was not necessary for him to answer her question ; his manner told the truth ; she pressed her hand to her heart and said not a word, but stood looking into Mrs. Bostwick's face with a blank gaze. Controlling himself, Pompey arose, lifted her in his arms and placed her in the lady's lap, like an infant ; got in the cart, and drove forward to the cabin, recklessly, as if they could run away from their sorrow. Mrs. Bostwick loosened Eleanor's dress and fanned her with her bonnet; she seemed holding her breath in a kind of spasm. When they reached the plateau she was still perfectly undemonstrative ; they lifted her out, laid her down on her bed in the cabin and sprinkled water on her face. She breathed, in long, convulsive breaths, but she would not speak nor give any sign in answer to their solicitations.

They chafed her hands and feet and forced water between her lips. After a time she recovered herself, but she said nothing, only drew the cover over her face as if she could not bear the sight of sympathy. The negro built a fire, and made a cup of coffee.

" You'll faint away yerself, missus, if yer don't take something," he said, to Mrs. Bostwick.

She drank the much needed draught.

" When did he die ?" she asked, softly, hoping that discussion of the subject might get Eleanor to weeping.

" Four days after you was took away, missus."

" How ?"

" Dey killed him. Dem gorillas shot him. You see, we got on der track and 'tacked 'em. We killed a great many —dat Captain, sartain, and many more. But massa, he was so eager to find his chile, I 'spect he not look out close for. hisself—he was shot. He didn' suffer much. Ah no, bless de Lord! He died as gentle as if he was gwine to sleep. An' he said, tell my chile, ' God bless her.' He said, ' Captain Bell, take car' my chile.' "

The sound of smothered weeping made the listeners thank God for the needed tears which might save the surcharged heart from being rent asunder.

" Where is he buried ?" asked Eleanor, after a few moments rising up, with a wan, stricken look, very painful to see.

" Come wid me, missa, I will show you."

She followed him to the grave, chosen in the loveliest portion of the plateau. A tree bent over it, and the sods were springing with grass. A rude brown stone, carved with his knife by Captain Bell, stood at the head. Pompey left her alone at her request.

It was long before she came back to the cabin. When she did, there was something mingled with her mourning of a sterner character.

" They have killed my father," she said. " My life is no

better than his; I want no better death. He labored for his
State and Country. I will continue his work. As long as
there is any thing that a woman can do, I will do it. I have
not a relative in the world who is nearer to me than a stranger.
The man I was once betrothed to, I now scorn and condemn.
The only relief it will be possible for me to find, will be to
suffer for the cause which my father taught me to revere."

And it seemed from that hour as if the spirit of the brave
old man had entered into the breast of his daughter.

CHAPTER XV.

LADY SECESSIONISTS

To go back a little and explain how these two Union
ladies happened to be held in durance vile by an enterprising
secessionist female. That unhappy night which found them
the prisoners of a band of outlaws, and fastened in the garret
of a forest-inn, found them also equal to the emergency. The
moment they were left alone, staring at each other forlornly,
with their hands tied behind them, their woman's wit began
to solve the rather difficult problem of an escape from such
custody. Eleanor's supple and slender hands soon insinuated
themselves out of the knot which bound them, and were ready
to free her friend's. The door would not yield, the window
was too small—it was only a glimmer of starlight through the
shabby roof which finally suggested that desperate venture.
With the strength of despair they tore away the rotten shingles, and by the aid of the bed crawled through; and here
they might well hesitate in their dangerous exploit, for to

slide down and drop into the darkness beneath was a risk, they could hardly guess how deadly. However, death was preferable to imprisonment, and only pausing to listen that all was quiet below, they committed their souls to God, groped their way to the eaves, and dropped. Fortunately, upon the side they had unwittingly chosen, the fall was but a few feet, after they had thus thrown themselves over the eaves, a heap of house-rubbish, decayed vegetables, corn-husks and straw receiving them kindly. Grasping each other's hands they fled, like deer, into the forest. Many times they fell, plunging into underbrush, stumbling over fallen trees, sinking into miry places—for the darkness within the wood was impenetrable. The only stars they saw on that dismal journey were the fiery eyes which twice glared at them stealthily out of the blackness of midnight, freezing their souls with terror. They had heard, while far within the shelter of the wood, the cries and curses of men in search; and these sounds had made the fiery eyes less frightful—yet it was awful to grope through that thick night, not knowing what beast of prey might be silently tracking them. Long after all sound of pursuit had ceased, they pressed onward, they knew not whither; they wanted to be far away when morning broke; besides, it was as fearful to remain still as to move on. Eleanor lost one of her shoes in a bog—the other gave out when caught in the briers, where Pompey afterward discovered it: her feet were bleeding at every step. Mrs. Bostwick grew so lame, that she could move only with the greatest effort; she had sprained an ankle in jumping from the roof, the pain of which she was at first too anxious to notice; but the long, rough tramp increased it intolerably, and finally she gave out, sinking down and saying she could go no further. Eleanor, herself suffering torture at each step, just then discovered that they had reached the edge of the forest and were stopped by a rail fence. On to this she assisted her friend ; and there the two sat until the increasing light in the east made them fearful of detection. Eleanor stood upon the top rail and reconnoitered. She saw the cultivated fields and the respectable farm mansion, and felt almost as if amid friends. The house appeared a great way off, when she looked at her friend's swollen ankle and her own bare, bruised feet ; they were both of them famished as well as fatigued, however, and the only hope of relief was in reaching the dwelling.

"Let us try and reach it before our enemies are up and stirring," said she, helping Mrs. Bostwick down into the field ; but when the lady attempted walking, no amount of heroism could enable her to succeed.

"You must sit here in this deep grass, where you will be entirely hidden, while I go to the house, and beg of them to send some one to bring you."

"Poor child, you can not get there yourself, I fear."

"Oh, yes, I can. I shall limp a little, but I'll make a crutch of hope. Good-by, Annie. I shall make all the speed I can. Try and sleep a little to pass away the time."

Thus Eleanor set out in the light of the rising sun. She was glad when she had made her way across the unsheltered field, not so much because the dry stubble of the harvested wheat cut her bleeding feet cruelly, as that she knew not what spies might detect her. Having crossed it, she came into the lane from which she afterward took her night flight; here the cool grass was like a bandage to her wounds, and she made better progress. It was two hours before she made the tedious mile to the door of the mansion-house. The family were at breakfast ; she heard the rattle of dishes; no one had observed her approach, and now, as she stood with her hand on the knocker she began to think of the strange figure she made, and of what construction might be put upon her improbable story. She, so accustomed to every honor and attention, the petted daughter of a wealthy aristocrat, had hardly bethought herself of the position in which she was now placed—that contempt and neglect might take the place of flattery and respect.

The thought of her friend, counting the slow moments. in her solitary concealment, gave her courage ; she seized the heavy knocker, and, in response to the summons, the girl-in-waiting, Kitty, came to the door, and stood, holding it partly open, looking at her from head to foot with a supercilious air. Alas ! poor Eleanor—she had tried to hide her bare feet beneath the folds of her dress, but the prying eyes of the girl fixed upon them relentlessly.

" What d'ye want ?"

" I want to see your mistress."

" She'll not put herself out to wait on beggars."

" I am not a beggar," said Miss Beaufort, in the tone of one accustomed to the control of such impertinence ; but as she denied the charge, it rushed over her that it was altogether true—what else was she ?—and she continued, with that bright trustful smile which was one of her charms—" at least, I have never begged before. But I am in trouble this morning. Tell your mistress a lady wishes to speak to her."

Kitty opened her eyes at the word " lady," but she didn't turn up her nose, this time, for two reasons : first, it was too flat for any such demonstration, and secondly, the polished voice and manners, and the winning smile, had made an impression upon her.

" I s'pose I can speak to her," she said, leaving Miss Beaufort on the steps, and returning to the dining-room, where she told her mistress that there was a cur'us lady, without no shoes, and a handkercher on her head, wanted to speak with her.

" She isn't a crazy creature, is she, Kitty ?"

" No mum.   She's as sensible as I am, this minute," which was saying a good deal in the stranger's favor.

" Bring her in here."

It was a moment of painful embarrassment to Eleanor, when she appeared before the assembled family ; the eyes of the lady were turned upon her with a cold suspicion which made the color burn in her pale cheeks ; two young ladies, daughters of the house, seemed oppressed with inward merriment, and the gentleman eyed her with interest.

" What do you wish ?"

" I wish kindness and protection, madam.   A lady and myself were captured yesterday by Horton's band of guerrillas ; we escaped from them last evening, and have been wandering all night in the forest.   Our shoes dropped from our feet. My friend is so ill and her ankle so swollen, I was obliged to leave her in the wheat-field running by the wood."

" Sit down," said the gentleman, handing her a chair. " Horton's band, hey ?   Didn't know they were in these parts. How came you to fall into their hands ?"

" They carried us off, during the absence of our men."

" Where from ?"

" From our home, I suppose over twenty miles from here," answered Eleanor, evasively, for the thought had rushed over her that these people would probably not sympathize with her, politically.

" Humph, what's your folks' side o' the question ?"

" We are for the Union," she said, without an instant's hesitation, looking him full in the face.

" That's just what I reckoned," said the gentleman.

" They served you right to carry you off—wish they'd have kept you," remarked his wife, tartly.

" I shouldn't think any mother could be so cruel as to

say that," replied the young girl, her lip trembling, despite of
pride.

"Don't mention us 'long side of a Unionist, if you please,"
said one of the young ladies, with a sneer.

"What's your name?" resumed the gentleman.

"Beaufort," she answered, without reflection that it had
become as dangerous as it once was honorable.

"Ha!" and he mused a moment. "Your father's name
Walter?"

She bowed assent.

"Where did you say they took you from?"

The sudden wily tone and furtive glance put her on her
guard. Remembering the public prominence given to her
father's sentiments, his escape from prison, and that there was
secretly a reward out for his capture, she regretted that she
had given his name at all. To this last question she made no
reply.

"Wife, give Miss Beaufort some breakfast. Fix her up
with shoes and what she needs. I'll take her home myself,
this afternoon or to-morrow. Did you say there was another
lady?"

Eleanor directed him where to find Mrs. Bostwick. As he
went out, he called his wife into the hall, and there gave her
some instructions, which resulted in her behaving decently,
though with icy coldness, toward the strangers. When her
companion was brought in, they were given breakfast, and
conducted to a chamber in the attic, where Eleanor was supplied with an old pair of slippers, and with liniment and
bandages for dressing her friend's swollen ankle.

Having been told that it would be impossible for Mr.
Simms to leave home that day, but that he would attend to
their case on the morrow, they were glad to throw themselves
upon the bed and sleep off some of their great fatigue.

They were grateful to Kitty for bringing their dinner to their room; that they were not esteemed worthy to sit at the table of a secessionist gave them more amusement than chagrin. With rest and refreshment, Eleanor's native wit recovered its power. She had been half-stupefied that morning; but now, as she thought it over in the solitude of the attic, the readiness of Mr. Simms to put himself to so much trouble on their account was plainly not without some motive stronger than that of kindness. In the first place, he had not the face of a generous man who would do such an act without reward; and again, that the whole family cherished an active and vindictive hatred against all Unionists was apparent. It was clear to her that he suspected her connection with the Union rendezvous, the existence of which had troubled the Confederates not a little; to detect the retreat of such famous persons as Captain Bell, Turkey Dan, and Walter Beaufort would be an advantageous matter to their host—a matter quite worth taking a day's drive for. Upon the plea of protection and care of the ladies, he could not be denied access; nor would honor permit his detention, however much her friends might have reason to suspect him.

"Annie, I'm afraid we shall be compelled to decline our kind host's escort; I think we must trust to ourselves."

"Why, Eleanor?"

"You would not be willing to peril our cause and the lives of our friends, by betraying the rendezvous?"

"Certainly not. If it comes to that, we can take our chance. We can die on the road, or go to prison. Only I wish our friends knew we were safe. They must suffer tortures of anxiety."

"If it wasn't for your ankle, Annie, we might steal out of the house this evening, and try and find help from some less savagely secessionist source."

"Ah, my ankle! I'm afraid it will keep me helpless a long time."

"It is very hot, and so is your face, Mrs. Bostwick. You are feverish. You haven't the health to endure these hardships as I can."

"I wouldn't mind the fever if I had the use of my feet."

But if they had any hopes of getting out of that house by stealth, they were cut off at twilight, when the mistress herself came up with some bread and tea, and, upon going out, locked the door upon her prisoners. This little act confirmed them still more in their suspicions.

"We have fluttered right into the spider's web," said Eleanor.

When, the following morning, Mrs. Simms came in, with a tolerable pair of shoes and a couple of sun-bonnets, and told her *guests* to prepare for their return, Miss Beaufort, thanking her for her hospitality and kind intentions, declined decidedly receiving any further favors.

"What do you mean by this kind of foolery, after the trouble we've been to?" asked the lady, angrily.

"I have my reasons, madam, which I am at liberty to keep to myself, I suppose. You can guess them!"

"You won't be allowed to gratify your whims!"—and the lady summoned her husband to aid in braving the fugitives into submission.

"You might as well go, now you've got a good chance. What in mischief's the reason you won't take up with an offer, better'n you've a right to expect?"

"Because, Mr. Simms, my father and myself are under the protection of friends whom I would not betray to as bitter an enemy as I feel you are,—no, not to save myself worse than my present trouble!"

"How are you going to help yourself?" he asked, throwing off his wheedling tone. "If you attempt to get back on your own hook, you'll be dogged, every step. If you should wait a month, you'd never make a move but you'd be watched."

"Then I will never make one. Thank you for the hint."

"What you going to do?"

"Trust in Providence."

"Humph — he don't have much to do with people of your stamp. You're here, and if you won't go home, you can stay here. We'll be on the look-out for whoever may come hunting after you. We'll keep you as a kind of bait to attract Unioners. And perhaps, by writing on to Nashville about you, we'll put the authorities on the right track. Wife, take care of your prisoners. We'll get pay for our trouble out of them yet."

Mrs. Simms was a practical woman, who believed in securing present and tangible reward for the board and lodging of her prisoners. That very afternoon she brought up a pile of sewing, and set Miss Beaufort to work to earn her keeping. Mrs. Bostwick was, for some time, unable to assist; but as soon as she was convalescent, she was furnished with plenty to do.

The poor prisoners were really glad of employment; they would have gone wild with the thoughts which crowded upon them and the longing for home, if it had not been for this relief. Then they were too proud to eat the bread of their enemies, although compelled against their wish to do so, without making full returns. Mrs. Simms found them profitable in a high degree; they saved the hire and trouble of a fall seamstress, and did their work much better than she was accustomed to finding it done—that is, in all plain sewing and embroidery. But when the impertinent daughters of the house brought their flashy dresses to be made and fitted, Eleanor contrived to ruin the fit, so that they never renewed the experiment—she had not been trained as a dressmaker, and she made no great effort on this occasion to learn the art.

The sympathy and lively chat of Kitty, who had taken a fancy to the ladies so much more refined than her own mistresses, was their only relief from the monotony of their days. She contrived to bring them many a dainty to spice the plain fare ordered by their keeper.

Occasionally Mrs. Simms treated them to a tirade, in the well-known present fashion of Southern ladies—a tirade, tacked together with hempen ropes, and smelling awfully of tar and feathers and brimstone; and occasionally her daughters amused themselves by a visit to the attic, where their rounds of silly abuse were very sparingly replied to by the prisoners.

In this manner days and weeks had dragged away, bringing no relief, and almost destroying hope, when the cunning negro crept into the wolf's den and stole away the lambs, and the angry secessionist had not the satisfaction of bagging a single Unionist.

CHAPTER XVI.

A WOMAN'S HELP.

ELEANOR BEAUFORT and Captain Bell were standing almost as they stood when their eyes first met, under the pine-tree on the plateau, in the "leafy month of June." Now the tree over their heads was brilliant with the touch of an October frost; at their feet trickled a little stream, and along it stretched the tents of the refugees, in the hollow between two hills, a most lonely, isolated spot, which Turkey Dan had chosen as their present abiding-place. It was evident, from the movements of the men, who were busy cleaning their muskets, repairing their clothing, boiling meat and parching corn, that they were preparing for an expedition.

The face on which the Captain now gazed had changed much in three months: the joyous smile and rich color had fled; the cheeks were pale and thin; and in place of the girlish brightness there was a fixed, calm expression that was almost stern. She was looking down upon the ground, leaning her head against the trunk of the tree; he watched her, until the tears came to his eyes, and his lip quivered.

"Eleanor, I can not bear to see you grieving so," he said, in the husky voice of a strong man moved by powerful emotion.

She looked up at him silently, and oh, so sadly.

"Eleanor, believe me, I would not intrude myself nor my feelings upon you, in the midst of your distress. Only— only you are so lonely—you share your grief with no one— you have no relatives to comfort you. Would to God

you would let me take a portion of your sorrow on myself—
let me mourn with you, for your dear father, whom indeed I
loved and honored as a son."

As he made this reference, with passionate earnestness, the
tears gathered on her eyelids and dropped upon her cheeks.
He made an impetuous motion as if he would have kissed
them off, but restrained himself, and took her hand, which
remained in his own like an inanimate thing.

" If it was almost impossible for me to keep silent before,
when I heard you laugh, when I saw you smile, when you
had others to love and care for you, how can I remain apart
now, and see you suffering, without offering the sympathy of
a heart that loves you—that adores you, Eleanor—that has
been yours every instant since the day I saw you first. Ah, I
will not tell you of my love, now, of my hopes—I only ask to
be allowed to offer you sympathy, protection. You are so
alone in the world ! You can not believe that it is a selfish
motive which prompts me to ask you, in this season of mourning, if you could not, if you would not give me the right to
protect you, to comfort you—the right of a husband."

She made a slight motion of surprise and refusal, but he
continued so hurriedly that he would not be arrested :

" To-morrow, you know, we go forth on a dangerous venture. But we are fuller of hope than we have been for
months. There are excellent tidings of promised relief. A
Federal division is about to force its way into this part of the
State to afford us the aid we have so long prayed for. I am
charged with some secret, important commissions. We are
full of courage and enthusiasm—we forget what we have suffered and only look forward to a bright future. Before I go
forth on this venture, I would like to place you in comparative
comfort and safety. You are aware that my father is with
us now, and that he is a clergyman. He would marry us,

and you would have the right of a daughter to his care.. He
would conduct you to a quiet home in a certain village, where
he and my mother would do all in their power for you.
However, dearest Eleanor, this they would do at all events.
I hold it forth as no argument why you should marry me."

She withdrew her hand and lifted her drooping head, looking into his eager, glowing face with such sorrowful eyes that
his heart sunk, despondent.

"Beverly"—it was the first time she had called him by
this name—" it seems to me as if my heart were as cold as ice.
I can not love you, nor any one, well enough to marry him.
I am devoted now to my country—it is all that gives me any
interest in life. Girl as I am, I believe I can work for her.
Oh, Captain Bell, if you want to break this stupor, to thaw
this ice, give me work to do. What are your secret commissions ? Can not you trust some of them to a woman's wit ?"

" So am I devoted to my country, but it does not conflict with
my passion for you. Ah Eleanor, you make me miserable !"

" Do I ?" she asked, searching his pleading eyes, " then that
is another trouble for me. I am sorry. And now, while we
are talking, let me tell you something I wish you to know.
Before this rebellion came, I was betrothed to a young gentleman. I thought that I loved him. But his course since
then has been such as to make me despise and condemn him.
He is now an officer in the Confederate army. I only regret
that I was such a child as not to read his weak moral character more plainly. I feel as if he, and all like him, were, in
a manner, responsible for my father's death. Judge, then, if
I can forget it ! And I will tell you further, Beverly, that of
all living men, you appear to me best and most upright. I
honor you, and am honored by your love. If I was any longer capable of love, I would love you. But I am not. Say
no more, Beverly—let me be your sister."

"Be my sister, then," he said, gently, pressing a kiss upon her forehead.

He picked up a crimson leaf with which she had been playing, and put it in his bosom.

"And now, since you are my sister, will you not go to my father's house and remain there until this struggle is over?"

"No—not yet. I can not rest. I want to take my father's place. I must do something. If I can be of no service in any other way, I will make my way to the North, and wait upon our sick and wounded soldiers in the Hospitals."

"I can not let you go so far away! No, Ella, remain here if you will not seek a more comfortable home. Who knows how soon your services may be needed to attend upon the wounded and dying of your own State? If the impending battle takes place, there will be work enough for all tender hearts and loving hands like yours. In the mean time, if it would make you any happier—but no, I will not mention it. I might place you in peril, for which I should be unhappy."

"Tell me what it is, Beverly. For if you do not lay out work for me, I shall seek it myself."

"You know I went away from here alone and in disguise, from which private tour I returned yesterday. I have been within a few miles of Knoxville. There, in the house of a friend of our cause, I met about a hundred of our best men. We had in view an important step, suggested by the Federal military authorities, which would require courage, skill and secrecy to take successfully. We are coöperating with the Federal army, and to aid them in their expected onset at the rebels in this State we have undertaken to burn all the important bridges on the East Tennessee and Virginia railroad. Captain F., of the First Tennessee Regiment, is the leader of the enterprise. I have been selected, with twenty-five of

my best men, to take charge of the bridge thirty miles from
here. Captain F. will superintend operations in the northern part of the State; in the mean time, he is riding about in
disguise, seeing that all things are in order. Now, I need a
trusty person to send to him with a message. I have not
time to go myself. Do you think you could be my courier,
Eleanor?—that you could ride on horseback, unmolested,
through an army-cursed, secessionist country for sixty miles?
—that you could even play the part of a saucy secessionist
lady, if such a ruse should become necessary?"

Her eyes lighted with more fire than he had seen in them,
of late days.

"Try me."

"I will try you. You shall have my favorite horse, and a
pair of revolvers, in case of personal peril. You're a good
shot, Eleanor?"

"Excellent."

"You must stop the first night at such a house" (describing
it), "near such a village; the family are my friends; they
will keep you over night, and perhaps afford you an escort
the next day. Can you ride there in a day? It is thirty
miles."

"Easily."

"The next night, then, will find you at your destination.
You must inquire for Colonel Walker, a Confederate contractor for army food. You can pass for a relative of his, if
necessary; he is the man, Captain F., prosecuting his plans
under this disguise. When you reach him, give him this."
He placed in her hand a strip of paper closely written over
in cipher.

"She sits on her horse like an angel on a cloud, or a bird
on a swinging-branch," said Turkey Dan, going off into a
strain of poetry, when Miss Beaufort, early the next morning,

amid the " God bless yous" and cheers of the whole company, set off on her welcome errand.

It added very much to his intense pride in the young lady's appearance that he himself had made her a present of the dress and shoes she wore, and the snug riding-hat beneath which her dark hair and sweet pale face shone out like a spirit's. He had obtained these things upon his last excursion below the mountains; and Eleanor had prized them more than she ever had presents before, not only because she stood in sore need of them, but because the kind heart of the rough hunter had chosen the black for her apparel which he guessed she wished to put on.

"I fret a great deal about her," continued Turkey Dan, to Captain Bell, by whose side he was standing; " I don't know what's to become of her. I'd work my fingers off to keep her comfortable; but she isn't fit to live with the likes of me and Sallie. I wish you'd take her under *your* wing, Captain; you're the only man I know that's fit to take charge of her. You'd be a fortunate man if you got that girl for your wife."

" Supposing I couldn't get her?" suggested Beverly, while a shadow fell over his face.

" I don't want to flatter you, Captain; but if you can't get her, no man can."

" I don't know about that. The Beauforts rank several grades higher than the Bells. When this trouble is settled, and she is restored to her estates and remunerated for her losses, she will match with the highest in the land."

" Now, Bell, you know that little lady is an out-and-out republican, every inch of her. If she don't take up with you, there'll be some other reason. I never seen Sallie think so much of anybody—and Sallie's a judge. Don't you feel a little afeard to let her go off alone so ?"

" I don't feel quite right about it," was the answer, as the young man looked uneasily after the rapidly disappearing figure. "But her mind needed some relief. I knew the ride, and the sense of having performed a service, would be beneficial, *if* no accidents should occur. Yet I do feel worried. I almost wish I had sent you ; but I needed you with me in this business we have on hand, and she wished to go so earnestly."

"Well now, Captain Bell, I'll jest tell you how I look upon it. Thar' won't nothing hurt that young lady. She's under the purtection of sperits, if ever a human being was. She'll be took car' of without our troubling about her—I just feel so."

Dan's "feeling so" was not any very tangible proof that Miss Beaufort's safety was insured ; yet his confident tone had a good effect in rallying the young man's spirits ; he had too much on his mind and hands to afford to indulge himself in melancholy forebodings ; he waved his cap as Eleanor turned a moment on the brow of a distant hill, down the further slope of which she then disappeared—and with a repressed sigh, shook off despondency, and went to his work.

With a mind bent only on the safe fulfillment of her message, Eleanor rode on, braced by the coolness of a lovely autumn day. She met many persons of all pursuits in the course of her day's journey, but passed on unmolested, and in most cases, not even spoken to, except to pass the compliments of the way. She had the appearance of a planter's daughter riding from one farm to another, paying visits, and as such she attracted no attention.

She reached the end of her first day's travel some time before dark, and was most hospitably received by the plain farmer and his family, to whom she gave Captain Bell's message of introduction. She found that the flame of devotion to country burned here all the more intensely from being repressed. The good man opened his heart to the sympathizing girl, and they talked until quite late.

That night she slept upon such a soft and snowy bed as she had not seen since driven from her own home; and the next morning the choicest breakfast which the farm afforded was served to her, and her pocket filled with luncheon. It was thought more prudent for her to go forward alone than to be seen in company with the farmer, who was pretty well understood to be a Union man. Encouraged by her yesterday's experience, she felt not a shadow of fear, and set forth cheerfully, followed by the best wishes of her kind entertainers. On, through small villages and along a pleasant country road she passed, until the middle of the afternoon, and she was within fifteen miles of her friend's destination. Now, as she was riding quietly along, she perceived, in advance of her, a great cloud of dust, and saw a banner flying, and soon came within full sight of a regiment of Confederate infantry, with a company of cavalry, completely filling up the road, with noise and clamor, their army-wagons following on with baggage, and two pieces of artillery leading the van. What to do she did not know.

A high rail-fence bordered the wood on either side, and behind these lay open fields, where she would be plainly visible. If there had been any by-road into which she could have turned until the regiment passed by, she would have had no trouble. As it was, she feared both rude jests passed upon herself, and perhaps suspicions of her errand, which might lead to capture and search. She concluded that she would turn and ride back until she came to some cross-road, into which she could find shelter until the enemy had disappeared. But at that very instant, a number of cavalry officers, riding in advance, appeared full before her, over the brow of a little hill which had kept them from her observation. She wheeled her horse to avoid them, when one of them called out:

"It's not necessary to fly, madam. We are not capable of harming our fair friends. Ride on. Our men shall not annoy you."

His tone was so courteous, and it occurring to her that a show of unnecessary alarm might cause them to suspect her. She obeyed the order. As she turned again, their admiring glances rested on her beautiful face.

"I'll ride back with you along the line, if you feel timid," said one of them, under the sudden inspiration of gallantry, awakened by so lovely and youthful a woman. She thanked him, and he turned and accompanied her, she keeping close to the fence, and wishing much for a vail to hide her countenance from the stare of so many men.

"Wall, Colonel, do you know who you've got in tow thar?" suddenly called out one of the company.

Eleanor looked over at the speaker; she recognized him at once, as one of the inhuman brutes who had sought to horse-whip her at the portals of her own house, and knew that she was recognized.

"That's old Walt Beaufort's daughter, the cussedest female rebel and spy in the hull State, Colonel. P'raps she can tell you where her father is;" the scoundrel was seeking his revenge for her courageous defiance of him on a former occasion.

"I can tell you where my father is," cried the young girl, a bright red spot springing to either cheek; "he is beyond your power, Colonel, or that of any other man. He is in his grave. Sent there by the murderous hand of an outlaw, like that creature who just addressed you."

"His life was forfeited to the Confederacy," replied the officer, a little sternly, and laying his hand on the bridle of her horse, he asked: "What is your business, Miss Beaufort?"

"I am trying to find a friend, if I have such a thing left in

the world.   But am I obliged to explain myself, if I choose
to ride from one village to another ?"

"Your principles and those of your family are so well
known, as also that you are connected with a most pestiferous
set of Union rascals, who make us great annoyance, that it
would be no more than prudent for us to take you into custody, and compel you to give the information which you
doubtless possess about Captain Bell and others."

"Believe me, Colonel, if I *had* such information, the rack
nor dungeon could not force me to say one word to the injury
of my friends.   I'm a quiet woman, going peaceably on an
errand, and I beg you to let me pass."

"Can't do it, madam.   I regret to inconvenience a lady.
I shall not subject you to any particular annoyance, but I
wish to ascertain from you some matters of great interest to
me.   I consider it fortunate to have met you."

Eleanor looked forward to the column of infantry, the
straggling wagons, the thousand impediments which beset her
way ; raising her riding whip suddenly, she brought it down
sharply on the officer's hand, causing him to release his hold
on the rein.   A word and a touch sent her horse flying forward.   At first the companies made way for her, until they
understood the command of the officer to arrest her progress,
and saw a dozen of the cavalry in hot pursuit.   Then they
attempted to check her course.   The animal which Captain
Bell had loaned her was, as he had said, his favorite, distinguished for power and speed.   Obedient to the urging of his
rider, he dashed through every obstacle, and many a soldier
whose hand was outstretched to grasp the rein went tumbling
to the ground.   On she sped ; but now the infantry was form-
ing across the road, and the wagons were still behind them ;
at this critical period she perceived a narrow lane running up
between two fields ; how it ended, or where, she knew not ;

into it she turned, and galloped fast, pressed closely by some of the best of the cavalry horses.   As she neared the foot of the lane, she saw that it was closed by a gate, which was probably locked; at all events, she had not an instant to spare in its unfastening; on she flew, and as they neared it, stooped, patted her horse's neck, gave him the word, and with a tremendous leap, powerful as that of a tiger, and light as a cat, he cleared the obstacle.   A hearty cheer went up from the soldiers as they saw the gallant feat; the courage of the fair girl won their admiration, whatever her politics might be.   Two of her pursuers followed her—the brute who had betrayed her, and the angry officer who did not like to be struck even by a woman.   Others stopped to open the gate, and a dozen rode into the field.   Running along the back of the wide field was an open forest.   If she could gain the shelter of this, she felt that she would be comparatively safe.   Eleanor did not think particularly of herself; it was not her own danger which put such energy into her efforts; she was thinking of the little scrap of paper concealed in the lining of her hat; of the ruin that would befall not only that single plot for the discomfiture of the enemy, but consequent thereon, the peril to the whole Union cause in the State of Tennessee; the lives that would be jeopardized, the disheartening reaction upon the now hopeful sufferers for their country.   All this pressed upon her mind as she heard the thunder of pursuing hoofs, scarcely a rod behind her.   As she approached the other side of the field, she perceived that it was bounded by a wide ditch which drained the land, and which was full to the brim from the recent fall rains.   Her horse was beginning to breathe a little hard, but she coaxed him on

"Stop, or I fire," cried a voice behind her.

She held up her faithful steed for the second leap; he flew over the gaping ditch and alighted in the edge of the wood. As she spurred him on she turned her head. The Colonel had attempted the leap, and his hard-ridden horse had come down headlong in the muddy water, with only his fore-feet clinging to the earth on this side; the other man had taken the risk successfully, and, as she turned, fired his revolver, which sent a ball whistling past her ears. Still flying, she drew her own revolver from her bosom, fired, and sent the scoundrel reeling to the ground. Then she saw that she had the best of the race; she plunged into the forest, and rode rapidly, until she came upon a bridle-path, which, she judged, led out somewhere upon the road she had been obliged to desert. Having at present no further cause for alarm, she rested her jaded horse, and went forward as rapidly as she could without tiring him out, in order to get free of the woods before dark.

It was deep twilight when she finally reached the road; all was quiet and dark; and at ten o'clock that night she paused before the little inn, at which Colonel Walker, contractor, was stopping while buying hogs, (unromantic, but true!) inquired for him, delivered the precious dispatch, received his warm and admiring thanks, and retired to sleep off the fatigue of an exciting day.

In the morning, upon relating her adventure to the disguised Union Captain, he advised her to wait where she was a couple of days, until the road was free from the soldiery. He knew their destination, and that their path would continue the same as hers for some twenty-five miles; it was best to give them time enough to have the way cleared of stragglers. She consented to the propriety of this; was introduced by the Confederate contractor to the good woman of the inn, as a sister of his, who had brought him information of importance; and was consequently well treated.

Well satisfied with the success of her mission, she started

on the .nird day to return to the mountains; which she
expected Captain Bell would have also reached about that
time.

What was her surprise and consternation, as she neared the
close of her first day's journey, to perceive, as she approached
the house of her Union friend, at which she expected to stay,
that his fields had been turned into a camp, from one of the
tents of which a Confederate flag was flying. She surmised,
at once, that it must be the same regiment she had passed on
her way down, and that it would be dangerous for her to be
recognized by any of its members. After a moment's reflection, she concluded to turn back to the village which she had
left a couple of miles behind, and try and find from there
some other road which would take her in the direction she
wished to go. This course she decided on, and turning back,
was almost in the outskirts of the village when she encountered a party of soldiers who had been in town on various
errands, returning to their camp. They proved to be friends
and companions of the miserable villain whom she had shot
dead in self-defense; they set up a shout when they saw her,
and immediately surrounded her. She spurred her horse and
attempted to break through them, but half-a-dozen of them
seized the rein at once. At the sight of the revolver which
she drew from her dress, they dropped it as quick; they were
not armed, save with their cavalry sabers.

"Let me go, or I'll shoot six of you," she said, resolutely.

Suddenly a powerful fellow, who had stolen up from
behind, hit her arm a savage blow with the back of his saber,
dashing the pistol to the ground. It was quickly picked up.

"We've got you this time, my pretty miss. We hain't
forgot that you murdered one of our boys t'other day. We'll
take you back to the Colonel, if you please. He wan't very
much tickled with the duckin' he got in that mud-puddle.

Sp'iled his uniform.   He won't be sorry of a chance to settle that little matter with you, I reckon."

When she found that further resistance was useless, she begged them to let go the reins of her horse, telling them she would go with them without compulsion.

" We ain't a goin' to trust that animal," laughed one of them.   " No, no ; you won't give us the slip this time."

" Better tie her hands, I reckon.   She's a perfect she-devil ; no tellin' but old Nick'll fly away with her.   I never see a gal git cl'ar of nine hundred men as slick as she did."

" Here, miss, put them pretty paws together."

They bound her hands with an old silk handkerchief, and led the horse and his rider unresistingly back to camp.

" Look here, Lieutenant, we've bagged that shy bird you heerd us tell on, t'other day.   You wasn't with us that time ; wish you had a-been, to see the fun.   Come and take a look at our gay prisoner."

The young officer to whom one of the men thus addressed himself turned from the steps of the farm-house, into which he was about to enter, and Eleanor, sitting pale and quiet on her horse, surrounded by ruffians, looked up to meet the distressed and astonished gaze of Sinclair Le Vert.

" Eleanor !" it was all he could say, as, rapidly changing color, he sprung down the steps to her side.

" Begone !" he cried to the discomfited men.   " I know this lady.   She is a friend of mine, and not to be treated thus."

With his saber he cut the handkerchief from her wrists ; then held out his hand to assist her to dismount.

" I would rather ride on," she said ; " these men had no authority to stop me."

" Impossible ; it is already nearly dark, and the road is beset with vagabonds."

"Give me back my revolver, and I will take care of myself, sir."

"Ah, Eleanor, how coldly you look, how cruelly you speak! I can not bear it—indeed, I can not. Wherever you may be going, stay here to-night. The woman of this house will take good care of you, and in the morning I myself will see you safely on the way. I have so longed for a chance to speak with you, to see you again. I am the same as ever—indeed I am; but I have been driven by the iron rod of a father's command. Ella, dearest, how thin and pale you are looking —and you are in black. Ella, how is your dear father?"

The question came upon her so suddenly, asked in that tender, familiar voice, the shock was more than she could bear. She burst into tears, and sobbed convulsively.

"What have I done? Can it be? Alas, poor Ella!" cried the officer, lifting her from her horse, with a feeling of grief and remorse that rent his weak nature. He guessed the sad truth—it was not necessary for her to speak.

The friends who had entertained her a few evenings previous, seeing her through the window, hastened to the door and drew her in.

"Take good care of this young lady, and I will see that you are paid for your trouble," said the Lieutenant.

The good woman of the house smiled.

"We want none of his money for taking care of *you*," she said, as she almost carried Eleanor into the sitting-room. "But we shouldn't object to their paying for some of the property they have destroyed. We have seen sad times since you were here, Miss Beaufort. They have given my husband and son the choice of being shot, or of *volunteering*. Queer kind of volunteering, isn't it? At my persuasion, they have joined the rebels, but it is only to go over to the Federals the very first opportunity they have. I tell them perhaps

they can do more good in that way. They may have a chance
to carry information to the Unionists, which would be better
than just standing up to be shot. But oh, me! what the
family's going to do I don't know. They've taken all our
corn and hay for the winter, all our cattle and hogs, burnt up
half the fences, and knocked things to pieces generally. They
camped down on us because we were for the Union. It'll
be hard times, this winter, hard times! But here I am, telling
my own troubles, when you're nigh about dead, poor child."
She untied Eleanor's hat, whispering, as she stooped to take
it off: "How did you get along with your business?"

"All right," was the answer, as, with a great effort, she
recovered herself, and smiled at her kind hostess.

"Did the officer say any thing rude to you?" questioned
the woman, wondering at her sudden fit of weeping.

"Oh, no. He used to be a friend of ours—our nearest
neighbor. It made me think of home and my father."

"There, there, don't speak of it," said the kind lady, seeing
her lip begin to tremble again. "These are awful times for
all of us. Come in the kitchen and wash your face in some
cold water, and I'll make you a cup of tea. I've got a little
that I keep for company that I like."

Eleanor bathed her burning eyes in the cool water, and
drank the strong tea; then she went back to the little parlor,
and sat there in the stiff cane-seat rocking-chair, looking into
the fire in the chimney, and thinking of home.

The voice and face of Sinclair had called up the past with
startling vividness. She seemed again to be in the spacious
parlors of her own house, with Sinclair sitting at the piano,
humming gay tunes and keeping time on the keys; with her
father at his desk in the adjoining library, and the merry
voices of Lina and Jim in the dining-room; luxury, and protection, and love enfolded her-in a soft atmosphere; she was

a brilliant, careless, triumphant girl. Swept away, as by a breath of wind, was the long summer, with its strange experience, its want, danger and privation, and its terrible crowning catastrophe.

> " Old dreams come back once more,
>   Old thoughts flow through my brain—
> I am floating by the shore
>   Of olden bliss again.
> I am floating by the shore,
>   But I can not touch the strand—
> No more—no more—no more
>   Shall my feet touch the shining strand
>   Of that beloved land!"

And swiftly, like the withering breath of a simoom, came back the desolate, struggling, forlorn, poverty-stricken, hopeless present. Then arose, like a star over the sea, the memory of Captain Bell, so humble, so pure, so unflinching in his love of all that was true and good, the refuge he had offered her, the simple yet earnest expression of his devotion to her. She thought of him with affection and gratitude—she felt that moment, that if she could return his love with such feeling as it wanted, she would accept his offer and become his wife. But no! her heart was sad and broken—it was no longer fit to mate with his.

"Eleanor, will you not shake hands with me—not meet as a friend, if nothing more?"

It was Lieutenant Le Vert who spoke; he had come into the parlor, and stood looking into her abstracted countenance.

"I can no longer look upon any of the enemies of my country as my friends," she replied, not noticing his extended hand. "I have suffered too bitterly."

"You *have* suffered, Eleanor, I see it in your face. If you knew how unhappy I feel about this, you would pity me."

"I do pity you," she said, with a slight curl of the lip.

"You sneer at me, Ella! Then it is plain you no longer love me."

"You say truly there, sir."

"How harsh you are! Very well, if you will be so ungenerous. I sought you this evening to say many things, but you will not hear them. I have still to tell you that your arrest was reported to our Colonel; who, it seems, is very angry with you for killing one of his men the other day. He says you shall be sent on to Knoxville to prison. I have been to see him. I told him you were a personal friend of our family, and used all my influence, but he was obdurate. He has ordered a guard around the house this night."

"My father was in prison four months."

"And you do not shrink from it! You have too much courage, Eleanor; you are not womanly enough."

"Our standards of womanly excellence differ—mine is of a different order from your sister Marcia's."

"I wish you were more like Marcia," said the young man, half impatiently, half admiringly, looking at the maiden, by whose personal beauty he could not but be enthralled, while he half wondered at, half feared the high traits of a character which he wished less noble.

Eleanor made no reply to this lofty wish; she was astonished at her own mental growth since the time when she had thought this man her equal.

"I am not quite so absorbed in this Confederacy yet," he went on to say in a low voice, "as to ignore all personal friendships that conflict with it. You may hate me, Ella, but I still love you too well to see you fall into trouble without an effort to save you. The guard at the back-door of this house is a fellow very much attached to me; he has consented to allow you to pass him. At four o'clock this coming morning,

when the hour is darkest, and the camp stillest, you must slip
out that door. I will be there to lead you safely to your
horse, which I shall take means to have stationed at a proper
distance out on the road."

"I thank you, Sinclair. If you can do this without com-
promising yourself with your superior officer, I shall be glad
to escape from this."

"It will be hard for him to fix the deed upon me, however
much he may suspect me. And have you nothing to say to
me, Ella?"

"I would like to hear of the fate of my servants, if you
know any thing of what has happened to them."

"Well, Lina is waiting upon Marcia now, I believe," said
Sinclair, blushing slightly. "My father has hired Pomp's
wife—he, Pomp, has cleared out, no one knows where. The
most of the field hands have scattered—some of them were
taken to the river to work upon fortifications."

"Thank you."

"And is this all?"

"All, I thank you. Good-night."

He retired, and Eleanor, confiding the plan of her escape to
her hostess, laid down upon the lounge in the sitting-room,
to rest until the appointed hour. At its arrival she was ready;
with a cordial embrace of her friend, who had risen and
warmed a cup of coffee for her on the coals of the covered
down fire, she stole through the door, took the hand reached
out to her in silence, and fled around the house, out upon the
road, and quite a distance along it, to where her horse stood
waiting, tied to a fence-post. Sinclair unfastened him, helped
her up, placed the reins in her hand which he held a moment
as if loth to let her go.

"Walk him gently at first, so as to arouse no attention—
there is starlight enough for you to pick your way. It will

soon be light. Perhaps I shall never see you again, Ella ;—I
am going into active service right away.   Good-bye."

" Farewell, Lieutenant Le Vert,"—and as he retraced his
steps to the camp, she walked her horse along the dim road,
without one regret at the parting which had just taken place.

A great shout of joy went up from Camp Union, when
their beloved messenger returned to them safely, the middle of
that afternoon.   The tears actually stood in Turkey Dan's eyes.

" We felt awful oneasy when we got back last night and
couldn' hear nothing of you.   I don't believe the Captain slept
a wink," and he lifted the weary girl down, almost tempted
to kiss her, as he held her in his long arms like a baby.

But Dan had never kissed any body since the night he
" popped the question " to Sallie ; so, after looking at her like
an elephant at a fawn, he set her down carefully, as if she
were tender as a new-laid egg.

" I *did* repent my temerity in sending you off," said the
Captain, taking her hands and looking into her eyes joyfully,
while Sallie, Mrs. Bostwick, Pompey, and all the friends
gathered about in an excited circle.

" I suppose you would have felt still more uneasy if you
had known that last night I was the prisoner of a Confederate
regiment.   I've had a narrow escape, but I've done my errand,
and here I am, ready for some other venture."

They would allow her no rest until they had heard the
whole history of her little expedition.

" And the friend who furthered my escape was the lover I
was telling you of," she added, in an aside to Captain Bell.

On a Saturday night, ten days later, the skies which bent
over Tennessee reflected the glare of five burning bridges, set
in flames simultaneously from one end to the other of the
State.   The daring and secret exploit of a few brave Union
men was most successfully completed.   But alas ! the Federal

army for which they had thus prepared the way, did not make its appearance. The danger of the friends of the Union was increased ten-fold, and no hand of power was extended to their relief. Peaceable farmers were shot down in their cornfields, and the rope was busy with its victims. The cloud of disaster hung now over the region of East Tennessee, surcharged with the fiery bolts of destruction ; while, as with one voice from thousands of heroic but embittered breasts, went up the cry—

" How long, oh Lord, how long ?"

CHAPTER XVII.

TURKEY HUNTING.

" IF I don't have luck this morning, the women-folks 'll have to go without their breakfasts. They made ruther a slender supper last night ; and I feel like doin' as the Injuns do—drawing my belt tighter, so's not to feel the holler spot," muttered Daniel Drew, as he crept out of his tent one December morning about four o'clock—shook himself, to be rid of the shiver creeping over him in consequence of one blanket and a sharp frost—swung his gun over his shoulder, and trudged off with long strides up the mountain side, through the chilly starlight.

After a tramp of two miles, he entered a wild forest, so thick, so gloomy, so utterly silent, so tangled above and beneath in primeval profusion, that it would seem as if no man's feet had ever before pressed it. Into this he plunged with almost as much *nonchalance* as though it had been broad daylight, avoiding obstacles by the same instinct with which a blind man feels the nearness of that which he can not see. Dan's senses had been sharpened by long training to at least twice the acuteness of an ordinary person's. After he had penetrated some distance into the wood, he sat down on a log, and waited a few minutes.

The gray light in the east brightened so that even within those shadows things began to be perceptible. Presently a ray of sunlight, like a golden arrow, pierced the foliage almost horizontally; and immediately, as if it had thrilled through a thousand sleepy nests, all kinds of soft sounds filled the quiet with musical clamor. The frost had not yet frightened away all the birds from that temperate climate, and now one and another chirped and shook his wings; a little ripple of wind ran murmuring through the leaves, and the very ground, as well as the air, seemed full of small noises, which only the ear of a poet or a hunter might distinguish. Dan listened, with his sunburnt face as full of delight as a child's; he loved this forest company. But there was work to be performed, and down on his hands and knees he went, crawling along until he got into the heart of a thick clump of bushes, where he brought his rifle down, and rested it before him. Taking from his pocket a peculiar whistle made of deer-bone, he fixed it in his lips and began a perfect imitation of the cry of the wild-turkey. Soft and wild the notes gurgled out, as if the heart of the bird were running over with passion and tender appeal. Away into the chilly shadows it flowed, dulcet and voluptuous, filling with warmth and melodious fullness the deep quiet. Then all for a brief space was silent; the cry began again, note rolling upon note, like one golden wave upon another, flooding the forest. In the next interval of silence, Dan heard the soft "cluck, cluck" of an approaching turkey; he could as yet see nothing; but as he resumed his call, a stately bird stepped out of a distant

cover, and drew cautiously near. Now it would step along
haughtily, then pause and listen; and now, as it came out upon
a little open spot, the morning sunshine struck its rainbow
breast, its sparkling eye, and its crimson crest; its head lifted
with mingled pride and suspicion, its bearing conceited yet
vigilant. It was on the look-out for the rival fowl, up so
early and calling its mate. The "cluck, cluck," came from a
female turkey, coquettishly hiding behind the tall, dry grass
of a little marshy hollow. Dan could easily now have drawn
a bead on the splendid fellow, but he was lost in admiration
of his favorite game, and wished to arouse still further the ire
and fire of the stately bird, which was wandering toward the
female while keeping its golden eye turned in the direction
of its supposed rival.

Presently Dan heard a light step in another direction, and
beheld, to his delight, another turkey and another walking up,
until quite a flock gathered about, some calling like himself,
some clucking in response. So fascinated was he with the
rare spectacle, that if it had not been for the thought of
the hungry little ones at home, he would hardly have
disturbed that royal company. Perhaps, too, the instinct
of the hunter was stronger than his love for the life and glory
of the forest. Suddenly, into the midst of that gorgeous flock,
poured the deadly shot; the sharp report of the gun startled
all other sounds into muteness; the blue smoke curled in the
sunshine; the smell of gunpowder overpowered the fragrance
of frosted leaves. When the smoke cleared away, there lay
two of the largest birds, the colors dying out of comb and
feathers, and a mist over the sparkling eyes; the others had
fled; the peace and glory of that woodland morning had been
desecrated.

Gathering up the fowls, and slinging them over his shoulder,
Dan only stopped to shoot a half-dozen squirrels on his way

back, for the children would be waiting for their breakfast, and there was only half a ration of corn-meal.

"It's cur'us that anybody'll be so mean as to build pens to catch turkeys in," soliloquized the hunter. "I call that the essence of meanness. Ef a person hasn't wit enough to shoot 'em as they ought to be shot, he should let 'em alone. Ef they could see such a sight as I see this mornin', they wouldn't bait with corn any more. After I've gone after a lot o' flour and stuff, I must make a business of hunting deer for the next week. Sallie and the rest'll have a hard time of it, after I'm gone, if I don't lay in a store of dried ven'son. Can't spend more'n a week, nohow. Things is comin' to a p'int at last. Bell sent me word I must hurry up, if I wanted to be in at the death. Old Zollicoffer's talking fight. Blast 'em, that's all we want! All we want is to fight! fight fair in an open field! This mean, bushwhacking work of firing at unarmed men from behind a fence, or in his own door, isn't the kind *we* take to. No, by thunder, we want to fight! I'm goin' to volunteer in the 1st Tennessee, and Sallie must take car' of the young ones till this scrimmage is over. I'll kill her a few deer, and she must look out for the rest herself. As for Miss Eleanor, she declares she's gwine to the war, too. I expect she will. It's just like her."

Looking down into Camp Union, he saw the smoke curling up from Sallie's cabin, and hurried his pace homeward. The tents which had whitened the spot had now all disappeared except his own, which he occupied in deference to the women, who were allowed the exclusive use of the one little cabin which had been roughly constructed, as the cold weather made camp-life more severe.

The occupants of the cabin were Sallie and her brood, Miss Beaufort, and a couple of new-comers, fleeing for a time from persecution. Mrs. Bostwick had been so fortunate as to have a shelter provided for her in Kentucky, whither her husband had safely conducted her. She had earnestly solicited Eleanor to accompany her, but the young girl had other purposes which made her cling to those about to engage in battle for their country. She had resolved to become a hospital-nurse, and with this in view, was to accompany Dan when he finally set out to join his regiment.

Pompey, with her full consent and approbation, had attached himself to the regiment as the servant of the officers; and they found him constantly one of the most efficient of their men.

" Where's Miss Beaufort?" asked Dan, as he threw the birds down in the open door; " don't tech them turkeys, Sallie, till she's had a look at 'em. Ain't them beauties?" he continued, as Eleanor came forward. " I did wish you were with me this morning to see the sight—a hull flock of 'em. The woods was right purty, at sunrise."

" Thought you didn't 'low women 'round where turkeys was," said Sallie, a little spitefully.

" Now you know *you* can't fool a turkey, wife; it's the only thing you can't do. But Miss Beaufort's extra cute for a woman. I believe *she* could hold her tongue if she was told to. If you'd been along, Miss Ellen, you could have taken off the head of one or two as easy as not."

" I should like the glory of killing a turkey," was the half-smiling reply.

" Speakin' of turkeys," added Dan, with his odd quirk of the mouth, " these two are mighty like that couple I brought you last spring."

A shadow swept over Eleanor's face; he was sorry in an instant that he had called up memories so in contrast with the present.

" I fell in love with you that day," he went on, trying to

banish the shadow, "didn't I, Sallie? And wife's never been jealous a bit. I' b'lieve she's in love with you herself."

"La, Dan, she's l'arned both them boys to read right smart," said the big woman, looking proudly at her eldest. "Come, husband, skin them squirrel, quick. What a lazy-bones you be! Don't you know Miss Beaufort's nigh about starved?"

"We'll brile them on the coals. They'll do in twenty minutes."

Before the twenty minutes had passed, however, there was an addition to the number for breakfast. Pompey, traveling by night, had come from Captain Bell, with a message for Dan to join his regiment as quickly as possible.

"Wall, Sallie, I don't know what's to be done for fodder. I'll go off to-day, and get a lot of corn-meal and salt; and you'll have to trust to the old double-bar'l for the rest."

"I'll take car' of myself, I reckon. I mostly have."

"That's so, Sallie; you're a brick."

"'Twon't take you long to git ready, Miss Beaufort?"

"Not long. I haven't as much baggage as I used to have when I went North to spend the summer."

While Dan was off after provisions, Eleanor again sewed into her garments the little wealth that was left her in the shape of her mother's jewels, for she scarcely expected to see this spot or this family again.

A rather showy brooch, of which Mrs. Drew had expressed admiration, she made a farewell present to her.

That evening, the trio bade the inmates of the cabin goodby, and set off in the darkness to make their way to Kentucky, to join the Union army gathering there.

As their forms disappeared in the night, Sallie drew the sleeve of her dress across her eyes ; whether the solitary tear she shed was for her husband " gone to the war," or for the young lady who had made herself so beloved, it would be hard to tell.

CHAPTER XVIII.

THE BATTLE OF WILDCAT.

IT was in the last days of November that Zollicoffer startled the people of the upper Cumberland valley, by his sudden movement from the Cumberland Gap through East and Middle Tennessee to the south fork of the river some fifteen miles from Somerset, Kentucky.   It was an enterprising move on his part, for which the Federal Generals were unprepared ; it gave him the control of the river and access to the adjoining coal and salt mines, at the same time threatening all the central portions of Kentucky, while affording him ample opportunities for retreat.   Here he was allowed to remain some four or five weeks, intrenching himself in a well-chosen encampment on three fort-like hills, and stripping the invaded country of grain, fodder and cattle.

How Generals Thomas' and Schoepff's divisions gathered about him here, how he came out to attack them with a force vastly superior, and how completely the rebel was defeated, losing his own life in the venture, are matters of history too recent to be interesting here.

It was on the Sabbath, the nineteenth of January, that the hills and ravines where were gathered those opposing forces were shaken with a storm such as their ancient walls had never before reechoed.

The windows of heaven were opened; the rain fell in tor-
.ents; the vivid flash and the loud roar of heaven's artillery
were constant and awful.   But it was not in the battle of the
elements above that so much of the terrible was consummated;
it was in the conflict of armies of human beings below, that
all which the mind can imagine of the sublimity of horror
was realized.   Hour after hour this storm arose and deepened.
in violence, swelling louder and more fierce, as eight thousand
of the enemy and four thousand of the Union troops drew
together with deadly shocks of meeting and repulsion.   Peal
after peal of cannon, with the sharper rattling of musketry
the whistling of shot, the crashing of shells, and the wild
shouts and cheers of excited men mingled in a tumult of
sound, to which was added the solemn accompaniment of
the thunder of heaven.

Now it was that portions of the opposing armies became
confused and blent with each other in the disorder of the elements of earth and air; and now it was that the same gallant
Captain, now Colonel F., who had led the raid against the
Tennessee bridges a few weeks previously, came face to face
with the rebel chieftain, and in answer to a treacherous shot
from his aid, turned and shot Zollicoffer through the heart.
And now it was that the 9th Ohio made one of the most
brilliant charges which have distinguished this war; pressing
forward as steadily as if they were on drill parade, over an
open space of two hundred yards, directly in the face of the
enemy's fire, and with a terrific shout of exultation, charging
with the bayonet the appalled foe, who turned discomfited
before the bristling walls of steel, and fled ignominiously.

In the mean time, the regiments of loyal Tennesseeans
were recompensing themselves for some of the wrongs and
delays of the past summer and fall.   Memories of the outrages they had suffered filled them with fierce revenge, and

they fought like tigers defending their cubs. From their position in the woods, which the 1st Tennesseeans had taken up, they had an excellent opportunity for the practice of some of their famous sharpshooting. Here Turkey Dan, as cool as if alone in the forest hunting deer, except for a dangerous spark of fire in his eye, picked off, one after another, at an astonishing distance, the gunners of a rebel battery, planted on a hill separated from the woods by a deep ravine. The balls from this battery came crashing through the tops of the trees, over the heads of our soldiers, doing little damage, but making a frightful threatening as they roared through the shattered branches.

"We must take that battery, boys," said their Colonel.

A loud cheer expressed the willingness of his men.

"It isn't so risky as it looks," continued their officer. "When we plunge into the ravine they can not touch us with their fire."

And so it proved. As they struggled across the marshy and over-flooded hollow, the cannon-balls flew far above them; they gained the hill, pressed up its steep acclivity with cries and cheers, charging the artillerists at the point of the bayonet, and taking the battery with scarcely the loss of a man.

All this time the chilly January rain poured down. But the hearts of the soldiers were warm with triumph as they found the enemy everywhere giving way before them.

The loss of their leader and the irresistible charges of the enemy were disheartening the rebels, who in the morning so audaciously attacked our inferior force. At first, as they retreated, they rallied and formed; but soon the rout was total and disgraceful. They were chased into their intrenchments, into which shells were thrown, and which would have been stormed immediately, but that night descended upon the drenched and worn-out victors.

While the soldiers gathered about the welcome camp-fires to catch some needed rest and refreshment before renewing the attack on the coming day, the surgeons were busy with their sad work.   Parties of those who had not entered into the fight went out to gather the wounded and dead.   Oh! this is the melancholy after-part!   The battle is over, and the country rings with joyous acclaim; while the dead lie in their unmarked graves, and the wounded linger through weeks of suffering, and arise to go maimed and enfeebled through a blasted life.   This is the dearest price of all the treasure we pay to secure the freedom and progress for which we fight.

Among those who rested not on that dismal and wretched night, was a woman, who searched over the wide extent of battle-field, carrying a little present relief to those not attended to by the surgeons.   It was Eleanor Beaufort, devoting her young life to scenes of horror, bringing pity and aid to the suffering.   By her side went Pompey, carrying a lantern, water and spirits; many a wounded wretch was lifted by his strong arm into a more comfortable position, while Eleanor moistened the fevered lips, and bade the sufferer hope for speedy attention.   Friend and enemy received like help; though she shuddered in her soul as some of the fierce eyes glared at her out of tangled masses of black hair, reminding her of the wretches who had so often imperiled her, within the last six months; yet her womanly heart could not refuse them succor as they lay there moaning and cursing in their pain.

It was not many hours before the wounded were gathered into the hospital tents; all who could be found, though a few might have escaped search, having fallen in tangled underbrush or weedy marsh.

Eleanor had a trouble of her own.   Turkey Dan had sought her, after the close of the battle, and told her that Captain Bell was missing.   He had not seen or heard from him since they were ordered out of the wood to take the battery. His company had acted under a Lieutenant. This officer knew nothing of his whereabouts; but some of the men said that he had been killed by a cannon-ball—that they saw him fall, just as they charged into the ravine, and could not pause to carry him off the field. This report was doubly probable, since the enemy had taken no prisoners, and time fled by without his reappearance.

"Come, Pompey, we must not rest yet," said the pale but unflinching girl; "if Captain Bell is any where where our soldiers have been this day, we must find him, dead or alive."

"My legs feel as if thar was a screw loose, somewhar," remarked Dan, "but I'm gwine along, if they drop out on the track. I tell you what it is, Miss Beaufort, if they've used up Captain Bell, you'd better believe thar'll be some more tall fightin' done to-morrow—by one Tennessean, if by nobody else."

Eleanor was oppressed by too sad a foreboding to have much to say; taking the path back to the wood in which his regiment was stationed that afternoon, they commenced, by the light of a lantern, a second search—they had gone over the ground carefully once before. After an hour's wearisome plodding, they came into a little hollow, half filled with water, across which a fallen tree was blown; and here the light flashed over the uniform of a man, lying motionless against the tree in a partly upright position, the lower portion of his body in the water.

"It is he," murmured Eleanor, growing white and weak. The sudden glare of light caused a slight motion and moan —he was not dead. He made an effort to lift up his head, drooped on its hard pillow, but could not achieve it.

"Beverly," cried the young girl, plunging into the water and bending over him, "ah, is this you?"

He smiled as he heard her voice, and opened his eyes—

his face was so thin, so pinched with pain, so pale, that it looked as if months of sickness had passed over it. She poured some brandy between his lips.

"I believe I must have fainted with loss of blood," he whispered.

Dan and Pompey came forward to lift him up. At the change of position, he could not repress a groan.

"It's my arm, boys."

The poor arm indeed, his right arm at that, hung dangling by his side, horribly broken and shattered. Though her blood was freezing with dread and anguish, Eleanor bound up the bleeding limb as well as she could with Dan's silk handkerchief, and the two strong fellows bore off the almost exhausted patient to the surgeons' tent.

"It must be amputated immediately; and it's doubtful if that will save his life—he has lost so much blood."

As this decision of the surgeon was listened to by the distressed girl, she begged permission to remain by his side until the ordeal was over.

"You can trust-me," she said, "if I do tremble a little now. It's because I'm so tired."

The surgeon looked into the young, fair face, blanched, but full of resolution.

"Is he a friend of yours?"

"Yes, a friend only. We have fought the contest of this summer side by side, doctor, and I shall stay by him now."

She was permitted to remain, standing by the surgeon's side and calmly obeying his commands. By the merciful aid of chloroform the patient was unconscious of the operation; and when he again rallied to the pain of the reality, the arm was dressed, and he said that he felt more comfortable. Eleanor was warned of the danger of his suddenly sinking, and was left to watch by him through the brief remainder of the far-spent night, administering stimulants constantly, and giving him that incessant care which he could not otherwise have had.

In the morning Turkey Dan paid them a brief visit; the army were to pursue the enemy, and he came to bid his wounded Captain and his devoted nurse good-by.

"If you die, Bell, I'll get mad about it. Don't you do it. If you do, I shan't overlook it," he said, with a rude attempt to conceal his own emotions at parting with his admired, almost idolized officer.

"How can I die, when I have Eleanor to take care of me," said the young man, simply, turning his wan, wistful eyes to her face with a look which betrayed his heart.

"Wall, Captain, I don't believe you *can*. But, Miss Ellen, you mustn't get tuckered out, neither, overdoin'."

"Pompey will see to that," she replied, cheerfully; and as she spoke, the faithful giant brought her the cup of tea which she needed greatly after the fearful night she had endured.

The bustle of preparation for pursuing the enemy grew louder in the camp and Dan was obliged to leave.

After a time Captain Bell fell into a profound sleep; and Eleanor stole away to pay a hasty visit to other sufferers who might be cheered by some little word or deed of kindness from a woman.

As she went up to one cot where a patient was tossing as if he could not bear the pain and confinement to which he was obliged to submit, she started with surprise upon perceiving the haggard countenance of Sinclair Le Vert. Left on the field by his own flying men, he had been kindly cared for by the enemies he had been taught to regard with unjust and vindictive hatred.

"Eleanor, where shall I see you next!" he exclaimed, holding out his hand eagerly. "How came you here?"

"How came *you* here, Sinclair?—fighting those who should have been, who wished to be your brothers. You will find me, now, wherever I can best serve my friends and country. Are you much hurt?"

"No—wounded just above the knee. The doctor says he can save my leg—and that I'm not dangerous. But it's confounded hard, lying here, and fretting, and knowing that our army is disastrously beaten, and all that."

"You are drinking the cup your own hand has filled."

"Now, Ella, *please* don't rebuke me, when I'm feverish and cross. I would almost be willing to have met with this accident for the sake of seeing you again. I havn't forgotten the past—nor I can't forget it."

"Do you wish for any thing I can get you?"

"Not now, unless it is a drink of water. Thank you. Are you going? You'll come again, often, won't you? It will cure me to see your face."

She almost pitied him, he appeared so uneasy, and appealed to her so beseechingly—even in his illness, his temper was so different from that of Captain Bell's, who bore his sufferings with such fortitude. She did pity him, with that humiliating pity we give to those whose weakness and sin appeal to us—not with the tender, earnest pity she lavished so overflowingly on the noble sufferer whose side she had just left.

"Say, Ella, sit down here, just one moment longer, won't you? I've something to say."

Her mind was half absorbed in fear that the Captain would awaken and need immediate attention; but she could not refuse the imploring voice and eyes. She sat down on the bundle of baggage beside the camp cot.

"Stoop a little closer, Ella; I don't wish those others to hear. I've been thinking that as I shall be kept in hospital some time by this wounded limb, and shall need a woman's

care so much, and as you are here amidst these rough men,
without any protection, perhaps it would be better for both of
us, if we should be married. I know you've felt bitterly
toward me, Ella; but now that you see me here, wounded
and a prisoner, far away from home, from my mother and
sister, I'm sure if you ever really loved me, you will forgive
me, and fulfill our engagement now."

"Then I never really loved you."

"And it will be so much better for *you*, Eleanor. Indeed,
I urge it for your sake as well as mine. This victory of the
North is a chance; its triumph will be short; perhaps by the
time I am well, we shall be retaken or exchanged, and if you
go back to your former home as my wife, your property will
be restored to you; you will once more be protected, surrounded by friends and company, instead of wandering about
in this wretched way."

"As for my estate, Sinclair, if that is what you are after,
you can have it, till such time as the United States Government recompenses its faithful adherents for their losses. As
for my marrying you to take care of you, there are other
worse sufferers than yourself, whose sufferings I feel deeper
sympathy; the sick and wounded in my country's cause,
claim all that I can do to serve them. The time has
not come when I can devote myself to pet nursing of an
enemy."

"Cruel, sarcastic girl! You used to be so gentle, Ella."

"And do you think, Mr. Le Vert, that my experience for
the last year has been such as to increase my gentleness? I
have suffered that which in this world will never be forgotten.
The impress is burnt into my heart and mind. If I have any
hope and tenderness yet in my nature, it is not for you or yours.
If you ever wish to see me in this tent, you must address me
as you would any other stranger nurse. I shall extend to you

the same charities that I would to any other helpless person. Let that suffice. Never *dare*, Mr. Le Vert, to act as if any other relation were possible between us."

As she left the tent, the Confederate officer tossed on his hard bed with no pleasant reflections.

"It's so strange," he muttered, "for *her* to persist in refusing *me*. She's ruining all her own prospects. How under heaven she expects to live among those miserable Yankees, I can not conceive. Take to school-teaching, perhaps; she knows enough. It's curious that the more she snubs me, the more I like her. I'm certain, quite certain, I shall never meet another girl her equal."

When Eleanor went back to Captain Bell, she found him wide awake, with a wild, uneasy look on his face, which softened down as soon as he perceived her.

"Don't run away from me, Miss Beaufort," he pleaded; "I feel as if you were lost, unless you are where I can look at you."

"You don't want to be selfish, do you, Captain? You know that there are a great many wounded men to be looked after;" she answered him playfully, for she felt rather startled at his restless glance and changed voice.

"I hope not; but my head is so light; I have such curious fancies come into it—and I feel terrified, too. It's a little strange, that a man of my courage should feel so helpless and so cowardly. Let me hold your hand."

"It's the fever, Beverly; and you have lost so much blood, you are like an infant. I will stay with you. Don't you give yourself the least uneasiness about any thing."

She bathed his forehead, gave him the medicine prescribed for keeping down the fever, soothing him in every possible manner, as she saw the fire gradually mounting to his brain.

"I wish I knew how the boys were getting along to-day,"

he said, late in the afternoon, ceasing his restless movements for a moment, and looking into his nurse's eyes with a piercing earnestness.

"I can tell you," said the cheerful voice of the doctor, who entered at the moment. "They are in full possession of the enemy's intrenchments and camps, without any further loss or trouble. All they regret is, that the enemy betook themselves across the river in the darkness, last night. They've run clear out of sight, leaving us in possession of every thing. Oh, if the roads were only so we could follow up our advantages!"

"Hurrah for the old flag!" cried the Captain, suddenly sitting up in bed, and making an effort to move the poor stump of a right arm; cheek and eye were burning fiercely, and his expression made Eleanor pale. The next moment he sunk back on his pillow; the doctor immediately administered a more powerful soothing draught; but the fever now raged uncontrolled; and no further word or look betraying any thing but the wildest delirium was vouchsafed to his anxious watcher.

When Turkey Dan returned to camp, that night, he had hard work to persuade Eleanor to give up her place for the next few hours to him. The surgeon had warned her that her friend's case was critical, almost hopeless, and she was loth to leave him. Exhausted nature demanded that she should take rest; the fearful excitement of the previous day, the wet, exposure and harrowing scenes of the following night, and constant duties since, had only been endured by her delicate frame because strengthened by the invincible will within. Prudence, and the desire to keep herself fit for further service, induced her finally to accept Dan's offer; and when once wrapped in her blanket in the tent given up to her use, the fatigue of youth and health overcame anxiety, and she slept as refreshingly as ever she did in her life.

Morning found the Captain in the same dangerous state, but no worse ; that day the wounded were removed to the boat, which conveyed them eventually to a hospital in Louisville. Turkey Dan was obliged to see his friend and Captain borne away, raving with delirium ; but Eleanor promised, as he wrung her hand at parting, to write to him as soon as the young officer was better or worse.

During that tedious journey down the Cumberland and up the Ohio, Eleanor Beaufort was an angel of mercy to the sick and wounded men. Wan faces would light up when her kind eyes rested upon them, and men would speak to her in whispers of their own far-away sisters and mothers, sure of her sweet sympathy. She wrote letters for all who were anxious to send personal word to their friends, and in many ways made herself efficient. The doctors, however much disposed to discredit women-nurses, got to rely upon her for the careful fulfillment of their most important instructions.

Lieutenant Le Vert, lying there among others in that crowded cabin, learned a new lesson in the capacities of a woman's heart and hand—obliged to see those gentle attentions which he would fain have concentered upon himself, bestowed alike upon the humblest soldier and the finest officer. It worried him dreadfully to see Miss Beaufort, of Beaufort-place, lavishing personal care upon Northern mudsills ; and to find his own cherished and luxurious self no more tenderly cared for than the honest Germans of the heroic 9th Ohio, who had routed his own regiment so utterly.

Yet, much as his base Southern pride and his selfishness cried out against it, he could not but appreciate something of the loveliness and nobility which partly astonished and wholly disconcerted him.

Would that more of the insolent Confederate officers, taken prisoners by our brave men, only to be petted and luxuriously

cared-for by their Northern admirers, and servilely attended
upon by our unwilling soldiers at the order of a secession-
sympathizing superior, could be taught the lesson which was
forced upon the stubborn mind of young Le Vert.

CHAPTER XIX.

THE HOSPITAL.

" How pretty you look, Eleanor !"

" Do you think so ?"—and she blushed slightly as she met
the eyes of the convalescent fixed upon her admiringly.   " I
am glad you think so, Beverly, for I got this dress expressly
on your account.   It's a compliment to the dress, however,
not to me."

" On my account !   Eleanor, don't you think it is cruel to
flatter me with such speeches ?   Beware how you put wild
thoughts into the brain of a poor, crippled man, who is only
too desperate already."

" So you really think I look pretty," she said, with a gay
audacity, very charming, but very different from her usual quiet,
melancholy manner.

She stood up before him, looking down in slight confusion,
but sparkling and animated in every gesture.   The room in
which the speakers were was the convalescing department of
the hospital—a spacious, airy room, now occupied by some
dozen or more of cheerful-looking patients glad to find themselves this far in the way to health and out-door liberty.
There was no one near enough to the window where Captain
Bell was sitting in an arm-chair, to overhear the conversation
between the young couple.   A glow of warm spring sunshine,
" the first of the season," fell within the casement, lighting up

the face and figure of the young girl. It was not wonderful that the convalescent was taken by surprise when she appeared before him. He had never seen Miss Beaufort, except in the plainest attire and under the most depressing circumstances— sometimes with patched shoes and a coarse dress soiled by exposure to the roughness of camp-life. Since she came to the hospital she had worn a plain black suit, which made her resemble a Sister of Charity. If she had appeared so lovable to him hitherto, under all vicissitudes, how his heart leaped now as he looked at her !

She wore a lustrous silk, black ground, with small white embossed flowers relieving it; corded with white silk, the flowing sleeves turned back with the same, and finished around the neck with a lace-collar of exquisite fineness.

Her round white arms gleamed out from undersleeves of lace, and were clasped with bracelets of pearl. She wore a pearl brooch at her throat. Her hair was arranged so as to do justice to all its glossy profusion, and in her hand she held a bouquet of white roses and buds.

"Where did you get all these beautiful things ?" asked the young man, a sudden jealous pang shooting through him. Perhaps she had accepted some wealthy admirer, who was to bear her away from the privations she had lately experienced.

The eyes of the maiden raised slowly and settled upon his face timidly; but when she saw its wretched expression she smiled again.

"I disposed of a few of my mother's diamonds, Beverly. I have held them very sacred ; I did not like to part from them, but I thought if my dear mother were looking down from heaven upon my actions, she would approve them. I think all things should be done becomingly and in proper order, and as I—had made up my mind—to—I—"

She paused in utter and overwhelming confusion. If the

young man's face had not been so pale, his eyes so hollow, his form so wasted—if her eyes had not chanced upon the empty sleeve of his coat, it is doubtful if she would have summoned courage to go on. As it was, after a moment's hesitation, she resumed :

"I have seen how hard it is for you to get along without your good right arm, Beverly—"

" Well ?" he questioned, as she paused again.

The rosy blush crept up over her cheek and brow, and the voice sunk low, as she murmured :

"And I have resolved to become your right arm."

He stared at her, catching his breath, and leaning forward. He did not dare to put the construction upon her words and looks which swept over him in a sea of rapture. It was like Lady Geraldine's visit to the poet Bertram :

"Said he : ' Wake me by no gesture, sound of breath, or stir of vesture,
    Let the blessed apparition melt not yet to its divine !
No approaching—hush, no breathing ! or my soul must melt to
        death in
    This too utter life thou bringest, oh, thou dream of Geraldine !'

"Ever, evermore the while in a slow silence she kept smiling,
    But the tears ran lightly over from her eyes, and tenderly ;
' Dost thou, Bertram, truly love me ? Is no woman, far above me,
    Found more worthy of thy poet-heart than such an one as I ?'

"Said he : 'I would dream so ever, like the flowing of that river,
    Flowing ever in a shadow greenly onward toward the sea !
So, thou vision of all sweetness—princely to a full completeness,
    Would my heart and life flow onward—deathward—through this
        dream of THEE !'

"Ever, evermore the while in a slow silence she kept smiling,
    While the silver tears ran faster down the blushing of her cheeks ;
Then, with both her hands enfolding (one) of his, she softly told him :
    ' Bertram, if I say I love thee—'tis the vision only speaks !' "

" Eleanor, are you mocking me ?"

In the eyes lifted to his he saw a pure and tender smile. She drew a little closer, bent, and kissed his forehead.

"Beverly," she said, "this is my wedding-dress—I hope—unless you should refuse me! And this," she said, drawing it from her finger, and giving it to him, "is my mother's wedding-ring. It will answer for her child."

It was sweet to her to see the rapturous happiness light up the noble, wasted face.

"Would you marry a useless cripple like me, Eleanor?"

"You have your left hand safe, dear, and that will answer the purpose of going through the ceremony. As to the other, all I ask is to take its place—it will be a poor exchange, at that, I fear."

The tears welled up through her sunny smiles.

"My blessed, precious Eleanor!"—it was all he could say, for there were tears in his own voice.

"Are you ready now to make me your wife?" she asked; "if so, here comes our visiting chaplain, and as you are discharged from the hospital to-morrow, I want the right to go with you wherever you go."

The chaplain making his way through the aparment, toward the young couple, in whom he had taken an especial interest, was left by Eleanor to the keeping of Beverly; while he stated the wishes of the pair, she sending a messenger in earch of Pompey, her ever-faithful attendant, to whom she had promised due notice of the event.

The other occupants of the room, and two or three of the favorite officers, were invited to witness the ceremony; they gathered about, while Pompey stood humbly in the background, gazing on his beloved mistress with his heart in his face.

With a solemnity befitting the feelings of the devoted young pair, the pastor pronounced the marriage rites; and never, in halls of luxury nor grand cathedrals, did the services make a more profound impression, or did the new-married pair receive more earnest congratulations. The invalids upon whom the beautiful bride had lavished such generous care, wished her joy, and bade her God speed with tears of sincere emotion.

"And, Massa Chaplain, please don't go way just yit," said Pompey, when the congratulations were over. "We've jes' got a few refreshments, if you'll do us de honor to partake."

In ten minutes a table was stretched through the room, and covered with a handsome supper by the delighted Pompey and a couple of waiters whom he had secured. Flowers, and a bride-cake were not wanting, nor any of the elegant dishes suited to such a repast. It was enjoyed by the convalescents with all the relish of improving health and the excitement and surprise of the occasion. The walls of that hospital, inclosing usually so much pain and gloom, had never been enlivened by a scene like this before. It was the ray of sunshine with which Eleanor, young and romantic, had seen fit to gild the great event of her life. She put far from her the thought of home, of the beloved dead, of the uncertain future, setting her woman's heart to the work it had chosen, of blessing the life of another.

When the feast was over, and the remnants distributed to the patients in other wards of the hospital who were allowed to partake, the young couple sat by the window, in the rich light of evening sunset and full moonrise, talking over the future. The bridegroom had but little to say; his whole soul was absorbed in contemplation of this new treasure which had so suddenly become his own. It seemed like a dream to hold that fair white hand, and see the golden circlet of wifehood glittering there. He was afraid to touch the drooping curls, the lustrous folds of the silk robe; he could not realize that this beautiful girl, whom he had worshiped from afar, was his own—his wife.

"How can I take care of such a frail, fair flower?"

"Have I not proven, in the last few months, that I could take care of myself, and others, too, Beverly? I don't want you to think of it. I married you to take care of you! But you haven't lost all, in losing your arm, dear; there are many things, worthy of you, left to you yet. And until you find something suited to your position, I shall look after you myself. There, there, don't speak. Then there's Pompey; he's certain he can support us both. But we will not tax his energies so much as that. We can live on what we have, and what we can earn, until the Southern Confederacy is blotted out of existence, and I am restored to the estate it has robbed me of. It can not be but that this shall sometime come to . pass. We will be rewarded for what we have lost. Cheer up, Beverly, I'm sure every thing looks very bright."

"It looks bright as heaven to me," he whispered; "only I shall grieve if I bring hardship upon you; I am afraid I am selfish in being so happy."

"If our beloved State was only relieved of her frightful sorrows," mused Eleanor. "We have hoped in vain that relief would have come before this. We must still remain fugitives from our homes, and our hearts be depressed by knowledge of what others, who are dear to us, must still endure."

"If it had been my *left* arm, Ella, I should not mind its loss so much. I would be in the army again, fighting my country's battles until the other arm was taken also."

"It is hard for you to remain idle, and see us yet so far from the triumph of our cause. I would willingly follow you to the field again, Beverly. But since you are compelled to give up your place, since your sacrifice has been consummated, let us be cheerful, and have faith to believe that our leaders and our soldiers are doing all that can be done—that glory and victory will soon rest upon our banners. We have both met with losses which nothing in this world can atone for—they are sacrifices on the altar of our country. Ah! my dear father! if he could have been here to-night!"—she brushed away the tears and smiled again—"but I will not be sad, Beverly. I will believe that he looks from heaven and sends us his blessing this hour.

"Look at the moon! How splendidly it rises, rolling its silver chariot up the blue sky. I little thought, when I sadly watched it rise last night, that it would be my honeymoon! It's shining in your eyes, my sweet wife! You look like a spirit of light—like an—"

"Angel!" laughed the young bride, softly; "that is the set phrase, isn't it, for new husbands to bestow upon their wives?"

"You may laugh, but I really believe you are a little angelic, Mrs. Bell!"

CHAPTER XX.

CONCLUSION.

It is little over three months since Captain Bell and his young wife left the hospital. They are living in Cincinnati, or rather in a cheap cottage in the suburbs. His health being still somewhat uncertain, and having as yet learned to make but awkward use of his left arm, he is doing but little. He is young and ambitious, and Eleanor has decided that he must study law; to this end she is working bravely, having obtained a situation as music-teacher in a female school. She has descended to that terrible degradation which her aristocratic Confederate lover was afraid would overtake her, if she refused his offer of secessionist protection! Being entirely unaccustomed to any set task, it is not denied that she is often wearied and discouraged; but she would not sacrifice the principles which have shed such luster upon her beauty and youth for a place beside Mrs. Jefferson Davis in that imaginary court which that lady has held in fancy for some time past.

Pompey, faithful as he is generous, clings to them; does the rough work of the little household, the marketing, etc., and a good day's work as a blacksmith steadily besides. He often tries to induce his master and mistress to accept his earnings; but Eleanor has told him to keep them all safely until such time as she returns to her liberated estate; or, that failing, until he thinks it safe to bring his wife and children to Cincinnati.

Struggling as they are with poverty, obliged to make a home amid strangers, it is yet their greatest anxiety to see their native State relieved from the terrible oppression which rests upon her. When our victorious army took possession of Nashville, they rejoiced as at the liberation of their State from further bondage. But distress and disappointment have come upon them, as they find that their hapless friends in East Tennessee are still subject both to the tyranny of an oppressive government and the horrors of a guerrilla warfare.

God grant that before many weeks or months they may return to the land of their love, to find traitors punished, lawless freebooters hung, the property of rebels confiscated to reward the losses of faithful Union men; to find Turkey Dan and his wife safe and well, and ready to return to their old occupations of hunting deer and bear instead of the more rightful bushwhackers.

May the lovely home of the Beaufort family arise again in renewed splendor from its present mire and desolation; and may the noble couple who have been willing to sacrifice ease, wealth, liberty and life to secure their State to the Union under which it had prospered, be repaid two-fold for their losses and sufferings!

When the history of this unholy struggle of ambition and jealousy against the fatherly hand of a beneficent Government comes to be written, there will be no chapter more embalmed by the tears of our children than that which does justice to the fidelity and persecution of the Union people of Tennessee.

A few days since, Mrs. Captain Bell received a letter from Turkey Dan. That he is more at home with the rifle than the pen, the style of his epistle made very apparent; but his friends cherish his missive as preciously as though written with a diamond point on square note-paper of velvet richness, with his initials stamped in the corner, along with the heraldic device of his family.

"CORINTH, Joone 2 '62.

"DEER MISES CAPTIN: So U an the Captin hev hiched Hosses hev U. Wal U R A full teem for the Uneyun an no misstake. U no the song we use to give with a full corus out in the Woods it was the Uneyun of hearts the Uneyun of Hands the Uneyun of States who can sever i hop U may bee as happy as me an Sally has allus bin wee never Quarl exsep wen she gits the gug all to herself but as U don tak any i spose U L git along like lams i gumped rite up and hollered when i got your leter that U was jined fur life i wood have ansured it previously but i hev bin doin Awl sorts of things i hev jest got back from helpin cotch morgan an his men jehossifat i wish U had bin thar tu hav seen em skedaddle i was Shot at sixtene times and wasn hit unce xsept twice thru my cap wich I didn mind as it was a old un an once thru the

Caff of my lage which is well now Wee took haf his men an Lutenent Wood who U no is une of the wust Skoundrils in the hull dod-blasted lott an wee think wee killed morgan but ant surtin since then i hev bin Sent out skoutin by gineral halleck to find out wats Beecum of Boregards army its the opinyun of sum of Us that the yurth Opend and swalowed it Up bekase the Old feller doun below got tired a wating fer halleck to send the Konfederates doun by Usuyel wa if thar any wars abov grownd i L find em see if i don't ime back in camp fur orders an tuke this Oppurtunity of lettin' U no i reseved U R leter an how tickkled i was   Sally drew will cri for goy wen i tel her.   awl i hop now is that U L bee back to U R Old home B 4 long an that U L make a trip to the mowntins an weel celebrate next 4th of July with as much eclaw as we did the last i promise U bar stew an wild Tur-key as well as plenty of Hale Columby so no more at presn as i hev jest been ordered to find out wether Boregards in richmon or tuther place i spose mises bell is ure rite arm now captin   i saw how matters was comin round   its awl rite an God bless U both.   xcuse mi riting vich is a litel stiff with handlin my rifle so much lately an wotever U do don't forgit ure frend an wellwisher an hopin the Uneyun will be Restored as good as new   DANIEL DREW."

ADDENDA.

" Let me speak, to the yet unknowing world,
  How these things came about ; so shall you hear
Of carnal, bloody and unnatural acts ;
Of accidental judgments, casual slaughters ;
Of deaths put on by cunning and forced cause ;
And, in this upshot, purposes mistook
Fallen on the inventors' heads ; all this can I
Truly deliver."—HAMLET.

THERE is so much in these pages calculated to excite
astonishment and perhaps doubt, in regard to the correctness
of some of their delineations of character, as well as of some
of the incidénts narrated, that it has occurred to the author
to place before the reader the original statements and docu-
ments upon which her conception and narrative are founded.
It will be found that fiction has added nothing to the enor-
mity of the bare facts.   Indeed, had the author introduced
scenes depicting some of the actual events which have written
the history of Tennessee (during the years 1861-'62) in blood,
the pages of the novel would have assumed the character of
a romance of Robespierre and Danton's reign—would have
repelled the reader by its truly horrible element.   When the
history of this war against treason is written truthfully and
without fear, the world will have a story to read which might
have been written of the Osmanli invasion of the Eastern
Empire, but which it will be difficult to reconcile to the
professed " civilization " of~the nineteenth century.

Chapter I—Danger to Unionists.

The Louisville *Journal* of May 31st, published the following notice of warning to one of the eminent Union men of
Central Tennessee :

" We don't know where Mr. Etheridge is at this time, but wherever
he may be, we would warn him of the danger of his returning to
Tennessee.   We could give him facts, which would convince him
that he can return only at the imminent risk of his life.   Instructions have certainly been given by General Pillow that he shall be

nung or shot, or otherwise killed at the first opportunity. He has been keenly watched for in all directions. Men were hunting for him last night in the cars, at or near the Tennessee line."

A letter from one of the oldest and noblest citizens of Nashville, written to a friend in the North, June 1st, read ;

"Things have sadly changed in Middle Tennessee of late. The Union men are fairly muzzled since their leaders have all bolted, with two or three exceptions. You can not conceive the villainy, the lying, the baseness used to intimidate loyal men, and ruin the State forever. We have held several meetings lately, but the result only convinced me of one thing : the poor of the Southern States are unworthy of liberty. The Governor has mustered into the service about nineteen thousand troops in various parts of the State, but generally near Nashville. * * * It is trying to think of commencing the voyage of life anew at the age of sixty, and to sunder every tie which clings around the fireside ; but, rather than bow my gray head to treason and traitors, I will starve alone by the wayside ; for if I can't get money to travel with, I will come as far as Cincinnati on foot. We get no news here until it is altered and revised by our ' Safety Committee.' ".

Chapter IV—A Spy Wanted.

The Rev. C. W. Charlton wrote, in June, to General S. R. Anderson, (the rebel commander in East Tennessee,) as follows :

"I wrote to Mr. Finley on yesterday, calling his attention to the fact that it was highly important to have at this place a shrewd detective. We must have such a man. Have you such a man in Nashville ? If so, send him on. East Tennessee will attempt to set up for herself. Of this you may rest assured."

Same Chapter—Secession Ferocity.

The statement of " Turkey Dan," of the number of men whipped (page 40) and hung (page 44) have so many con: firmations, that we hardly know which particular account to adopt. Parson Brownlow's book is painful in its statements of these wretched tragedies, He says, among other things,

"They came sometimes with two coffins, one on each cart, and they took two men at a time and marched them out. A poor old man of sixty-five and his son of twenty-five years were marched out at one time and hanged on the same gallows. They made that poor old man, who was a Methodist class-leader, sit by and see his son hang till he was dead, and then they called him a d——d Lincolnite Union shrieker, and said, ' Come on, it is your turn next.' He sunk, but they propped him up and led him to the halter, and swung both off on the same gallows. They came, after that, for another man, and took J. C. Haum out of jail—a young man of fine sense, good address, and of excellent character—a tall, spare-made man—leaving a wife at home with four or five helpless children. My wife passed the farm of Haum the other day, when they drove her out of Tennessee and sent her on to New Jersey—I thank them kindly for doing so—and saw the poor widow plowing, endeavoring to raise corn for her suffering and starving children."

Rev. John McLeon Collins was arrested at Memphis, Tennessee, April 25th (1861) and thrown into a loathsome dungeon. He says :

"While confined in that city, I was compelled to witness the enormities perpetrated in obedience to the behests of those who ruled the mob. One hour in the morning, from six to seven, was allowed me to stand at the window-grate, and at such times their whippings and head-shavings were indulged. *Here I saw, from the 27th of April to the 6th of June, eighty-five men whipped and their heads shaved, and forty-three hung, because they refused to take an oath of allegiance to the Southern Confederacy. And on the 19th of May last, one of the most beautiful and accomplished young ladies this county can boast of, was stripped to the waist, thirteen lashes laid upon her back, and the right half of her head shaved,* simply because she had purchased a ticket for Cairo, and was congratulating herself that she would soon be in a land of freedom. These crimes, which make the blood curdle in our veins, 'and rouse a vengeance blood alone can quell,' were regarded as small matters by the *Avalanche*—altogether too insignificant to be noticed.'

The *Avalanche* was the leading secession sheet of West Tennessee. Neither it, nor any other journal allowed an existence at that time, took any notice of these terrible tragedies. A community which had learned to witness the flogging of slaves, male and female, with feelings of satisfaction, were not supposed to be particularly concerned in the flogging of a Union female.

Chapter VI—The Prison.

Prison Life in Tennessee would find material enough at hand for a volume which would at once startle and excite men to execration. Brownlow in his narrative states:

" Upon the 6th day of December they marched me off to jail—a miserable, uncomfortable, damp, and desperate jail—where I found, when I was ushered into it, some one hundred and fifty Union men; and, as God is my judge, I say here to-night, there was not in the whole jail a chair, bench, stool, or table, or any piece of furniture, except a dirty old wooden bucket and a pair of tin dippers to drink with. I found some of the first and best men of the whole country there. I knew them all, and they knew me, as I had been among them for thirty years. They rallied round me, some smiling and glad to see me, as I could give them the news that had been kept from them. Others took me by the hand, and were utterly speechless, and, with bitter, burning tears running down their cheeks, they said that they never thought that they would come to that at last, looking through the bars of a grate."

Chapter VII—Knights of the Golden Circle.

The document given on page 70 is a perfect transcript of one issued by the Order, dated from Louisville, May 24th (1861). Those Confederate scoundrels—of whom a vagabond journalist named Bickley was the chief—made no secret of their schemes. Bickley wrote a letter to the Kentucky Legislature, dated also from Louisville, in May, in which he said:

" There are now nearly eight thousand Knights in the State, distributed through every county, and the organization is growing daily in favor and importance, and the work will be pushed with the utmost vigor until the tri-colored flag of the Confederate States floats in triumph from the dome of the Capitol at Frankfort; and if, perchance, Kentucky should be tied to a Northern Confederacy, cursed and blighted with the fanaticism of Abolitionism, the organization will invite and carry from the State ten thousand families of Kentucky's best citizens, and plant them on the broad and fertile prairies of the noble State of Texas, where the K. G. C., in that State, will meet them with open arms and warm hearts, and welcome them to a State where every man's constitutional rights are respected."

Chapter VIII—Whipping Women.

The instance already cited of the young lady of Memphis being stripped to the waist and flogged, is confirmed by other instances of a similar revolting character. Parson Brownlow in his New York address said:

" They whip them, and, as strange as it may seem to you, in the counties of Campbell and Anderson they actually lacerate with switches the bodies of females, wives and daughters of Union men —clever, respectable women. They show no quarter to male or female."

Chapter XVI—The Bridge-Burners.

The burning of the bridges in East Tennessee was an exciting and interesting episode. The detail given in this chapter of the part performed by Captain F. (Fry) is in consonance with the facts of that event, which transpired on the night of November 3d. The facts of the case were not known even to the majority of Unionists until they were divulged by Brownlow, on his arrival in Nashville, in February, so well kept was the secret. The substance of his revelations was thus given by the Louisville Journal:

"Chaplain Carter and Captain Fry, of one of the Tennessee regiments, in the latter ipart of October, made their way in disguise and over hidden paths to the house of a prominent loyalist within eight miles of Knoxville. Here they convened about one hundred trustworthy and devoted men, to whom they represented that a Federal division was about forcing its way into the Eastern District, and that, in order to insure the success of the contemplated expedition, and prevent the reinforcement of the Confederate forces then guarding the Gap from either the West or East, they were authorized by the Federal military authorities to prepare and execute a plan for the destruction of the principal bridges on the East Tennessee and Virginia Railroad.

"Most of those present at once signified their willingness to co-operate with them, and it was accordingly arranged that parties of fifteen to twenty-five, armed and provided with the necessary combustibles, should proceed as secretly as possible to the vicinity of the bridges selected for destruction. Captain Fry, assuming the character of a Confederate contractor, professedly engaged in the purchase of hogs, under the name of Colonel Walker, traveled from point to point, personally superintending the preparations.

"So well were the plans laid, and so successfully carried out, that, although the most westerly of the doomed bridges was no less than *one hundred and seventy-five miles* from the most easterly, the guards at all of them were overpowered, and the structures fired within the same hour of the same night—that is, between the hours of eleven and twelve of the night of the 10th of November. The bridges were readily set in flames by means of ropes dipped in turpentine and stretched from end to end. Captain Fry was himself present at the burning of the Lick Creek bridge."

Same Chapter—The Female Messenger.

A letter written from the camp of the 1st Tennessee regiment, in the fall of 1861, mentions the following incident:

"One of the features of the 1st Tennessee regiment is the person of a brave and accomplished young lady of but eighteen summers, and of prepossessing appearance, named Sarah Taylor, of East Tennessee, who is the step-daughter of Captain Dowden, of the 1st Tennessee regiment. Miss Taylor is an exile from her home, having joined the fortunes of her step-father and her wandering companions, accompanying them in their perilous and dreary flight from their homes and estates. Miss Taylor has formed the determination to share with her late companions the dangers and fatigues of a military campaign. She has donned a neat blue *chapeau*, beneath which her long hair is fantastically arranged, bearing at her side a highly-finished regulation sword, and silver-mounted pistols in her belt, all of which gives her a very neat appearance. She is quite the idol of the Tennessee boys. They look upon her as a second Joan of Arc, believing that victory and glory will perch upon the standards borne in the ranks favored by her loved presence. Miss Captain Taylor is all courage and skill. Having become an adept in the sword exercise, and a sure shot with the pistol, she is determined to lead in the van of the march, bearing her exiled and oppressed countrymen back to their homes, or, if failing, to offer up her own life's blood in the sacrifice."

STORY-TELLING IN MAUM GUINEA'S CABIN.

MAUM GUINEA,

AND

HER PLANTATION "CHILDREN;"

OR,

HOLIDAY-WEEK ON A LOUISIANA ESTATE.

A SLAVE ROMANCE.

BY MRS. METTA V. VICTOR,
AUTHOR OF "ALICE WILDE," "UNCLE EZEKIEL," ETC.

BEADLE AND COMPANY,
NEW YORK: 141 WILLIAM STREET.
LONDON: 44 PATERNOSTER ROW.

INTRODUCTION.

Negro life, as developed on the American Plantations, has many remarkable as well as novel features. The native character of the black race under the Slave system is toned down rather than changed. We find among the slaves all those idiosyncrasies which distinguish the negro type in its native land. Superstitious, excitable, imaginative, given to exaggeration, easily frightened, improvident and dependent, he forms a most singular study ; and, so differently do the negro character and the relation of slave and master impress different observers, that the philanthropic world is greatly at a loss for some settled opinion regarding the normal condition of the African in the drama of civilization.

In writing of the race, I have sought to depict it to the life. Seizing upon the Christmas Holidays as the moment when his exuberant, elastic nature has its fullest play, I have been enabled, in the guise of a romance, to reproduce the slave, in all his varied relations, with historical truthfulness. His joys and sorrows ; his loves and hates ; his night-thoughts and day-dreams ; his habits, tastes and individual peculiarities, I have drawn with a free, but I feel that it is a perfectly just, hand. There will, indeed, be found so much that is real in the narrative, that it will scarcely be deemed a romance by those who read to be informed as well as to be pleased.

The several slave-stories given are veritable historical transcripts. That of Nat Turner's insurrection is drawn from the most reliable authorities. That of the leading character, with slight embellishment, is drawn from a life history, stirring and novel though it be. The various descriptions of barbecues, negro-weddings, night-dances, hunts, alligator-adventures, slave-sales, are simple reproductions of what is familiar to every Southerner.

"Maum Guinea" has not been written to subserve any special social or political purpose. Finding, in the subject, material of a very novel and original nature, I have simply used what was presented to produce a pleasing book. If the moralist or economist should find in it any thing to challenge his or her attention, it will be for the reason that the book is a picture of slave-life as it is in its natural as well as in some of its exceptional phases.   M. V. V.

MAUM GUINEA,

AND

HER PLANTATION "CHILDREN."

CHAPTER I.

FLIRTATION.

"Gay as the indolent poppy-flowers,
   Sleepy and sweet as they,
With love, like a golden butterfly,
   Deep down in her heart at play."

Daughter of Egypt, vail thine eyes!
I can not bear their fire.—BAYARD TAYLOR.

By dark bayou and cypress-swamp,
   By rice-field and lagoon,
Her soul went wandering to the land
   That scorches in the moon.—ALDRICH.

"You go 'long, 'Perion !"

"I wan' to, druffully, but I *can't*."

"W'y ?"

" 'Cause my feet is fastened to de yearth, Miss Rose."

"I don' see nuffin keepin' 'em—'less it's cause dey so big, you can't luf 'em."

"Dem's massa's own shoes I's a wearin', anyhow, t'ank you; I 'mired de buckles in 'em, dis mornin', and he says: ' Go 'long, take 'em ;' and den he gibs me dis note to bring ober, safe and soun', and tell no tales. I wears massa's shoes, and eberybody knows *he* got han'some feet. No, no, Miss Rose, 'tain't dat; it's suthin else is a fastenin' ob 'em. Can't you guess ?"

"Laws, no—course I can't."

"It's 'traction—'traction of grabity tow'd de lubly bein' in whose presence I now revolbe."

"Laws, Mister 'Perion, you uses such obbrobrious language!"

"We's had opportunities, Miss Rose; we ain't common folks. 'Sides, I's 'spired by de occasion."

"'Spec's if you was conwersin' wid Miss July, de likes ob me couldn't understand it at all,"—and the crimson turban of the young mulatto girl gave a coquettish toss, and the black eyes flashed at him a quick, sidelong look.

"Now *don't* go to saying dat," answered her companion, with a gesture of distress. "You knows I nebcr speaks to July 'less I can't help it. Course, bein' fellow-serbants, and eatin' to de same table, I has to be perlite to her. But I guess I knows who I wishes was missus' maid, 'stead of dat pert niggah."

"*I* wouldn' belong to nobody but my own young missus. She's de bestus young lady in de hull Lousiany State. Don't you t'ink she's *berry* han'some?"

"She's mighty han'some for a white lady—mighty han'some, and I don' wonder young massa t'ink so; but I know who suits my taste better!"

"Who, now?"—with the most innocent interest.

"W'y, de lubly bein' who waits on her, in course,"—with a flourishing bow.

Again the crimson turban was tossed.

"Laws, Mister 'Perion, you is such a flatterer!"

The young colored man leaned against the gate-post, surveying her admiringly; her lithe, slender form, clear, yellow complexion, and flashing eyes, were doubtless his ideal of female beauty.

"Tru███'t flattery, Rose."

"Hadn████ttah let July know w'at you been sayin'."

"You knows you's better lookin' dan July. Wish you wouldn' refer to dat indiwidial ag'in, Miss Rose; it hurts my feelins."

"Oh, it does!"—with provoking incredulity. "But you see, Jim was ober here, Sunnay night, and he tol' me you and July was gone to meetin' togedder."

"Oh, gorry, Jim'll get thrashed for tellin' dat story. I had a sprained ankle, and couldn' go nowhar. I was as oneasy as a fish out of water all de ebenin', for I 'spec' he come and tell you some lie. Hope you wouldn' have nuffin to say to *him*, Rose—he's nuffin but coachman. Massa don' set no great store by *him*."

"He plays de banjo bestus eber I heard—Jim does."

It was very cruel of the girl to make this assertion so coolly; Hyperion kicked the gate-post, and looked sullen.

Although it was the middle of December, the rich sunshine of the South melted over the landscape, of which the figures of the speakers made at this moment a vivid and picturesque part; the girl, graceful in form and motion, with her red head-dress, and gold ear-rings glittering with every movement; the boy, dressed in the extremest elegance of a *valet*, in his master's left-off clothing, lounging indolently; both of them belonging to the finest specimens of mulattoes, young and handsome. They preferred the full warmth and light of the noonday sun, to the shadows on either side of the tree-bordered avenue, at the foot of which they stood; and as they basked in the bright day, they seemed a natural part of the bloom and gorgeousness of the climate.

The road which ran past led through a rich and level country, divided into such extensive plantations, that only two or three other dwellings were anywhere visible besides the low, large cottage which stood at the head of the avenue, a veranda extending around the first story, and trees embow-

ering·the broad roof, making, with its French windows, and
vine-wreathed pillars, an attractive residence. Glimpses could
be had of the out-buildings, and negro-houses further back,
but the profusion of shade was such that these objects were
almost hidden, showing just enough of themselves to give
life to a scene which might otherwise have seemed lonely,
from the absence of neighbors.

While the servants stood at the gate, happy in their broad
flirtation, the curtains were parted from one of the upper
windows, and a young lady looked forth, her pink lawn dress
and dark hair fluttering in the light breeze.

" Rose !" she called, after leaning out a moment, to be sure
that there was no one at the front of the house whom she
did not wish there.

" Laws, dar's missus, callin'. 'Spec' dat answer's writ
a'ready,"—and the young girl ran at the summons, leaving her
companion thinking how " mighty quick that young lady mus'
be at writin',"—when the truth was, she had been longer
composing the brief note than its limits seemed to warrant.

The missive came wavering down into a rose-bush as Rose
reached the spot. The writer watched till she saw it deposited in Hyperion's vest-pocket, and himself mounted upon the
horse that had borne him from a neighboring plantation, when
she disappeared from the window.

" Don' belieb any more dat Jim's lies. You kin see for
yourself my ancle's lame, else massa wouldn' 'lowed me to
ride dis hoss. Will you be to home next Sunnay night?—
'cause I got suthin berry pertikler to say, Rose."

" Ef I don' make no promise, I shan' break none. Jim
said he'd hab his banjo ober to mammy's cabin, Sunnay
night."

" Berry well, Miss Rose. You can dance to banjo all yer
life, if you want to. Shall I gib Jim your complimens ?"

He straightened himself so finely on the spirited horse, and
looked at her so fiercely, that the saucy laugh went all out of
her brilliant face, and with downcast eyes she murmured:

"Laws, no. I don't care a straw for Jim, nor his banjo
neder. I 'spises him, he's so set up about hisself. He may
come to mammy's ef he wants to—*I* shan' be dar. I shall
be down beside de spring, under the hill, 'less it's too cold.
Dar's a nice bench dar, and nobody spyin' roun',"—and with
a flash of her eyes at him, to see how he received this
information, she darted off toward the house.

Hyperion's face shone like gold in the sunshine all the way
home. He was so full of anticipations of the "berry pertikler" communication he had to make, that the reins fell on
the neck of the horse, who walked home at his leisure, mind-
ful not to overheat himself. When the *valet* came in sight of
his young master impatiently pacing the portico, awaiting his
return, he suddenly gathered up the reins and dashed up
the carriage-path, with a speed which intimated he had ridden
post-haste.

"You've been absent twice as long as you ought, you
rascal."

"Gorry, massa, I didn' wan' to kill your favor*ite* hoss.
'Sides, the young lady took time to do her writin',"—and
Hyperion handed the dainty note, confident of its mollifying
influence.

In this he did not miscalculate, being motioned away by
the eager hand which took the missive, the seal of which was
instantly broken, and the young gentleman engaged with the
contents. The smile which broke over his face proved these
to be of an agreeable character; he read the few words over
and over, and finally kissed them, before he deposited them
in his vest-pocket. Yet this important note was a simple
acceptance from Miss Virginia Bell, of Mr. Philip Fairfax's

invitation to a Christmas festival which was to be celebrated in the neighborhood. All that charming secrecy which had invested the manner of its delivery and reception, was only that consciousness which attends every little act of two persons who have just begun to dream of that which they have not yet put into words. There was no more reason why Hyperion should have conveyed his message as subtly as if it had been a challenge to a duel, and its answer have been dropped as cautiously as if it had been the key to a conspiracy, than there is why two young people should blush when they chance to meet each other's glances, or tremble when their hands touch accidentally. These are the indescribable " airy nothings " which make the first stage of courtship so charming—delicious in experience, and hallowed in recollection.

Philip walked up and down the portico, thinking nothing, but dreaming every thing sweet and vague, the blood coursing through his heart to a music which thrilled every nerve—the music of his own hopes; though his step kept time unconsciously to the melody which floated from the direction of the stables, whither Hyperion had taken the horse. His *valet* was singing; though remarkable, even among the rich-voiced colored people, for the purity and power of his voice, it seemed to the young master as if it had never poured forth before so deep, unrestrained and joyful a strain. And perhaps it never had; for the colored man was dreaming, too; and his memory was welling and full of the gold of somebody's smile—the toss of a crimson turban, the glitter of a pair of ear-rings, darting through all his visions.

" 'Pears to me yer mighty happy to-day."

" Well I is—'spects because it's comin' Cris'mas," answered Hyperion to the colored woman who addressed him; and so surprised was he to think she should speak to him at all,

that he stopped and looked at her. " It's comin' Cris'mas,
Maum Ginny."

He was on his way back to the house, and paused before
the cook's cabin, in the door of which sat the woman who
addressed him. She was a tall, good-looking person, also a
mulatto, although two or three shades darker than the boy,
almost entirely without the laugh and sparkle which sets off
the dark features of her race so pleasantly ; stern, even com-
manding in appearance, with a strange look in her eyes which
might be sadness or might be hate, or both—nobody could
read it. She was usually so silent that Hyperion felt especially honored by her addressing him, waiting for her to say
more.

Maum Guinea was a new-comer, compared with himself. *He*
had been born on the plantation, and brought up with his
young master, changing gradually from his plaything, to
be teased and worried like a good-natured dog, to his
servant and *valet,* with all the ease and privileges of a
favored house-slave.

Maum Guinea had been with them but five or six years,
Colonel Fairfax having purchased her during one of his visits
to New Orleans, his former cook having become too old to
move with the desired alacrity. She had the confidence and
respect of the family in a high degree, and was liked by all the
slaves ; though to the latter she was an object of mystery and
conjecture. Her moody silence in the midst of their thoughtless gayety, her ability to keep her own counsel, the gloomy
fire of her eyes, awakened their awe, while her gentleness to
the sick, her skill in nursing, her accomplishments in cooking,
and the many favors she contrived to do them all, inspired
their affection.

Maum Guinea's advice was law with house-servants and
field-hands. They came to her in their joys and troubles,

and she gave them a kind of wise sympathy, asking none in return for her own cares, if she had any.

"Plenty ob good times, Cris'mas," continued Hyperion.

"*I* don' like it ; it's black to me—blacker 'n my own blood."

She spoke this with such sudden fierceness, and a look of such terrible passion leaped out of her eyes for an instant, that the laugh was frightened out of her companion's face. He scraped the ground with his shoe, not knowing what reply to make, though his curiosity was keenly alive.

"Mos' folks likes it, specially collud pussons," he continued, at length ; "nuffin to do, den, but play an' dance and hab good times. Gorry, I guess dem poor field niggers glad ob it.'"

Maum Guinea did not appear to hear him. Her sudden fit of communicativeness was over, and her eyes were fixed on the distant sky with a far-away look ; after waiting a short time, he moved on, not thinking it safe to interrupt her mood.

"'Spec's you found Rosa well?"

He wheeled around suddenly and met her half-smiling look—a look which never grew into a real smile—with a puzzled, embarrassed air.

"'Clare for it, Maum Guinea, I b'lieves you know *eberyting* going on—eben what one's t'inking."

"Birds sing sweet afore Valentine—ask Massa Philip," she replied, rising and going in-doors, muttering to herself, when there, "blackbirds better not try to sing—no use—no use !"

"I's got a more importan' questing to ask massa," whispered Hyperion to himself—"old massa, too ; ef it was only young massa, shouldn' car'. Gorry, but I hates it ! I orter to do it dis berry day, while Massa Philip so tickled wid his letter ; p'raps *he'll* ask ole massa for me,"—and he turned the corner of the house, whistling softly, and stealing a subtle glance out of the corner of his eye to see if Mr. Philip was still in the favorable mood. That young gentleman was leaning against a pillar of the veranda, looking off in the direction of Judge Bell's plantation, and smiling as if he saw a certain beautiful face through all the intervening space; he looked handsome, with that expression in his features, though he was not a particularly handsome man. His complexion was sallow and his features irregular; but his hair was glossy and abundant, his form good, and his air frank and pleasing.

Hyperion—he had given this fanciful name to his *valet*, on account of his flowing curls, purple and shining, and with scarcely a trace of the original wiry kink — subdued his whistle, approaching his master with the air of one who has a favor to ask. .

" How now ?" asked the latter, pleasantly, when he finally perceived him, after he had stood several moments near him. " Speak out, what is it ?"

" Oh, Massa Philip—" here the *valet* stopped, shuffling his foot on the ground ; a vision of the coquettish turban again inspired his courage, and he proceeded : " Oh, massa, nex' week comes Cris'mas, you know, and I 'spec's—'spec's—"

" What, you rascal ! you haven't come to me to beg spending-money, have you ? It's only last week I gave you five dollars, and you ought to have a hundred dollars of your own by this time. Can't afford to have you so extravagant—I really can't,"—and the young gentleman shook his head gravely.

" Oh, Massa Philip, 'tain't de Cris'mas money—I's got plenty ; it's—it's—"

" Been playing off any your old tricks, ha ?"

" No, massa ; but you see it's comin' Cris'mas, and I was a t'inking as how Massa Fairfax he don' like to let any his people go 'way from home to get married."

"Why, no, certainly not; it's a bad practice," answered the young man, growing serious, while a shadow fell over the brilliant face of the "boy;" "but I hope *you* don't think of getting married, at home or abroad, Hyperion?"

"I *was* a t'inking, do I hadn' spoken to her 'bout it, nor wouldn' till I'd asked *you*. 'Twon't be no trouble to you, massa; I'll jes' step ober and see her once-and-a-w'ile, and she's a berry, berry nice pusson, and t'inks a heap of me."

"How do you know, if you haven't asked her?"

"Oh, massa! I *guesses* it,"—with a sly chuckle.

"Who is it? If you want to be so foolish as to get married, why don't you take July, here at home? that would be sensible."

"July!"—with a queer contortion—"she's such a bad temper, massa,"—peering up at the window to see if that person was within hearing—"'sides, she's 'gaged to Jim."

"I don't think the Colonel will consent to your marrying off the plantation; and I don't know as I shall let you marry at all—bad practice. But you haven't told me who it is."

"It's Miss Bell's Rose, massa."

The young gentleman flushed up in the guiltiest manner; he couldn't help it, for the shrewd eyes of the poor fellow were reading his face.

"Oh, it is, is it?"

"Yes, massa; and maybe 'twill be all in de family, arter all—hi! hi!"

"Clear out, you rascal! Go and dust my clothes, they need it."

"But, massa—"

"Well! well! clear out, I say. Maybe I'll speak to the Colonel, though I guess you're capable of managing your own business. It isn't best to be in too much of a hurry about it, though."

· "I know, massa; but Cris'mas is comin', and it's a good time to get married."

"What, so soon? Short courtship, hey, boy? And all the better for that," he added to himself, thinking of somebody else, and of the ceremonies and delays attending " marriages in high life."

CHAPTER II.

CHRISTMAS EVE.

Joy for the present moment! joy to-day!
Why look we to the morrow?—SARGENT.

Hi, pretty Kitty! hi, jolly Polly!
Up with the heels, girls, fling, lassies, fling!
Hi, there! stay, there! that's not the way, there!
Oh, Johnny, Johnny,
Oh, Johnny, Johnny,
Ho, ho, everybody, all around the ring!—SYDNEY DOBELL.

Christmas comes but once a year,
And when it comes, it brings good cheer.—OLD SONG.

These eight days doth none require
His debts of any man;
Their tables do they furnish out
With all the meat they can.—OLD SONG.

"Wildly and gorgeously flashes the fire,—
The squeak of the fiddle flies high and higher."

IT was Christmas Eve. The sound of the fiddle floated through the darkness over Colonel Fairfax's plantation. Guided by this, as also by the fitful flash from distant bonfires, we might come upon a curious scene. The field-negroes were having a grand frolic. As none of their cabins would allow of much dancing within their limits, and there were twenty or thirty ready for a regular " break-down," they had chosen an open shed belonging to the sugar-house, which they had brilliantly illuminated by fires in the open air. About

these were gathered all the aged and rheumatic, whose dancing
days were over, toasting their unshapely feet at the glowing
embers, and looking on at the more active revelers.   The
air was almost balmy, soft as spring, but damp enough to
make the warmth of the blaze welcome to those who were
not exercising.   Fantastic as the flames whose light played
and quivered around them, were the groups which they
revealed — uncouth creatures, the most of them, even the
younger ones; while the old seemed more like caricatures of
humanity than realities.   Yet all of them—the young and
stout, and the old, distorted by hard labor beyond their
natural ugliness, branded by servitude, withered by years—
were as gay and free from care as a meeting of chattering apes
in a Bornean forest.   They had none of them lost that rich
capacity for enjoyment which is the boon and blessing of
their race.   They were happy in their new clothes, in their
week's holiday, the warmth of the fire and the exhilaration
of the music.   Each one had received a new suit that very
day; the homely cotton gowns and trowsers were new, as
were the shoes; and some were bedecked with turbans, gorgeous as the poppies of the Orient.   And some of the dandies
—for even among field-hands on a sugar-plantation, there are
dandies—flowered out in vests of superfluous brilliancy, which
they had purchased for themselves from their allowance of
spending-money.

Perched on a box at one end of the shed was the musician:
an old negro with white wool and wrinkled face, who evidently felt the importance of his position, for he rosined his
bow, and screeched it across the strings, until the anticipation
of the dancers was wrought to a pitch with his highest note.
The red hue of the fire gave a weird glow to the rolling eyes,
and shining faces; the soft, oily chuckle of the girls and the
easy laugh of their partners sounded pleasantly on the air.

Everybody was laughing at the least provocation, or none at all. Some ancient crone, with her knees drawn up to her chin, before the fire, has said something, at which all her companions " hi! hi!" " hi! hi!" and some stalwart dancer has hurried up the fiddler, whose answer is followed by a chorus of " yah! yah! yah!" " yah! yah! yah!"

In the mean time, somebody sings:

> " De ladies in de parlor,
> Hey come a rollin' down—
> A drinkin' tea and coffee;
> Good morning ladies all.

> De gemmen in de kitchen,
> Hey come a rollin' down—
> A drinkin' brandy toddy;
> Good morning ladies all."

At which everybody laughs, and the fiddle squeaks violently.

" Say, dah! hain't ye got dat fiddle ground?"

" Min' yer bisness, and don' be in a hurry. 'Fraid I shall break a 'tring if ye hurry me,"—and Uncle Zip grins to himself, at the thought of the discomfiture he has threatened.

" Berry well. Me and Chloe is a going to get along widout yer help,"—and the speaker catches a girl around the waist, sets up a clever, lively whistle, and they begin to hop and jump in a grotesque jig, the steps of which could never have been set down in any " art of dancing." The fiddle gives a triumphant squeal, which extinguishes the whistle, Uncle Zip's head drops on his breast, his monstrous foot beats time, his arm moves methodically, and out jumps an invigorating reel, which sets the beaming, giggling, uncouth couples into wild and indescribable feats of motion.

There seems, in all the features of this fantastic picture, a harmony; the dark sky, the flashing, leaping flames, the crimson glow, the grey head-dresses, the black faces, the bright eyes, the shrill, merry music, the untutored gestures.

Fast and faster flew Uncle Zip's bow, and wilder grew the
frolic, until musician and dancers paused from sheer exhaus-
tion.   The performer refreshed himself from a jug which
stood on a box beside him, the gift of the company in part
reward for his arduous labors.   Some of the old women
began to rake out sweet potatoes from the embers, which
those disposed took in their hands and munched; there were
also corn-cakes, baked on hot stones; and eggs which had
been stolen or purchased, and saved for this occasion.   It was
rumored by some that there was a pig to be roasted; but this,
it seems, had been reserved for Christmas-day proper, when
there was to be a barbecue, and good times generally.

In the midst of the first "recess," while these refreshments
were being handed round, a group of house-servants approached, led by the tall figure of Maum Guinea.

"Oh, dar's Maum Ginny.   Oh, I's glad," cried the children,
some of whom had been permitted to keep up and see the fun.

"How is yer, Maum Ginny?"

"W'at yer got? w'at yer got?"

The whole crowd pressed around, knowing by instinct that
she came for their benefit, as she never went to merry-
makings for her own.   July, the chambermaid, was with her;
and Hyperion, looking much less bright than on the day we
made his acquaintance, though he was dressed with an
elegance that made the "niggahs" stare; likewise Rose and
another girl from Massa Bell's plantation, and one or two
others.   Maum Guinea carried a large basket, covered with a
cloth, and Hyperion, with another man, two large buckets
full of steaming coffee, seasoned with sugar.   The girls
brought tin-cups to drink from.

"Here, chil'un," said the cook, "is my treat."

As she spoke, she uncovered the basket, which was heaped
with cold ham, buttered biscuits, and any quantity of small

sweet-cakes. To the cries of delight she made no response, not even smiling at the thanks and flatteries which overwhelmed her, but went quietly to work distributing the dainties in such a way as to secure to each a fair portion.

"Oh, Maum Ginny, how could you 'teal so much nice t'ings?" asked one eager urchin, as he grasped the cakes she gave him.

"Didn' 'teal 'em," she replied, indignantly; "bought ebery t'ing wid my own money—eben de eggs an' sugar—an' bake 'em myself."

"Oh, Maumy, you is awful good."

"Woll, woll, neber mind dat. I's got no pickaninnies spend money fur, and ole women don' need finery."

The eager creatures grunted and chuckled their admiration and satisfaction. In their eyes, Maum Guinea, although colored and a cook, was almost as superior a being as any of the white race they had ever seen. They regarded her with almost the same awe and adoration which they would have bestowed upon a *fetish*—they believed that something of a supernatural character attached to her.

While the others were eating and resting, Hyperion bribed Uncle Zip, with a piece of silver, to continue his playing; and he and Rose, Jim and July, danced French-four, half-cotillion, and some of those regular dances which they had copied from the lessons set them by the ladies and gentlemen at whose balls and parties they served as attendants. Very well they danced, too; especially Rose, who had something of the mixture of fire and languor which distinguishes the Creole women. Hyperion was distressingly graceful and impressive; while Jim bowed lower, and threw out his heels more freely than was admired by the critical eye of the *valet*. But, of course, a coachman could not be expected to rival a *valet* in refinement and elegance. Alas, for Hyperion! alas,

for Rose! though they gradually warmed to the music, and
entered into the spirit of the dance, there was evidently something wrong with them. The glow which had lighted up
their golden faces, as they flirted in the sunshine, but a few
days previous, was softened down by a decided shadow.
Sometimes, when she looked at her lover, a slight quiver
would weigh down the lashes over her dark, liquid eyes, and
compress her lips; while his gaze followed her every moment with a sad, unsatisfied longing.

They had met by the spring, on the previous Sabbath night,
as they had agreed; and there, very much after the fashion
of whiter and freer lovers, had, all coquetry aside, solemnly
promised to marry each other—provided, they were allowed.
They knew very well that it was against the rules to marry
off their own plantations; but they were both especial favorites
and pets, and relied upon carrying the matter with the young
white lady and gentleman, whom they suspected of a tender
interest in each other; and when they parted at the spring, it
was with the hope of being married this very Christmas Eve.

Rose's imagination had already selected the very dress, out
of her young mistress' wardrobe, which she was to beg for
her own wedding-dress—a corn-colored tissue, with crimson
trimmings, which was now in its second season, and which
she had always admired exceedingly. She felt certain, too,
"that Miss Virginny would give her a real gold ring," to be
married with, and a wreath of flowers for her hair, and plenty
of cake to make merry with. They would be married
Christmas Eve, and then they would have a whole week to
spend together—a whole week of regular honeymoon; and
after that—why, they could see each other pretty often, and
perhaps, before many months, they would belong to the same
family, with a bride and groom to wait upon, and every thing
so nice and happy.

This was the pretty dream they had cherished when they parted; but when they met again, a few days later, their prospects were changed. Miss Virginia had no idea of allow ing her favorite maid to marry, and be having interests of her own, which might interfere with dressing her hair and humoring her caprices at all times—at least, not at present— not for a year anyhow. She was going to Saratoga next year, and should need Rose as much as her trunks or purse, and Rose might be ill or something—no, no, decidedly—not until she returned from the Springs. By that time, matters might be arranged, if they were still so foolish as to wish it, so that they could marry; a contingency might arise—here Miss Virginia blushed, and looked out the window, confused by the pleasant thought which had swept across her mind, sweet as a breeze from a garden of roses. It was but a thought—nay, but a fancy—for no lightest whisper had yet been breathed; but it awoke a bashful, tumultuous stir in her pulses, and set her to dreaming, so that she leaned against the window-sill, forgetful entirely of the downcast girl, who, with tearful eye and heavy heart, was striving to keep on with her embroidery, and not injure it by the rain which dripped over her cheeks.

Poor Rose! her brilliant hopes had been blotted out, corn-colored tissue dress, gold ring, and all. During that half-hour, almost for the first time in her life, she wished she were not a slave—which was very unreasonable in her, for there are many free white people who can not marry whom they please nor when they please, nor have a silk tissue dress to be married in. Turbulent thoughts swelled her bosom, and once or twice a defiant glance flashed through her tears at the young mistress whom she loved, and who was usually indulgent to a fault. Virginia made a pretty picture as she leaned against the window-frame, the dark braids of her hair,

heavy and shining, framing a face of delicate oval, tinged
with the warmth of a southern climate; lips like rubies;
cheeks just a shade brighter than the clear brunette color of
neck and brow; the fancies of eighteen summers floating in
her eyes, the anticipations of maidenhood heaving her breast
with a breath quick and tremulous. She was young, wealthy,
beloved; ease and happiness were her birthright, and it would
have been cruel for her to have been robbed of them thus
early. She looked kind, too, and gentle; indolent, as a
southern temperament is apt to be, but not ill-tempered. Her
air was that of a person of refinement and intelligence above
that of ordinary young ladies.

"Oh, dear! I hope the dress-maker won't dissappoint me
about my ball-dress," she said, at the close of her reverie. It
was natural she should think of the festival, since Philip
Fairfax was to be her escort, and that her thoughts should
finally settle upon her attire, which was to be so charming.
"You must go and see her to-night, and find out how she is
getting along with it, Rose;" and, singing to herself, she
glided out of the room, forgetful of her momentary vexation
at her maid for wanting to marry.

Hyperion had had no better success with his suit; indeed,
rather worse. The old Colonel chanced to be in a bad
humor when the matter was proposed, and had not only
utterly refused to hear of his marrying off the plantation, but
had insisted on his taking July if he wanted a wife.

"July's sixteen now, and not much to do. It's high time
she was doing her share toward keeping up the population,"
said the matter-of-fact master. "She's a good-looking wench,
too; I don't know what better you could ask, boy."

Mr. Fairfax had not the same reason for favoring the
match which Philip had, as he did not suspect the state of
affairs between the young people. He was a good master—a

model master—but a strict disciplinarian, and would not allow such irregular proceedings as having one of his slaves go to a neighbor's plantation in search of a partner.

Almost discouraged, Hyperion returned to Massa Philip to get him to intercede for him, and was told that it was not wise at present.

"Wait a while, you rascal, wait a while. I'll see that you aren't obliged to marry July, if you have such a bad opinion of her. Maybe you can get Rose yet, if you are patient; there's more Christmases coming."

This was the shadow which had fallen upon the slave lovers—a light shadow, compared to darkness which might be, but which gave a sad, cold look to the faces usually so vivacious, and drew the sharp eyes of Maum Guinea upon them with no common interest, as they threaded the mazes of Uncle Zip's not very intricate music.

"'Tain't weddin'-cake," she said, meaningly, as she offered them of the stores in her basket when the dance was finished; "But I guess yer can eat it. Pr'aps, when Maum Ginny bakes weddin'-cake for de young massa, some oder folk'll get der share too."

"Laws, how you do go on!" ejaculated Rose; but she sighed afterward.

In the mean time, if one couple was in the shade, another was in the light. Jim, the coachman, was in exuberant spirits; he flung himself around so, during the dance, that there was danger of his getting himself into a fatal tangle—in fact, once, leaping up and hitting his long heels together in the air, he came down differently from what he expected, to the "inextinguishable" merriment of the whole company, from the toothless negress mumbling over the ashes, to the pickaninny rolling on the ground near by.

"Tell yer what, Maum Ginny," spoke Jim, after Rose,

rolling his eyes mysteriously, and chuckling at July, who rolled her eyes also, and smiled like a sunflower, "yer may sweeten a hoe-cake for *us*, and we'll be eberlastingly obleeged to you, t'ank you, and do as much for you on suitablum occasion."

"Ho! ho! dat so, July?"

"Yis, Maum—we jis' made it up."

"To-morrer ebening I 'spec's we'll need de preacher. My complimens to yer, Mister Hyperion, and hopes you and Rose won't refuse us der perliteness of yer countenance, to stand up with us,"—and he flourished a bow, to which the *valet* replied with one still more impressive.

"T'ank you, Mister Jim, I don' know as I's any engagements as will pervent my doing yer the honor of bein' yer groomsman—dat is, ef yer goin' to do it up brown, as der coachman of a fust family oughter."

"Oh, I's got a w'ite dress," spoke up July.

"And I calkerlates to spend t'ree dollars in refreshments, and I 'spec's missus will give us a bottle of wine, like as not— July missus' maid, and missus said she might chuse a partner, ef she liked."

"You'll come, Rose?" asked the bride-expectant.

"W'y, yis, I s'pose so."

It was hard for Rose to stand up at somebody else's wedding, instead of her own; but she choked down the lump in her throat, and began to question July about her dress and "fixins," as the visitors gathered up the now empty buckets and basket, and left the "niggers" to finish the ball.

Maum Guinea promised Jim she'd bake them a splendid cake, with frosting on it; for the family was going to take dinner out on the morrow, and she should have less than usual to do.

When they came to the cook's cabin, a cheerful light shone

through the little square window; none of the party were
sleepy, and she asked them to come in and sit awhile; so they
went in, squatting themselves upon the floor in a semicircle
about the fire. There was a good deal of screeching and
laughing, pretended anger and rude flirtation among the
young people; but the mistress of the cabin had grown silent,
gazing into the deep, red heart of the fire with a steady, stern
look, which almost made the superstitious creatures about
her tremble, when they chanced to observe her in the midst
of their merriment.

There was something in Rose's soul that night—we suppose
she had a kind of half-in-half gold-colored soul, seeing there
was so much white blood in her veins—which brought her
into sympathy with the quiet woman near her; she gradually
sidled up to her, though she still held her lover's hand, and
finally dropped her head against the stately bosom of the
cook.

" Oh, Maum Ginny," she cried, looking up, half-frightened
at her own boldness, " tell us a story. I do like stories so ;
and you tell such queer ones. Tell us suthin 'bout *yerself*,
Maumy, when you was a girl 'bout my age."

Maum Guinea started as if a hissing snake had suddenly
sprung out of the glowing coals; but she was soon calm
again, shaking her head in refusal.

" Chile, chile, hush !"

" Jim, you tell us 'bout dat big snake you cotched last summer," interposed July, who was proud of the exploit of her
lover, as well as a little frightened by Maum Guinea's voice.

" Well, you see," he began, nothing loth, " massa sent me
out in de swamp to—"

" We's all heard dat, forty times ober," murmured the
valet, who always held himself superior to Jim, and did not
hesitate to criticise.

"Sent me out in de swamp, wid an ax, to cut some bark to make wash for Bill's foreleg, which was swelled; and I found de right kind of tree, only der was a big black wine twisted around der trunk, w'ich I t'ought I'd cut down; but w'en I teched it wid de ax, golly, didn't it untwist itself mighty quick time, and stan' right up on its tail, and look me in de face, sassy! Yer see it was a snake, de biggest eber *I* see—w'en it stood up it was just my height, and as ugly as it was big. He look at me so wicked, golly, I t'ought my time was come. I couldn' lif' han' nor foot, but jes' look him in de eye; yes, sir "—mysteriously—"dat snake was de debbil hisself, sure 'nuff, and he put a spell upon me, so I couldn' help myself. His eyes were as green as grass, and he winked at me so sassy—he *did;* you needn' stick your tongue in yer cheek, 'Perion; if you'd been dar you'd *see*—and den he jes' drew back a little, and I don' know now how it happen, but de ax it flew up itself, for I couldn' lif' it, and hit him on de neck and cut his head cl'ar off. It was de debbil, sure 'nuff, for he hollered 'ouch!' when his head fell off; but I didn' stay to bury him, nor to get de bark nudder. Golly, I wouldn' go in dat swamp ag'in for a silber dollah."

"We's mighty glad you's killed de debbil, Jim," said a shining, good-humored-looking fellow, the darkest of the group of mulattoes; "'kase we all feel easy in our mind now."

They all giggled at this sally; nevertheless, three or four of them, with dilated eyes, stole furtive glances under the bed and into the corners of the room, as if they expected his majesty might still be alive and near at hand.

"Somebody tell anodder story—suthin *new*, that nobody else eber heard," suggested another.

"Don' tell any thing skeery," said July, creeping closer to Jim.

"'Kase might make July's hair stand on end," suggested

the wit of the company again; "an' eberybody knows it's so kinky, hain't no end to stand on."

"It's 'traiter yourn, anyhow," retorted the young lady.

"Look-a-heah, chil'ren, 'tain't more'n 'leben o'clock, and nobody can't go to bed till de blessed Cris'mas comes in. S'posin' somebody tells each oder de *trute*—suthin as has happened to hisself, some time anodder. We's all slaves, and we's all been sold once or more, 'ceptin' 'Perion here. Les' tell suthin 'bout w'ere we cum from, w'en we's little, or w'en we had anodder massa," said Jim.

They all looked at Maum Guinea.

"Go on, chil'ren," said she; "ole woman'll listen."

"But you ain't ole, Maumy," said Rose, "and you know more'n any de rest."

"Woll, woll! let oders tell dere's first. Dar's seben ebenings comin', and we can tell lots ob stories. Who'll begin?"

"Draw cuts," suggested Hyperion.

Jim brought the broom out of a corner, and pulled as many splints as there were persons present; Maum Guinea, who declined to take part in the lottery, arranged them in her hand so that but one end should be visible—the one who drew the shortest splint to tell the first story. The lot fell upon Johnson, a house-servant from the Bell plantation, a slender, thin, rather sullen-looking man of about thirty, with glittering, Italian eyes, and a good deal of the nervous white element in his temperament.

"Mister Jonsing, please purceed."

"Don' be bashful, Mister Jonsing."

"Let him alone honey; he's a-getting ready."

Johnson looked over at Rose; her hand was in Hyperion's, but her eyes were fixed upon him coaxingly; although his fellow-servant, she knew nothing of his history previous to his arrival at Massa Bell's, two years ago.

• "Oh, yes, tell us," she pleaded, with lively curiosity.

" 'Twon't be nothin' to make you laugh," was the answer.

"We don' want to laugh, jes' now," said Maum Guinea, gravely; " it's going on to Cris'mas now, and we oughter be singing hymns of glory. If you've any thing heavy on yer mind, maybe you'll feel easier for sharing it, dough—w'en it lays *too* long, it grows so heaby, can't be lifted nohow."

" If I must, I must," said Johnson, and his auditors crowded a little closer about him, opening both ears and eyes, excepting July, who was dropping asleep on Jim's shoulder, dreaming of her wedding-dress.

CHAPTER III.

JOHNSON'S STORY.

And the slave, where'er he cowers, feels the soul within him climb
To the awful verge of manhood, as the energy sublime
Of a century, bursts, full-blossomed, on the thorny stem of time.
                                                    LOWELL.

Her freezing heart, like one who sinks
    Outwearied in the drifting snow,
Drowses to deadly sleep, and thinks
    No longer of its hopeless wo.—IBID.

The great King of kings
Hath, in the title of his law, commanded
That thou shalt do no murder.—SHAKESPERE.

"I WAS born and brought up in Ole Virginny. My mudder was a slave, and my fadder was a Member of Congress. I belongs to one of de fus' families—got good blood in my veins—say my fadder could make a speech as smart as any-body in the city of Washington. My mudder was only fifteen year ole when I was born. She was a house-servant, but only light work to do; use to sew for missus, and tend de chil'ren; use to hab good times 'fore I was born; but after dat, times was not so easy. W'en a missus hates a slave wuss'n pison, times ain't easy for de slave, s'pose ye know. My mudder was *berry* handsome—handsome as Rose dar—jis' sech soft, shinin' hair and eyes, and skin as white as mos' anybody's. I can remember how she looked when I was a little fellow tumbling in de dirt, or in de porch wid massa's *oder* chil'ren—his real ones, I mean. She used to sing so beautiful—all de people lub to hear her sing—put de fretfullest baby to sleep wid her singin'. 'Spec' she was happy and kerless for a w'ile; but by time I got ole enough to notice, she use to cry more'n sho laugh. She would sit and sing, holding missus' baby in her lap—her own would be put out to black nigger to nurse—and de tears a-rollin' down her checks all de time I was cuttin' up and rollin' 'round in de grass.

"You see, missus was awful cruel to her. W'enever massa was away in Washington City, w'ich he'd be months at a time, she'd whip her, and starve her, and freeze her, and eberyt'ing she could do, 'cept to kill her outright. You see, missus wasn't berry handsome, and my mudder was; my mudder could read and write, too, and was rael ginteel; and missus hated her 'kase her husband liked her so well. Ef he hadn't favored her beyond the rest, and give her presents, and sot her up 'fore his own wife, I don't s'pose missus would 'ave got so bad. She used to try to make her husband sell her 'way down South; but he wouldn't do it—swore he'd sell hisself fust; and the more lies she told 'bout de poor slave-girl, and de more trouble she tried for to get her in, de more massa took her part. I don' blame Missus Jonsing now so much as I did once—but 'twas wrong, all round, and dat's a fact.

"Woll, you see, my mudder she lub massa berry much—she *lub him* orfully. W'en he'd been gone and come back, and she heard his voice 'fore she seen him, I've noticed her pressin' her han's to her heart, and gettin' faint-like, and **then** lookin' so happy—dat's w'en I was a growin' boy, and she were more'n twenty year ole. She nebber tell him how bad mi..sus use her—how her back all scarred up with whipping, and her feet froze wid bein' kep' out one col' night all night. She was 'fraid massa would sell her, rudder dan see her used so bad; and she'd take it all, sooner'n be sold 'way from him.

"Woll, missus she find out way to make slave-girl more misablum still. She quit a-whippin' and a-starvin' her, and took to gibbing it to *me*. She hoped to make my mudder run away wid me, and nebber come back no more.

"My mudder was proud of me. She teach me to read and write all she knew; she ·made my clothes nice, and keep me clean, and w'en massa come home from Washington City, she'd fix me up, and contribe to hab me 'round, so he'd see how much I growed, and how bright I was; but he didn't seem to keer—only to be put out about it; and den she'd cry ober me nex' time we was alone togedder, 'cause he didn't want to see me 'roun'. I s'pose he didn't like to see me 'roun', when he was kissin' his *oder* chil'ren, and showin' 'em de nice presents he'd brought; but my mudder was a foolish slave, and it made her feel bad; and de fact is, 'twas all wrong all 'roun', anyhow.

"Woll, missus she treat me so bad, I got thin and trembly, and was all de time in a kind of scare; my mudder use to set and cry ober me at nights, w'en she could get me wid her, w'ich wasn't often, and sometimes she talk to me—oh, real bad—'bout Missus Jonsing; her eyes would shine till I was scared, and would begin to cry, and ask her not to look so; but I felt some drefful bad feelings in my own heart, and once I told her I was goin' to kill missus when I got big enough. Den she try to hush me up, an' say I mus'n' t'ink such naughty, wicked t'ings. But I did t'ink 'em.

CHRISTMAS EVE FROLIC—*Page 17.*

"Woll, one day, I was ten, 'lebing year old, missus got oberseer to whip me for breaking a dish, and he happen to jerk my shoulder out of j'int, and den, I tell you, my mudder, she couldn' bar it no longer; she took me in her arms, and went before missus, and gib her sich a talking to, missus turned as w'ite as a ghost, and she had her out to de whipping-post less'n no time, to have ' de sass took out of her.' So, w'en we bof got well enuff to crawl aroun', my mudder she took me, one night, and we run away. I t'ink she t'ought she'd go de right way, and she'd get to Washington City, and tell massa how t'was, and beg him to sell her an' me away. But she got lost in de woods; dar was snow on de groun' de second night we was out; she gib me all de biscuit and meat she had in her pocket, I 'spec', and we wandered 'roun' and 'roun', days and days, and she put her petticoat ober me ob nights; and one night she sung and sung so sweet to me, dat I stop crying and fell 'sleep, t'inking of de angels, and de next mornin', when I woke up, my mudder was dead.

"Yes, she was cold and dead, sure enough; and dar I set and hollered and cried, till bym-bye some men who was a-huntin' come 'long, and dey found us, and took me out de woods; and 'bout a month after I wer' sent back to Missus Jonsing—but my mudder nebber troubled her no more.

"Missus wasn't quite so bad to me after dat, but she nebber liked me berry well. I was a right smart boy, so spry and knowing, they couldn' help having me 'round great deal. I use to wait on table and on company. I got lots of complemens and kicks both. I kep' up my readin' and writin' w'enever I had a chance, and I larned a little cypherin' from the new oberseer, who took a fancy to me; and massa tol' me once, mebbe I'd get to be oberseer myself some day. I was always kind o' quiet for my age, and the older I growed the quieter I got. You see I was t'inking of suthin more and more since my mudder was dead. Sometimes missus would ask me what made me so sullen; if I wasn't well took keer of and comfortable. I t'ink she was kind o' 'fraid of me. I use to look at her, w'en I stood 'hind massa's chair at table. She was a proud-looking woman, but she wasn't handsome. Sometimes, w'en she'd meet my eyes, she look kind of startled; 'spect dar was more in 'em than I meant myself, for all dis time I was t'inking, t'inking.

"Tell you, my frien's, w'at I was t'inking about: *I'd made up my mind to kill my missus.* Don' be so scar't, Rose. You see, I'd got it fixed up that I ought to do it. She'd killed my mudder, or de same, and w'en one pusson kills anodder de law hangs 'em. Woll, I knew, in course, I couldn' prove she'd killed my mudder, so I was bound to take de law in my own han's. You see, I *felt* so, and you can't expect poor, ignorant black folks feel t'ings right; t'was wrong, berry wrong, but fact is, ebery t'ing was wrong, and I couldn' get it right, nohow.

"Woll, Missus Jonsing, she got so she couldn' bar to have me 'roun' de table, and she got massa to gib me kind of assistant's place to de oberseer; and so I hung 'round, in and out de house, till I was 'bout twenty-two year ole; and still I hadn't had no berry good chance to do what I meant to.

"Howsumever, dar was anodder reason. Dar was a girl in de house dat I'd got to t'ink a heap of. She was right young and pretty. I wanted her for my wife, and she t'ought a good deal of missus, and I couldn' somehow bring myself to do de job, w'en she was 'round. I t'ought a *great deal* of Chloe, but she didn't seem to keer for me. She was berry sprightly, and I was so quiet-like, she didn' take to me. Last I found out she was belonging to young massa, missus' oldest son, jis' a year older'n me—my half-brudder he was, if he wouldn' like to be tol' of it. So den I made up my mind for certain.

"'Fore long, I had a chance. Massa and his son bof went to political meeting, over in de town, to be gone all night. 'Twas bright moonlight—bright as day—but I wasn' going to wait. She always kep' her door locked, but de window was open, for 'twas a warm night, and I climbed up on de roof of de porch, and got in de window as still as a mouse. I had an ax in my hand. I could see all about. Missus was sleeping on a bed. 'Long side de bed, on de floor, lay Chloe; she was sleeping, too. De bed stood out in de room, so I could step 'round de oder side, and not wake Chloe.

"'My head was as hot as fire, and my heart as cold as ice. I raised de ax. Jis' den Chloe riz right up like a sperit, and looked at me. I reckon she couldn' scream, she was so scar't; she raised her hand, as if forbidding me, and de ax kind o' sunk down. I couldn' kill missus, and she lookin' at me wid dose eyes.

"'Ef it 'twan't for *you* I'd do it,' I muttered; and den I jis' gib up, and turned 'round and went out de window, jumped down, and stood still a minute. I 'spected Chloe'd tell on me, and den it would be all up wid me; anyways, I didn' want to stay no longer. I'd made up my mind to run away, w'edder I did or didn' make out w'at I wanted. I had de key of de stable, and I'd got a hoss out in de lane, waitin'. So I stood jis' a minute, and den I fled, and I nebber see'd de ole plantation sence. I could write so well I'd writ myself a pass, and I rode dat night and de nex' mornin', w'en a couple of w'ite men met and stopped me. I showed my pass, and I got to Norfolk someways, and I had money, and paid my passage to New Orleans on a vessel w'at was going right away; and I've had all kinds ob times sence den, but nebber no good luck. I don' belief Chloe eber tol' on me, for I see de paper myself w'at massa advertised me in, an' dar wasn' not'ing said 'bout dat; but I got took up

for a runaway, somehow, at las', by somebody as was hard
up, and mus' sell somebody else's niggah, 'kase he'd none of
his own. I was sol' by a man dat hadn' a speck of right to
me, to a hotel-keeper in New Orleans; but I was 'fraid of
bein' found out in dat conspicurous situation, and made myself
so 'tickalerly disagreeable, dat he sol' me to Massa Bell—and
dat's how *I* come down to Lousianny, Miss Rose, sartain."

CHAPTER IV.

CHRISTMAS.

Hark! hear the bells, the Christmas bells! Oh, no! who set them
        ringing?
I think I hear our bridal-bells, and I with joy am blind.—ALDRICH.

        For, borne from bells on music soft,
            That solemn hour went forth from heaven,
        To stir the starry airs aloft,
            And thrill the purple pulse of even.

        Oh, happy hush of heart to heart!
            Oh, moment molten through with bliss!
        Oh Love, delaying long to part
            The first, fast, individual kiss!—OWEN MEREDITH.

        And had he not long read
        The heart's hushed secret in the soft, dark eye
        Lighted at his approach, and on the cheek,
        Coloring all crimson at his lightest look?—MISS LANDON.

        Capricious, wanton, bold and brutal lust
        Is merely selfish; when resisted, cruel.—MILTON.

IT was late Christmas morning before any one stirred on
the Fairfax plantation. There were no children at the old
mansion-house, to waken with the first crow of chanticleer,
and drag papa and mamma out of bed, to look for mysterious
treasures dropped by their patron saint through the dark
watches of the night; and everybody, white and black, had
kept Christmas Eve with such fervor that Christmas Morn

took them unawares. When the drowsy creatures began, one by one, to creep from their resting-places on cabin-floors, a sense of pleasure stole into the dullest brains. No work, no care, no punishment—nothing but eat and play; not for one day only, but for a week. They must enjoy themselves now enough to last them a whole year. The oldest negro, thrusting his white wool out-of-doors to wish merry Christmas to his next neighbor, was as much of a child as the radiant, rollicking, funny little grandchild darting between his legs, his ebony countenance suffused with the consciousness that he was going to have 'lasses with his hoe-cake for breakfast. There is no doubt but that the 'lasses with which that pickaninny besmeared himself, gave him as much joy as little Florence Bell's wax-doll, cornucopias and miniature tea-set gave her. It is those who are contented who are the richest.

Old Zip, being wide awake himself, resolved that no laggard should slumber longer; so he took his fiddle, and marched up and down the negro-quarters, playing and singing vociferously:

"Old Zip Coon, berry fine feller,
Plays on de banjo, coon in de holler."

"Berry fine fellow—ho! ho!" said a young darkey, scornfully, as the musician came up to him—"but I show him a trick or two!" and, turning back into his cabin, he brought forth a bran-new banjo, and began playing a bran-new tune, which Zip had never even heard, and which drew out the settlement, as the smell of clover draws bees.

"Wah did you get dat?" asked the old fiddler, with evident jealousy.

"Bought 'em," said the young competitor, thrumming away triumphantly.

"Banjo berry good for common niggers; but banjo ain't fiddle,"—and Uncle Zip resumed his playing with an energy

which extinguished the new tune, and compelled the banjo
to fall into rank and play second fiddle.

The shrill squeal of a fat porker soon blended with the
music, as a couple of men entered a pen in the rear of the
cabins, and seized the victim which was to be offered, a
smoking sacrifice, to the day's festivities.

The grand feature of this day's frolic was to be a barbecue
in the edge of the woods which skirted the plantation.   Even
the house-servants, such of them as could be spared, were not
averse to joining in the wild novelty of this favorite sport,
which was to begin at noon and end at midnight, and was
engaged in by the hands of several of the plantations, each
of which contributed its share to the furnishing of the feast.
As they had slumbered until long after sunrise, there was no
more than time for the women to bake the breakfast-cake,
wash the children's faces, and get their own finery in order,
and for the men to get the necessary " traps" together, by the
appointed hour.   The weather was propitious—still and
bright, and just cool enough to be exhilarating.

In the center of a cleared space, which ran a little way
back into the wood, the ceremonies began by kindling a huge
fire, in which the tamarack-branches crackled and the pine-
knots glowed, in a manner especially delightful to these dark
children of the sun, who loved both the heat and the light.
The luxury of toasting their shins was enjoyed with the most
delightful laziness by the elders of the frolic, who shook their
heads, rolled their eyes, laughed queerly, and made brief
observations or told fantastic tales which taxed even their
own wonderful credulity.   All those who were not singing
or dancing or fiddling, had enough to do in watching the
motions of the men engaged in the important work of getting
the feast rightly to " doing."   Ebony babies rolled around
like balls in the dry grass, and older urchins lugged small

branches, with tremendous efforts, adding fuel to the flames, in the center of which began to deepen and vivify the hot logs which made the reliable foundation of the fire, before which sticks were set up, from which were suspended two huge " porkers," to be roasted whole, after the fashion of a barbecue.

Musical as the sweetest strains of the violin, was the continual splutter and sizzle of fat which began to drop from these. It filled all senses with rich anticipations. Under its inspiriting influence, the young folks began to dance with a vigor fully equal to their performances of the previous evening; while there was a much larger crowd and a fuller band of music. Uncle Zip's fiddle had been reinforced by two banjos and a tambourine, to say nothing of a tin-pan and a *kettle*-drum. And the music thus produced was of no mean character. Rich, lively, melodious, full of golden rhythm and delicious sensibility, it moved the African blood to responsive beats; it was simple and natural as their own feelings, and as gay: while it had about it an originality distinct as that of the race from which it emanated. All the splendor of their native clime is in the golden melodies of the negroes.

Although the roasted porkers were the principal item in the bill of fare, there were accessories. In a large pot, which swung over a small fire of its own, some score of chickens were giving forth a savory odor. They were under the superintendence of a Dinah who understood the art of stewing fowls. Let not the inquiring reader trouble his mind as to the means by which these delicacies were obtained; they may have been raised by some provident resident in the negro-quarters, or they may have been taken surreptitiously from the hen-houses of masters—it matters not.

There was also another rare dish, upon which was concentrated all the care and skill of the best cook in the party.

Two or three enterprising persons, instead of engaging in the dance, the night before, had gone forth secretly, and their skillful hunting had been rewarded by that daintiest of all game, in the estimation of the colored people—an opossum. Stuffed with a stuffing compounded by the cook aforementioned, rolled in leaves and grass like a mummy in its swathings, and buried in ashes among hot stones, "possum up a gum stump" was expiating his folly in having been so foolish, notwithstanding his reputation for discretion, as to fall into the hands of the enemy. There were also some fresh fish, caught that morning in a creek which wandered through the woods at some distance from the spot, and just brought in by the exultant darkey who had secured them, which were put to bake in the same primitive manner. Eggs there were by the bushel—let us not be inquisitive, either, as to where they came from; and two or three women, as the crisp brown skins of the porkers announced their arrival at the stage of perfection, went busily to mixing up corn-dodgers, which they set up to brown on pieces of board before the fire, or laid upon hot stones. For drink, there was a caldron of coffee—for on the Fairfax plantation, the slaves had an allowance of coffee through the holidays—a jug of whisky for the men, and plenty of molasses-and-water for the pickaninnies.

No wearisome formality presided, like a garlanded skeleton, at this feast. When all was done, stalwart carvers brandished huge knives, with which they sliced off savory and unctuous portions of the roast for one and all; children lay on their backs, devouring "chicken-bones," and screaming to "mammy," for more. There was much shouting and laughing, grabbing from each other, chasing after the stolen morsel, and screams of merriment smothered in rich mouthfuls of good things—there was, withal, a great plentitude of eating. Neither appetites nor capabilities for fun were at all delicate.

The shining faces of the urchins shone still more with grease
and delight. The girls shrieked and giggled, and the beaux
kept them shrieking and giggling. Grotesque, wild, uncouth,
like the creatures themselves, was their mirth; but it was
sunny as the sky, beaming with good-humor, broad and
pleasant, good to look at—not a touch of malice, not a sign
of quarreling, not a case of downright drunkenness. Oblivious to the scars of the past and the toils of the future, these
children of the sun basked in the pleasure of the present.

It was nearly dark as the feast was finished; the young
people were too full of supper to care about recommencing
the dance immediately; there were plenty of remnants to
make out a second feast when appetite should demand. As
the twilight deepened, the fire was made to burn the more
brightly; far up in the bright blue heaven the Star of Beth-
lehem glittered over the wild, fantastic group, as hopefully
as over those fairer and finer creatures gathering to places
of more refined enjoyment.

Far away into the forest flashed strange gleams of light,
chased by stranger shadows. Birds and beasts, in wonder
and trouble, flitted deeper into the recesses of the wood, in
search of their accustomed repose. Quaint stories were told,
and listened to with open mouths, and big, credulous eyes.

It was at this hour that the party was honored by a visit
from the bridal party. Jim and July had been married in
the afternoon, as Rose was obliged to attend her young
mistress to a ball in the evening, and could not be spared
except through the day. She and Hyperion were neither of
them with the party now, having other duties to perform.
But they had stood up at the ceremony, and had helped eat
the cake and drink the wine furnished for the occasion.

All giggling and radiant, the new-married pair, attended
by a group of house-servants, came to receive the congratu-

lations of their friends, and to bestow a patronizing glance
upon the barbecue.

July was resplendent in a white dress, white cotton gloves,
a string of mock-pearls about her neck, and a wreath of
silver flowers about her head.   Her hair was long enough to
braid, though "kinky" and coarse.   She was a good-looking
mulatto, though nothing approaching to Massa Bell's Rose in
beauty or grace.   Jim wore a gorgeous waistcoat, had a sprig
of flowers in the button-hole of his coat, and also sported
white cotton gloves.   The bride received the attentions of
the company with little tosses of the head and affected airs,
well satisfied to be the observed of all observers.

"Mighty sorry yer didn' get here soon 'nuff to have a bit
o' 'possum," said one of the proud hunters who had added
that animal to the feast.

"Oh, we's had cake and wine," replied July, carelessly;
but Jim, who liked 'possum as much as his neighbors, looked
rather sorry too.

"Yer ain't too proud to take a cup o' coffee, if ye *are* a
bride, I s'pose," said one of the women, offering that beverage to the new-comers.

"Nor to dance a right smart break-down," added Uncle
Zip.   "Come, Jim, lead out de bride, and I'll play ye de
libeliest tune eber you danced to.   Boys, be sure you keep
time; play libely," he continued to the banjos, etc.

The fiddler's arm must have ached, as well as the legs of
the dancers, by the time that jig was through; for it was as
"lively" as he had promised.

After two or three dances, and having exhibited themselves to the universal admiration, the bride and groom
departed, amid the good wishes, jests, and broad sallies of
their entertainers.

High blazed the bonfire, loud rose the music, and gayer

than ever grew the frolic, as the evening deepened into night.

In the mean time, Christmas festivities were not confined to the colored people. Colonel Fairfax and his family dined with a neighbor. The dinner and its after-amusements were prolonged into the evening; but at dusk, Philip excused himself, to return home, finish his preparations, and make himself happy, by escorting Miss Bell to a ball which was given in a village a few miles distant.

This ball was to be a very select and brilliant affair—a private ball, indeed, given by a number of young gentlemen who invited their friends themselves; and just such an occasion as is especially enjoyed by young Southern people, who are very fond of dancing *festas*.

Philip went, in the family-carriage, for Miss Bell. Hyperion had consented to take Jim's place as driver, Jim being "berry pertickelerly engaged" that evening at home—a service he was not loth to perform since he knew that Rose was to accompany her mistress, who would need her aid in dressing, after arriving at the scene of festivities.

Mr. Philip found Miss Virginia well and in good spirits. After a few words of greeting, and many injunctions from her tender-hearted mother about her health, and not to allow the child to take cold, nor to over-exert herself, and to the driver to be careful, etc., all of which was eagerly promised, the young gentleman helped his partner into the carriage; Rose, with a huge band-box in her lap, took a seat beside the coachman, and they drove rapidly away.

Only those who have been similarly situated can appreciate the happiness of that brief ride to the unacknowledged lovers, who felt and thought so much and said so little, and who were so surprised, when the carriage drew up before the illuminated hall, to find that they were at the end of the drive.

" How do I look ?" asked tne young lady anxiously, as her waiting-maid put the finishing touches to her dress, before one of the mirrors in the dressing-room.

" I nebber saw missus look so well before," whispered Rose—" it's trute, Miss Virginny ; you do look oncommon han'some.   Dar ain't a lady come in dis room yet, can compare—dat's so."

" You flatter me, because you love me.   I suppose I look well to *you*," answered Virginia, in a low voice ; yet she could not help looking pleased, and hoping that she *did* appear to the best advantage—for was not *he* to approve or disapprove ?

If Virginia had been as vain as she was beautiful, she would have felt that she was destined to be the belle of the ball.   Her dress was very becoming ; and anticipations of enjoyment added unusual brilliancy to her always handsome features.   Her slight figure seemed to float in a rose-tinted cloud ; her attire being a very full and fleecy robe of the finest texture over a skirt of pink silk ; a bandeau of pearls on her rich and elaborately braided hair, a few flowers in her bosom, and her fan and handkerchief costly and dainty. When she joined her partner at the door, she knew well that he was pleased with her, by the admiring glance which he could not forbear ; the faint flush which rose to her cheek added the crowning grace to her loveliness.

Breathing the perfume of flowers, bathed in light, floating to delicious music, the hours of that brilliant ball stole swiftly away with Virginia.   She was admired, and overwhelmed with attentions.

Perhaps a curious feature of the scene, to a stranger, would have been the crowd of dark faces at the dressing-room doors, which opened into the dancing saloons.   The maids who had attended their mistresses, were privileged to peer in upon the festivities; and a group of eager, delighted countenances, of all shades of color, were visible at each.

Foremost among these, and almost pressed into the ball-room by the crowd behind her, was Rose, enjoying the triumph of her young lady with pure delight.

" By gracious ! what a handsome girl !" exclaimed a tall, dark gentleman with whom Philip was conversing, as his eye suddenly fell on Rose.

" Which one ?" asked Philip, his thoughts full of a certain young lady.

" There, in the door—a slave, I suppose. A superb creature ! The handsomest mulatto I ever saw !"

" Yes, she *is* pretty," responded his companion, carelessly ; " she's Miss Bell's waiting-màid, if I mistake not."

" Oh, ho ! is she ? I'm going to visit Judge Bell to-morrow. I have business with him—one reason of my being here at this time."

Philip Fairfax was not especially delighted with this information. The gentleman had been attentive to Miss Bell, had danced twice with her, had made himself very agreeable to her ; and he was a person to be feared as a rival—considerably older than Philip, but more self-possessed, a good talker, elegant in his manners, aristocratic in his bearing, known to be wealthy, and one of the first gentlemen in New Orleans.

But, for the present, the gentleman's eyes were fastened upon Rose. She wore the dress which she had coveted for a wedding-dress—the corn-colored tissue with crimson trimmings. Her soft, glossy black hair was tastefully braided ; that indescribable grace, which no thoroughly Caucasian blood could ever emulate, pervaded every movement and curve of her form ; her clear complexion looked that of a rich brunette, in the lamp-light ; while the luster of her eye, the sparkle of her smile as she watched her beloved mistress, gave a beautiful animation to her face. She was, indeed, dangerously handsome—not handsome only, but refined, gentle, womanly, also ; touched by that pensive grace which makes the vivacity of her race so charming, by contrast with the previous moment.

" A superb creature !" murmured the gentleman to himself.

Yes, a *creature*—a slave—that was what that beautiful woman was.

Again the gentleman danced with Miss Bell. She had met him at her father's house the previous year, just after her first return from school. He was a stranger to many of the company, being only a visitor in the village, and was one of the most distinguished of the guests. Virginia was as naturally flattered by his attentions, as Philip was naturally annoyed.

" Give my respects to your father, if you please, Miss Bell, and tell him I shall do myself the pleasure of calling upon him to-morrow—that is, to-day," he added, laughingly ; for it was two o'clock when he bade her good-night.

Philip stood by and heard it, and saw the young girl's smile ; and it was, perhaps, under the influence of the passing jealousy aroused, that he gathered courage, during the drive home, to decide his fate—to utter the important words, to receive the important answer.

Very tired, but very happy, was Virginia, as she sought her chamber in the first gray light of the expanding morning. Her heart was in such a tumult, soul and sense so thrilled and startled by a new bliss and a new reality, that there was a prospect of her not getting to sleep at all. She, who had gone forth half-trembling with a vague expectation of a crisis impending, had returned from the ball—*engaged*. Yes, " engaged," she whispered to herself, blushing, even in the quiet of her room ; that epoch so interesting to maidenhood had come, had passed—she was actually engaged. Philip, on the way home, urged alike by love and jealousy, could no longer refrain from putting into words the question which had trembled in his heart so many days. And Virginia had answered it according to the prompting of her feelings, earnestly, joyfully. The momentary pleasure she had taken in the admiration of the distinguished stranger, melted away like mist before the full sunlight of this real passion. Her lover had no reason for jealousy; he went to his dreams, contented. If the driver, in gallantly assisting the maid to the ground, had found a chance for a sly kiss in the starlight, it was no more than the happy couple they attended upon had also found opportunity for—that first, shy, blissful kiss which seals the betrothal, and is kept forever as a precious memory.

It was with the recollection of that kiss burning in her cheeks, that Virginia joined the group around the late breakfast-table, which was not served until high-noon. Her mother was too busy to observe it, and the young girl's conscious looks passed undetected. She made haste to cover her own joyous secret, by giving her father the message of Mr. Talfierro.

"Talfierro! you don't say so! the devil!" growled the Judge, evidently less pleased than troubled; at which his daughter was surprised, for she remembered that he had been a favored guest the previous season. "I did not expect him so soon, by several weeks," he added, in a kind of apology, seeing Virginia regarding him. "However, it's all right. We'll make him welcome."

"Everybody is welcome, during the holidays. The more, the better," said the wife, as she passed the Judge his coffee.

"Yes, yes, of course," he replied, recovering his cheerfulness. "Well, my daughter, I trust you did credit to the family, last night—your first ball, eh?"

" Dat she did, massa ; dat she did indeed, sir," answered Rose, with emphasis, she having come into the room with a bouquet of flowers, in time to overhear the question. " De handsomest young lady dar, by all odds. Dar's more'n one t'ought so—Massa Philip Fairfax for one, and here's his complemens, brought by 'Perion, and dese yere flowers, out de hot-house."

Virginia blushed so violently as she took the bouquet, as to fix the eyes of her mother suspiciously upon her ; however, she had nothing serious to fear from the scrutiny, for she knew that Philip was a favorite with her parents, and that there were none of those hateful financial difficulties in the way, which disturb so many matches otherwise " made in heaven."

Hardly was the midday breakfast over, before the promised visitor appeared. But Virginia had ample time to attend to her toilet for the dinner, before she was summoned to the parlor, as her father and Mr. Talfierro had a long business-talk in the library, while she was dressing. In the mean time, Rose had very provokingly been called away, just in the midst of arranging her mistress' hair, to bring cigars and sherry into the library, when there were plenty of other servants who might have done that service just as well. It was very provoking of papa very—and Philip expected every moment.

CHAPTER V.

SCIPIO'S STORY.

Look out upon the stars, my love,
  And shame them with thine eyes,
On which, than on the lights above,
  There hangs more destinies.
Night's beauty is the harmony
  Of blending shades and light;
Then, lady, up—look out, and be
  A sister to the night!—PINCKNEY.

Oh, Miss Minny, but I'm 'feared we'll have to part—
I've done broke my banjo, and you've done broke my heart.
                NEGRO MELODIES.

THE same company that had listened to Johnson's story, on Christmas Eve, were gathered again in Maum Guinea's cabin, the night after the ball. She had treated them to a supper of roast fowls and sweet potatoes, with pound-cake and coffee for dessert; the fowls she had bought with her own money, and Mrs. Fairfax had given her the other things.

The supper was cleared away, the fire flashed up cheerfully, and the whole company joined in singing song after song, accompanied by a banjo played by Scipio, the good-natured fellow who had congratulated Jim on ridding the world of the devil. Hyperion sung some songs which his ready ear had caught from the parlor—fashionable airs which had not yet descended to the kitchen; hymns, also, of that vigorous and exciting character liked by the race, were given with great fervor, and when they were sung, Maum Guinea joined in with a clear, high voice that thrilled a person through and through but to hear.

When the music was exhausted, the stories began. Again Maumy arranged the "cuts" in her hand, and all drew, except Johnson, who, having told his story, was "out of the ring." The lot fell to July.

"Laws-a-massy! I ain't nuthin' to tell," she murmured, quite overcome by the idea. "Nuthin' nebber happened to me, 'cept gitting married, and you all knows dat."

"Wa'n't you nebber sold?" queried one of the group.

"Laws, yes, twò, t'ree times; but dat ain't nuthin'. Fust time, I was a baby, and can't 'member nuthin' 'bout it; den I was sole to a lady to play wid her chil'ren, and she brought me down to Lousiany; and den she died, and missus bought me, and allers keep me."

"An' so you nebber did nuthin' but git married, hey, July?"

"No, nuthin' nebber happened to me, 'cept when I see a spook one night in de garden. T'ought I was clean gone *den*, sartain."

"How dat spook look, July?"

"Laws, I don'no how it look; I didn' stop to see. All I see was suthin white, and heerd it moanin'! 'Spec's it was missus' chile as died a long time ago."

"Oh, my!" ejaculated several, with fearful glances out of the window.

"S'posin' 'twas," said Maum Guinea; "sperit of little innocent chile would do no hurt, I'll warrant."

"Don't talk 'bout ghostesses," pleaded an apprehensive fellow, who looked big and stout enough to vanquish a score of the dreaded phantoms.

"Woll, July, ef you hain't got de gift of tongues, spokin of in de good book, course you can't be 'spected to use 'em," said another. "We'll hab to draw ag'in—dat's so!"

The lot this time fell to Scipio. He gave a desponding groan, shaking his head and making all kinds of contortions.

"I's in de same fix as July," said he, "only I ain't eben got married."

"Sho! Scipio, 'tain't fair," remonstrated Johnson; "I's told mine, and now de rest wants to back out."

" No, certing, 'tain't fair !" cried several.

" It's de solum, blessed trute, dough, dat I hain't no more nistory'n an alligator. I don' know who my mudder was, who my fadder was; w'edder I's got a blood-relation on de face of dis yearth, w'at name my own maumy gib me, w'ere I cum from, nor w'ere I's going to. All I know is, might as well laugh as cry. I's a happy nigger, naturally. Don't make no difference to me w'edder I was hatched out of an alliga-tor's egg, 'or w'edder I had member Congress for *my* fadder, long's as I've 'nuff to eat, don't have to hurt myself workin', and nuthin' don't happen to my banjo—yah ! yah ! yah !—

> "Oh, if I was but young ag'in,
> I'd lead a differen' life ;
> I'd take my money and buy me a farm,
> An' take—Rosa for my wife !"

And flourishing his hand across his beloved banjo, he bowed to Miss Rose with a gallant air.

" No you wouldn't," said Hyperion ; " gib you to un'er-stand, Mister Scipio, *I's* got a word to say about dat."

" Oh, ho ! has you ?" quoth Scipio, resignedly, while John-son drooped his head on his hand and looked steadily into the fire. It was plain the young lady had plenty of admirers.

" Come now, Scip, tell suthin," pleaded a girl by his side.

" Woll, I s'pose I can tell a lie, if I can't tell truth ?"

" But we 'greed to tell true stories," said Johnson.

" Oh, gorry, that'll go hard—'gin de grain," said Scipio, with another contortion. " Howsomeber, I'll try, an' if it makes me sick, Rose dar 'll have to take car' o' me. Woll, de fac' is, I was born onlucky. I got more w'ippins w'en I was a young'un, dan would 'ave sarbed massa's hull plan tation, if dey had been properly diwided. Yer see, I was allers getting into trouble—standin' on my head 'stid of my heels, as a boy oughter ; if missus send me of an errand, I

nebber get back, 'cause it allers happened so many cur'us
'tings to keep me—couldn' raise no chickens, 'cause I 'tole so
many eggs; and if dar was comp'ny to dinner, I allers upset
de dishes and drop de gravy 'bout on de carpet; an' I kep'
de little pigs squealin' awful, and lame de turkies t'rowin'
'tones at 'em; so I got lots of w'ippins, and dey made me
smart—dat's so—and I hain't got ober it yet.

"Woll, I was such a bodder, massa sen' me to be sold. I
kicked and hollered dreffful, for I t'ought bein' sold 'was wuss
'an bein' w'ipped—yer see, I was but half-growed den, and
I'd heerd de niggers talk 'bout being sold down to de rice-
swamps, w'ich I t'ought was in de bad place 'bout w'ich
Aunt Dinah used to pray and sing on Sunnays; an' I kicked
so, dey tied my legs togedder, just as Cuffee ties chickens to
take to market, and put me in a wagon and drove me to
town; and I looked 'round, and t'ought wasn't so bad as
dey'd make b'lieve. I see lots o' t'ings berry interesting, and
w'en dey come to big room w'ere dey was a-sellin' niggers,
up on a high place, I gets up purty good spirits, and was
berry quiet and perlite, 'specially as massa said he'd t'rash
all de skin off me, if I didn' behabe myself fust-rate. W'en
dey put me up dar, and de feller begun to turn me roun'
and praise me up, I t'ought to myself: 'Gorry, I guess I's
some punkins, arter all!' and w'en I see a good-natured
lookin' gentleum a-steppin' up, and lookin' at me purty much
as if he'd a mind to buy me, I giggled, and put my t'umb on
my nose, much as to ask him to please take me; and he
smiled, and turned to de feller w'at was a-hollerin' me off:

" 'Tricky?' 'quires he.

" 'Oh, he's chock-full of life and sperits,' says de oder;
'he's bilin' ober wid health and strength—*he'll* nebber be one
of de sullen kind,'—and de gentleum took a fancy to me,
it 'pears, for dey struck up a bargain widout much trouble.

"He was a mighty nice gentleum, and he wanted me for a kind of body-serbant like, to wait on him 'bout de house and go wid him 'way from home; and I like him, berry much indeed, berry. But I was born onlucky. Gorry, didn' I play him tricks, till he didn' know w'at he was about? He didn' like to hab me w'ipped, and he uses to keep a little 'orse-w'ip, and wollop me hisself, w'en I was outrageous; but I 'spect he didn' lay it on hard enough. I made him more trouble dan my head was worth—dat's so. I kindle de fire in de liberary wid de paper he'd been a-writin' on; I tip de inkstan' ober t'ree times a week reg'lar; I cotch my toe in de carpet ebery time I bringin' in de glasses, w'en he hab gentleum wid him; I 'teal his newspapers w'at he put away berry karful to make kites of; I tar' my clo'es and dirty 'em so, I neber fit to be seen w'en I was wanted in de parler; I puts massa's cologne on my own wool, and tries to shabe myself wid his razer, and get found out by cutting my face orful. He threatens to send me to de w'ippin'-post, and to sell me to de rice-swamp; and I allers so sorry, and promise so hard, he puts it off till nex' time. And so I grows up wid troubles enough ebery day to make my wool as w'ite as a sheep's; but it didn' pervent my keeping fat and comfo't-able, 'kase, as I said, it's better to laugh dan cry.

"But oh, lordy! w'en I got to be a nice young feller, and was full-growed, and had got ober t'aring my clo'es and tripping my feet in de carpet—w'ich I ain't quite recobered from yet, seein' as how, if I go to back out perlite, as a serbant oughter, I's sure to cotch my heels, dey is so uncom-mon long—w'en I'd get ober dem troubles, oh, lordy! den's w'en de ser'us troubles begun. Ladies and gentleum, has you eber been in lub? Dat tender sentiment is ondescribable, and I shan't agitate yer feelings by dwelling on it at dis time. Lub, ladies and gentleum, lub, is like a snappin'-tortle—ye'd

better let it alone, or ye'll get caught 'fore you know it,"—
here Scipio paused a moment, his hand wandering tenderly
over the strings of his banjo, while the girl next to him
hitched a little closer and regarded him admiringly—he was
evidently lost in retrospection.

"Woll, next house to massa's—he libbed in de city ot
Charleston, dose days—was a girl w'at allers set my heart to
palpitatin' so, I was sure I was gettin' de St. Witus' dance,
or suthin of de kind.   Ah! my stars! but Dinah was a
flirt!   She use to wait for me to be openin' der side parler
winders 'fore she shook her duster out ob de side winders;
and Sunnay afternoons, w'en she'd got her fixins on, she use
to walk by, berry slow, and cast look out de corner of her
great black eyes, till I 'clare I couldn' stand it.   I learn to
play de banjo purpose to gib her serenade of a moonlight'
night—and she use to lean out de garret winder, and drop
hollyhocks and roses down, jes' like w'ite ladies does under
similar circumstances; and den I go home, happy as a pickaninny in a tub of 'lasses, and t'ink so much 'bout her, nex'
day, dat I make more mistakes'n eber — hand massa his
slippers w'en he ask for his cigars, put his coat on wrong side
out, and show visitors into de dinin'-room, 'stead of de parlor.

"One Sunnay ebening I knock at de basement door of her
house, and 'quire for Miss Dinah; and w'en dey show me in
de kitchen, dar sat anodder gentleum, a-puttin' on airs and
t'inking hisself mighty nice, 'cause he'd got a ring on his
finger and a great big gilt chain ober his west.   Yer oughter
see dat girl dat ebening, w'at a coquette she was; smiling
at me an' den at him, and makin' herself agreeable to bof of
us, and we a lookin' at each oder, and speaking so dreffn.
perlite, 'twould have excruciated you to see.   Woll, t'ings
went on so, for a monf or more; ebery ebening I was out,
I called on Miss Dinah, and dat ar' rascal was allers dar too

and daytimes she was allers gibbing me 'tickler 'couragement, out de winder and in de back porch.

"One night, de moon was like a silber doller, and eberyt'ing was lubly as a rose, and I took my banjo and got ober de fence 'tween de two gardens, and begun to play berry sweet under her winder, and I heerd her raising it, and jest as I turn my face up to kiss my hand to her, she empty a pitcher of water slap in my face. Den I heerd her giggle; den I heerd somebody outside de fence giggle too, and I looked and seen dat imperdent darkey peeking tru' and larfing at me. Gorry! I couldn' stand dat, no how! I flings my banjo at his head, and den I jes' gib one jump ober de fence, and I chase him, and cotch him, and I gib him such a pounding as he nebber got before; but de wust of it was, de watch come along and put us in de watch-house, and massa had to pay to get us out. He ask me how I came to be dar, and I up and tol' him de hull story, and he larfed at me, an' didn' scold—jes' said I ' musn' place my 'fections on de fair sect—dey was like eggs in July—berry onsartin. Yah! yah!

"Woll, I found de fair sect berry onsartin, indeed—least-wise, Miss Dinah. She nebber speak to me arter dat, 'cause I pounded her fine beau half to deff; an' mebbe it's best she didn', for massa died of yaller fever dat berry summer, and I was sold wid de rest de serbants, soon arter, and I'd had to bid Dinah a long farewell, any how—

"Oh, far'-ye-well, far'-ye-well,
    Far'-ye-well, my Dinah,
I'm goin' down to New Orleans,
    Far'-ye-well, my Dinah.

"Woll, I've had seberal different kind of times sence den, but trouble don' hurt me. It rolls off my min' like water off a duck's back. If I haven't got a wife, I've got a banjo, and dat never scratches nor bites, and is allers agreeable."

"Laws, Scipio, some females wouldn' scratch or bite," suggested the fair one by his side.

"Dasn't trust 'em," was the grave response.

"Better stick to yer banjo," muttered Maum Guinea.

"Ho! yes! ye'd better stick to yer banjo," said a woman of middle-age, the housekeeper from the Bell plantation; "w'at's the use o' wife or chil'ren, w'en you don' know w'en dey may be took away. I's had a husband, and four chil'ren, but I hain't one now."

"Was they took away?" whispered July.

"P'raps, if I draw the cut nex' time, I'll have to tell ye Scipio, play and sing 'Uncle Gabriel,'" she continued, as if to change the subject.

So Scipio began one of their favorite banjo-songs:

"Oh, my boys, I'm bound to tell you,
　　　Oh! oh!
Listen awhile and I will tell you,
　　　Oh! oh!
I'll tell you little 'bout Uncle Gabriel;
Oh, boys, I've just begun.
Hard times in ole Virginny.

Oh, don't you know ole Uncle Gabriel?
　　　Oh! oh!
Oh, he was a darkey Gineral,
　　　Oh! oh!
He was chief of the insurgents,
Way down in Southampton.
Hard times in ole Virginny.

It was a little boy betrayed him,
　　　Oh! oh!
A little boy by the name of David,
　　　Oh! oh!
Betrayed him at the Norfolk landing ·
Oh, boys, I'm getting done.
Hard times in old Virginny.

They took him down to the gallows,
   Oh! oh!
They drove him down wid four grey horses,
   Oh! oh!
Brice's Ben he drove de wagon,
Oh! boys, I'm getting done.
Hard times in ole Virginny.

There dey hung him and dey swung him,
   Oh! oh!
And dey swung him and dey hung him,
   Oh! oh!
And dat was de last of de darkey Gineral;
Oh, boys, I'm just done.
Hard times in ole Virginny.

"Tell us *your* story, Sophy," said Rose, when the chorus died away.

"Hush! not to night—dar ain't time. You and I mus' be going back 'fore long."

"Sophy," continued Rose, half under her breath, "did *you* ever hear of black folks rising up and murderin' their masters? You know I can read, and I come across a little book once, hid away in Missus Bell's bureau, and it told—oh, it told such a drefful story."

"Hush!" cried Sophie, sharply, and glancing out the window, and around the room, as if fearful that the "walls had ears;" her face was blanched to a kind of yellow white, and she shuddered visibly. "Musn' talk 'bout such t'ings, honey," she said, more calmly, a moment later. "Dey's bad, berry bad, and our massas wouldn' like to oberhear sech talk —we'd all be punished, like enough."

"I believe you do know suthin, Sophy—I've t'ought it before," continued Rose, searching the countenance of the woman earnestly.

Rose was bright and intelligent, could read faces, and had

gathered up many curious bits of intelligence already, young
as she was.

"Don't you be tryin' to find out w'at you no bisness to
know," was the evasive answer. "W'en my time comes to
tell my story, mebbe you'll find out some t'ings I've heard,
and some I've seen. Come, Rose, we'd better be going."

"W'at a sleepy-head dat July is," exclaimed Rose, rather
contemptuously, as she discovered that personage was sound
asleep on Jim's shoulder. "I could stay awake t'ree hours
yet."

"S'pose you could, sake of bein' wid 'Perion," replied Jim,
laughing; "but July don't have to keep awake to be wid me
-yah! yah!"

"Oh, you get out!" cried the company.

"I's willin'," he returned, shaking his bride by the shoulder,
"'specially as we's all goin' coon-huntin' to-morrow night,
and will have to keep wide awake den. Good-night, ladies
and gemmen."

Well pleased with the promise of a coon-hunt, the party
broke up, leaving Maum Guinea to the desolation of her
solitary cabin.

There was no necessity for Hyperion's gallanting Rose
home, as Sophy was fully capable of accomplishing that duty
without his help; but he could not be made to realize it;
so Sophy started on ahead, well aware that the young couple
could dispense with her very close attendance; and so
smartly did she trudge along that she gained the gate at the
foot of the avenue fifteen minutes before the sauntering lovers
overtook her. The Christmas holidays were halcyon days
for them.

CHAPTER VI.

A HUNTING PARTY.

I will sing thee many a joyous lay
　　As we chase the deer by the blue lake-side,
And the winds that over the prairie play
　　Shall fan the cheek of my woodland bride.—HOFFMAN.

Mine are the river-fowl that scream
　　From the long stripe of waving sedge ;
The bear, that marks my weapon's gleam,
　　Hides vainly in the forest's edge.
With what free growth the elm and plane
　　Fling their huge arms across my way,
Gray, old ; and cumbered with a train
　　Of vines as huge, and old, and gray !—BRYANT.

Cursed be the heritage
　　Of the sins we have not sinned !
Cursed be this boasting age,
　　And the blind who lead the blind
O'er its creaking stage !—OWEN MEREDITH.

SATURDAY was cool and cloudy—a delicious day for
hunting ; and a party of ladies and gentlemen, consisting of
the Bells, Fairfaxes, Mr. Talfierro, and one or two others,
concluded to celebrate Christmas week for that day, by a
grand hunt. A good many of the colored people were
engaged in a similar manner ; several went with their masters
to assist in the labors incident to the occasion ; and parties
of negroes also went off by themselves in search of their
favorite game of coon and opossum. The wood, in the edge
of which the negroes had held their barbecue, was one of
those dense forests peculiar to Louisiana and Florida, filled with
tangled thickets, vines, dangling mosses, treacherous swamps ;
open ground in many places, where the hunting could go on
without so much difficulty ; in others, dark and impeded by
underbrush, with an occasional lagoon, or creeping stream.
It was the place of places for the hunter ; he could have his

choice: shy deer, fierce catamount, artful wild-turkey, tempting birds and water-fowl, or vulgar coon. There was one objection to the company of ladies—the nature of the ground would not permit of riding; and they were supposed hardly fitted to endure the fatigues of an expedition on foot. But the two who accompanied this party scorned that plea. Virginia Bell was an accomplished pedestrian and an expert shot; while Kate Burleigh, her friend, was a wild, dashing creature, as fond of hounds and hunting as the men—who carried a knife in her belt, and handled her rifle as easily as the best. The two together felt themselves equal to a catamount, and it is a question if Kate would have fled from a bear, even, without a trial for the mastery. However, they did not intend, in case of over-weariness, to be a drawback to the ambition of their escort.

Four or five miles in the wood was a lovely sheet of water, along whose margin the magnolia dropped its fragrant blossoms, in their season; and which at all times was fragrant with the spicy pine, and beautiful with aquatic plants. Here there was always a boat moored, and fishing-tackle prepared; and the ladies proposed, upon reaching this spot, to take to the water, recruiting themselves by angling for fish, while their comrades went on as far as the game or inclination led. Each of them had a trusty slave to bear her rifle, and to row the boat, when they should reach the lagoon, remaining in attendance upon their wishes during the day. Johnson was Miss Bell's attendant, and Kate had a servant equally trustworthy.

It was the intention of the party to lunch on the banks of the lake—perhaps to dine there also; for if game was peculiarly tempting, they might remain out deep into the night.

Colonel Fairfax took Hyperion, Jim, and two or three stout negroes with him, and half a dozen dogs; Judge Bell was similarly attended : there was Philip, and a couple of his young friends, and Mr. Talfierro, who was, at present, a guest of Judge Bell's. As the whole company, with rifles and hounds, plunged into the deep shadows and flickering lights of the wood, they were in high spirits, the day promising so especially well.

"Haven't seen you for some time, Judge," remarked Colonel Fairfax to his neighbor, as they found themselves jogging along, side by side, the young people in advance, and no one near them, except Hyperion, who was just behind, but quite unheeded by them. "I suppose your work was finished some time ago—sugar ready for market?"

"Yes; got along very well this season; but did not have more than two-thirds the crop I had last year. I was disappointed, for I had made my calculations upon having a better one. Unlucky for me, *this* season in particular."

"That's a fact; we're all on short allowance this year. The sugar-crop is an uncertain reliance, anyhow. One tip-top season, and then two or three poor ones, generally."

"I shall have to begin planting in a week or two," said the Judge.

"Got to plant this year, eh?"

"Yes, I've ratooned two seasons. So I had to save a part of my cane for planting, which reduced the product still more. However, I hope to come out all right next time."

"Is your guest, Mr. Talfierro, from New Orleans?"

"Yes, that is his home," answered the Judge, growing a little moody in his manner, despite of his ardent love of hunting, which usually exalted his spirits to the highest exhilaration.

"His appearance is very prepossessing."

"He's a great favorite ; and I like him, myself, very much —still, I didn't care to see him, at this time. Fact is, he holds my note for five thousand dollars, due a month ago, and I haven't a thousand dollars ready money. My crop fell short of my expectations."

"Of course he will wait. You are good for the amount, and it wouldn't be kind of him to press you for it. He can afford to take the interest and wait for the principal."

"Well, I thought he would do so, and I didn't give myself much trouble about it. But he's rather close in business matters, after all."

"If that's the case, you'll have to sell some of your negroes."

"To tell you the truth, Colonel, that's just what he wants me to do. He wants to buy from me."

"Then where's the difficulty? You can spare two or three or four of your field-hands, as well as not, I should think. An easy and economical way of paying the note that bothers you so."

"I expect I shall have to do that—sell some of my negroes —but I'll have to find other buyers, and that will give me some trouble. Mr. Talfierro has no plantation, and does not want working negroes. The truth is, Colonel, he's taken a fancy to Rose, and he wants *her*."

"Sho!" ejaculated his friend.

Neither of them noticed the convulsive start, the sickly pallor of the mulatto-boy, trudging along within ear-shot of their conversation.

"He's bound to have her."

"What does he offer?"

"Oh, the most extravagant price—twice as much as the girl's worth. If he wasn't rich and unincumbered, he wouldn't think of being so foolish. He'll give me four thousand dollars for her, and wait my convenience for the balance of the note."

"Four thousand! a fancy price. She'll never bring you

more than half that, again—perhaps not half. I should think
you'd be tempted."

"Well, I *am* tempted. But I don't like to sell Rose.
She's a house-servant. I've had her a good many years; and
the worst of it is, my daughter is so much attached to her.
Virginia would cry her eyes out, if I were to dispose of her
favorite maid."

"Girls cry easily, Judge; you mustn't give too much weight
to their tears; they dry up soon, fortunately. She's a nice
girl to have about one's house, Rose is—good-looking, bright,
and tidy. But four thousand dollars is a big price; she
won't bring it many years. She's in her prime now—healthy
and attractive."

"Yes, Talfierro swears she is the handsomest mulatto he
ever saw. He's really quite bound to have her."

"You've got another young girl growing up—that Chloe
of yours—can't she learn to take Rose's place in waiting upon
your daughter? She'll soon learn to like her just as well."

"Chloe's a nice girl—smart and tidy. But Virginia seems
to be peculiarly attached to Rose."

"Well, if you can afford to humor her in the fancy, I suppose it's all right. But girls' hearts are not easily broken;
don't be too tender of 'em, Judge. They're like India-rubber :
they take impressions, but they don't stay,"—and the Colonel
laughed easily. "Have you noticed, Judge, the danger there
is of you and I being brought into family relations ? Say,
neighbor, what do you say to that ?"

"I *have* been a little suspicious lately, Colonel, but haven't
thought much about it, either. Well, friend, I'm agreed,"—
and the neighbors shook hands, laughing and well pleased.
"They're a fine couple, if I do say it. Couldn't either of 'em
do better."

"If Miss Virginia has a lover to take up her thoughts,

she'll soon be resigned to Rose's loss," continued the matter-of-fact Colonel. "Four thousand dollars would buy her lots of wedding-finery. Howeve·, it's not for me to advise you, neighbor Bell."

"I suppose Virginia could be reconciled, but—but—the fact is, I don't just like to sell that girl. ˙ She's very much attached to all of us, and she's so—so young—and—" here the speaker hesitated, ashamed of his own natural impulse of virtue and humanity.

"We can't afford to humor the feelings of our negroes, Judge; it's a bad idea. They're a careless race, and don't suffer much from sentiment. I suppose Black ˌEagle, my pet horse, felt badly, when he was taken to strange pastures last year, but I was obliged to sell him. You know that the girl will, in all probability, be well treated, and have an easy time of it. She will be doing. very well, very well indeed. Like as not, she'd be eager to go, if she knew what the state of the. case is. Better ask her."

"I think not," responded Judge Bell, shaking his head.

"There! they've started something—a deer, I do believe," cried his companion, and the two hurried on ; while the slave, who had heard every word which they uttered, followed with a dragging step, carrying the basket on his arm as if it weighed a thousand pounds.

Trudging along over knolls of sand, checkered by the lights and shadows playing through the trees ; and through hollows tangled with vines and long, dry grass ; catching their feet in the bare roots of palmettoes, washed out of the loose soil, the eager hunters now hurried on, silent and alert, rifles ready and eyes on the watch. Virginia kept up well with Philip's easy stride ; she had taken her light rifle now from Johnson, who had hitherto relieved her of its weight. Kate kept with Colonel Fairfax, of whose skill she had a high opinion, and all pushed forward, each one emulous of the chance of the first shot.

As they glided along in silence, the faces of the lovers were brilliant and eager; they almost forgot that they were alone together, with soft mosses beneath their feet, and bright birds twittering in the branches above them, with the cool breeze of the light clouds kissing their cheeks at intervals, and all the soft, low noises of the deep forest about them; they were good hunters, both of them, and they would have forborne the sweetest opportunity for whispered words, in this moment of anticipation, to have seen, in the deep shadows before them, the starry eyes of a deer.

"Here is a track," whispered Philip, stooping down and pointing out to his companion where the light hoof of some passing animal had recently cut the dewy grass.

"And here is the mark of his horns against this tree," responded Virginia, showing where the bark had been rubbed up, on a water-oak near by.

"I declare, Miss Virginia, you are as sharp on a trail as an Indian," murmured her lover, admiringly. "Let us go on in this direction. I see the track again, here, and here."

They stole along, their hearts beating so loudly that they fancied almost the distant game might hear them. At that moment the baying of the dogs which attended the other members of the party announced that they were on the trail; the couple paused to listen. For a time, they heard only the sighing of the wind in the pines, or the soft dropping of dew or withered flowers from the tall magnolia trees; then the baying of the hounds again, the crack of a rifle, and the next instant they heard a rush in the underbrush a little to one side of them; and, turning, saw a noble buck standing disconcerted and motionless at thus being suddenly confronted by enemies, as well as pursued. That brief pause gave Philip time to swing his shot-gun into aim and fire. The deer tossed his head defiantly, and dashed away, right past them, for the hounds were behind him.

"Too bad," murmured Philip, and they started in pursuit. The deer sought the covert of a close thicket not far away; but that, which was small, was already nearly surrounded by dogs and men; and he suddenly turned, retraced his steps, and dashed by them again.

As his form stood out a moment, well defined, on a slight rise of ground, Virginia fired, and, by the stagger of the buck, as he bounded off, he was evidently wounded.

"Your shot told, Virginia," cried Philip, and he dashed on, in hopes of getting another chance himself.

A mighty tumult resounding through the woods proclaimed that the game was being closed upon. The negroes yelled, the hounds ditto, the men shouted; and the barking, screaming, the cheery cries, and the quick discharge of two or three guns, proved that the buck was brought to bay. Following the noise, Virginia reached the spot where the splendid game lay dead, scarcely a moment later than Philip. To her was given the principal honor, for it was her fire which had first wounded the deer and disabled him from successful flight.

"I will hang his antlers in the hall, in commemoration of the feat," said Judge Bell, patting his daughter proudly on the head.

Elated with this successful beginning of the day's sport, the party began to realize that they needed a little rest and refreshment before again taking up the march. They were not far from the lake, where the ladies proposed to await the return of the others, and to its banks they all now repaired, to partake of the lunch which the servants had brought with them. A cloth was spread upon the grass, under an oak, whose farthest branches were mirrored in the lake ; and around this gathered the company, waited upon by their house-servants, while the rest of the negroes lolled in the shade, at a respectful distance. The murmur of the water, just rippled by the breeze, darkening and brightening as the fleecy clouds swept overhead, made pleasant music in their ears, giving an extra relish to the cold ham and fowls, the biscuits and claret, which formed the lunch. The plainest viands have an unwonted charm, when partaken of by a tired hunting-party in the open air, and here were plenty of delicacies, as well as substantials.

"What is the matter, Hyperion — are you sick ?" asked Virginia, near the close of the repast, as he came near her to offer her the wine. She had been watching him for some time, concerned for him, as he looked so ill and haggard, performing his duties by force of will, and without a particle of his usual vivacity.

"No, not berry. Nuthin' much."

"Shall I tell Rose you had the blues to-day ?"

Even that magic name awoke no sparkle on the dull face.

"T'ank you, missus, you berry kind."

Nobody else noticed the sudden and singular change which had come over the favorite slave—the pet boy—the pinched look of the nostrils, the contracted lines about the mouth and eyes, the listless movements.

"Isn't it perfectly charming here ?" exclaimed Kate, as the two ladies found themselves alone, an hour later. "I could stay here forever."

"Oh, yes, very beautiful ; I always loved it," answered Virginia.

Nevertheless, she would have liked to have been with Philip at that moment, if her physical endurance had been equal to a whole day's hunting.

"Come, boys, get out the boat, and row us across the water."

The slaves obeyed; the little boat was drawn up where
the ladies could get into it; they took seats, and the rowers
lazily dipped their oars, with just enough outlay of energy to
keep the boat in motion. The fishing-tackle was not found
in very good order; but they caught two or three scaly
prizes, which they avowed their intention of having for supper.

Dreamily the boat flitted to and fro, amid broad-leaved
plants; the young ladies talked, as girls will, much nonsense
and some poetry; they dipped their hands in the water—fair
hands, which floated, like water-lilies, drawn along by the
current of the boat; they sung, and chattered; they laughed,
they watched the wild-birds; and all this time, Johnson and
Hyperion, silent, preoccupied, melancholy, rowed them whither
they listed, not once striking up their usual merry boat-song
of—

> "Gineral Jackson mighty man,
> Waugh, my kingdom, fire away—
> Fought on sea, and fought on land,
> Waugh, my kingdom, fire away."

"W'at de matter wid you, 'Perion? Needn' tell me—
dar's suthin done gone wrong," remarked Johnson, as the two,
having safely landed their fair voyagers, were now obeying
further orders by gathering up dry underbrush to make a fire.

"Don't ask me, Johnson, *don't*. If de worst happen, you'll
know it soon enough; and if it don't, no use fretting."

"Hope notting bad won't happen to *you*, ole feller," said
his companion, earnestly; everybody liked Hyperion, and
Johnson had experienced so much trouble himself, that he
knew it was no light matter which had come over his friend.

"'Tain't *me*," was the brief reply, and that was all the *valet*
could be induced to say.

"Give us a roaring, dancing, beautiful fire, Johnson; it's
getting dark, and there's no signs of the hunters yet. We

are going to surprise them with a glorious supper, when they get back. Are there dishes enough in the baskets, boys?"

"See what we have killed! Did you think we were so skillful?"—and Virginia held up half-a-dozen birds which they had shot in the last hour, while the boys were preparing the fire.

"Go, get the choicest part of the venison, Hyperion—some for broiling, some for roasting; and you, Johnson, find some stones to bake the fish in. Is there plenty of pepper and salt and wine, and are there any sandwiches left? Oh, here's biscuit enough to last a week, and all kinds of nice things. Maum Guinea knows how to calculate the appetites of a hunting-party. Hurry, boys, we're bound to have a grand feast."

Darkness came down over the forest; but the fire blazed high and bright. The cheeks of the young ladies glowed with excitement. They trilled merry snatches of song, as they assisted in the preparations going on for a supper in the woods.

There was danger of the haunch of venison being over-roasted, for it was full nine o'clock before the cries of the hunters announced their return. They came, making their way through the night by the aid of blazing pine-knots, which they bore aloft; and they were not sorry, as they gathered about the beacon-fire on the lake shore, to see the cloth laid, and to receive a hospitable invitation from their fair friends to stop and sup. The birds were done to a turn, the fishes rolled out of their leafy coverings, white and tempting, the venison was all that it ought to be, considering who killed the game; seldom was an impromptu feast more keenly relished than by the famished hunters, who had returned laden with the trophies of the day's sport. The dogs looked on with asking eyes, and were rewarded for their excellent services by many a sweet bone and dainty morsel.

While they were yet at supper, several negroes passed, with guns and axes, in a high state of excitement.

"Oh, massas, we's treed a coon!" they shouted exultingly, as they hurried by.

Philip, and two or three of the younger gentlemen, were not as yet so wearied, but that they concluded to join the negroes, and be in at the death of the coon. Snatching torches, and heedless of the remonstrance of the ladies, though promising not to be away over half an hour, they joined in the pursuit of the poor little worried coon.

"Dar, dar, he's in dat tree, sure 'nuff; I seen it move, and de dogs is barking all round it," cried a darkey, exultingly.

"Whar's de ax?"

"Needn' cut um down," cried another. "I see him berry plain, right in dat crotch up dar, and I's gwine to shoot um."

"Shoot away!" shouted Philip, laughingly, without much confidence in the skill of the negro, who blazed away with his old gun, and was answered by a cry which thrilled the group with horror—not that of a poor coon, in distress, but of a human-being.

"Good heavens! you've shot a man!" exclaimed Philip.

Groans of anguish descended from the tree; they waved their torches, but could see nothing distinctly, for the thickness of the branches. It was the first impression of all that they had come upon some negro runaway, who had been skulking in the deep forest, and who had hidden in the tree, fearing discovery by the hunters.

The teeth of some of the negroes began to chatter, and their eyes rolled apprehensively; they had heard strange tales about these refugees, and knew not what desperate character they had chanced upon.

"Oh, Lordy! Lord be mussiful to me a sinner! Oh,

Lordy! I's killed! I's clean gone killed, no mistake! oh, Lordy!"

"That's Uncle Zip's voice, as sure as I'm alive," said Philip.

"It's Uncle Zip!" echoed all.

"Zip, is that you?" called Philip.

"Oh, laws-a-mussy! Oh, Lordy! yis, its me!"

"Are you much hurt? Can't you come down?"

"Oh, I's killed, sure 'nuff! Oh, no, I can't come down. I's shot right in de shoul'er—can't stir, oh—oh—ouch!"

"Well, you are in a bad box, old fellow—no mistake," said Philip. "Boys, how shall we get him down?"

"We's hab to climb up dar, and try if we can luf him down easy," was the suggestion, which was finally adopted.

Two stout negroes climbed the tree until they came to the wounded man, about whose waist they tied a rope, and let him down as gently as possible; but not without much groaning and crying from the poor old fellow, who was really in a good deal of pain.

"How came you up in the tree?" inquired his young master, after he had given him a little brandy from a flask in his belt.

"Oh, massa, I don' want to tell," was the whimpering reply.

"Gorry, I knows," cried one of the negroes; "it's a bee-tree."

"Oh, ho! oh, ho!" cried the others.

Now, it was a well-known fact among his neighbors in the negro-quarters, that the old fiddler had been enjoying, for some weeks, an unfailing supply of honey. They had suspected that he had discovered a bee-tree; but, if so, he had no idea of sharing his prize; the selfish old rascal kept his store of sweets to himself, much to the envy of his friends. They had kept watch on his proceedings, in hopes of tracking him

to his treasure ; but he had been too sly for them. And here
he was now, caught in the sweet trap in this cruel manner.
When his companions averred that it was a bee-tree, he
groaned more terribly than ever.

"Cheer up, Zip," said Philip, kindly ; "you're not killed,
by any means ; you'll be all right in a week or two."

"Oh, oh, Lordy ! 'tain't dat, massa. I don' mind de shot
so much, dough my shoul'er hurts awful ; but dey'll 'teal all
my honey."

"Never mind your honey, my boy. You've paid pretty
dear for your bee-tree. Let it go, and be thankful you're not
killed outright."

"Oh, massa, I can't play de fiddle no more berry soon—
can't play de fiddle on New Year's, nohow ; and it hurts
awful. But dat ain't de worst. Oh, massa, wish you'd tell
'em let *my* bee-tree alone."

"Well, well, the boys shan't have your honey. But it'll
be all gone before you're able to come here again. You'd
better be got home now, as soon as possible."

Several of the negroes were obliged to abandon the pleasure of capturing the coon, and assist in carrying home poor
Zip, whose chief grief was in the discovery of his treasure.

"Oh, my bee-tree, my bee-tree ! Boys, let my bee-tree
alone !" was the burden of his moans, as he was assisted back
to his cabin.

The party by the shore now hastily broke up ; Colonel
Fairfax hurrying down to see to the dressing of the negro's
wound, and to send for a surgeon, if necessary. It was high
time for the sport to be ended, the hand on the clock telling
Sunday morning before any one was in bed. By the flickering fire which faded and expired in intensest darkness, before
the gray of dawn took the place of its uncertain glimmer,
all night, like an animal of the forest, crouched Hyperion.

CHAPTER VII.

SOPHY'S STORY.

God works for all. Ye can not hem the hope of being free,
  With parallels of latitude, with mountain-range or sea;
Chain down your slaves with ignorance, ye can not keep apart,
  With all your craft of tyranny, the human heart from heart.
                                                LOWELL.

And on the lover of her youth,   •
  She turned her patient eyes,
And saw him, sad and faint and sick,
  Beneath those alien skies.

She saw him pick the cotton-blooms,
  And cut the sugar-cane—
A ring of iron on his wrist,
  And round his heart a chain.—ALDRICH.

From the hearths of their cabins,
  The fields of their corn,
Unwarned and unweaponed,
  The victims were torn.
By the whirlwind of murder
  Swept up and swept on,
To the low, reedy fen-lands,
  The marsh of the swan.—WHITTIER.

HARDLY had Maum Guinea dished the breakfast on Sunday morning and sent it to the house, before the door of her cabin opened, and Hyperion entered, looking so changed from the saucy and elegant *valet* he usually appeared, that she almost dropped from her hand the coffee-pot from which she was about to take her own allowance.

" Now, chile, you's sick, sartain ; and you've come to look for suthin to cure you. W'at's de matter ?"

He dropped into the chair which sat by the little kitchen-table, and leaned his head into his hand without making any reply.

" W'at's de matter, chile ? speak !" she said, very kindly, for he was a favorite with her—perhaps he reminded her of some one of her own kin, whom she had some time cared for and loved.

"It's all *here*," he said, at last, pressing his hand on his heart.

"W'at is it, honey? Tell Maum Ginny, and mebbe your heart'll feel lighter. But drink 'dis coffee, fust—'twill kind o' set you up, and gib you stren'th."

"I don't want nuffin' to eat or drink; my throat is all choked up wid such a lump, I couldn't swaller a mouf'ful, Maumy."

"Woll, now, jes' speak right out, w'at de trubble, darlin'?"

"Oh, Maum Ginny, dey're talkin' 'bout sellin' Rose."

"Sellin' Rose!"

"Yis, I heerd 'em myself. Massa Bell, he's offered four t'ousand dollers for her; and he's hard up for money, and Massa Fairfax he say—' Sell her, sell her!' "

"Oh, dey wouldn' sell Rose. Miss Virginny wouldn' let 'em." She tried to speak cheerfully, though her hands trembled as she pushed the dishes about, pretending a carelessness she did not feel.

"Dey spoke 'bout dat; and dey said, ' Miss Virginny soon get ober it'—Miss Virginny would get ober it, but *I* nebber should, Maum Ginny,"—he raised his eyes to her face with an expression which pained her corded and scarred old heart, albeit it was used to torture.

"Who wants to buy her?"

"That gentleum from New Orleans we see here yesterday, —dat berry proud gentleum wid de di'mond buttons in his shirt,"—poor Hyperion had noticed, with the appreciative eye of his calling, the glittering brilliants which bedecked the splendid gentleman.

"Has he got a wife?"

"No"

"Curse 'em!" exclaimed the woman suddenly, drawing her tall form up, while her eyes flashed with vivid fire, "curse 'em, I say! curse 'em all—buyer, seller, de whole w'ite race!"

"Oh, Maumy!"

"Don' you curse 'em, chile? Ain't dar dark spot in your bosom, jes' as bitter as gall? Oh, dey'll sell our chil'ren, w'en dey wants money! Massa Bell better sell his own girl! She ain't so good nor so purty as Rose. *She* wouldn' bring four t'ousand dollers, ho! ho!"

"Oh, Maumy; how you talk!"—the young mulatto-man had not yet become so familiar with secret and long-suppressed feelings like these, as not to be startled when he heard them uttered. "But I wish I was a w'ite man."

"Oh, yis!" scornfully, "you'd be a human bein' then, you know."

"I could help myself—I could do suthin. Now I can do notting—notting at all—my hands is tied. I laid out in de woods las' night—all night, t'inkin' about it. De stars shone like de glory hallelujah, de lake kep' whisperin', till I'd most a mind to jump in, and not hab to t'ink so hard any more. Oh, how I did wish I had four t'ousand dollers to go and gib Massa Bell, and take Rose and marry her as we's promised to each oder. But I hadn't no money—I could nebber earn any —not if I work my fingers to de bone all my life, I won't have any money, 'kase it's all massa's, and I b'long to him. I can't take a wife, and hab her all *my own*, to take care of her and de pickaninnies, and be proud of dem, and feel der *mine*. I can't be notting—I can't hab notting—I'm a slave, Maum Ginny, dough I nebber knew what it meant, till I hear massa Bell talk yesterday. Oh, Lordy, how I wish I had some money!—if I had pile of dollers big dis room, I'd gib it all to buy Rose 'way from dat gentleum. Oh, I wish I had

some money. Oh, Maumy, what shall I do?—my head is
all a-fire."

"Don't take on so, honey; drink dis hot coffee, 'twill
clar yer head," she urged again, coaxingly. "Leastwise, don't
gib it up yet. I don' belieb Miss Virginny'll let Rose go.
I'll go to her, myself, and tell her dis berry ebening—I'll go
to Massa Bell, and I'll shake my fist in his face, and tell him
if he sell dat girl 'way to New Orleans gentleum, he'll nebber
prosper long as he lib. I'll scar' him out of it! Taste yer
coffee, do, chile."

A drowning man catches at straws; and Hyperion, holding
himself so high an opinion of the cook's character and influence, felt cheered by her promise to interfere in the matter.
He drank the stimulating beverage which she pressed upon
him, and felt his spirits rise into a degree of hope.

Judge Bell had not said that he was positively going to
dispose of Rose; he had expressed reluctance to part with
her, and if he could get Maum Guinea, Miss Virginia, and
perhaps young Massa Philip to intercede for her, she might
be saved from the fate which threatened her — she might
some time be his wife, as Philip and Virginia had promised.
How willing would he be now, to wait a year, or two years,
if he could be certain that she would then be his! Would
he not even be resigned to giving her up entirely, if he could
know that she would never fall into the hands of that diamond
gentleman?

The Sabbath is a day not particularly observed for its
religious character upon extreme southern plantations. Some
of the Creole planters work their slaves alike upon that and
other days; but generally it is kept as a kind of lazy-day.
But during Christmas week, it was holiday like the rest; the
sound of a banjo, accompanied by lively singing, came from
a cabin not far from Maum Guinea's; the ambitious young

performer having it all his own way, now Uncle Zip had been laid up by that unfortunate mistake which had caused him to be treated no better than a coon.

"He Zip Coon now, sure 'nuff," said one darkey, shaking with laughter when he heard of the mistake; "guess he won't want to sing 'Cooney in de holler,' any more—he holler loud 'nuff hisself,"—at which piece of humor all his hearers ya-yahed in their soft, hearty way. A negro can laugh as easily as he can breathe; and as for his wit, he has not arrived at that stage of development, including the morose, envious, analytic, comparative, sarcastic and irreverent, in which wit comes into play. A negro is seldom witty—it is only the gold-colored descendants, infused with the tingling sharpness of the alien blood, who are ever known to be more than good-naturedly humorous.

"He's had honey on his hoe-cake ever since frost come," added another. "Sarved him right, setting up in his bee-tree like a bar', so cross and selfish."

"Woll, he won't eat no more *dat* honey, boys; 'kase I staid behind las' night, and took a bucket and brought it all 'way; we'll have a time wid dat honey dis berry arternoon. Git my ole woman to bake us lots o' cake, and we'll jis' have a feas'—no mistake."

The sound of the banjo drew out the indolent creatures from their late breakfasts; woolly heads were thrust out of doors to see what kind of a day it was going to be, and little groups gathered about on the fences and the steps of the houses. Colonel Fairfax's plantation was considered a model by his neighbors; among other things, the negro-quarters were arranged with more comfort and system than was common. The cabins, all of a size, and uniform in appearance, were ranged down either side of a broad alley, with little garden-patches in the rear, and the alley itself serving as

play-ground for the children, and hall-of-assembly for the
whole population, during their hours of social recreation.

The banjo-player sat on the steps before the door of one
of these huts, with an admiring crowd about him, singing
in a rich voice, which it was a pleasure to listen to—

John, come down in de holler,
Oh, work and talk and holler,
Oh, John, come down in de holler,
I'm gwine away to-morrow.
                    Oh, John, etc.
I'm gwine away to marry,
                    Oh, John, etc.
Get my cloves in order,
                    Oh, John, etc.
I's gwine away to-morrow,
                    Oh, John, etc.
Oh, work and talk and holler,
                    Oh, John, etc.
Massa guv me doller,
                    Oh, John, etc.
Don't cry yer eyes out, honey,
                    Oh, John, etc.
I'm gwine to get some money,
                    Oh, John, etc.
But I'll come back to-morrow,
                    Oh, John, etc.
So work and talk and holler,
                    Oh, John, etc.
Work all day and Sunday,
                    Oh, John, etc.
Massa get de money,
                    Oh, John, etc.
Don' cry yerself to def,
                    Oh, John, etc.
So fare-you-well, my honey,
                    Oh, John, etc.

The words of this melody were certainly not marvelous
for wit or elegance, but they were characteristic, and the
music was delightful—when half-a-dozen voices joined in the
chorus it was inspiring; to these homely, hard-worked,
monotonous-lived creatures, it was their one great enjoyment

—the one expression of the oriental warmth and sunshine still flowing in the undercurrent of their sluggish blood.

The tinkle of the banjo fell on Hyperion's ear, as the blows of a whip fall. on a naked back; he could not bear the torment; and making his friend Guinea promise to go with him that afternoon to Judge Bell's, he went away into the house to attend his young master, who was just rising after the unusual fatigues of the previous day.

"Heigho," yawned Philip, in dressing-gown and slippers, seating himself before a fire which the chilliness of the day made desirable, "every bone in my body aches. I believe I trudged thirty miles, yesterday; had a splendid day, though! Bring my breakfast to my room, boy; I'm not going down this morning."

"What's the matter with *you?*" he asked, as Hyperion arranged the coffee, toast, ham and eggs upon a little table near him. " *You* had an easy time, old fellow—nothing to do but wait upon the ladies. What's the matter? Has Rose been giving you the mitten?"

"Oh, no, Massa Philip; de trute is, Massa Bell is talkin' of—of—" his lip quivered and his voice choked up so that he could go no farther.

"What is he talking of?" queried the young gentleman, his curiosity aroused.

"Of sellin' Rose," sobbed Hyperion—and breaking completely down, he cried like a child.

"Whew!" said Philip, with a long whistle, "that *is* bad!" The "institution" under which he had grown up had not so murdered all natural sympathy in him, but that he, young man and lover as he was, felt a passing fellow-feeling for the distressed mulatto "boy."

"Oh, I guess that can't be so," he added, presently, sipping his coffee, "she's been in the family so many years. Miss

Virginia can't spare her. I don't see what Judge Bell should
be wanting to sell Rose, for ; he can well afford to keep her,
and she's a good, obedient girl."

"Dat New Orleans gentleum offer a big price for Rose,
massa."

"Aha! that's it, is it? Too bad! too bad! Ought to be
ashamed of himself!"

He went on with his breakfast, and seeing with how little
spirit his *valet* was performing his light duties, he said, gayly :

"Never mind, boy, 'there's as good fish in the sea as ever
was caught.' If they send Rose away, I'll keep a sharp look-
out for some other pretty girl, that will suit you just as well."

"Don't want no oder," was the trembling reply.

It was evident that Philip Fairfax, with all his good
feeling—his young, generous nature—did not regard the fact
of a slave losing the object of his affection, and losing her in
such a way too, in the same light which he would have
viewed it, if somebody had come along and forced from *him*
his right and title to the heart and hand of a certain fair
young girl, who was dreaming of him at that hour, even with
her prayer-book open before her. In the eyes of hard
masters, slaves are brutes, to be worked as much as will
"pay," like their horses and mules ; in the eyes of kind
masters, they are, at best, a sort of children, to be looked
after and made to do their tasks. Philip was kind ; he
would have been sorry if his pet "boy" had complained of
the toothache, or the loss of some trifling treasure ; he was
sorry for him now ; but he did not take his case to heart, and
judge it as he would have done his own—how could he? If
he had done so, he would have pulled the key-stone from the
foundation of the whole splendid theory of slavery.

"Oh, massa," pleaded the *valet*, throwing himself upon the
indulgence to which he was accustomed, when Philip had

finished his repast, and had fallen to whistling softly, looking out the window, and thinking about his betrothed, "won't you speak to Miss Virginny about Rose, yerself?"

"Yes, yes, I'll speak to her, if that'll satisfy you. But what good will it do? It isn't likely Miss Virginia will have much to say about it. Of course she will want to keep her dressing-maid, if it's possible. She'll coax her bear of a papa sweetly, without any asking, I'll warrant you. But if he's bound to make a good bargain, *I* can't help it, Hyperion, my boy. It's *my* policy to be as agreeable as possible just at present; it wouldn't look well for me to presume to interfere in family matters, already; don't you see? ha! ha!"—and he laughed softly.

This was too reasonable to be denied; and it was not the province of a slave to argue with his master—so Hyperion held his peace.

Late in the afternoon he and Maum Guinea set out for the Bell plantation. He had promised Rose to visit her, Sabbath evening. Sophy, the housekeeper, whom we have before mentioned, had invited both them and Maum Guinea to take tea with her, in her kitchen; it was her turn to "treat," she said; they had accepted her invitation with alacrity, knowing they should have a good time; for Sophy was only inferior to Maum Guinea herself, in the art of cooking, and being stewardess of the establishment, she could afford to give them a fine supper upon so important an occasion as Christmas week.

As they knocked at Sophy's door, the young man's heart sunk and felt cold within him. He had not seen Rose since this awful shadow had fallen between them; he did not know whether she was yet apprised of her danger; he did not know, he almost feared, that the girl might want to accept of the brilliant lot in store for her, as the favored slave of so wealthy and handsome a man, with whom she could lead a

life of idleness, and be decked out in all the finery her tropic
taste coveted.   Yes, Rose herself might choose it!   All kinds
of fears pressed upon him, until he felt sinking, and leaned
against the casement for support.

It was his affianced herself who opened the door.   She
knew they would come to Sophy's first, and she was already
there, waiting them.   How handsome she looked!   So gay,
so happy, so proud—for she was dressed in her best, and her
mistress had given a new brooch for a holiday present—a
great, gold brooch, with a bit of paste-brilliant in the center
which sparkled with the rise and fall of her shapely breast.

She knew she was looking well; her lover almost shrunk
before the blaze of her beauty; there was just that dash of
coquetry, that bewitching coolness, showing through sunny
breadths of smiles, which a handsome woman can afford to
assume, and which it requires no refinement of schools to
teach her—it is her nature, white or black, rich or poor.

"She don'no nuffin 'bout it yet, dat's clar," whispered Maum
Guinea, in an aside as they entered, "and don't you tell her
any t'ing just now.   You and she be as happy as yer can,
once more, anyhow; and perhaps it'll all be right yit.   I'll
go out and speak to Massa Bell w'en I gets a good chance."

Happy!   Yes, even with all that dark doubt of the future,
the mulatto-man experienced a perhaps even more intense
pleasure in the society of the woman he loved; his eyes
followed every movement of her lithe form; he smiled at all
she did and said; and if he did not talk much, Rose knew
that he felt much, for she read the language of his eyes.

It was so pleasant in Sophy's large, light kitchen.   She
had invited Johnson, and two or three others, also; her
guests were sitting about, laughing and talking so naturally,
that Hyperion began to feel as if he had had a bad dream,
and was just waking up to his every-day experience.

The table was drawn out in the middle of the floor, and a coarse white cloth covered up all marks of its uses in cooking; two or three kinds of sweetmeats, in glass dishes, graced the board; and a plate of butter, a luxury at the South. A turkey was basting before the fire, and the odor of white-flour biscuits came from the bake-kettle on the hearth, blending with the matchless fragrance of coffee; these, with the sweet potatoes roasting in the ashes, were to make a supper worthy of the times, and all the more keenly relished, since it could be enjoyed but at one portion of the year.

It was already well understood among their friends that Rose and Hyperion were "engaged," and were to be married if their owners would allow. With jest and merriment they were placed side by side at the table. The unusually luxurious fare, and the natural good-humor of the company, made the occasion one of great delight. Even Maum Guinea was cheerful, hoping in her heart for the best. Rose found the "merrythought," or, as they called it, the "wish-bone," on her plate; and she and her lover made their wish, pulling the bone apart to decide whose wish was to be fulfilled.

"I've won—I've won!" cried Rose, gayly, while her companion's hand fell heavily down, and his face wore a look of disappointment at which all the young people laughed.

He did, indeed, feel deeply disappointed; for he was not above the superstitions of his people, and placed great faith in all such matters as this. What he had wished for may be easily inferred.

"What did you ask fur, Rose?" queried one of the party.

"Oh, I ain't goin' to tell, 'cause if I do, I shan't get it. It breaks de charm."

"Oh, do tell! you'll get it, all de same."

"No, I shan't. Mebbe I wished for a silk dress to wear wid my new breas'-pin, and mebbe I didn't. I shan't tell."

Another pang shot through her lover's heart at these laughing words. She had wished for a silk dress, the foolish, giddy thing, and perhaps she would have one sooner than she expected.

After supper, Maum Guinea slipped out, and was absent half an hour, while the rest of the company sat about, laughing and singing, the girls helping their hostess to wash up the dishes and put the room to rights. The work was all finished, and the party gathered about the firelight in a half-circle, when Maum Guinea returned.

"He's partly promised—I'm pretty sartain it'll be right," she whispered in answer to the mute question in Hyperion's eyes.

The words pierced through him, like arrows of sunshine, with a sharp joy. He had so much confidence in the woman that he felt almost free from apprehension; he squeezed Rose's hand, so that she cried out, to the jest and amusement of the rest; he immediately began to talk, to tell funny stories, and to sing his best songs in his "happiest manner." Rose grew very proud of him, he was so witty, such a splendid singer— her eyes glanced triumphantly from him to the company, as much as to ask, "Who has such a nice young man as I has?"

When he had exhausted his sudden flow of jollity, the visitors began to press Sophy for the story she had partly promised them. She seemed reluctant, but finally said:

"Woll, woll, we'll draw cuts—and if it falls to me, I'll tell my story."

To their satisfaction the lot fell to her.

"Suthin about yerself, you know—suthin true, the way we agreed."

"If I tell you any thing 'bout myself, you must all promise to nebber, nebber tell to noboddy what you hear in dis room to-night."

"Oh, we won't nebber tell," they exclaimed, eagerly, their eyes beginning to expand with curiosity, and a kind of delicious terror of they knew not what.

"You mus' promise on de Bible," she said, rising and bringing an old, well-worn copy of the New Testament. "'Cause I's never told dis story afore, and if you should let it out, you might git me into trouble."

Each one laid his hand on the book, and promised not to tell, and then they gathered closer, almost trembling with eagerness to hear a story so important that it must be kept such a profound secret.

"Dar'll be some terrible things in it; but you musn't get scar't. It's passed and gone now, w'atever it is. Set up clost, fer I mus' speak low. Wouldn' like to be oberheard, nohow."

In a kind of half-whisper, enough in itself to make what she said impressive, and which chilled through her susceptible audience like a breath of north wind, Sophy began her story :

"I was born in Southampton county, in ole Virginny; I lived on massa's plantation all de time; I was kind of kitchen-girl, and done chores, and learned to cook, and w'en I was fifteen I was married. Me and my man, we had a cabin of our own, and lived togedder berry comfortable. Massa's farm was a tobacky farm. My man's name was Nelson. He was good to me, and t'ought mighty sight o' me, and w'en I had my fust baby—laws ! he was de tickledest and de most sot-up nigger you eber saw. Ah, Lord-a-mighty, don' I recolleck dat yit ?

"He was good to me ; but somehow anodder he got into trouble wid oberseer purty often ; I 'spect he was sometimes a little sassy. You knows some hosses and oxen dey hab to be drove, and whipped, and scolded more'n oders, to make

'em go de ways dey's wanted—dey's kind o' stubborn.
Woll, so it was wid Nelson. I 'spect he'd got some notion
in his head 'bout not liking to be ordered 'roun' so; and our
)berseer was mighty cross man, allers knocking niggers
about.

"One day, w'en my baby was 'bout t'ree months ole, I'd
got done de work at de house; 'twas summer ebening, and
warm, and I'd come home to cook my man's supper, and
nuss my baby. Troo' de day I hab to leave my young'un
wid all de rest, in care of old brack woman too ole to do
much work. Dey keep de babies in a kind o' pen, w'ere dey
could crawl 'round widout much tendin'—I could go and
nuss it once in a w'ile—woll, I come here at night, and got
his supper ready for him, and den sot down in de door to
play wid my little one. I felt berry nice dat time, 'kase de
head-cook had gib me piece of cold chicken and rice-pudding
for my man, for helpin' her right smart wid de big dinner fer
company: and I was t'inking w'at a treat it would be to
Nelson. But Nelson didn' come home. He usually got
home by dark, summer days; but de clocks strike nine, ten,
and he didn' come. I began to stop singing, and to feel drefful
oppressed 'bout breathing. I t'ought mebbe it was because
de night was so warm. Little Sam was soun' asleep, so I
laid him down on de bed, and started off to look for my
husband. Suthin took me right straight to de corn-house;
and as I came clost to it, I hearn somebody groanin'. I
knew 'twas him, and I flew and tore open de door, and dar
he .ay. De oberseer had gib him awful whipping—awful!
and den, here de weather was so warm, he'd jist turn de salt
and-water over his back, and let him lay.

"I helped him up and got him home; he didn't eat no
cold chicken nor no rice puddin' dat night. Massa scold de
oberseer for whippin' Nelson so hard, 'kase he was one of

his best hands, and he couldn't go to work ag'in fer 'most two weeks. After dat he let my husband alone fer a long time; but dar wasn't any good feeling between de two. I use to beg Nelson not to aggrawate him, 'cause he was a bad-tempered man, anyhow, and he wouldn't gain nothing but blows and cusses by going contrawise to him; but he was spunky too, Nelson was, and once-and-a-while de fire would blaze up dat he tried so hard fer to keep down. I knew he did try, for *my* sake, 'cause I begged him so hard.

"Our Sam was a beautiful pickaninny: so round, and fat, and shiny, and so full of fun. W'en he got big enough to roll around and kick, to laugh, and, bym-bye, to holler ' Pop, Pop!' w'en his fadder come home, den Nelson grew more happy-like. He lubbed his boy so much, he forgot his bad feelings tow'd de oberseer; he didn't set no more of ebenings glooming over de whipping he got. Massa liked him berry much, 'kase Nelson had more sense'n most niggers, and he use to get him to do all de pertikeler jobs 'bout de farm. Sometimes he'd gib him few shillings silber; den Nelson he'd buy suthin for his boy, and he got him a red calico frock— real turkey calico—the purtiest you eber see.

"One day I was up to de house wid Sam; Nelson was pickin tobacky in de field. Sam was goin' on two year old, and use to play about de yard or kitchen w'ile I was working 'round. I'd jist dropped de taters I was peeling, and run out to see w'at he was doing, w'en I met massa and a strange gemman walking through de yard, and dey stopped to look at my boy, and dey praised him up wonderful. He had on his red dress, and I wan't surprised dat dey t'ought him a right smart, purty chile; but I didn't t'ink notting farder, for 'tain't often, yer know, dat masters sell little chil'ren 'way from der mudders. Bym-bye I heard de gemman say, kind of low:

" ' I'll give you five hundred for him—not a cent more.' ,

" My heart jumped right up in my mouf; I went and picked my boy up, and stood a-looking at 'em, wild-like.

" ' Sophy,' says massa, kind of laughin', but shamed-like, 'how'd you like to give up your boy to this nice gemman here ? He'd be took good care of—jest as good as you could give him.'

· " ' Oh, massa !' dat was ebery word I could say; but I didn't belieb him den, 'kase he was a kind of laughin', and I t'ought he was tryin' me for a joke.

" ' I've partly promised him to dis gemman ; so you may wash him up and get him ready, for he's got to leab in two hours, in de stage.'

" ' Oh, massa, I can't ! I can't !'—I kind of screamed it out, which made him a little angry, for he spoke more sharp.

" ' Pshaw !' says he, ' don't be foolish, Sophy. He'll be well treated. You see, dis gemman has got a girl has lost her baby, and she wants anodder, and she'll be extra kind to it. *You'll* hab anodder in a month or two, and den you won't mind de loss of dis so much,' and he laughed. ' One'll be 'nuff for you to take care of; don't be selfish, my girl. Go and get de boy ready, and bring him back here ; and be spry 'bout it—ain't no time to spare. I'll show you de girl as is to keep him, and you'll see she's a nice pusson.'

" ' Can't I take him down to de field to bid his pop good-bye ?' I asked.

" ' Dar won't be time ; besides, it'll only make you both feel wuss. W'en your oder baby is born, you won't miss dis. Come, Sophy, be spry.'

" I went to my cabin wid my boy. I tried to get out a little apron to put on him, and to wash his face and hands. But I was too weak ; I jist staggered to de bed, and set down and cried ober him, and kissed him. T'ree, four times I tried to get up, for I knew massa would be awful mad; but I *couldn't*, and dar I sot w'en he come after us.

" ' W'y didn't you bring him up to de house? De stage is going by in a few minutes. You don't behave yourself berry well, Sophy,' says he, and he takes my boy out of my arms, and walks out of de room wid him—and dat's de last I eber see of Sam.

" I sot dar, kind of stupid; and bym-bye I heerd de stage-coach coming 'long de road, and it stopped afore de house. I tried to get up, but I was too weak. Den, w'en it started on again, I flew out like a wild creature, and up de lane to de gate, jes' in time to see it whirlin' ober de hill—and dat was all. I guess I kind of fainted, till I come to, and heerd old Bess, de head-cook speaking to me, and she put her arm round me and lifted me up.

" 'Nebber mind,' says she, ' you'll get use to it.' *I's* had five sold away, in my time. Come, I'll go back to your cabin wid you. I's got a little sperits here will rewive you up.'

" ' Nelson ! Nelson !' was all I said.

" ' Yis, he'll take it harder dan most men would. But he'll get ober it. Don' fret, honey. Eberybody has trouble. Las' year, massa hisself had a purty little girl die ; your baby ain't dead ; cheer up, honey.'

" ' I wish it was dead,' I muttered.

" She took me in de house and made me drink some brandy, and staid wid me as long as she could, till she hed to go back and get supper. Den I sat alone, t'inking what Nelson would say w'en he came in, and his boy gone. It didn't 'pear to me as if 'twas so ; I'd git up and look in de bed, see if Sam wasn't dar, fast asleep—den I set down ag'in, and wisk my husband nebber would come home.

" I heerd him comin' along, whistlin', and he puts his head in de door, and calls out :

" ' Sam ! Sam ! here's poppy cotched a squirrel in de fence.
Come, Sam !' Den he looked at me, and says he, ' Is he
asleep ?'—den, for de fust time, I bust out a-cryin', and he let
de squirrel drop, and looks round sharp, and says : ' W'at's
happened ?—is de boy hurt ?'

" ' Oh, Nelson, massa's sold him, and dey's took him far
away.'

" He dropped down on de step 'sif he was shot, and
nebber spoke. I crawled up to him and leaned my head on
his shoulder, and dar we sot 'most all night. He didn't say
much—he wasn't no great talker no time—and all he t'ought
not eben I could tell. But arter dat he was changed berry
much. He was so silent and stubborn, I was almost 'fraid
of him ; but he did his work well—nobody complained of
him.

" Well, w'en my next baby come along, I felt a little happier. It was a boy too, and I 'spected Nelson would get over
his trouble, and take to de new pickaninny. He did. He
was softer to it dan he'd eber been to Sam ; he never spanked
it, nor got fretted wid it. But de did'nt seem to play wid it
so much, and he nebber come home whistlin'—ef I heerd him
whistlin' far off, w'en he turned into de lane he allers stopped.
'Peared like as if he was allers afraid, w'en he opened de
door, he shouldn't see no pickaninny dar. He was still, and
hard-working, so dat eben dat ugly oberseer couldn't find
much fault wid him.

" Dan was a likely boy, too—we called our second, Dan'l,
after de good man in de Bible, who was took up from de
den of lions, as de hymn says—jist as pert and healthy as
little Sam had been. He was a favorite wid white and brack
folks, jist as bright as a dollar, and so full of funny tricks.
We tried not to set our hearts on him, for he'd be sold
away too ; but it 'peared as if de harder we tried not to, de

closter he grew to us. We knew de smartest chil'ren sold de fust.

"Well, frien's, Dan'l was spared to us till he was nigh six years old; and den massa had a bad crop, and a hard time, and he was getting more slaves dan he could 'ford to keep and Dan was sold, wid a hull lot more, large and small.

"I asked massa to sell us 'long wid our child; but he so so much store by Nelson, he didn't want to part wid him; 'sides, de cook was gettin' ole, and I mos'ly took her place. So our boy went away, and we nebber knew whar, nor w'edder he be dead or libing now.

"Massa sot great store by Nelson, and it was sorry times for massa dat he did. Berry fine to like him, 'kase he honest and work hard; but he was a-playin' wid fire, w'en he sole *his* chil'ren away. My man wasn' like some niggers; he couldn' b'ar everyt'ing, and nebber seem to feel it. He couldn't laugh and sing, and take t'ings easy, no matter what happen. He didn' like knocks and whippins, and raising chil'ren for market, like as they was chickens and pigs.

"I wonder if dar's anybody 'round?" continued the story-teller, after a moment's pause. "Set up closter, my frien's, and fust let me look out a minit,"—and she went to the door, peered forth into the darkness, returned, and resumed her narrative in a half-whisper:

"Not long after Dan was gone from us, Nelson begun to go out nights. He'd steal away after I was in bed, and wouldn't come in, sometimes, till nigh daylight. If I asked him whar he was, sometimes he'd say, huntin' coons; and ag'in, fishing; but he never brought no fish home, and I didn't believe him. 'Peared to me dar was suthin pertikeler on his mind, but he wouldn't tell me what it was. Sometimes, when de oberseer had gib him a kick or a blow, he'd speak of it at night, and laugh in such a strange way, it

made my flesh creep. I didn't know what to make of Nelson. Dough he was my own husband, and good to me, and
we'd bin faithful to each oder, and lubbed each oder better'n
most men and wives, I didn' understan' him, in dose times.
But I knew he was troubled, and I lubbed him all de more.
I knew he had only me, now Dan'l was gone, for we'd had no
more chil'ren, and I tried to be a good wife to him. I nebber
scolded him for staying out, but tried to get him as good
breakfast as I could; and I didn't pry into his business, only
to say dat I wish I knew what was on his mind, 'kase I
might comfort him. Den he'd shake his head, and say I
shall done know all when de right time come.

"T'ings go on dis way five or six months. One Sunnay
he go ober to neighbor's farm, in de woods, to have a fine
time, roasting a pig, wid some der hands. De niggers all
like barbecues, and I was glad he was going—t'ought 'twould
cheer him up a little. So he starts off a little 'fore noon,
and 'twas two o'clock at night when de door opens, and my
husband speaks in a whisper, telling me to get up and dress myself, and be ready, ' for mighty t'ings are to be done in de land.'

"Scar't and trembling, I got out and slipped on my frock,
not knowing but de judgment-day of de Lord was at hand.
W'en I was dressed, he come in, and six men wid him. De
moon was just going down, and shone in de little square
window, so I could see der faces. Dey looked awful—all
scowling, and der eyes burning: and dey had guns and big
knifes. Nelson had de big butcher-knife w'ich I used in cooking, sharpened up. I begun to cry and pray, when one nigger.
I knowed him well—'twas Nat Turner, over to Travis', das
all de brack folks t'ought was a prophet—hushed me up.
Did yer eber hear of Nat Turner? Yis, Ginny, *you* has—I
see it in yer face. Nat Turner, he spoke in a clear, awful
whisper, dat went straight tru' me, and he says: ' Do work

of de Lord begins dis night. I've seen it in de heavens--I've read de signs of de times : dar's been wonders in de sky, and drops of blood on de corn. De Holy Spirit has bid me arise, and prepare myself. I am to slay mine enemies wid der own weapons; de black spirits contended wid de white in de heabens, and I see, de blacks victorious. Cheer up, woman. Your chil'ren shall no longer be sold from your bosom, nor your husband lashed at de whipping-post. I am come to repay. "Vengeance is mine, I will repay," saith the Lord.' Oh, Lord-a-mighty ! he looked so turrible when he was a-talking; he said many more things, which I can't tell you as he said 'em. 'De Savior has ordered it, dat I be de liberator of my people—dat I lift 'em out of de hand of de oppressor. Dis night, we will begin His work. Not one white man, woman or chile, will we leave alive in South ampton county ; we will conquer it, as did Washington in de Rebolution. W'en de Lord say unto us, "Smite !" den will we smite. We will not torment 'em wid de scourge, or wid fire, nor defile der women, as dey have done wid ours. But we will slay dem utterly, and consume dem from off de face of de yearth.'

" ' Oh, Nelson,' said I, clinging to him, as dey begun to go out, for de moon was sinkin', and dey were in haste to be off, ' w'atever you do to massa and missus, don't kill little Katie.'

" ' Yes, we must not spare one—not one—not de baby at its mammy's breast,' he said, shaking my hand berry hard. ' Good-bye, Sophy. We'll be back after you, w'en it's all ober. Keep quiet. Don't let on you know anyt'ing. You shall be rich and happy—no more a slave. If de worst comes to de worst, fly to de Dismal Swamp. Dar will be frien's dar.'

"I still hung on to him. ' Don't murder Katie,' I whis-pered, ' I love her.'

"'So do I,' said he, 'but de Lord's work must be done.'

"I was just like ice, wid fright and horror. When dey went out, I stood shivering in de dark. Purty soon, I t'ought I heerd a scream, but I wasn't certain; den, in a few minutes more, I heerd 'em go to de stables and take out all de horses, and ride away. I darsn't stir, till mornin'; den, wid de first light, I heerd old Dinah screeching wild and loud, and going out, I met her coming from de house, wringing her hands, and her eyes sticking out. 'Come! come!' she says; Oh, Lord-a-mercy! Oh, Lord-a-mercy!' I knew already, but I kept still, and run after her into de house. Dar, just dragged from der beds, in dêr night-clo'es, was massa and missus, stone dead, der throats cut, like as dey were pigs, and de carpet soaked full of blood. I jist gib one look, and run into de little bedroom off deyr's, war I knew Miss Katie slept. Oh, Christ! I see it now! I nebber shall forget it! Ebery night, w'en I wake up in de dark, I see her, jest as I see her den—dat beautiful chile—lying in her purty bed, murdered—her dimpling t'roat all cut straight across, and de blood gluing her shining curls to her neck and check. She was so sweet and kind, Katie was, and only ten years ole. She was like my own pickaninnies to me. She'd allers been fond of me, 'kase I took care of her w'en she was baby, de first year I was married. Dar she lay, de innocent—no mudder, no fadder, to straighten her little limbs, and wash dat cruel blood away. I sot down on de edge of de bed, and held her hand, and cried ober it, and kissed her poor little face. De whole plantation was awake, and takin' on awful. Most of de men had jined de insurrectioners, and gone off, and de women was hollerin' and prayin'. De oberseer was dead too, and I felt glad when I heard it. But I couldn't feel glad when I looked at little Katie. I t'ought over how I felt when I found my husband, most killed with whipping, and de salt brine on his bleeding back—w'en I heard de stage-coach rumble away over de hill wid my little Sam—w'en Dan'l was took away—w'en I had been flogged myself—I t'ought of all our wrongs and hardships, and I couldn't blame my husband—I knew he b'lieved he was doin' de Lord's work—but I wished dey had spared dear Katie.

"Dar was an awful time after dat," continued the narrator, her voice rising, but still in a whisper, high and sharp. "Oh dar was an awful time All Mr. Travis' family was mur dered too; and de're niggers joined ours, and dey rode on to de next plantation; dar dey killed all de white people, and got more help, and dey went 'round about to ebery house, all night, all day, all next night, all next day—for eight-and- forty hours de work went on. At ebery place de slaves rose up, and aided dem; they murdered de're own masters and missuses, and be berry chil'ren dey played wid. Dey b'lieved Nat Turner was a prophet, and de time of der deliverance was at hand. Yes, dey b'lieved it. Dey obeyed him, w'at he told 'em. All de dark spots slaves hide 'way in de're hearts, and say nuthin', come to light den—all de fires break tru' de ashes den, and blaze up turrible. Do you t'ink it was right, my frien's?"

"Yes," said Hyperion.

"No," said Rose.

"Woll, de most of 'em t'ought it was right, w'edder it were, or not. Liberty is sweet, even to poor brack slave— and in Virginny dar's plenty of white blood mixed wid ours, you all know. Dey murdered der own fadders, der own brudders and sisters, no doubt, many times; but w'at were dese, more dan oders, 'cept to make 'em feel more spiteful.

"We waited in fear and trembling; praying and crying we waited. Oh, dose were awful days!—awful for de poor white women and chil'ren, dat had fled for de're lives, w'en

dey heerd w'at was going on. Dey were hid in de woods,
night and day. I saw 'em myself, lots of em, w'en I went
off to hear what I could hear. I pitied 'em—more'n dey'd
ever pitied *me*. I took meat and bread to some dat were in
Travis' woods, wid de're chil'ren most starved.

"I begun to t'ink that Turner was sure 'nuff a prophet—dat
new times was coming for poor brack people; I begun to
dream of undependence and liberty, such as had been our
masters', and if it hadn't been for little Katie, I'd have felt
joyful enough to sing hymns of triumph. I could sew, and I
took one of her white dresses and made her a little shroud,
and put her in a box—for nobody come to bury the dead, and
we women dug a grave and put her in. Some de foolish
nigger-girls dey help derselves to missus' jewelry and fine
clothes, and put 'em on, and dance and cut up; but I made
'em put 'em back and behave derselves—leastwise, till dey
heard how matters was going.

"So we waited. At night we would see ghosts and hear
turrible cries. Some of us didn't dar' to go near de house,
'kase of de corpses dar. And I, after little Katie was buried,
didn't want to go nigh. De dead bodies begun to corrupt,
for 'twas hot August weather; but we women-folks couldn't
bury 'em. So we waited—Oh, Lord-a-mighty, yes!

"'Twas four nights now, and I was lying awake in my
cabin, thinking over things so fast I couldn' sleep, and the
latch raised softly and Nelson come in. I was so 'fraid of
sperits, and awful things, I'd kept my lamp a-burning, and I
could see how tired and sad he looked.

"'It's all up, I'm afeard,' he said, in answer to my first
question. 'We got along well enough, till they stopped agin
our will, at Parker's—we ought to have pushed on to the
village before they heerd the news there; but we didn't. The
whites got after us. They've scattered us, now. I come

back here, in hopes of finding Nat and getting wid him again
—I'd have some hopes, if I could get wid him.'

" ' Oh, Nelson, what'll we do ?' I cried; but he looked so
worn and fagged, I wouldn't tell him how heavy my heart
was; I sot some milk and potatoes on the table, and he eat
like a starving man.

" ' Sophy, I must go,' says he, as soon as he'd done eating.

" I begged him to let me go wid him, w'atever happened ;
but he wouldn't hear to it den ; he said I'd be a drawback,
'kase dey might get wid Nat, and get to fightin' de whites
ag'in, and den women-folks would be in de way.

" ' You jest hold your tongue, and don't let on dat you
ever knowed what was goin' on ; and you won't be harmed,'
says he. 'If I don't get back for you—if it's a failure after
all, and de Lord widholds His help—den, if you don' hear
from me, jest wait your chance, ef you have to wait a year,
and run away he fus' opportunity, and make your way to de
Dismal Swamp—it's only twenty-five miles from here, and
you'll find frien's, dar !'

" He wrung my hand most off, and I clung to him like a
burr, but he broke away, and went out into de night, and I
crept back into bed to purtend to sleep, as if nothin' had happened. De next day many white men rode up to de house,
all armed wid swords, pistols and guns ; and dey buried
massa and missus, and dey dragged off every colored man dar
was, w'at had nothin' to do wid de troubles at all.

" After that, dar was white men all de time riding ober de
country, and soldiers 'way from Norfolk and Richmond, dey
come to help put down de blacks. Oh, Lord-a-mercy ! dem
was awful times !

" Dey done and gone and butchered our people widout
judge or jury—hundreds and hundreds was shot, which was
a mussiful death, quick over But shooting was too good for

any but de innocent—dem dey suspected as having **had any-t'ing** to do wid de insurrectioners, dey hanged, and whipped, and burned—yes, burned—oh, Lord !" here the story-teller drew in her breath with a strange, inward gurgle and shriek, which made every one of her auditory jump to their feet and sink back again.

"Dey burned Nelson," she continued, after several moments of silence. "I'll tell you how 'twas. You see dey came, great lot o' white folks one day, and dey took me, and dey tell me my husband was arrested, and in Jerusalem jail ; and dey say if I 'fess w'edder he was guilty or not, and tell all I know 'bout Nat Turner, dey wouldn' punish me, dey'd let me be in peace—but if I didn' tell every word I knowed, dey would whip me till I couldn't stand. I tol' 'em, I shouldn' say nothin' agin my own husband, and I didn' know nothin' 'bout Nat Turner—I'd never see'd him but once, and I didn' know nothing 'bout him, good or bad. I knew w'at was comin', and I prayed deep and still to de Lord above to pity me ; but I wouldn' tell on Nelson. Dey stripped me stark naked, tied me up, and whipped me till I was most dead ; but I wouldn't 'fess. I fainted away, and dey throw pickle on me, and left me ; and next day dey come back and tie me up ag'in and whip me on my raw back, and den dey turn me round and whip me t'odder side, till I was raw all round. I kin show you de scars, dey're on my breast, dey're on my back. But my lips was shut, only I screamed at fust ; till I got beyond dat, and passed away to anodder world—a hell of misery, where it 'peared to me I'd lived a hundred years, wid devils yelling 'round me, and red-hot fire a falling on me all de time. So at last dey give me up, 'kase dey t'ought I was dead anyhow. But I come to ; de old cook, who was so ole and foolish dey let her alone, she nussed me up ; and dar I lay, day arter day, so sore I couldn' stir, wondering what

dey'd done wid Nelson. It 'peared as if de wish to hear 'bout
him, to walk to de village and see him, if he was still in jail,
gib me strength to get well. It was t'ree weeks before I
could crawl; den I set out, and crept along as best I could;
it was fifteen miles to Jerusalem, whar de jail and court-
house was, and it took me nigh two days to get dar. I asked
de jailer let me see my husband; he swore at me, and giving
me a kick, told me to 'cl'ar out! I'd never see him
again, till I see him in h—!' I asked him w'at dey did wid
him; he wouldn' tell me, but I found out afterwards, one
way and 'nodder, dough some folks was 'human enough not
to want to let me know. Fust dey tried to make him 'fess,
as dey did me, by flogging. Dey tied his han's and feet, and
bent his knees up to his shoul'ers and fastened dem wid a
stick; den dey rolled him on de floor like as he was a bar'l,
and dey lashed him more'n two hundred times. W'at you
s'pose he t'ought of? S'pose he t'ought of Sam and Dan'l,
s'pose he t'ought of blows and kicks—woll, woll! it's over
now, nigh onto thirty year. Dey kept him in jail 'bout
two weeks; and he had his trial; and dey proved on him,
dat he was a ring-leader—dat he was Prophet Nat's right-
hand man, and dey was going to hang him; but de mob got
hold of him, and dragged him from de officers, and swore
hanging was too good for him—and so—that's what become
of Nelson!

　　"'Spect I was kind o' crazy-like for a w'ile—next thing
I knew, I was lyin' on little Katie's grave. Ole cook found
me, and made me eat; and in two or t'ree days a change
come ober me—I was kind o' lifted up out o' my misery.
It come into my head dat Nat Turner was in de woods
clost by, and dat he would starve to def. You see dey
hadn't found him yet, and dar was hundreds a lookin' for
him. De whole country was in a trimble; women couldn't

sleep a-nights, nor men lay down der guns, till Prophet Nat
was found.

"It come. into my mind to carry him food, and I made a
pocket in my dress, and put in bread and 'taters, and went
a-wanderin' roun' night and day, purtendin' I was getting
yerbs and fire-wood. Dar was lots of white folks, eberywhar
keeping watch, all de time, on ebery road, and in de woods.
Once I heard a whisper, just a short piece off—it was daytime, den, and de whisper called me—' Sophy !' and I looked
sharp and saw a man's face, peering out of de ground, as it
were, and I see in a minit it was Nat Turner's, and I answered
him low-like—purtending to pick up sticks ! 'W'at is it, Nat ?
I see ye—can I help you any ?' And he answers back—' Come
to-night, and bring me food—I'm starving—don't speak now,
pass on.' So dat night, I went ag'in, berry cautious, and I
round him, whar he'd dug a hole beside a log, and crawled in,
and hid de place wid leaves and bushes, and I gib him suthin
to eat, and told him what had happened to Nelson, and all
de news I could—and he tol' me if I ever see his wife, to tell
her 'bout him'; and I darsn't stay but a minit, for de woods
was full of men, night and day. In dis way, I brought him
food two, t'ree weeks; once I went, and he was gone.. Nex'
day I heard, he'd been taken, and was in prison. Den we
was told he had been seen, and driven out, but had escaped.
Ten days later, dey rea'ly cotched him, and den I knew 'twas
all up wid him. De mob tried to kill him on de way to jail ;
but he had his trial and was hung.

"When he was hung and dead, dar was rejoicing in de
land. De white folks breafed free ag'in. He died like a
man—Oh, he was a prophet, sure 'nuff, Nat Turner was ; but
he couldn' overcome dis yere wicked worl'—de time wasn't
ripe.

"I went to see his wife, arter he was dead. She'd been a

purty cre'tur, young and bright; wid good white blood in her, too. They'd just been whippin' her cruelly to make her give up her husband's papers. I tol' her w'at I'd done for Nat in de woods, and she t'ank me heartily.

"Bruised, and beaten, and sore, no money, no home, no massa or missus, no chil'ren, no husband—woll, I hung 'round de ole cabin a spell, and den I starts for de Dismal Swamp. I couldn' bring myself to hire out to Southampton people, and nobody claimed me yet; dough I heard de relatives of massa and missus was comin to 'tend to de property, which made me hurry off de faster. So I foun' my way to de Dismal Swamp, and I live dar one whole winter, wid a band of run-aways; and de hunters got on our track one day, and dey cotched me, and put me up at auction and sold me—and I'm a libin' yet.

"Sometimes I wonder if I should know Sam or Dan'l if I should meet 'em down in Lousianny—dey's growed big men now. But all I's looking forward to is to lay my poor, scarred body in de yearth, and go up to glory, see if I can find my husband dar."

It was some time after Sophy finished her story before any one felt like speaking. Then they all promised her faithfully never to repeat what they had heard—and slaves, it is proven, can keep a secret.

No one could rally his spirits enough for a song or jest; the young people stole out; Hyperion gave Rose a squeeze, and a kiss which had something so earnest in it, that she neither giggled nor frowned; and he and Maum Guinea turned silently and walked slowly home beneath the eternal smile of the midnight stars.

CHAPTER VIII.

ALLIGATOR STORIES.

" Strange stories they tell,
  By exotic fires,
Of the monsters that dwell .
  Where the pyramid aspires—
Of the uncouth crocodile,
  God of the ancient Nile."

The alligator, swimming in the lonely lagoon,
Strains his dull ear to catch the banjo-tune.
                                NEGRO MELODIES.

PHILIP was hardly sorry, upon second-thought, to hear that Mr. Talfierro was after a slave-girl instead of a wife, for that gentleman was reputed immensely wealthy, and had just that incense of fashion and family hanging about him as would have made him a formidable rival with the parents, if not with the daughter. If Mr. Talfierro had offered to cancel his claims upon Judge Bell, by a proposition for the hand o his child, the old gentleman would hardly have had grace to withstand the temptation of so brilliant an alliance, even if the girl's fancies did seem at present to be fixed upon another object.

But this dangerous person seemed to be so confirmed in his bachelor habits, that not the sweetness and beauty of Virginia had any deeper effect upon him than to draw out his most graceful compliments; and against these she was well fortified by the assurance of somebody else's devotion.

Talking the matter over, that Sunday evening, in a sly nook of the deep-windowed parlors, the lovers came to the conclusion that it would be safe for Philip to ask the father's consent to their engagement, upon the very first opportunity; and this opportunity occurred immediately.

Judge Bell was in the adjoining library, and wanted the help of Philip's younger eyes in finding a certain book upon an upper shelf; and while Mr. Talfierro listened to Virginia's piano in the parlor, her lover "screwed his courage to the sticking point," and very manfully and handsomely, asked the approval of the father to confirm the betrothal.

Contiguous estates, fair fortunes, neighborly proximity, and an amiable, promising young gentleman, were not to be slighted; and the Judge had no objection to offer to the suit of the elated lover.

When Virginia glanced up from her singing, at Philip's return to the parlor, she saw, by his gay smile, that the matter had been favorably settled.

And now, indeed, her heart overflowed with happiness, as a bird's breast overflows with song; she could no longer keep silent the bliss within her; but when she sought her chamber that night, and found Rose waiting to undress her, she confessed to her faithful attendant the blushing story.

"Oh, I am so happy, Rose. We will have a splendid wedding! And you shall be married the same evening. Yes, I've set my heart upon that, as one of the accessories—to have you and Hyperion married at the same time. You see you will belong to the same family then—and it will be so nice— you to wait upon me, and your husband upon my—" here she stopped short, with a vivid blush, and made haste to let down her hair to cover her confusion.

"I's much obliged, missus, I'm sure," answered Rose, look- ing equally happy. "Hope you won't hab *berry* long engage- ment—don't see no use in your putting it off *berry* long."

Virginia laughed at this *naive* betrayal.

"It'll take me some time to get ready, you know. Philip is anxious enough, seeing there is no particular reason for delay; but I'm going to take time to have everything right. One can be married but once, you see—and it ought to be done properly. There will have to be so much sewing, and so many preparations. And I'll have to take a trip to New Orleans, to do my shopping. Oh, won't it be delightful— buying the dress and veil, and ordering bonnets and gloves. I can be ever so extravagant, and papa won't grumble; for it will be the first wedding in the family; and he'll see the propriety of having it in style. We shall have to make our needles fly, Rose; this nice, cool weather is just fit for sewing, and I must have dresses of everything pretty. When I go to New Orleans, I'll buy *you* a wedding-dress, too. What shall it be, Rose ?"

"I don' hardly know—I t'ink I should like a real sweet pink—but I'd rudder ask 'Perion w'at *his* taste is, 'fore I decide for sartain. You's berry kind, Miss Virginny,"—and she cast a gratified look upon the young lady, as she tucked up her hair in its little lawn cap.

Utterly unconscious of the danger which hung over her, the slave-girl curled down on the floor beside her mistress' bed, her usual place of repose, as glad with pleasant anticipations as the heiress whose fair hand seemed to have power to confer so much delight.

Both awoke from their cloudless dreams as only the young and careless can awake. Virginia went to breakfast, to be smiled at more fondly than usual by her mother, and to be slyly rallied by her father, to the discomfiture of her appetite, and the risk of upsetting her cup or meeting with some other table-accident.

There was a great dinner in the afternoon, and music and dancing in the evening. Virginia was so busy with dressing, receiving guests and entertaining them, that she could hardly dispense to Philip his share of favors; which almost made him wish that the holidays were over, and he had her to himself in the usual peace and quietness of those spacious parlors.

Rose, too, was very busy, waiting upon ladies, happy and animated, enjoying the occasion even more heartily than the guests. She was in her element, smoothing out handsome dresses, flying at the bidding of this and that elegant lady, listening to the music in the hall, bringing refreshments to the parlors, and always finding time to admire her own lovely young mistress, and exalt her above all others.

Once, passing through the hall, after dancing had commenced in the evening, she encountered the handsome gentleman from New Orleans, who had been at the Judge's so much within the last few days. There was no one near but the musicians, who could hear nothing but their own accords, and when he paused, she paused too; thinking that he wished some service.

"Rose," said he, with a smile, "did you know you were mine?"

She gave him a startled glance; she did not comprehend him at all, and thinking finally that he was attempting a jest, she smiled too, replying:

"How is dat, Massa Talfierro?"

"I bought you—are you glad? You will have easy times with me," he answered, much delighted with her apparent acquiescence in the bargain, for he was a fine gentleman, of delicate susceptibilities, and hated scenes.

"Laws, massa, might a made a better choice," she replied lightly, and glided by; she was used to be jested with by gentlemen, and the idea did not occur to her that he was in earnest.

Such a fact would require time to make an impression upon her; if she had been told by the Judge himself, she would have been incredulous at first; she knew she was a favorite; and she no more dreaded leaving her *home*, than one of its own children dreaded it.

Now the Judge, in finally consenting to the bargain, and
still before the papers were signed, had requested the girl's
purchaser to convey the news to her himself; as he had a
kind of impression that there would be rebellion, or at least,
tears and remonstrance ; and Mr. Talfierro, secure in his
good opinion of his powers of pleasing and persuasion, had
been willing to do this.

It was true, as a general thing, that girls in Rose's condition were not over-scrupulous, and that they were delighted
with change and novelty—willing to go, whenever sold, if the
new master were more liberal than the old.

He took it for granted that Rose had understood him, and
that, like others of her class, she was careless of change, and
satisfied with her lot; and he returned to the Judge with the
intelligence of her saucy acquiescence.

" She's a spirited creature—she can give jest for jest—she'd
as soon try the world in a new place as a kitten or a dog,"
remarked her expectant owner.

"I'm really glad she took it so quietly—I hate a fuss,"
responded the Judge.

In the mean time, while music and feasting went on in the
mansion-houses of the plantations, it was kept up with more
vigor if less grace in the cabin, and out in the open air.   Far
and wide resounded the tinkling banjo and the merry violin,
answering each other from one estate to another, while the
light of bonfires never died out.   Coons and opossums fell
daily victims to relentless pursuers, and their lifeless bodies
were offered a savory sacrifice at the barbecues which were
nightly held.

Hogs which had become wild in the woods, and no longer
belonged to any one in particular, were lawful game—
chickens, wherever they could be bought or stolen, and all the
small prizes of the forest which the negroes could trap or

hunt. Seldom had there been so merry a Christmas time as this, some of whose events we are recording The planters generally had cut and ground a tolerable crop, and were disposed to humor the slaves who had toiled eighteen hours out of the twenty-four, during "grinding-season." The weather had been propitious; not a rainy day, so far; the air cool and bracing, the days and nights calm and bright. The whole country, black and white, seemed determined to enjoy itself to an amount of social pleasure which should atone for any degree of isolation or privation during the year.

The light and music which streamed from Judge Bell's mansion, on Monday night, was reflected back from the fiddle and bonfire which made echo in a distant part of his plantation. A group of negro men, field-hands the most of them, were gathered around a huge fire, at which an opossum and a pig were roasting. There were no women present, and consequently, no dancing; but one of them had a fiddle, and with the universal love for music which characterizes them, they interspersed their wild and often silly stories with songs and melodies, some of them merry as the leaping fire, and some of them plaintive and touching beyond expression.

This group of revellers was composed of some of the smartest and most skillful of the out-door slaves—the most of them good hunters and fishers—who had been off for a day's sport, unencumbered by those who could not aid them to advantage.

They stretched their brawny limbs about the fire, delighting their sensitive shins with the warmth, and talking in uncouth accents, laughing musically, watching the pig roast, and also the pumpkin, and carefully attending to the 'possum, wrapped in leaves and gently baking amid ashes and heated stones. According to their own statements, some of them

had had wonderful adventures, the most of which had never
extended beyond the swamps and woods of their own plantations.   But they were full of reminiscences of turkey-hunts
and "painters," and strange experiences of alligators—some of
the latter stories bearing evident marks of having descended
from their Congo mothers, in the original shape of croco-
diles, here softened down to our less formidable tribe.   A
fetishish and hobgoblin air had some of these remarkable
traditions, grotesque and ridiculous, with not enough reason
in them to pin the airiest faith to ; but they were delightful
to these vivid, untrained imaginations, and perhaps the wild-
rolling eyes and big-mouthed credulity of the hearers were
all in keeping with the stories.

One told about a turkey-hunt in which he took the most
conspicuous part ; but, as hunting wild-turkeys requires more
caution and delicate skill than seemed to be in his organization, perhaps he exaggerated his personal importance.   His
auditors swallowed his story as good-naturedly as they would
have done the wild-turkey itself; and after it was finished,
the negro with the fiddle sang a favorite song of the planta-
tion-lands in Louisiana and Georgia, the chorus of which is
a curiously-correct imitation of the peculiar cry of the turkey-
cock when he calls to his distant mate—a soft, guttural.
resounding utterance—and in the chorus the whole party
joined—

    "Chug-a-loggee, chug-a-loggee, chug-a-loggee chug !"

"Look-a-heah, niggas !   S'pose an alligator come out of
de cane-brake as big as dat cypress log dar — guess you
wouldn't sing chug-a-loggee !" said a "boy" who had just
dropped into the circle.

"Wha' for ?" exclaimed half a dozen of the darkies in
chorus, as they sprang to their feet and rolled their eyes in
an extraordinary manner.   Each one, standing as immovable,

for the moment, as a post, still rolled his eyes so as to catch a full view of the entire vicinity.

"Yah! yah! Ef you ain't the skeeriest niggas in dis parish!" exclaimed the "boy," as he fairly exploded with laughter at the statuesque figures before him.

"*Alligator!*" he suddenly screamed, in a frightened voice, as he bounded up in the air and started back.

"*Alligator!*" frantically screamed every darkey, as they disappeared in the darkness like shadows over the greensward.

"Yah! yah! yah! Oh, gorra mighty! Yah! yah! yah! Dis nigga will jes' die wid larfin'! Yah! yah! *Alli*—yah! yah!— *gator!* Yah! yah!" and the black joker rolled over on the ground, in his explosive enjoyment of the fright he had caused. He first tumbled head over heels, like a coon tumbling from a tree; then ran his head into the ground; then "fetched up" against a tree, to steady himself. Suddenly, he listened:

"Hark! W'at's dat? It's something *sizzlin'!* It's de pig, sure!"—and he went forward to the fire, to find the pig fairly frying before the hot embers.

"Dis'll *nebber* do! Pig spilin', and de niggas gone! Oh, Lord! dar's de 'possum cookin' like an old shoe. Niggas! Hoo—oo—oo—oo!"—and his rich voice died away in the darkness like a retreating song. Presently a shadow flitted in the distance—then another, and soon all the negroes were again before the fire. Seeing the imminence of the crisis, every one hastened to relieve the burning pig and 'possum. When all was right again, they sat silently down. At length one of them said:

"Conundibus, wha' for you cry out '*alligator!*' when dar's no alligator 'round in de winter?"

"Yes, dat's just what *I* wants to know," said another.

"It's my 'pinion de circumstances is mighty s'picious!"

said a third darkey.   "Dar's de tail ob dat 'possum *clean gone !*"

This brought them all to their feet again.   The 'possum-tail gone!—that was a calamity!   Conundibus was a rascal, that was clear.   The darkies approached him threateningly. With a wild " Yah! yah! yah!" he disappeared in the darkness, whither the others dare not follow him.   Muttering their odd and wild imprecations upon " de young dog," who was " eber cuttin' up de feelin's " by his practical jokes, the party was soon laughing and jabbering like a set of parrots, over their now thoroughly-cooked feast.   Pig was taken from the spit and placed on a great sugar-pan, which served as a platter ; potatoes were raked out of the hot ashes ; 'possum was carefully laid upon an old earthenware dish especially reserved for the delicacy.   Its tail was gone! and Conundibus was voted to be a " berry serious rascal."   When all was ready, the violin struck up a clear, ringing air, and the negroes, standing around, joined hands as they uttered in concert a wild chaunt, half song and half recitative, which it is almost impossible to put into words :

	By de dark lagoon,	(*Recitative.*)
	Huah! Huah! Huah!	(*Chorus.*)
	By de cane-brake's track,	(*Rec.*)
	Huah! Huah! Huah!	(*Cho.*)
	By de cypress swamp,	(*Rec.*)
	Huah! Huah! Huah!	(*Cho.*)
First voice.—De darkness sleeps—		(*Tenor solo.*)
Second "	De winds make moan—	(*Bass "*)
Third "	De waters dream—	(*Soprano "*)
Fourth "	De stars keep watch.	(*Alto "*)
	Hark! Hark!	(*Staccato chorus*)

(*Violin plays a plaintive melody, imitating a woman's song.*)

First voice.—My wife is dar, ober dar !	
Second "	My mother is dar, ober dar !
Third "	My sister is dar, ober dar !
Fourth "	My true love is dar, ober dar !
	Hark! Hark !

(*Violin plays a low but joyous strain, which dies away on the strings.*)

By de dark lagoon—
By de cane-brake's track—
By de cypress swamp—
Huah—huah—huah !
Huah—huah—huah !
Huah—huah—huah !

This last chorus was prolonged until it seemed to melt into the still air. The singers then all shook hands, and the feast began. In a moment all was a bedlam of enjoyment. Song, dance, joke—each followed rapidly, even as the negroes eat of the pig, potatoes and hoc-cake ; for, let the spirit of fun be ever so exuberant, it did not, for a moment, stay the feast.

"*W'at's dat ?*" suddenly exclaimed one of the darkies astride of the cypress-log, having a pig's leg in his hand, while his well-filled mouth almost stopped his utterance.

Instantly all was still as death ; then all eyes opened wide as shutters—all mouths gaped—each negro's arms and fingers stiffened at his side, and knees perceptibly quaked.

"De debbil hisself!" shouted the darkey from the log, and, with a wild " whoop !" he disappeared in the woods.

"De debbil ! Oh ! oh ! oh !" was heard on all sides, as the darkies vanished in the darkness, leaving the feast deserted. Then there came slowly forward—what was it ? An alligator, apparently ; yet it walked *erect*, as if standing on its tail. The monster came slowly forward, uttering a noise something similar to a pig's grunt, until it stood by the deserted feast. It walked around the board, passed through the fire, knocked the embers aside, and, finally, bent down before the feast. The breast between the fore-legs parted, and the head of Conundibus looked out, his cheeks fairly wet with the tears of his suppressed laughter. Then he protruded his hand to seize a morsel of the delicious pig, and was in the act of bearing it to his mouth, when—crash, crash, fell the blows

upon his alligator's head.   It was the turn of Conundibus to
be frightened.   He burst from the skin, to find one of the
darkies, armed with a club, ready to dash out his brains.
His sudden appearance, however, apparently from the very
monster's bowels, caused the assailant to stagger back in
horror.   Conundibus, throwing the skin over on the stupefied
negro, made for the woods, while the thick recesses were
rendered fairly jubilant with his laughter.

But his laughter proved his frolic's ruin ; for the negroes,
secreted in the darkness, sprang out, and soon had him
prisoner.   They dragged him forward to the fire, to find the
fellow with the club carefully examining the hollow skin, to
be assured there was not another darkey within its ample hollow.   The capture of the "serious rascal" revealed all, and
although the darkies had had their feast almost spoiled, so
clever was the trick that they soon forgave the joker, and
the feast went on.   Alligator stories became the theme of
discourse as the pig continued to disappear.

"Whar did you get dat big skin, Conundibus?" said the
negro whose club had so nearly finished the apparition.

"You jes' tell me wha' for you come back to see dat I
wasn't an alligator—you jes' tell dat afore I answers any
interrogums," said Conundibus, anxious to learn how it was
possible for any negro to get his courage up to the point of
assailing "de debbil."

"W'y, you see, I t'ought it was only de old cane-brake
alligator waked up from his snooze jes' for to get sunthin' to
fill his stomach aside ob stones.   I t'ought he jes' *smell* pig,
and come out ob de mud, and he so stiff he couldn't walk, so
he come along on his tail.   I knowed 'twasn't de debbil,
'cause *I* saw de debbil once, and he was a horse, wid a cow's
head and a chicken's tail, and had a church bell on his back.
Dat I *knowed* was de debbil ; and so I knowed dis yere wasn't

de debbil widout he been habin' children. T'inks I, if he *been* habin' children, I better kill 'em, else de family get *so* big dat ebery nigga's house must have a debbil in it—yah! yah! yah!"

Conundibus half-suspected his friend (John Cottontop, as he was called, from having something on his head that was neither hair nor wool, but looked like a black cotton ball) knew that the apparition was not the devil, nor the old fabled cane-brake alligator, who was supposed to have haunted the swamps on the plantation for many a generation. Cotton-top was not considered remarkably brave, for he always *would* run at the cry of "*alligator!*" and would make others run; yet, it was a fact, that John was one of the best alligator hunters on the place—that he killed more of "the varmints," and made more money from the sale of their oil and skins, than all the rest of the negroes put together. The truth in this case was, John had first run, as was his failing; but the thought of oil and hide always would give him courage again; and, in this instance, having caught a glimpse of the appari-tion before he ran, he had returned to bag his game in the usual way, by hitting it on the head from behind.

Conundibus proceeded to narrate his adventure in obtaining this particular hide:

"You see, darkies, de alligator, which isn't so plenty as dey used to was, is goin' off like de Injins—nobody knows whar; but I believes," he said, with a knowing shake of his very woolly head, "I believes dar is a hole *somewhar* dat goes in de groun', and dat de alligators, and Injins, and deer, and 'possums goes in and finds anodder place better'n dis, 'cause dar isn't no niggas nor poor whites dar to pester 'em. *Dat's* my most perfound comprepinion."

"Your what?" said Cottontop, greatly interested in the deep insinuation of the philosophic Conundibus.

"Oh, look heah, nigga: I can't gib you sense any more'n de oberseer can give your head good nigga's ha'r!" was the rather tart reply. Cottontop was silenced.

Conundibus proceeded: "Woll, dis yere old 'un wouldn't clear out wid de rest. He staid behind and cum ashore ebery night las' year, to stick his nose in massa's groun', out of 'cause he couldn't help it, I s'pose. I war down in de swamp by de lower bayou one Sunday, you see—you needn't roll your eyes so ober dar, you nigger preacher wid de fiddle —one Sunday, jus' to see whar de light cum from perhaps, or whar de dark went to ebery mornin', when what should I see but dat alligator dar, trablin' aroun' on Sunday like a gentleum wid a big chaw of tobac' in his mouf. By golly, I struck out ob dem woods and across to de houses in a hurry, and jes' let de boys know it. So we went back, and dar he war, sure enough. We tried to head him off, but de smart old fox would go towards de bayou anyhow; so we kept pesterin' him, and makin' him snap his tail like a whip, until he had knocked de bark all off on it—you see dar it is all gone. I knowed if he got in de water he was gone for good, so I jes' got straddle his back. You know when a nigger gits on an alligator's back, dat dey jes' stops, and swells up and blows like a bull, dey gits *so* mad. So de ole feller stops, and de way he stirred up de groun' was a sin. De shadow of his tail knocked two niggers down, and he struck out his face for anodder nigga's heels, and almos' kotched 'em. Gosh! dat nigga wouldn't been a chaw tobacker for de beast. You see *I* was de boss ob dat boat, 'kase I was on deck— yah! yah! and de critter couldn't shake me off. De ole fool didn't know enough to lay down an' roll ober. He got blowed all out wid his fussin' 'roun' to get me off. De boys put out both his eyes wid de pike-spear; den I took de spear and put it right under dis foreleg yere, and dat did de job for him. He jes' lay right out and whined like a dog, and den died. Dat's all."

"Who got de ile?" said Cottontop.

"I didn't stop to see *dat* dirty work!" said the story-teller, with a kind of mock dignity. "De boys dragged de beast up to de houses, and arter de skin war off I jes' took it. Dat's all."

"Dat ain't nuffin. I's killed a houseful of 'gators, I has," said a short, thick-set, scrubby-headed looking darkey, celebrated chiefly for the quantity of pig he could eat and the big stories he could tell. "I's made 'em carry me across de lagune *many* times. "I's got an alligator bridle to ride 'em wid. I's got an alligator skin at de hut on rockers, and ebery one ob *my* pickaninnies was brought up in *dat* skin. I's got—"

"Look-a-heah, Pluribus, you isn't got one t'ing. You isn't got a piece of pig about you, have you?" said Conundibus. The injured Pluribus could only be silent, and in two minutes more was fast asleep on the greensward, literally surfeited with the pig he had devoured..

"I don't b'lieve w'at dat nigger say about ridin' de alligators across de bayou," said Cottontop. "I once heard tell dat de mails on de Mississip was carried up and down by boys on de alligator's back—dat dey went so fas' you could only see a streak through de water; but I don't believe dat, nohow, 'kase I *knows* de beast is de slowestest critter dat eber did live. Why, I'll tell you: once I was goin' across de bayous in de oberseer's skiff, to de ole rice plantation. W'en I got to de bayou, dar was jus' about two hundred little alligators creepin' aroun', jes' hatched out in de sand. De ole alligator was out on de mud. I went ober to de old place, staid dar all night, come back nex' day, and de old alligator had made only jes' about twenty rods, dat's all

But, I tell you, dey is great in de water! I jes' went ober
der holes in de skiff, and I b'lieve dey could beat me wid de
best boat. I once took ole massa and anodder gentleum
ober to see de ugly beasts in der holes. Oh, de Lord! De
gentleum was so skeered dat we pulled ashore, and he got
sick a-hearin 'em beller, and grunt, and splash."

"Cottontop, w'at you kill so many alligators for?" said
one of the listeners.

"None of your business!" said the apparently offended
negro alligator-merchant, for such he was; and to his hand
was the growing scarcity of "the animals" owing more than
to any other cause. The fellow hunted them chiefly in the
winter with great success pecuniarily. He would travel
around in the daytime and discover where the creature had
buried itself for the winter's torpor. The spot was always
indicated by a round ridge on the surface of the ground.
Having marked the spot, he would return at night, build his
fire, open the mound, cut off the alligator's head, open and
disembowel him. The fat of the ribs and flesh he would
"try out" in his pans, and before morning would return
loaded with skins and oil. The skins he sold at a good
price, for fancy leather, and the oil he disposed of at a very
paying rate, for machinery lucubration. In this trade he had
amassed a snug sum of money, and was, therefore, quite a
"respectable darkey"—notwithstanding the negroes, for some
reason, did not like the manner in which he had procured
his wealth. It was whispered around among the slaves
that Cottontop had twice offered his money to the old master
to induce him to give Maum Guinea her freedom. The
superstitious blacks believed that his wish was to get rid
of the old cook; but, if such an offer had been made, it
was from the negro's knowledge of the negro's heart—because
he read in the old woman's face the secret of her agony

and penetrated the dark shadow which rested upon her soul.

———

The small hours wore on, and one by one, the black revellers fell asleep by the fast-dying embers. As Cottontop concluded, the fiddler arose, took his violin down from the bush, from which it hung in safety, and, one strong stroke across its strings started the black assembly suddenly into life. Each black arose, and in a moment, standing there before the almost expired fire, they formed into the mystic ring of clasped hands to chaunt again their wild chorus:

> By de dark lagoon—
> By de cane-brake's track—
> By de cypress swamp—
> Huah—huah—huah!

The words rolled out on the air and died away in the distance as if speeding on their way to other lands—as if to pursue airy paths to far Africa, to awake on the banks of the fabled streams of Negro-land the responsive

> Huah—huah—huah!

at once the revelation of the slave's misery and his hopes of the future.

When the grey streaks of morning pencilled the east, over the low lagoons, the Cypress-swamp barbecue was among the the things of the past—only capable of sending one pleasant thril. to the negro's breast as its memory was recalled.

CHAPTER IX.

THE FUGITIVES.

And the nightingales softly are singing
   In the mellow and moonlighted air ;
And the minstrels their viols are stringing,
   And the dancers for dancing prepare.

None heeds us, beloved Irene !
   None will mark if we linger or fly.
Amid all the masks in yon revel,
   There is not an ear or an eye—
Not one—that will gaze or will listen ;
   And save the small star in the sky,
Which, to light us, so softly doth glisten,
   There is none will pursue us, Irene.
Oh, love me, oh, save me, I die !—OWEN MEREDITH.

These lovers fled away into the night.—KEATS.

VIRGINIA was in her chamber, standing before the mirror,
clasping a pearl necklace about her throat.   Her cheeks were
flushed, and her eyes brilliant with delight; for it was New
Year's morning, and on the little pier-table were various
parcels which she had just opened—the gifts of parents and
friends.   The handsomest of these was the necklace—sent by
Mr. Talfierro as a bridal as well as New Year's present, with
his compliments and congratulations — the Judge having
informed him, on the previous day, of the approaching marriage of his daughter.   Philip's gift also was there—a richly
ornamented guitar, which he had been to the village expressly
to purchase, and which was the only thing he could find in
the little town which he thought would please his betrothed.
More elaborate and costly presents he intended to select upon
his visit to the great city which he also found it necessary to
make before the occasion of the wedding.   There were books,
and perfumes in fancy cases, dresses, and pretty trifles in
profusion ; so that the young girl had hardly known what to

admire most, until the little parcel containing the pearls was unfastened, and then her delight was complete. Very charming it looked, glistening about the slender throat—fine and softly rounded, if not so fair as the jewels—the graceful pendants rising and falling with the motion of her breath.

"Mr. Talfierro is such an agreeable gentleman—so tasteful and generous," she murmured. "Look, Rose, what Mr. Talfierro has sent me," as she heard her waiting-maid enter, and caught a glimpse of her dress in the mirror. "Oh, I am so much pleased with it—it will be so pretty for the—the wedding," she continued, still looking in the glass at the fair reflection before her.

It was not until she felt the skirt of her dress grasped strangely that she turned and beheld Rose crouching at her feet as if overwhelmed with terror, her eyes dilated, her lips parted, and trying in vain to gasp out an articulate word.

"Save me! save me!" she presently sobbed or rather shrieked out.

"What from?" asked Virginia, looking toward the door, a half formed thought of a poisonous serpent or a rabid dog rushing into her mind; but seeing and hearing nothing, half fearing the girl had gone suddenly insane, so wild was her expression.

"Oh, Miss Virginny, you can save me, and you will!"

"Certainly I will," spoke the mistress, soothingly. "What is it, child?"

"It's him—it's dat New Orleans gentleum—your fadder has done gone and sold me to him."

"Sold you, Rose? Oh, I guess you are mistaken."

"I wish I was, Miss Virginny. But dey's bof' told me now. Your fadder says so hisself. I's to go to-morrow airly,"—and sob after sob broke distressingly from the dark, panting bosom.

"If papa has sold you, he has done very wrong," cried Virginia, flushed and indignant: "He knows I can not do without you!"

"In course you can't, Miss Virginny. Who'd do your beautiful hair, or your lawn dresses, I'd like to know!"

Poor Rose! She was thinking of Hyperion, of herself—of her faithful lover and her hated owner—but she felt instinctively, in that hour of desperation, that it would be in vain to appeal to "white folks" on common grounds of sympathy, and she grasped at the idea of her being useful and necessary to Miss Virginia, as a drowning man grasps at a straw. The momentous question of the slave-girl's fate resolved itself into the critical problem of "who would do her missus' hair, and clear-starch her muslins."

"At this time of all others, Rose! So much to plan and do —and all the sewing and embroidery. I shall just tell papa flatly that I can not and will not get married, if I am compelled to part with you."

"Oh, do! do tell him, dear missus," and for a moment a gleam of hope shone over the beautiful, wild, imploring face, like sunset out of a summer storm-cloud; but it was swept over by a second gust of despair, as she added: "Ah! ah! he tell me de papers done been signed."

"Well, we'll get them *un*-signed then," said Virginia, resolutely. "I'll ask Mr. Talfierro himself; I'll appeal to his gallantry. *He* certainly can not have as much need of a lady's-maid as I,"—and she half-laughed in the midst of her irritation. "If he wants a housekeeper, he can find plenty, more fit than you; while I can not possibly dispense with you. I have learned you to do every thing so nicely—and besides, I like you so much, Rose, dear,"—and a sense of gratitude and love filled her heart at the instant, as she remembered the faithful, untiring, affectionate attentions of the girl through so many years.

"Rose's heart would done break to be sold away from her own young missus,"—and the speaker pressed her hand on her heart, as if there were already a sharp pain there.

"Get up, Rose; and don't cry—at least until we see what can be done. I'd rather Mr. Talfierro had kept his pearls, than that he should have vexed me so. It does not seem like New Year's morning any longer—I'm so out of humor. However, we needn't fret, either of us. It can not be, and it *shall* not!"—and the young lady threw down the necklace with a very decided movement. "Look at my pretty presents, Rose, while I go speak to my father."

She went out of the room; but the girl did not look at the pretty presents—not the glittering of jewels nor the lustre of a silk robe glancing out of its wrapper of tissue-paper could light her eyes with a passing curiosity; she sat upon the floor, motionless, her hands folded in her lap, her glance bent upon the carpet, the rich tints and flitting changes of her brilliant countenance faded to a dull, dead yellow.

In the mean time, Virginia found her father alone in his little office-room. The family had breakfasted, and the compliments of the day had already passed; something of the pleasure which parents experience in bestowing good gifts on their delighted children still irradiated his countenance.

"Hey, puss, what now? Any thing wanting?" he inquired, as his eldest and pet child came towards him with some hesitation.

"I came to speak about Rose, father.

"Rose! Yes, yes, I expect a scene, Miss Virginia—but please be brief about it. The deed is done, and can't be undone."

He spoke a little nervously. It was evident that he did
not feel as if he had been doing exactly the right thing. He
knew, first, that the girl was a great favorite with his daughter,
and that she would be very unwilling to give her up; and
secondly, his conscience, as a man, was troubled, for he knew,
much better than his child, the object of the purchase, and
he could not *quite* persuade himself that the mulatto-girl,
always modest and virtuous thus far in her young life, was
just the creature for that kind of a sale. He had taken the
liberty of disposing of her, body and soul, and yet, curiously,
he did not feel entirely easy about so plain and common a
business transaction.

The idea of modesty and virtue in a Louisiana colored-girl
might well be ridiculed; as a general thing, she has neither;
and who is to blame for it we do not propose to argue. It is
doubtless a great blessing to the colored race that it is held in
slavery for the salvation of its soul and the precious boon of
its enlightenment; and if such a state of morals prevails in
the far South, we suppose it to be only one of the branches
of the above inestimable blessing. Rose happened to have
grown up with more than her share of excellence for the
reason that she had always been more of a companion of the
young daughter of the house, than a common servant; and
there had been no grown-up sons; and the family of Judge
Bell lived quietly, and with more than the ordinary degree
of refinement for that latitude. Thus, by reason of her
seclusion, and her constant association with the ladies of a
gentle household, it came to pass that the slave-girl Rose
blushed as easily and kept herself as charily, as her friend
and mistress Virginia.

"Well, papa, I don't see how I am to get along without
her. I shall never, never find anybody to take her place,"—
and the young lady burst into tears

"It will be inconvenient for a while, I know; but litt.e Dinah will soon be grown enough to do all that Rose does. She's large enough, now, to make a very nice little waiting-girl."

"She can't embroider, nor sew worth looking at; and I'll 'ook like a fright with her at my hair—and now, just when—"

"It *will* be bad for you to be looking like a fright now-a-days, puss. But I guess we can manage that."

"Besides, father, I think it is cruel to send Rose off among strangers. She is such a timid thing—and so much attached to us. She seems distracted with the very idea. Indeed, indeed, papa, it makes me unhappy to look at her."

"I'm sorry for Rose, and for you, too, little one. I hate to part with her myself. She is honest and faithful—a good girl. It was only necessity that induced me. Girls of your age do not know what business-troubles are. To satisfy you that I was obliged to do as I did, I will tell you that Mr. Talfierro held my note for five thousand dollars; that he came here to collect it; that I had not the money; and that he offered to cancel the whole amount, in return for Rose. He seems to have taken a fancy to her; and he is rich and can afford to indulge his fancies. In fact, he is determined to have her. He went so far as to threaten the prosecution of the debt, if I didn't accede to his manner of settling it. Now, the girl isn't worth half that in market; it's a fancy price, and I could not afford to refuse it."

"I wish Mr. Talfierro had never seen us! I wish he had his necklace back. I don't like him a particle," cried Virginia, with girlish petulance.

"He has not done such a bad thing for you, my dear. I am so pinched for money this season, that if he had not done as he has done, I don't see how I could have provided you with a suitable outfit. Reflect upon it, Virginia. I should have been compelled to raise five thousand dollars. Now I am not only free from that, but the portion of that sum which I had managed to lay by, I can afford to use for your benefit. It will not be an unpleasant thing for you to take ten or twelve hundred dollars to the city to go shopping with. You can soon make another girl available, without the extravagance of keeping a five-thousand-dollar waiting-maid. Don't you see?"

"Yes, I see; but I'm sorry for Rose—I can't help it, father. She was engaged to Philip's man, and they seemed so attached to each other—it's not right to separate them. I had promised her she should be married at the same time with myself."

"Pooh! pooh! girls' nonsense! Soon get over it, both of you."

"I can't bear to tell her that she really has got to go," continued Virginia, lingering in the room, as if still hoping for a revokal of the sentence.

"The best way would have been to have said nothing about it, till the time came for departure. An hour would have sufficed to pack her trinkets. If I'd been wise, I should have thought of it."

"She couldn't have even said good-by to Hyperion."

"Well, the fewer good-byes the better, in such cases. They are excitable creatures, the whole race of 'em. They will wail one moment and laugh the next. I suppose they'll make a great fuss, and get over it all the sooner. You can tell Rose, for her comfort, that you will be in New Orleans in a few weeks, and then you will come and see her."

"You've no idea, father, how she seems to feel about it."

"Nor I *can't help it!* It's no use talking, now,"—he spoke more sternly. "Bid her prepare herself, and do not hint at the possibility of her remaining. Be decided, and you will save yourself a scene."

Virginia withdrew, and with reluctant footsteps sought her chamber. As she entered it, Rose stirred for the first time; raising her head, she looked in the tearful face of her young mistress.

"No use tellin' me de news," she remarked—and getting up, went quietly to arranging the room.

That day the Judge's family were to dine with Colonel Fairfax. The festivity was to serve as the introduction to that feeling of relationship and mutual interest natural to the present state of affairs. The betrothal of the young people was already avowed in both households. Philip had stimulated Maum Guinea, by a gold dollar, and still more by one of his golden smiles, to do her handsomest in the culinary department, and to Hyperion he had given warning to exercise his utmost skill. The dinner was to be succeeded by evening gayeties, to which a few more young people were invited.

The peculiar circumstances attending this little party kept Virginia in a pleasant flutter of anticipation. If it had not been for the sad, dull face of the girl who flitted about her with unusual assiduity, doing every thing kind and careful, but speaking little and shedding no tears, she would have been extremely happy. But she could not, in the selfishness of her own joy, quite shut out the distress of her slave. Her voice trembled when she addressed her, calling her "Rose, dear," and "her darling Rose," to testify her own unwilling ness to give her up.

"Make me look as well as possible," she said, as Rose took down her rich hair to dress it for the *fête;* "I wish Philip not to be ashamed of me. Besides, it will be the *last* time you will dress me. It's *too* bad! I *hate* Mr. Talfierro!"

"So do I," whispered the slave-girl, under her breath, and

a single flash broke from under her drooping lashes, like the glitter of a dagger.

"Will you go with me over to Colonel Fairfax's, or will you stay here and be getting yourself ready for your jour- ney?" asked Virginia, when ready to descend from her chamber, bright and beautiful as tasteful and loving hands could make her.

"I'd like to go 'long wid you, missus."

"I thought perhaps it would be better for you, and for *him* too, not to see him, Rose," continued her mistress, gently.

"Oh, no! no! I must see him, and Maum Ginny."

"If you wish it, you certainly shall. You can go over with us, and stay until we return. It will not take you long to arrange your little affairs here."

The slave-girl did not smile bitterly, with the mockery of the white nature, at the idea that people in her position, no matter how faithful their service, were not burdened by the accumulation of many effects—her whole being was preoccu- pied by one feeling, to the exclusion of every other less- absorbing passion.

When they arrived at Colonel Fairfax's, Rose went imme- diately to the cook's cabin.

"Oh, Mammy!"

The words burst out of her heart with a sudden cry; it was all she said as she sat down on the wooden stool by the table, covering her face with her shawl. The cook raised herself to her full height from over the savory dish she was preparing; her black eyes seemed to shrink into half their size and double their intensity, as she fixed them upon the drooping form before her.

"Ho! ho! I 'spected as much."

"Did you know it?" asked the visitor quickly, dropping her shawl.

" De curse is a-falling, chile."

" Oh, Maumy !"

" It always falls—sooner or later. W'at' you got black blood in you veins fur? It's pizened—since the days of Noah, its pizened. It burns in our veins like fire—it's got de fire of de burning lake mixed up in it. When white blood runs wid dat, it's wuss still. Ho ! chile, I knew well 'nuff w'at you'd come to."

" Does *he* know it ?"

" Woll, he heard it. But he hoped ag'in hope. Hasn't lived as long as Maum Ginny, or he'd know better. *I* never hope nothing."

She went on with her cooking.

" Can't you save me, Maumy ?"

" Me, chile ?"

" You can do so many things, Ginny !"

" Can't make black blood white."

There was nothing said for the next few minutes. The cook was in all the hurry and bustle of dishing up a grand dinner. Her assistants were coming in and out, hurrying between the cabin and the mansion. She scarcely glanced at her forlorn visitor; but once, as she added the " finishing touch " to a spicy soup, she muttered :

" 'Twon't spile *their* appetites any."

It was not until all the various courses had been sent in, and the dessert was on the table, that there was any quiet in the kitchen. Even then Hyperion had not come in, though he knew Rose was there ; as it was part of his duty, on that day, to assist in the dining-room.

After the coffee had been sent in, there was comparative repose. But the cook did not dispose herself to conversation. She drove out the slatternly girl who came to wash up the kettles and pans, and went at that work herself with a vigor

which soon put an end to it. Beyond offering a cup of
coffee and a plate of dainties to Rose, she scarcely spoke;
and when her tasks were finished, sat down without tasting
of food, and stared into the fire. Rose did not feel hurt by
her manner; she knew that her own grief was working in
Maum Guinea's breast almost as powerfully as in her own;
and indeed, she was herself in a sort of stupor, hardly real-
izing the passing moments, but only wondering when Hyperion
would enter and speak with her.

The brief winter twilight had descended when he did so.
Shadows lurked in the corners of the cabin, chased restlessly
by tongues of light that seemed to seek to sting them, as the
fire flashed up or sank apart. A vivid glare from the falling
embers revealed the mulatto-man's face, as he opened the
door and stepped in, opposite to Rose. It was full of gloom
and despair. With a great sob, she rose and threw herself
upon his bosom; and there, for the first time since she had
learned her fate, tears came to her relief, and she wept out
the dreadful weight which had oppressed her all day, choking
her throat and burning her eyelids. He passed his trembling
hand again and again over her wavy, silken hair; he had no
words of comfort, for there was no comfort in the world for
them. He could not say "peace, when there was no peace."

A long while they stood thus, until her weeping became
less vehement. The sound of music reached them, thrilling
through the darkness, from the brilliantly-illuminated mansion

"Come, Rose, Miss Virginia wants you in de dressing-
room."

"You come back here, chil'ren, fust chance you get," said
Maum Guinea, as they went out.

After they had left, she stirred up the fire, put on fresh
fuel, put various dishes to warming, made a fresh pot of
coffee, and set the little table with a good supper. It was,

perhaps, nine o'clock when they returned together, to have a few last words of endearment and farewell, with only their beloved "Maumy" for a listener. The time had come for her to express herself. Closing the door carefully, she spoke in a low, steady voice :

"Quit yer crying, chil'ren, and make up yer minds to *do something*. Why don't you run away?"

They looked up at her in fear and surprise; her form seemed the expression of a concentrated will; her eyes were bright and resolute, as a panther's when her young are threatened by the hunter.

"I'd be afraid," whispered Rose, with a shudder.

"Would you be afraid, if *I'd* go 'long?" asked Maum Guinea.

"No, Maumy, not wid you and 'Perion."

"Where could we go?" asked the young man.

He had lifted himself up eagerly, and looked ready to meet the emergency; but it is not strange that he asked where they could go—they had not that dreaded, dreary refuge of the Dismal Swamp, to which many a desperate fugitive betakes himself; the country was open and settled; the river, a day's journey away. There was only the temporary refuge of the dark and tangled forest lying along the edge of the plantation; they might reach that, and if they escaped immediate arrest, might make their way, by night-journeys, to the river; and there would be the double danger of detection, and the great difficulty of securing a passage on any of the boats.

"I's got my plans, and they are doubtful 'nuff, too. But if you'd rather run the risks, than see Rose go off to New Orleans wid dat new owner, why, we'll try—dat's all. Don't make much difference to me whar *I* am. I's as well off here as I can be anywhar, now; but if it be a help and

comfort to ye, to have my company, why, I'm goin' **along.**
Dey may tear me to pieces, if dey want to—I'm going. I
didn't t'ink I'd ever sot my heart on anyt'ing in dis yere
world ag'in ; but I've grown to like you two—'pears 'most as
if you were my own ; and if you want Mammy to go wid
you, she's going. And now, we can't stand it to hide in de
woods, 'less we eat something. Set down and make a good
supper ; ye'll need it 'fore we's tru' wid this."

She began to pour out the coffee as she spoke. They
obeyed her with a kind of blind, bewildered obedience. Hope,
too, sprung up, at her words ; and those, whose dry throats
had refused to swallow a morsel through the day, now ate
with considerable appetite. She forced upon each the second
cup of strong, stimulating coffee, and herself partook of the
same.

"An' now," said she, as they concluded the hurried repast,
"you bof go back to de house. Rose must stand 'roun', whar
she will be seen ; and you go to your master's room, 'Perion,
and draw up your papers as a free colored man. You must
write like Colonel Fairfax, and sign his name. You's pert at
writing, and you can do it. Put on your silber watch and
all your little fixin's, to look respectable, and take all de
money you have. I hab a hundred dollars myself. It will
buy our passage, if we get to de boats. I'll be your maumy—
Rose'll be your wife. Den you get back here—I'll be ready."

Half an hour later, the three stood in the field running
along beyond the negro-quarters. Maum Guinea had sent
the young folks on first, remaining behind only long enough
to cover the fire and fasten the door of her cabin, as if she
had retired for the night.

"It's full ten o'clock ; they'll be going home in two hours.
You'll be missed den, sartain ; but probably not before dat.
'Perion, did you help yourself to Massa Philip's revolver ?"

"I did. But I wouldn't use it 'gainst any of *dem*. I t'ought of painters, or wolves, maybe, in de woods."

"And I have a knife," continued Maum Guinea. "Here, Rose, put dese yere biscuits in your pocket—mine is full. Come along."

She strode on as rapidly as if the sun lighted her footsteps, followed by Hyperion, dragging Rose by the hand, who had to run to keep up with them. Fantastic clouds, rugged and black, fled across the starlit sky—not more swiftly and violently than the poor fugitives beneath fled across the open fields. When they came to the edge of the great forest, they paused for a moment.

"Which way?" whispered Maum Guinea.

"Towards de lake," replied Hyperion. "Dar is a cave I found one day, clost by de water. W'en it begins to get daylight, I can find it, and we can crawl in dar."

"Oh, dear! w'at if dar were painters in dar, 'Perion?"

The young man pressed the trembling fingers of the timid girl—poor creature! so cowardly, so superstitious, so sensitive to cold and darkness, it was no wonder she trembled with fright and chilliness. The firm grasp of his hand reassured her, as they entered the gloomy wood. The real difficulties of the flight were just begun. Not a gleam of the dim starlight penetrated the shadows, except at intervals, where it would glimmer upon the water of treacherous marshes. Stumbling over logs, becoming entangled in brushwood, with nothing but instinct, as it were, to tell them the direction they should take, they made their way slowly and painfully; in doubt then, if they were really going toward the lake, but anxious, at all events, to get as far into the forest as possible, before the daylight should come to the aid of their pursuers. If they had ventured to light a pine-knot torch, they might have made much more rapid progress, and been sure of their route; but their flight might be already discovered, and the light be a snare to draw attention upon them. So they pressed forward, stumbling, crawling, running, as they could, through the thick darkness. After many hours of such journeying, they were rejoiced by coming suddenly upon the banks of the lake; they heard its soft ripple, and saw its waters flash back the evanescent gleam of beclouded stars. It would be in vain to search for the secret opening to the cave in such a night as surrounded them. Weary, and holding in their panting breath to listen for the dreaded sounds of pursuit, they rested upon a decaying log, waiting for the first gray light—they knew it could not be far distant. An owl in a tree overhead hooted dismally, as if in derision of their hopes and fears; at every cry of his, or the least twitter of birds in their nest, or the snapping of a twig beneath the light foot of some passing animal, Rose would cling to her lover, and his arm would tighten its grasp about her. The wind grew more chilly toward morning, and, despite her shawl, she shivered with the cold; for she was but a tropical plant, house-reared at that, tender and easily blighted.

Maum Guinea drew her knees up to her chin, and rocked herself to and fro to keep warm, and perhaps to keep down thought! Foolish fugitives! trembling in the cold and darkness. For what had they fled from comfort and plenty, from fire, food, kind masters, and easy service? Reckless, ungrateful, improvident creatures! Hyperion had spent his whole life on the Fairfax plantation; he had always been petted, done little work, and had especial indulgence. How had his masters wronged *him*, that he should repay them thus, by betaking himself off, at a loss to them of eighteen or twenty hundred dollars. The man had his own thoughts, as he sat there one long hour of that winter night. He had not studied Master Philip's mirror in vain. He knew that he looked as much like that dashing and chivalrous young gentleman, as one half-brother is apt to look like another. He did not know who his mother was, and Colonel Fairfax was not as proud of him as of his legitimate son; though he had always done him the justice to regard him as a fine piece of property. The Colonel had just given a festival of rejoicing over the betrothal of one son, and Judge Bell, that excellent citizen, had just sold this girl here by his side, to whom *he* was affianced, to raise the means of bestowing his daughter with becoming *éclat* upon that favored son.

That splendid reasoning faculty, developed to such a subtle degree of fineness in the brain of the pure-blooded white, had not as yet attained such power in this six-eighths mulatto-man; he did not deduce from these facts the overwhelming arguments which proved their righteousness to the entire satisfaction of the owners, at that moment engaged in bitter denunciation of his baseness—perhaps he did not reason at all; it was all passion with him, and not logic; he loved the dark beauty who clung to him in the shadows—he hated that rich gentleman who had come up from New Orleans to buy that which her love had promised to him; and under the impulse of these two wild passions, he had fled. Any one can read, at a glance, his want of wisdom and his wretched ingratitude; no one can blame the two gentlemen who denounce him with such harshness, as they stride up and down the portico, and wait for their horses to be brought by the first red streak of morning. We feel that they have been robbed and disappointed. One has lost two of his very best animals, and the other will have to meet a five thousand-dollar note under intensely provoking circumstances. What is most conducive to the financial prosperity of a nation at once becomes right—and what is best for the financial interests of these two individuals is, of course, right, and they have our sympathy. No human understanding could be so dull as not to comprehend the excuse they had for impatience and occasional light-swearing; the deep chagrin and irritation which took the place of the jovial good-humor of the previous evening.

In the mean time, " the rain falls upon the just and the unjust "—the same red streak of dawn which shows them the road glimmering across the country, shows to Hyperion familiar scenery which indicates his proximity to the place of refuge. They travel along the edge of the water for a half-mile further, and then the man creeps on his hands and knees, passing under bushes and tangled vines, while the women wait and tremble, for it is growing lighter every moment. Birds begin to chirp and flutter, the soft, gurgling notes of the wild-turkey resound through the wood, a bar of gold is lifted from the eastern gates, and morning is let in— the bosom of the lake flashes rose-red ; little frosty points glitter here and there on trees and clumps of dried grass—suddenly there is a great crash in the underbrush not a rod away, and Rose flings herself into Maum Guinea's arms, screaming:

" We's caught! we's caught!"

" Hush, chile," whispered the woman, sternly, " it's only a deer!"

Ah, yes! it was a beautiful deer coming to the lake for his morning draught; but at sight of the group he had startled, he bounded off, as startled as they—and Rose drew a long breath of relief.

The fright made them all nervous; it seemed to Hyperion as if there was a mist before his eyes which prevented his finding what he knew was there, while Maumy pressed in her arms the timid creature whose heart fluttered wildly against her own—keeping, at the same time, a keen glance wandering in every direction.

" Oh, 'Perion, I's afraid it's not here at all!"

"Don't say so, Rose; I know it is here, somewhere."

" Hark !" said Maum Guinea, " I hear a horn !"

Hyperion straightened himself up to listen.

" Yes," he replied, " they are in the woods now."

" T'ank de Lord ! here is de cave ! Quick, Rose, Maumy !"

The woman stooped down and crawled through the low opening from before which he had parted the dripping moss and dried vines. It was all darkness and uncertainty before them, detection and despair outside.

Hyperion quickly followed, replacing the door which nature had hung before the grotto, as carefully as possible. They crept back as far as they dared, and sat huddled together on the damp, cold rock which floored the cavern. All was doubt and night about them, though they could watch the gleam of day which pierced the curtain at the entrance. As the sun rose higher, there was more light about them ; they could dimly discern their surroundings ; so that Rose could convince herself that no crouching panther was near, to spring upon them unaware.

Dismal hours crept by like slimy snails. Fatigue overpowered the young girl, and with head on Maumy's bosom, she slept, her hand still clasped by her lover, whose eyes were fixed upon her face, constantly—a face delicate and pretty, even with the brilliant eyes shut in slumber, and in this wan light looking white and clear as marble.

It was afternoon when she awoke, quite ready to eat the dry biscuit, and the slice of ham, which Maum Guinea drew from her ample pocket. While they were partaking of this considerately-provided lunch, they heard sounds which arrested every faculty, holding it in strained suspense.

The horn which they had heard in the morning resounded through the woods, so close at hand that it seemed almost at the entrance of the cave.

It was followed by the voices of men, and the barking of a dog. By the shouts and excited conversation, it was plain that the party thought themselves on the track of the fugitives.

"Do you s'pose dey would bring dem turrible dogs?" whispered Rose.

"Never!" responded Maum Guinea, emphatically; "neider of our masters would do *dat*."

"I's got lead 'nuff here to kill a couple of bloodhounds," muttered Hyperion, grasping his revolver, while a fierce fire burned in his eyes.

"I'm not 'fraid of *one*," answered Maum Guinea, looking at her knife, "but massa wouldn't do *dat*. Dey don't keep 'em, and dey wouldn't be known to borrow 'em. 'Sides, dey don't want to tear dis yere purty flesh—'twouldn't be worf' five t'ousand dollars, after de dogs had worried 't,"—and she laid her hand on the girl's shoulder. "If 'twas only my ole bones, 'twouldn't matter."

"Dat cursed Bruno will hunt me out, dough," suddenly exclaimed the man, almost aloud; and surely enough, the next moment, whining and barking around their hiding-place, the dog came.

They heard him scratching at the vines, and then he bounded through the frail barrier, and ran up to them with a rejoicing look. He was a fine, large animal, owned by Philip, and had always been an especial favorite with Hyperion, whose liking he had faithfully returned. Totally unconscious of the peril in which he was placing his friend, he leaped around him caressingly, with quick cries of excitement and pleasure.

"Lie down, sir! be still!" said the man, in a low, stern voice; but the dog was too much excited by his discovery to obey with his usual alacrity.

In that time of danger, Hyperion would have shot down the animal, much as he liked him, but the report of the pistol would be yet more fatal. Maum Guinea, powerful and self-possessed, seized the dog's head, and drew the sharp meat-knife which she carried, firmly across his throat.

"Poor Bruno!" murmured Rose, as he rolled over in death.

And then the trio waited in such suspense as is agony of itself.

The dog had so torn and trampled the vines which previously concealed the entrance, as to make its discovery an easy matter; and doubtless the men were close upon his tracks. A man parted the bushes, peered in, stooped, crawled through the opening, and stood before them, regarding the group with a curious and mingled expression. It was Johnson, of Judge Bell's plantation—they were discovered! Hyperion might have killed him, but he would have been compelled ultimately to surrender, and it was not in his heart to kill any one of his pursuers—unless it might be Rose's new owner. He looked in the agitated faces before him, and his eyes finally settled upon the girl's. She threw up her hands, imploringly:

"Jonson," she whispered, "*you* will not tell on us?"

"Good-bye, Rose; if you get off from here, don't forget Jonson."

He turned abruptly, and had just made his way out, and pulled the bushes hastily over the spot, when others came up, and they heard him say:

"Where's Bruno? I've been chasing him up, as he seems to be on track of suthin; but he's gone off in dat thicket now. 'Pears to me dat brush looks rudder suspicious. Dar ain't nothin' to be seen 'round here. Let's 'xamine dat brush-heap,"—and the party went away, leaving the fugitives another respite.

The sound of pursuit did not again approach so near them ; but they had been too thoroughly alarmed to recover even the small measure of repose they had enjoyed through the morning. The afternoon wore away wearily. As the darkness began to close up the mouth of the cave, poor Rose's courage almost gave way. She was cold and hungry, thirsty and weary, her bones ached, and her flesh quivered ; her mind was full of apprehension of wild animals which might be coming home to their lairs ; she thought of Miss Virginia, and her pleasant chamber full of warmth and light—and again she thought of Mr. Talfierro, and nestling closer to her lover, borrowed from his superior strength and courage, energy to endure her trials.

When it was quite night, they crept forth, to drink of the waters of the lake, and to stretch their cramped and chilly limbs. It had been discussed whether they had better start that night, and try to make their way to the river, or wait where they were for a day or two, until the woods had been thoroughly searched, and the chase abandoned. As they had enough food to keep them from perishing, for a couple of days, and were now probably more secure where they were for the present, they decided to remain one day longer in their hiding-place. When they had quaffed the water for which they had been longing many hours, and eaten the one biscuit apiece which Maum Guinea distributed, they gathered branches of hemlock, and armsful of dry grass, which they carried into the cave, to make their damp resting-place more endurable. In order to break off branches where the disturbance would not be observed by any passing eye, Hyperion climbed trees, and selected them from the upper portions. It was a relief to them to have something wherewith to busy themselves, and they were almost sorry when their work was done.

A little while they sat on the bank, listening to the soft plash of the water, and looking at the dancing stars, glimmering like shivered diamonds in the bosom of the lake. Maum Guinea sat a little apart from the young couple, lost in her own peculiar reveries; while they, thus together, whose lips and hands could touch at will, were happy, despite the threatening circumstances which surrounded them.

"I t'ink we're going to have good times, 'fore long, Rose," whispered her lover. "If we get on a boat, and get safe to a free State, den we have no more trouble. We'll be married right away; and we'll keep house of our own—nobody only you and I and Maumy. Maumy will cook, and you will sew for ladies, and I will do—oh, many t'ings! We'll live right nice. No rich gentleum won't come for to buy you dar—we'll be married man and wife like white folks. And our pretty pickaninnies won't be sold 'way from us dar, Rose."

The girl laughed, and slapped his cheek; if there had been light, he might have seen the rich blood, which thrilled through her frame at his words, rush into her cheeks with a dark glow which had a beauty of its own.

So they talked and caressed each other, until the bitter reality of their situation was almost forgotten.

"Come," said Maum Guinea, after a time, "we must sleep what we can to-night; for to-morrow night, de Lord willin', we'll be marching for a better land dan dis."

Ah! a better land.

They crept back into the cave. The fragrant hemlock, and crisp, elastic grass made a comparatively comfortable couch; Maumy made of her bosom a pillow for Rose, and the three slept securely in their novel bedchamber.

"Oh, I's so tired!" exclaimed Rose, in her childlike manner, as the long hours of the succeeding day crept onward, with nothing to vary their monotony. "Maumy, don't you remember you partly promised to tell us a story 'bout your self? I wish you'd tell it now. Do, Maumy, I's so tired."

"Better not tell it, 'till we're safe away from dis yere country. 'Might make you low-spirited, chile; and you'll need all your courage."

"I'd rudder you'd tell it now. When we get 'way from here, I don't want to hear t'ings to make me sad—want to forget 'em. Do, Ginny! my head aches, and the time is so long."

"I never have tole it to nobody," muttered the woman.

"Maybe you'd feel better to tell it to *us*, Maumy."

"Ah! I never 'spect to feel better on dis yearth, chile. Folks gets where dar ain't any comfort for 'em, sometimes. But seeing I'm yer maumy now, sartain, and have took up my lot wid yours, whatever happens, maybe I'll tell it to ye."

She sat silent a few moments, as if making up her mind to the effort. Dew dripped from the dark rocks above them; the only light was the dull glimmer at the mouth of the cave; the dreariness of the place was indescribable, and her mood was just desperate enough to impel her to the narrative which hitherto had never passed her lips. With her two eager listeners gazing into her strange, expressive face, Maum Guinea began her story.

CHAPTER X.

MAUM GUINEA'S STORY.

Soft my heart, and warm his wooing,
What we did seemed, while 'twas doing,
  Beautiful and wise;
Wiser, fairer, more in tune
Than all else in that sweet June,
And sinless as the skies
That warmed the willing earth, thro' all the languid skies.
  SYDNEY DOBELL.

And closer, closer to her heart,
  She held the little child,
Who stretched its fragile hand to feel
  Her bosom's warmth, and smiled.

But she—she did not own a touch
  Of that fond little hand—
Great God! that such a thing should be,
  Within a Christian land!—ALDRICH.

" WHEN I was a little girl I lived on de banks of de James
river. 'Twas a purty place, and we b'longed to a right nice
family; we use to pride ourselves on our family. We held
our heads mighty high 'kase we b'long to Massa Gregory.
De house was big and han'some; dar was flowers all about
it, and gardens, and de lawn in front run straight down to de
river. I use to set under de big trees and see de water flow
by, all blue and full of gold sparkles. Nebber, nebber do I
look up to de Almighty's heaben above us, w'en it's bright
and full of stars, but I minds de James river, and de days
w'en I was a girl. I was a wild kind of a cre'tur—not bad,
but full of fun and mischief; I was happy all day long; and
I was so pert dey let me be, and didn' ask me to work not
enough to hurt a chicken. Massa was a pleasant man; he
'lowed his slaves to l'arn to read, if dey want to, and to go
to meetin'; he nebber whip 'em, 'less dey was awful bad, and
prowoked him to it. Missus was a Christian lady, jest as

sweet and pious as de Lord ever made. She took a liking to
me, and she learned me to read de Bible, in her own room;
and she taught me how it was wicked to do wrong, and w'at
it was to be good and do right. I had no parents, dat I
knew, and she sort of petted me and kep' me 'round her,
doing light work for her, like sewing and such, and I had
more'n half my time to myself. She dressed me nice, and
taught me to be tidy and careful. I loved her so much, I
tried to do jest as she wanted, but I was wild, and I used to
play too much, and tear my frocks and lose things. Den
she'd scold me so softly, it broke me down worse dan if she
was ugly, and I'd cry and try to do better. Her eyes wasn't
berry strong, and she learned me to read so well, I had to
read de Bible to her mos' ebery evening, and always on de
Sabbath day. I didn't like it, 'cause it was so solemn, and·
I'd rudder be in de kitchen, cuttin' up, or out on de lawn a
lookin' at de flowers and water; but I wouldn' let on I
didn' like it, fear I'd hurt her feelings. She'd t'ink it was
awful if I'd say I didn't like de Bible. I _did_ love it, only it
was so sober, and I was so full of fun; and it use to make
me feel pleasant and patient, and I was fond of hearing my
missus pray, too—she use to pray for _me_ well as for white
folks, and for her servants as if dey was her chil'ren. She
was so beautiful, I never tired looking at Missus Gregory;
not dat she was young, for she was growin' past middle-age,
but her face was so sweet, and she allers wore such fine lace
on her caps and about her throat and wrists, and her cheeks
were so pale and fine, and her. hands so white, and she was
so graceful and such a perfect lady. I've nebber seen her like
to dis day.

"She tried not to make too much of any of her yearthly
idols, but her heart was sot on her boy. Most while, w'en I
was a growing girl, he was up North at college. He was an

only chile, and fadder and mudder bof t'ought dar nebber was anodder like him. W'en his letters use to come, dey would read 'em so eager and laugh ober 'em; and bym-bye missus would 'teal up-stairs and read 'em again, and kiss 'em, and sit wid 'em in her lap, looking out de window and smiling to herself.

"One winter we was going to hab grand times at Chris'-mas, for young Massa Dudley was comin' home for good and all. He'd done got tru' wid school, and was comin' home a young gentleum. Missus was glad, 'cause he was not going back; and we was tickled, 'cause we t'ought dar would be gay times wid young massa in de house.

"De cook, she was busy for weeks. She took me in de kitchen, mornin's, and made me help her stone raisins and chop apples, and beat eggs and mix up cake—den was when I took my first lesson in cookin'. I liked to go dar, 'cause de merry clatter of de dishes, and all de nice articles she was at liberty to use, made it pleasant; and she'd gib me bunch of raisins and piece of citron or orange for being good 'bout helpin' her. We made cake 'nuff for a weddin'; and mince-pies, and ebery t'ing nice dat would keep; and jest afore de day, all sorts of t'ings besides. 'Peared as if ole cook 'membered ebery dish dat massa Dudley liked 'specially well, and dat was good many, for w'en he'd been home of holidays he'd commonly been blessed wid a growin' appetite.

"Laws! day 'fore Chris'mas, w'at a lookin' for de stage dar was! Even missus couldn' keep 'way from de winder, and little Peter, de waiter-boy, he sot out on top de fence on a little rise of groun', to be de first to tell de news. Dinner was nigh done bein' ready, and Dinah was beginning to fret; I'd gone and put on a clean frock to help wait on table, and missus had pulled de parlor curtains open fifty times, w'en Peter gib a shout, and we all run, and de stage come a-rollin'

'long and stopped 'fore de house. 'Tain't much, to hear me
tell de little pertickelers; but it was much to *me*, in dem
days, and I's nebber forgot de smallest circumstance. W'en
Massa Dudley sprung out de stage, light as a feader, de people
dey all rushed 'round a-kissin' him and shakin' hands—ole
nurse she hugged him right 'round de neck, and he laughed
and was mighty good-natured, but hurried 'way from us up
to de porch, where missus was standin' wid her shawl 'round
her, waiting to welcome him home. *I* didn' speak to him,
nor shake hands like de rest; and w'en dinner was on de
table, I didn' like to go in de room to wait on it. He looked
so *perfeck* w'en he sprung out de stage, dat I jus' shrunk
away and didn' dar' to speak to him. Sassy as I was; and
full of laugh and fun, I hadn' a word to say, but jus' stood
back so he wouldn' notice me.

"I's a-going to tell you jus' how foolish I was; I shan't
spare myself. W'en de bell rung for dinner, I went into
cook's bedroom, off de cabin, and took a look in a little glass
she kep' hanging dar. 'Twas de firs' time in my life I had
t'ought 'bout how I looked. Ah! w'at a silly chile I was!
as if it made speck o' difference to Massa Dudley how a
nigger look! but I'd been sp'iled and petted, and I was jus'
sixteen year ole, and nebber had felt serious, 'cept on Sundays,
since I was born. I t'ought my pink frock was mighty purty,
and I tossed my goold ear-rings for all de worl' as Rose tosses
her's when she feels sperited and bright. I was proud of my
hair, 'cause 'twas long enuff to braid, and real shiny; but
w'en I looked in de glass I wished I wasn't nigger at all. I
wished I was all white 'stead of part.

"Dey had a merry dinner—so much talk, so many t'ings to
tell; and Massa Dudley, he tell such cur'ous stories he keep
'em laughing half de time. I could see how proud his
mudder was. He was so glad to be to home, his eyes shone

and his cheeks was red; he was as gay as a kitten, and he praised all de dishes, and eat 'nuff to satisfy ole cook, almost. I couldn' look up, hardly, I felt so shy, which was new for me; and w'en dinner was mos' done finished, he noticed me, and says to his mudder:

"'Who you got dar? a new girl? Bless me, if it ain't little Ginny grown up like a sunflower! She makes you a nice maid, don't she, mudder?'

"'Yes, Ginny is a great help to me. She's my right hand, said missus, and den I felt happy to be praised by *her*; but I darsn't look up, and young massa laugh, and say:

"''Twas right new to see a bashful darkey.'

"Woll, dey had a merry Chris'mas; nebber was a merrier Chris'mas on de ole Gregory plantation; young massa made de house as bright as a streak of sunshine; dar was company, and music, and feasting, till after New Year's. I had a good time waitin' on de company, and seein' all de frolicks, 'sides having presents and a share of all de niceties. I felt happy; but 'twas a queer feeling, not like I used to w'en I romped on de lawn and cut up all kind o' mischief; I was quiet and proper, so dat missus praised me, and was pleased de way I waited on her visitors.

"After dat I was more her favorite dan ever. She learned me to sew nice and 'broider, and I 'broidered pair o' slippers for her son, w'ich she wanted to give him; I read to her evenings, and it wasn't so tiresome to me den, 'cause de weader was cold, and I couldn' go a-rambling over de lawn and down de river, as I did in summer. I was so quiet and orderly, and read de Bible so willin', missus t'ought I was going to be good Christian girl, and she said I might jine de church if I wanted. But I said I'd wait till spring.

"Woll, it come spring. De flowers begun to blow open in de soft mornin's; de sky was full of purty clouds, de winds talk, de birds sing, and my heart—poor, foolish, colored-girl's heart—grow fuller and fuller, till I couldn' breaf no more in de house, and one warm night, just afore dark, I run down to de edge of de water, and stand and look at de little sparkles of sunshine not quite gone 'way on de ripples; and I heard somebody come whistlin' and singing to hisself along de bank. I wanted to run back, but I couldn' stir a step; my heart beat so hard, and I jus' purtended I didn' see him, and w'en he come close by I didn' look up at all; so he stops side of me, and says:

"' Look up, Ginny. I've been home three months, and I've never seen your eyes yet, you shy little thing.'

"I had to mind him; and I 'spect he saw right tru' my eyes what was in my heart, but I couldn' help it to save my life.

"' You've got han'some eyes, Ginny,' says he, ' dey're de softest and brightest ever I saw,'—and den he stooped, picking up pebbles and t'rowing 'em into de water, and bym-bye he asked me what I was looking at so steady, when he come along; and I told him I loved de James river, and I often come and look at de water w'en it was full of sparkles. He made me talk, and I got over bein' so bashful, and felt so strange and happy in his company, and he kep' his eyes on my face, and smiled so sweet, and we stood dar till it was quite dark, w'en he said:

"' I declar', you're quite a girl, Ginny—mudder is learning you too much. You must give me a kiss, Ginny, to pay for being so purty,'—and he put his arm around my waist, and kissed me, and laughed a little.

"I run away, frightened and happy too. W'en I got near de house, missus called me out de window to come up and read my evening chapter. I could hardly see de words, dey danced so, and I couldn' tell one t'ing I'd been a-readin' 'bout w'en I got tru'. I sot by de window, de Bible in my lap, and I got looking at de stars, and t'inking of Massa Dudley, and I didn' hear missus till she'd spoke to me twice.

"'Ginny,' said she, again, very stern for her, 'I see suthin to-night that displease me very much.'

"I hung my head, for I knew den she'd been looking out de window, and seen us togedder down by de river; I hadn' t'ought nor done nothing wicked, but I felt 'shamed and guilty for all.

"'Mind, Ginny,' she said, 'I don't blame *you*—it's my son dat's to blame if any thing wrong should happen. But I want to warn you. I shall speak to him also. You mus' remember what you've learned in dat Holy Book—if you sin you won't be ignorant, for I've taught you your duty. I want you to be a good girl and a Christian. God has made you of a different color and race from us; but he has given you sense enough to know what's right and proper. Some missuses is willin' der slaves should do wrong; but I am not. Be a good girl, and you shall have a worthy husband from among your own people one of dese days. Don't forget what I've said, Ginny.'

"Dear missus! she was almost a saint. I wanted to kneel down and kiss her hand, and promise to mind her faithfully, but my t'roat choked up, and I went out silent. If I'd followed her advice, I'd saved myself lots o' trouble. I did mind it for a while—but 'de heart is deceitful above all t'ings, and desp'rately wicked,' and I 'spect mine was one of de worst. Leastwise, it deceived *me*. What I was doin' 'peared to me right at de time. I wasn't sorry, I wasn't 'shamed—only I didn't want missus to know it. Dat spring and summer I was berry happy. I use to take my sewing and set under a great elm tree by de water's edge, singing softly to myself— never 'flecting 'bout de future—jus' as gay and karless as de birds overhead; only once-and-awhile I'd take fits of thinking, and den I'd be way down low-sperited.

"So one day I was sewing in missus' chamber, and I wasn't very well, and I got dizzy and couldn't sew for a little w'ile, and she took notice of me. I t'ink she was as angry as she ever 'lowed herself to be; and I t'ink she was more hurt at her son dan she was angry wid me; for I know she talked to him dat evening long time, and nex' day he went off to an uncle's, and didn' come back for a fortnight.

"I was dreadful hurt and grieved to t'ink missus 'spised me, and couldn't abide me 'round her any more. She didn' let me read to her, nor set in her room to sew; but made me go to Chloe's cabin, and dar I lived till my baby was born. 'Twas a little girl, most as white as anybody's chile. Missus nebber come to see it, dough she sent me nice t'ings for it to wear and for me to eat when I was getting well. Den it was I 'gan to 'flect on what I was and what I'd done. If I'd been like mos' niggers I shouldn't a cared a speck; I'd taken it easy and been idle and karless. But somehow I was allers deeper in my feelings dan most colored folks; and missus' teaching had made me more so.

"My baby was the purtiest little cre'tur that ever lived. I loved her. If I was to tell you a t'ousand times you couldn' guess how much I loved her. W'en she was asleep, I'd sit and watch her all de time; w'en she was awake in my lap, I'd look into her eyes and never get tired. She had such beautiful eyes—blue—yes, chil'ren, her eyes were blue as Massa Dudley's—and so soft and smiling; and her head was covered with little black shiny rings of silky hair; and, though she was dark-complected, she had red lips, and rich dimples in her golden arms and neck. Every body said she was a perfect beauty.

"I'd a been perfectly happy with my baby, only I wanted

Massa Dudley to see her, and he never come near us. She
was born in the winter; and the first time I saw him after it,
was when I was setting up at the window, quite well, and
holding up little Judy, trying to make her laugh. He went
by de cabin, wid his gun on his shoulder, going a-hunting,
and he looked up and laughed, and asked me how I was
getting along; but he didn't notice baby, only wid a queer,
quick kind o' look, and den he hurried on as if he was 'fraid
of something.

"I didn' see him to speak to him till spring-time come
again; but I comforted myself t'inking how purty Judy was
growing, and how we'd 'joy ourselves playin' on de lawn, in
de grass, w'en warm weader come. So one day I was setting
on de door-step of our cabin, and Massa Dudley come along,
and dis time he stop and speak to us; it was jus' a year from
de time he first spoke to me down by de river, and my heart
was full, a-t'inking of it, 'fore I heard him coming.

"'You're better-lookin' dan ever, Ginny,' says he, wid his
ole smile. 'You make a right nice maumy. Is dis your
b_by? She's a bright little thing. I'm sure Madam Gregory
needn't have scolded us so for our naughty doings. Your
baby'll sell for a t'ousand dollars by time you're ready to
wean it. It's good property. Never seen a nicer darkey,'-
and he laughed and chucked me under de chin, and went off
whistlin'.

"It was a bright spring day, full of sunshine; but it grew
suddenly dark to me—dark and cold. My heart grew cold.
Yes, chil'ren, it grew so cold, it's never been rea'ly warm
since. Only the feel of the children's soft hands in my bosom
has kept it warm at all. I sot still till night, till ole Chloe
call me in, tellin' me Judy would cotch cold. I went in and
warmed my baby by de fire whar supper was cooked; I
rubbed her little cold feet, and nussed her, but half my comfort

in her was took away—done gone forever. I knew now, dat
de purtier and de smarter she was, de more likely I was to
lose her—de brighter she was, de more money she was worf!
Den I had my own selfish trouble. I loved young massa—
loved him jus' as well as w'ite folks love—mighty sight better
dan de most. I 'dored the very yearth he trod on—and it
broke my heart to hab him speak so to me. I oughter have
'spected it—I'd no reason to 'spect anyt'ing else. I knew I
was a slave—a poor, ignorant colored person; an' dat I'd no
business to feel hurt. Folks would have laughed to know I
felt bad 'bout his speaking so. 'Course he'd act so and feel
so. I was a fool, and I knew it. I didn't blame him, 'cause
I'd nothing to blame. I only loved him all de more, and
wished he'd come about and be as kind to me as he used
to be.

"But he didn't take much notice of me dat summer. I
guess his mudder talked him out of it—'sides, he was 'way
visiting good deal, and by fall it began to be talked on de
plantation dat Massa Dudley was goin' soon to bring a bride
to de ole Gregory mansion.

"Everybody but me was tickled 'bout it—de darkeys like
weddings and merry times, and dey's allers pleased when sich
t'ings are coming off. My heart was sore; but nobody knew
nuffin' 'bout it. I was so quiet and humble—not sassy and
set-up, like some of de girls—dat missus took me back
into her favor. I t'ink she was sorry for me, dough she said
nothing. I was 'round de house a good deal, sewing and
waiting on her; but I couldn' keep my baby tru' de day; it
was sent off, wid de oder babies, to de pen for ole Chloe to
mind; I had it to sleep wid me nights, and I went to nurse
it once or twice a day to de pen. I felt cu'ros 'bout my baby;
I couldn' b'ar to have it 'sociate wid de oder little niggers in
de pen. I made its clothes good, and it was always clean

when I give it to ole nurse; but it would always get dirty rollin' 'round and playing wid de rest. Nobody knew how I felt about it, and Chloe would jeer me for keeping it so fine; but dey t'ought it was 'cause I could sew so nice, and oder women jus' had rags on der chil'ren.

"Some time in de summer, wid missus' advice and consent, I jined de church. De church was a great comfort to me, and I t'ink it relieved Massa Dudley's mind, too; he was glad to get rid of me so, for he knew I was of a terrible passionate disposition, and he hadn't cared to see me 'round much, after he'd got engaged to be married.

"'Read your Bible, Ginny, and be a good girl,' he says to me, kind of mock-solemn, wid dat naughty laugh dat allers make him look so han'some, but dat showed de Lucifer dar was in him—it was de day he was going off for to bring his bride home.

"I forgot w'at de good Book says about doing good to dem dat despitefully use you; my cheeks got hot, and my eyes flashed fire, for I t'ought he was kinder making fun of me, and de more I loved him, de more I couldn't b'ar it.

"'Give my respects to your wife. I hope I shall like her mighty well!' I answered back, so spiteful dat it sobered him down, and he shook his finger at me, and said:

"'Take car', Ginny! don't you go to being naughty—if you get ill-tempered, we may have to sell you!'—and he walked off so haughty, as masters can walk, w'en dey walk over brack people's feelin's.

"It didn't put me in a very good humor for seeing de bride. I kep' brooding over it all de week de family was away. I worked hard, dough, to keep from getting bitter, and I done my work right well. I made de bride's chamber look beautiful, and I helped Dinah wid de cake and fixin's, doin' almost better dan she. I'd been considered to

hab good taste, for a slave-girl; I could draw patterns for
embroidery, and my needlework was beautiful; so I sot to
work to see how well I could make t'ings look de day dey
was all 'spected back. I put flowers in de wedding-chamber
and parlors, and set de table splendid—de butler he jus' stand
back and let me fix it.

"Woll, I t'ink a woman is a woman, if she *have* got brack
blood in her. W'en all was done, I went and changed my
own dress. I made myself look jus' as handsome as I could.
I had some corals missus had gib me, and I put 'em in my
hair; I had a silk dress, and I put it on, wid some bows of
red ribbon. I'd never worked enough to spile my hands,
and I was proud of 'em 'cause dey was slender and soft.
Den I dressed up little Judy in a w'ite frock, wid a string of
beads round her neck and bows on her shoulders, and I
brushed out her ha'r till it was all in shiny rings down onto
her neck; I got a bouquet of flowers, which I intended to
give to de bride when she come in de hall; and I waited wid
de rest of de serbants.

"Dar was a great time when Massa Gregory drew up wid
his wife; and after dem, young massa wid his bride. De
whole plantation was a laughing and shakin' hands, and wish-
in' 'em joy, and ole Dinah was a-making herself very conspicuous, as usual. I stood back to see how de bride looked.
I'd a burning curiosity to see if she was beautiful, and as
much of a lady as my missus. Dey say jealousy makes
people's eyes sharp. De minit I looked at her I knowed she
was a cold-hearted, selfish kind of a woman, who'd married
Massa Dudley 'cause he was rich and good family. She was
'bout nineteen or twenty; tall, rather pale, with gold-colored
hair and very delicate features. She was a good form, and
would have passed for a beauty most anywhar; but *I* didn't
t'ink she was beautiful. She was too quiet and cold—she hadn't

no color nor sparkle 'bout her. I t'ought she was tired of all de 'gratulations and hand-shaking, and so on ; but she was too artful to show it, and smiled pleasantly at everybody. I stood in de hall, holdin' Judy's hands, wid my flowers all ready to pursent w'en she come in. I was de last to speak to her. She took my bouquet very gracious, and den she stooped and patted Judy on de head—she wanted to seem good-natured, to get de good-will of de people.

"'W'at a lovely child !' said she ; ' is she yours, girl ?'

"I don' know w'at demon made me answer :

"'Yes, mine and Massa Dudley's.'

"Nobody heard me but she, I spoke so low ; she cast a glance at her husband, and then back to me—I knew I was as handsome as she was, any day, and I didn' care—I felt so wicked jus' den.

"She made no answer, of course ; she was surprised at my impudence, and I ought to have been punished for it, I know ; but her eyes spoke as plain as words, before she swep' by me :

"'I'll have you whipped and sold before long, girl.'

"I was sorry de next minit—not on my own accourt, but Massa Dudley's, and my own dear missus. I'd made an enemy, widout gaining anyt'ing by it—not dat I s'posed she'd t'ink of it long, or car' for it—such t'ings too common ; but I was too han'some, and had been too impertinent 'bout it, to be 'scused as a common case.

"I was sorry I'd said it, 'cause I felt I'd done Massa Dudley an injury ; I loved him too well to want to harm him ; I'd a laid down my life for him, any day, dough he cared no more for me dan if I was cattle ; it was only w'en de w'ite blood in me took fire and blazed up, dat I did sich hateful t'ings. White blood proud and 'vengeful—brack blood warm and kind. I 'dored him wid de wild heart of brack woman, and sometimes I hated him wid proud heart of white woman

—for, ye see, de blood is mixed in our veins, chil'ren—its all
mixed up and fermenting, and it makes trouble. Dem blue
eyes of Miss Dudley Gregory was cold and sharp as steel—
dey went tru' me wid a pang, and dey made me feel wicked
for a spell. But I was a member of de church, and tried to
be a Christian; I prayed de Lord forgive me, 'fore I went
in de dining-room, and I got de ugly feelin' down. I was
sorry; I would have begged de young missus' pardon, if I'd
had a chance. All I could do was to be submissive and
humble—to put de *pert* all out my manners; so I waited on
de company jus' as well as I knew how, and paid 'tention to
nothing but my work.

"Dar was dancing and music dat ebening; de parlors were
lighted all up like de sun; my breast was sad, I didn' know
why, but I kep' 'way from de house, setting under de oak
down by de river, listening to the murmur of de water, wid
little Judy fas' asleep in my arms. De sound of de water
kind o' got in my head, and whirled and sung so sorrowful—
hark, chil'ren! do you hear de lake out dar talking?—it's
saying de same t'ings now.

"Bym-bye, de house settled back in de ole ways; 'cepting
dar was no more company coming and going; young missus
was fond of showing off in such times, and Massa Dudley
was proud of her looks, and dressed her splendid. She
wanted me for dressin'-maid, I had such taste; but I begged
Missus Gregory to let me off, which she was kind enough to
do, and 'lowed me to gib up waitin', and take to cookin'. I
didn' fancy cookin'-work, but it kep' me from de house, and
give me peace of mind; it was hard, and sp'iled my hands,
but I wasn't proud any more, and I prayed every night for
de welfar' of de whole family. I *couldn'* like young missus,
but I could pray for her. I never knew whedder Missus
Gregory like her new daughter, or not; I t'ink she know she

was vain and selfish; but she was so kind and charitable, she would try to have good influence widout saying much 'bout it.

"Woll, time run along, winter and summer, winter and summer, t'ree, four years. Judy growed into a bright little girl, trottin' round, taking care of herself. If I say it, who was her mudder, de sun never shone on anodder such a chile—she was beautiful as an angel—*everybody* said so. Her eyes were as dark as blue eyes could be, wid long, drooped lashes; and her hair was just one soft fleecy cloud of shining rings, blowing 'bout her face; her mouth was red as a strawberry, and her skin was handsomer dan any white chile's could be—a sort of brown, not dark, rich and smooth and velvety, wid de red in her cheeks like peaches—and her motions! seemed she didn' move nor walk like common chile. She loved de grass, and trees, and talking water, well as her maumy use to; she use to frolic 'bout on de lawn like a bird, her little red dress darting 'bout in de light and shade. Missus Gregory give me purty bits of bright calico and muslin for her frocks, and I use to set up nights to make 'em han'some. Warm weather, she wouldn' have no shoes—'twan't allowed, and her little round feet were so purty and dimpled, I was prouder of 'em dan as if dar were open-work stockings and kid slippers on 'em.

"All dis time, dar didn' come no heir to de Gregory plantation; Massa Dudley give up hopes of dar ever being one, and it worried him more dan he was willing to let on. Missus Dudley didn't car', 'cause she'd rather keep 'bout in gay company, and be admired, dan be shut up in her chamber having children; only, when she see her husband was disappointed, dat made her jealous if she see him looking at oder people's babies. She was jus' as jealous as she was selfish.

"If little Judy come 'bout de house, she'd drive her away.

and when missus would reprove her, said she couldn't abide
de nigger chil'ren round her—dey'r place wasn't in de house
—dey made her nervous, de little brats did. Dar was nothing
'bout Judy to make any fine lady nervous—'less de angels
demselves make 'em so. I bathed her every night, and
brushed her curls, and kept her neat and tidy as a rose. She
was a good chile; she loved everybody; her lip would
quiver when de han'some pale lady spoke so cross to her.
But Missus Gregory got so she like to have little Judy come
to see *her ;* she taught her to read, and let her run 'bout her
chamber much as she mind to. You see, missus was in a
decline; she didn' 'spect to live long, and she'd got over the
aversion she once felt for poor little Judy; she couldn't go
out of her room much, and she liked de chile's company; it
'mused her, and passed away de time.

"I's always b'lieved 'twas missus' soft manners and heav-
enly face made my chile so gentle and obedient; she sort o'
caught some of the dying grace of that dear missus.

"'Spect Missus Dudley never got quite over being jealous
of me and spiteful at Judy. I knew well 'nuff 'twas her
first put it in Massa Gregory's head dat I ought to be
married.

"'Twas a shame,' she said, 'for me to be wasting my bes'
days, widout a husband! W'at good would I be to de estate,
living single?'

"So Massa Gregory, Massa Dudley, and young missus, dey
all said I must pick out a husband from some de hands on
de plantation. I jus' told 'em I *wouldn'*—I didn' want no
husband—I'd work hard for 'em as long as I lived; but I
begged dem not to 'sist on my marrying. Somehow, I
couldn't bring my mind to it; I'd smothered my passion for
my master; I'd scourged it and whipped it down; and now
I was living quietly, wid my chile and my Bible for company,

and I didn't want to rile up all my peace, taking up wid a man I didn' car' for.

"I went to missus 'bout it; and she put her foot down for once, dough everybody else commonly had der own way, dat it shouldn' be—dey should let me alone—if I didn't meet anybody I wanted, I needn't get married.

"So dey let me alone for awhile, till dar come a great trouble and grief to me—my dear missus died. It broke my heart to see her go; but she went so patient and willin'. She didn' forget poor slave-girl in dat solemn time. She made her husband and son promise never to sell me nor my chile, whatever happened.. She left me her Bible, and several little trinkets she knew I'd prize; and she put round little Judy's neck a string of old-fashioned gold-beads she'd worn herself. Here dey are, now, chil'ren—look at 'em—I allers keep 'em in my bosom, day and night.

"'Bout a year after missus died, ole massa said I mus' marry—couldn' have no more foolin'; I was de healthiest, bes'-looking girl he owned, and I mus' have a husband. I cried 'bout it, but I couldn't help myself. White masters owns brack folks' feelin's as well as der bodies. So I was married to Jackson, massa's teamster, who had wanted me long before, but I'd given him de mitten out-and-out. He was right black—no w'ite blood in him, good-looking and kind-tempered, and he loved me and little Judy faithfully.

"We had a little cabin of our own fixed up more comfor'-able dan de most, 'cause I had a way of keeping t'ings nice, and Jackson like to see 'em so. I did de cookin' for de house —de most of it—wid a girl to cl'ar up and do de drudgery; den I had a good-sized room of my own, 'sides de kitchen, wid a table and set o' chairs, and walences 'round de bed, and a stand for de Bible, and a bit o' carpet. Little Judy was six years ole when I married Jackson.

" Woll, we had chil'ren—four in all. I took good car' of dem ; but dey never seem to me *my own*, like Judy. Dey was nice pickaninnies, some mos' as brack as der fadder, some more like der maumy — but dey was no more like Judy dan dark is like light. I couldn' help being kind to my husband, he was so good and 'tentive to me—had allers liked me ever sence he was little, and I was so good to his chil'ren—but my heart clung to my own chile more and more, wilder and wilder—oh, Lord of mercy, how I did love my Judy !

" Jackson liked her, too ; he wasn't jealous 'cause I favored her ; he sort of worshipped her—he told me, of'en and of'en, she was an angel, and he was 'fraid suthin would happen to her. Ah ! dat was an echo of my own heart. I didn' dar' to breaf when I t'ought of it. She was too purty, too good, too 'telligent for a slave. She could read any book she laid hands on. She knew all the hymns and psalms in the hymn-book missus give me for her. She was so innocent and pious. Sometimes she played wid de worst little niggers on de plant-ation ; but she never seemed to take harm from 'em—dust wouldn't stick to her.

" When she growed old enough to be useful, I couldn't keep her all to myself. Missus Dudley wanted her in de house. She made her wait on company, and take care of her room, and do light chamber-work. I saw Massa Dudley look at her strange sometimes. He had no chil'ren, and I b'lieve his heart yearned after her. He needn' bin ashamed to call her his daughter—she was fair enough for a king's daughter. She wasn't to blame for her brack blood. And if she'd been sent up North, 'way from her maumy, no person could have told dar was a drop of it in her veins.

" All dese days I was a-working. I sewed nights for rest de serbants ; I raised chickens and wegetables of my own, dat I never tasted—I sol' 'em in de market, and laid de money 'way—not even Jackson knew 'bout dat money. He s'pected I had some, but he didn' know how much, nor where I kep' it. When missus died, she gave me twenty dollars in gold, out of her own purse-money. Dat was de beginning. You see, I had it in my mind to buy my girl's freedom. Judy shouldn't be a slave. Long as she was a little girl, I didn't mind it; but I'd allers been resolved she shouldn' grow up to be a woman, and a slave—ever since de first hour her lips touched my bosom, I'd had it in my mind. Many colored persons don't feel so; but I'd had opportunities for reading and t'inking—and, oh! I'd had plenty opportunities for *feeling*. She *wasn't* a nigger, and she *shouldn't* be a slave! De Lord hadn' set de brand of bondage on her, and man shouldn' do it.

"If I'd had my choice, I'd rudder see her married to a man as black as Jackson, than be any white massa's missus; but I'd hopes of better things dan either for her. If I could buy her freedom, could take her up North, and put her in some school, or get some white family to 'dopt her, I was bound to do it. I was resolved not to let my own feelings stan' in de way—I'd give her up—she should be free white woman, marry good white man, and her chil'ren, and her chil'ren's chil'ren, should be free. On dis my heart was sot. For dis I worked w'en I might have been idle. I took no rest. I 'couraged her to get books from massa's liberary, and read and study, so she'd have a start if she ever got in a school. She did read and study many books—it was de only deceit dat dear chile ever practise—she was so fond of books, she'd borrow 'em widout leave, 'cause massa wouldn' have allowed it. Sometimes she'd read aloud to me, when I was sewing, fine stories 'bout happy white lovers, and I t'ink to myself she should some day be as fine and as happy as dey.

"I had an ole chany tea-pot dat had been t'rown away at de house, whar I use to keep my money—gold and silver, mostly gold. Many times each year I'd count it over and over, to see how much dat golden grain had growed. Fifteen year I was a-laying up dat money—fifteen year, and I had twenty dollars to begin wid. Dar was a heap of it. It got so much, I couldn't count it; and I darsn't get nobody to do it for me. So I bought an ole 'rithmetic at a book-stall in de village, for Judy to study, and I worried over dem figgers myself, till I could get 'long and count my money. De day Judy was fifteen year ole, I counted it, and I had a t'ousand dollars. I knew massa would hold her worth more'n dat; but I 'spected he'd remember his promise to his dead wife, not to sell her, and mebbe he'd feel kindly, and willin' to let me have my own chile for dat. I could hardly keep from going right to him and asking him; but de nearer I come to parting wid Judy, de harder it was; and I t'ought, as nothing happened, and she didn' seem in danger, I'd work another year, and try and get her a little something to send her 'way up North wid. I'd give my promise to massa to come back, if he'd let me go 'long; and if I couldn't find de right folks to 'dopt her and send her to school, I'd 'prentice her to some dress-maker, so she could get her own living, and be a respectable free white woman.

"Judy was so pious and so modest, she didn' think of her looks; she didn' guess how han'some she was, and how every one turned to look after her when she passed by. I didn' want her to stir out, hardly, I was so 'fraid somebody'd want to buy her, or some de colored boys would be stepping up to her and askin' de privilege of her company. Yer needn't feel hard, 'Perion, 'cause I didn' want her to mate wid a colored man; dar was none on massa's plantation dat I felt towards as I do towards *you*—dey was coarse kind of young men, and had no learnin', and dey wasn't worthy of my Judy. Heigho! do you hear dat water in de lake keep a-moaning, Rose? I wish dis knife was out in de middle dat lake—it's horrible de way dat knife keeps a-lookin' at me!

"Did you ever hear a clap of thunder burst in a cloudless sky?—w'en de sun is shining, and dar ain't no signs of a storm? One day, 'bout t'ree months after Judy was fifteen, I heard dat clap of thunder break. De blue sky dat was over me and my chile showed a little cloud no bigger dan a man's hand, and dat was de beginning of de storm. Don't look at me so, chil'ren! I'm a withered and branchless old tree, knotted and scarred—for ye see, de lightning struck me, and I couldn' never bear green leaves again."

Maum Guinea rocked herself to and fro in terrible silence, while her listeners dared not interrupt her mood, by expressions of the interest which they felt. Rose wanted to press the clenched hand to her pitying bosom, but she could not break upon the tide of recollections which were rising in the story-teller's soul.

"Hark!" whispered Hyperion, suddenly.

The three started, every faculty strained and held in suspense. There was some person, or persons at the ingress to the cave—the vines were carefully lifted aside, some one bent down and forced his way in, and, just as Hyperion sprung to his feet, revolver in hand, a well-known voice exclaimed:

"Don't shoot—it's me—Johnson."

He stepped forward and shook hands with the party.

"I've come to pay you a friendly visit," he said, smiling, as Hyperion returned the threatening weapon to his pocket. "Couldn' rest, 'less I know how you was gettin' along. See here, Rose, w'at I brought you!" He tossed a great apple into her lap, and another into Maum Guinea's; then he drew from beneath his jacket a loaf-of bread, some slices of cold meat, and a small flask of brandy. "If you should get sick in dis damp hole, de liquor'll be useful," he said.

"W'at's our massas doing 'bout us, now?" was the first question.

"Dat's w'at I come to let you know. You see, 'twasn't easy for me to get off, 'specially in de daytime, jes' now, w'en everybody's eyes is sharpened; but I was 'fraid you'd be gone by night, and I'd miss you. I jes' want to tell you to stay where you are for a spell yet. You're safer here dan anywhar else at presen'. I'll try and keep you from starvin', and let you know when I t'ink it's least bit safe for you to try to get off."

"De Lord bless you, Johnson!" said Rose, earnestly. "How's Miss Virginny?"

"She's better dan any de rest; but she ain't to be trusted, 'course, 'cause 'tain't for her interest. But she told me, confidentially, she didn't care much if you wasn' found—she hoped you would get off—"

"Dat's my own dear missus, all over," interrupted poor Rose.

"But de rest of dem, dey're awful mad. De Judge, he's mad 'cause his plans all upset, and Massa Talfierro down on him wid a vengeance; and de Colonel he raving—he's quick-tempered, you know, anyways. He says you're an ungrateful dog, 'Perion—ha! ha!"—and there was something bitter in Johnson's laugh, as if the thought of ingratitude did not appeal to his better principles.

"Ungrateful son, he means, 'stead of dog," muttered the *valet*.

"Massa Philip he takes it easy; whistles w'en his fadder scolds, and says you ain't to blame for running away with a girl so purty as Rose; only he's deuced if he knows who's going to tie his cravat for him, and twist his mustache jes' de right twirl."

"Poor Massa Philip! I *did* hate to leave him widout nobody to take right kind o' car' of him," said the soft-hearted "boy," with an accent of self-reproach.

"As for Massa Talfierro, he's bound to find Rose. He's hired men to hunt, and he'll help pay de expenses of finding · de runaways. He's a kind of man dat never gives up. He's mad as blazes 'cause he hain't had his own way—he's use to it, dat's plain—and he don't mean to be fooled by a lot o' niggers. He's swore he'll have dat devilish girl yet—so you see w'at's before you, Rose,"—the girl shuddered, and clung to her lover's arm instinctively. "I shouldn' wonder if he did w'at he said. I'm boun' to do all *I* can to save you, Rose, and dat's why I'm here. Don't you stir 'way from here jes' yit. Dey's got watches at all de river landings up and down for a good ways; dey's adwertised and got everybody lookin'. Jes' you stay here and keep quiet. I'll try and t'row 'em off de track. By time dese yere perwisions gone, I'll try and make another trip out here. I must hurry back, or I'll be s'pected. I don't want to be s'pected, 'cause I can't help you so well. Be quiet, and stop till you hear from me."

He shook hands with them, and was gone. The party felt despondent enough; the dangers of their undertaking overwhelmed them; they brooded over them in silence and misery till the twilight deepened again into desolate night; but in all three hearts was the courage to meet death rather than surrender the hope they had cherished.

"Go on with your story, Maumy, please. I shall die if I set here thinking and dreading about myself all de time."

CHAPTER XI.

MAUM GUINEA'S STORY CONTINUED—JUDY.

The shrouded graces of her form ;
The half-seen arm, so round and warm ;
The little hand, whose tender veins
Branched through the henna's orange stains
The head, in act of offering bent;
And through the parted veil, which lent
A charm for what it hid, the eye,
Gazelle-like, large and dark and shy,
That with a soft, sweet tremble shone
Beneath the fervor of my own.—BAYARD TAYLOR.

A weight seemed lifted from my heart,
    A pitying friend was nigh ;
I felt it in his hard, rough hand,
    And saw it in his eye.—WHITTIER.

Uncertainty !
Fell demon of our fears ! The human soul,
That can support despair, supports not thee.—MALLET.

" I'VE told you before, dat Miss Dudley Gregory was a gay
woman, fond of company and dress. 'Peared like, as time
went on, and she had no chil'ren to take up her mind, she
grew more extravagant dan ever. Nobody dressed so fine as
missus. She mus' take trips every summer up North, and
have lots o' spending money, and trunks full new clo'es ; and
winter-time she must give parties and keep house full of
visitors all de time.

" Woll, de Gregory plantation was sort o' wearin out.
Dar had been too many crops of 'baccy raised on de land ;
It was a-growing barren ; and de income of de estate wasn'
nigh what it used to be, and de expenses was more, 'cause
missus would live in high style. Every little while, of late
years, dey'd had to send niggers to market, 'stead of 'baccy.
De proud ole Virginny planters could raise good crop of
niggers, if de land was barren. Massa Gregory couldn' afford

to feed all de pickaninnies on de place. Every little while he
sold a nice, growin' chile, and sometimes a field-hand he didn'
need. Dat's de way me and Jackson lost our oldest chile—a
fine boy. He was sold de year before w'at I'm telling you
of took place. It was mighty hard to let him go; it made
us sad a long time; but we had de consolation of knowing
he was tol'ably well off—he was only sold to de nex' village,
to wait on a lawyer who wanted an errand-boy; and we saw
him sometimes, and knew he was well took care of.

"One fine April day I was busy making pound-cake and
other fixin's for dinner and tea; dar was company at de
house, and dar must be extra nice dinner. Judy was settin'
in de door of our own room, working a collar for missus. De
door was open 'tween de two rooms, and as I flew round,
busy 'bout my work, I could see her, where she sot, and I
kep' thinking I never saw her look so purty. Her head was
bent over her sewing; her hair fell in curls all down her
cheeks and neck; her cheeks were bright; her little w'ite
apron was tied neatly over her dress, so as not to soil her
work, and she was singing to herself very soft and low.

"'Dar, didn' I tell you?' I suddenly heard missus say,
right in front of de cabin.

"I looked out and saw her standing wid a strange gentleum looking at Judy, who was so busy she hadn' noticed 'em
at all.

"'Didn' I tell you she'd beat anything you ever saw?'

"'She's confoundedly purty, that's certain,' answered de
gentleum wid her.

"'De handsomest colored-girl I ever saw,' kep' on missus.
'I wouldn' think of letting her go; but I *must* have money,
and Dudley says he can't afford to let me have any more.'

"'But will he part wid her?'

"'Oh, I'll worry him into it. She's no use to us, in

pertikeler. I'd rather have the money; and she's just de girl
for your wife, George—*you* can afford to keep her.'

" ' Yes, she's jus' de girl,'—he laughed w'en he said it, and
looked at my chile wid dose hateful eyes—I wanted to tear
'em out dat minit.

" ' Judy,' called missus, 'I shall need you to help wait on
the dinner—don't forget.'

" ' Yes, ma'm,' said Judy, raising her eyes, so innocent and
smiling.

" ' W'at eyes!' muttered de strange gentleum—and de two
walked away, leaving me as weak and cold as water, and
Judy singing away as merry as ever. Not dat I rea'ly feared
missus would make out what she wanted, for I knew massa
had promised his dead wife; and I t'ought anyhow, I could
buy my own chile myself, if de worst come. But reason as I
would, I couldn' help feeling cold and trembly; I didn' know
w'edder I'd got de pudding and sauce right or wrong; and
all de time she was singing to herself, happy as a lark.

" W'en dinner was sent in, I hurried on a clean dress, and
tol' Judy to stay whar she was—*I'd* wait on table dat time.
I wanted to keep her out of sight, and I wanted to find out
who de stranger was, and as much as I could from what
might be said at dinner.

" ' Why didn' Judy come,' asks missus, w'en she see 'twas
me.

" ' She's got a bad headache, ma'm,' says I, 'and I'll jes'
take her place.'

" She give me a prying look, but I 'peared not to notice it;
so I waited 'round, and listened to every word dat was spoke.

" Massa Dudley, he complained of hard times, and made
some remark 'bout his wife's extravagance dat made her very
angry; dey sometimes let der bad feelings show out towards
each other, w'en dey was provoked; dar was half dozen

guests ut de table; but de man I had marked set nex' to massa, and appeared kind of confidential. I found out he was cousin of missus's, very rich, and he had a wife, but she wasn't wid him. He was de baddest-lookin' man I ever see ; a middle-aged man, wid han'some features, only such a bad mouth, and such ugly eyes. He drunk a good deal of wine, and was coarse and loud in his talk, dough he was so very rich—he wasn' a gentleum, and I didn' believe he b'long to any true branch of de ole Virginny stock. Howsumever, massa was mighty polite to him, and paid him extra 'tention ; 'cause he wanted to borrow money, I guessed, and I wasn' far from right.

"Dat night I didn' sleep, t'inking over matters. Nex' day Judy was sent for to come up to de house. I jes' went wid her, pretendin' I wanted my orders for dinner. W'en we come on de portico, dar sat Massa Dudley and Massa Raleigh, de stranger, and missus, waitin' for us. Missus she give me look dat paid back de one I give her de day she first set foot on dat spot—she'd never forgotten it, and she was going to pay it back wid interest.

"Massa Dudley didn' dare to look me in de face, nor my chile ; he kep' his eyes fixed on de rose-vine front of him, and says, pleasantly :

" ' Well, Judy, how'd you like a new home, and a new missus ?'

"She didn' know what to make of de question ; she looked at him and me and all 'round ; but when she met Miss Dudley's eyes, she seemed to get afraid of something, and she caught hold of my frock, and said :

" ' I shouldn' like to leave my maumy at all, master.'

" ' Oh, you're a big girl, Judy—too big to talk about your maumy. Everybody leaves der maumy some time,' said he, making light of it.

"'W'at does dis mean, massa?' I asked, boldly, looking him full in de face.

"'It's not for servants to be putting questions,' said missus, tartly. 'I presume we understand our business.'

"'It means dat wife, here, and her cousin Raleigh have been striking up a bargain. He wants Judy, and she has consented to give her up. His wife is a nice, kind lady, and she'll have a splendid home.'

"'Didn' you promise your mudder, on her death-bed, you'd never sell us?'

"His eyes sunk; he had to clear his t'roat 'fore he could answer:

"'Well, *I* haven't sold her; I got fadder to make her a present to my wife, and *she's* sold her—she never promised. But you needn't fret, Ginny. You'll see her every year, when dey come here on a visit; and she'll have nothing in de worl' to do, but wait on a lady. She couldn' be better off.'

"'She couldn' be better off. Miss Raleigh will be very fond of her," said the stranger, with a kind of laugh dat made me feel as if I wanted to t'ar his heart out wid my teeth—all dis time he was a looking at my poor, modest, purty chile, as if he couldn' keep his eyes off her.

"She was frightened and pale; she kept close to me, and didn' speak, only once to missus, so pitiful:

"'Oh, please, missus, don't sell me 'way from maumy.'

"'I'd sell her, too, if my cousin wanted her; but he's got a good cook, and don't want to be bothered wid anodder. I wish he did.'

"'Couldn' you take Ginny, too?' asked massa, suddenly. I saw he pitied me, and was acting agin his conscience; but he hadn't strength of mind to stand out agin his imperious, selfish wife; he'd allers let her have her own way too much, till she'd got so she usually mastered him—'sides, I believe, he did need money dreadfully. Anyways, 'twas all *her* work —I won't blame Massa Dudley more'n I can help—I'd loved him once, as nobody else ever did love him.

" ' No! no! she'd be in de way,' was the short answer.

" I knew why he didn' want de poor girl's maumy 'round.

" ' How much will he give you for Judy?' I asked missus.

" ' Eighteen hundred dollars, cash down,' she said, coldly.

" ' *I'll* buy her,' I cried out. ' I can't pay you all, now; but I will—so sure as God lets me live, I will—and I'll give you a t'ousand dollars to-day, all in silber and gold.'

" ' You!' said dey all, surprised.

" ' Yes, me! a t'ousand dollars—and I'll sure get de rest.'

" ' A t'ousand dollars won't do,' said missus, as hard as a rock. ' It will just pay my debts and leave me nothing to go to de Springs wid.'

" ' Oh, missus!' said I, falling on my knees, ' don' refuse to let a mudder buy her own chile. Fifteen years I've worked day and night, and sot up late, and saved and contrived to get togedder enough to buy my own daughter. Don' go for to let anodder have her, after all I've done. You can take a t'ousand dollars and wait for de rest.'

" ' A t'ousand dollars won't do,' said she again; ' 'sides, I want to get rid of her. I've no reason to like to see her 'round,'—here she gave her husband a hateful glance, and he blushed.

" I'll give two t'ousand—come, let's bid!' said dat brute man to me, dat 'fernal stranger, laughing at de joke of bidding 'gainst a nigger.

" ' I's got no more to bid,' says I, ' but you oughter be 'shamed of yerself, t'aring a child 'way from her own mudder. Come, Massa Dudley, ain't you going to put a stop to dis? Won't you take my money, and give your wife what more she needs, and let me keep my Judy?'

"'I'll give twenty-five hundred, now my blood's up, bid· ding agin a nigger,' jeered Massa Raleigh. 'I shall be angry wid you, cousin Dudley, if you disappoint me in dis matter. I've quite sot my heart on making my wife dis purty present.'

"'I can't afford to throw away fifteen hundred dollars at dis crisis,' says massa, not looking at me, 'and all for a whim of Ginny's. Her daughter ought to be glad to get so good a place; and she may have to go, sometime, under less favor- able circumstances—for, by George, if affairs go on as they have lately, the Gregory estate will be in de hands of creditors before long. Yes, madam, dough you don't seem to know w'at your doing,'—and he gave his wife a fierce look.

"'Den don' make a fool of yourself, t'rowing 'way my cousin's offer,' she says, as calm and cool as could be.

"'I can't help you any, Ginny,' said master, after a moment's waitin'; 'I'm sorry, but I'm 'fraid Judy'll have to go.'

"I got up off my knees, and I 'spect I looked mighty fierce.

"'Dey say dis is a Christian land, massa; dat it is a good place to bring poor headen niggers to give 'em de light of de Gospel. I's had dat light, and I don' see yet w'at kind of Christians dem be dat spekilates in der own flesh and blood. I s'pose it's Christian to sell your own daughter, Massa Dudley. Look at her! She's de only one you ever had, to my knowledge, and you's done gone right well to sell her for money.'

"'Cl'ar, out, girl!' cries he, springing up off his chair in a rage—and de stranger laugh, and missus she laugh very soft and dreadful—oh, how I hated her, w'en I heard dat laugh.

"I took Judy by de hand, and we went home. 'Fore dinner, word came she mus' be ready to go in de mornin';

de papers was signed and dar was no use making a fuss. De
chile was done broken-hearted; she jes' sot and cried all
day—she didn' want to go off wid strangers, 'way from her
maumy. But she didn' guess de worst, as I did. She was
so pure and modest, she didn' dream w'at she was took 'way
fur. Her heart wasn't wrung by de anguish dat filled mine.
Ye see, I'd brought her up so pious, I knew she'd be shocked
and grieved to def. My brain was a burnin' up t'inking o
it; but I tried to keep calm, for I'd made a plan.

"Jackson didn' come home to dinner; he took his grub
wid de hands in de field, and I couldn' see him till mos'
night. 'Fore he come back, I wanted to fix my plans, so's
to tell him and get his help. I knew he'd help me, if it cost
him his life. He 'dored Judy, and it would jes' kill him to
see her carried off by dat bad man.

"Woll, I let de chile set and cry: I didn' say much to her,
for I was too busy in my mind. W'en Jackson come home,
I hurried up his supper, and den I tol' him de whole story.
He 'proved my plan, and was eager to help me. He wasn't
selfish, my husband wasn't; he showed he had a good heart,
when my troubles come.

"Dar was a sloop a-loading with tobacky, not more'n a
mile down de river, below us. I knew about it before; dat
it 'spected to sail next mornin' early—it was bound for New
York. I was goin' to take Judy and go aboard dat vessel.
I didn' much fear but I should be able to bribe de capt'in to
tak' us. I'd jes' seen w'at money could do wid an ole-
family gentleum like Massa Dudley; and I t'ought if it could
make him sell his own daughter, it wouldn' fail to make a
poor capt' in take a good price for stowing 'way a couple of
colored women 'mong his tobacky. If we got safe to New
York, dar was plenty of things I could do. I could hide
Judy 'way in somebody's school, who'd never know who she

was nor whar she come from, and I could get my own livin',
easy. Jackson was to try and git 'way wid de chil'ren, and
find me, soon as he dar.'

"I took down de ole tea-pot full o' money. I made a belt
and sewed in five hundred dollars in gold, and fastened it
round my waist. I put a hundred and fifty dollars in my
pocket to buy our passage—I wasn' going to let the capt'in
know I had any more. I put a belt round Judy wid a hundred dollars, so if anything did happen dat we got separated,
she'd have a little to help herself. De rest I left in Jackson's
car', for my oder chil'ren—to keep it sacredly till he saw a
chance to run away, and den to use it to help dem pickaninnies get der freedom.

" W'en he and I had talked it all over, we felt better. He
said he'd rudder give me up, dan see Judy carried off by
Massa Raleigh.

"W'en we'd settled it, den I took Judy and told her w'at
I was going to do. She was so glad, she laughed and cried
togedder. She was wise and careful, too; I wasn't afraid to
trust her. I made her go to bed early in de evening to get
rest; den I got out her clo'es, and went to overhaulin' 'em,
mending 'em and folding 'em up; so if any body was spying
'round de window, dey wouldn' suspeck my purpose. I knew
well 'nuff, missus would come spyin' 'round; and sure 'nuff,
'bout nine o'clock she burst in sudden, to see w'at I was
about.

"'W'ar's Judy?' says she, by way of 'scuse, 'I want to
give her some little things to fit her out for her journey.'

"'Much obliged to you, missus,' says I, curt enough, 'de
poor chile's cried herself to sleep. I made her go to bed,
against her journey to-morrow, and I'm mendin' up her
things. You may keep yer presents—she wouldn' take 'em
from you.'

"'Oh, very well,' says she, in return. 'You've got a t'ousand dollars have you, cook? Rea'ly, you're richer dan I am. W'ar do you keep it?'

"'Out at interest, of course,' says I; 'de lawyer dat's got my boy, is taking car' of it for me.'

"'Oh!' says she, and out she went.

"I didn' pray to de Lord to forgive me for dat lie. I didn' hardly believe dar was a God any more—I felt so bitter. Why did He make brack people, jus' to see such troubles? Why did He 'low me to bring up my girl pious and modest, jes' to let white man take her and defile her when he'd a mind to? W'at de use of trying to be good?

"I tell you, I had a great many thoughts dem hours. Bym-bye, I put my candle out, and I take my youngest pick-aninny on my lap. It was a little girl, only two year ole—a nice chile, dat I couldn' b'ar to leave. But I had to. I had to jus' leave her in de hand of Providence; and how could I trust de hand of Providence, w'en I saw w'at it had done for me and mine? I sot a-holding my sleeping baby 'till two o' clock. Den I woke up Judy, and we was ready in a few minutes. We put on our bes' clo'es, so's to look decent w'en we got to de city. We kissed de chil'ren, fas' asleep, and shook hands wid Jackson. Dar was no time to cry and talk on.

"He opened de door very soft; it was a dark night; it had begun to rain a little; we was glad of dat; for de sound of de rain and de wind blowing, kep' everybody from hearing us. I put an ole shawl over Judy's head and shoulders, and we slipped out on de lawn, and down to de river's edge. Jackson darsn't go 'long; t'ought our chance was better alone. I knew de way right well; I'd gone over it since I was a girl, and I kep' hold Judy's hand, and we run. De river it rushed on, sobbing like, for de wind was blowing—it was an old friend, dat river was, and I hated to part wid it. 'Pears to me, all de time to-night, dat lake out dar, is de James river.

"It was pitch dark still, w'en we come to whar de vessel was; but dey was stirring aboard of her, 'cause dey wanted to take advantage of de wind, and get down de river quick as possible. Judy begun to tremble so, I could hear her teeth chatter w'en we come onto de little dock, whar de light of de ship's lantern fell on us—I trembled too in every j'int, but I wouldn't let her see it—for I knew right well if the capt'in *should* refuse to take us, my chile was lost—I'd have to go back wid her and give her up. Woll, dey seen us standin' dar, and dey hollered out rough, ' W'at did we want?' and I tol' 'em I'd a special message for de capt'in and I mus' speak to him. So de capt'in swore at us a little, and hollered to me to speak out; but I tol' him it was private; and finally he let de han's help us on, and den I took him aside and whispered to him w'at it was. I tol' him me and my daughter wanted to go to New York; and if he'd give us passage in his vessel, and not let on we was dar, if anybody come to ask, I'd give him a hundred and fifty dollars in gold. His eyes twinkled w'en I showed him de money. He asked if I had any more. I told him not anodder dollar; but I was willin' to give all dat to get safe to New York wid my daughter. Woll, I believe he was a Yankee capt'in; he didn't love slavery, and he did love money—so we made de bargain easy.

"He swore all de officers in Virginny shouldn' tech me· and he took us down in his own little cabin, and told us to be easy in our minds.

"Oh! how safe we felt w'en we got down in dat little close place—it was paradise to us; but we wasn't sorry w'en we felt de vessel in motion, and knew dat we was actually sailing for de ocean. I t'ought of my poor, forsaken pickaninnies, but I couldn' grieve den, I was so glad my chile was safe.

" W'en it come broad daylight, de capt'in had breakfast sot in his cabin; he give us two poor scared women a cur'ous look, w'en he come in; but w'en he saw Judy, he jus' seem astonished.

" 'Jerusalem !' says he; and den he whistled to hisself, and says he :

" 'You don't say dat young lady's a slave,-do' you ?'

" 'Yes, massa, I's sorry to say she got 'bout two drops black blood in her.'

" 'Woll, she's good enough to eat to *my* table,' says he. 'Here, boy, put on two more plates, and give us something decent for breakfast.'

" He made us set down and eat wid him; he was jus' as 'spectful to my Judy, as if she'd been a lady, and dat made me take to him mightily. He wasn' fine gentleum; his hands was hard, and he talked purty rough; but he was a manly looking person, quite a young man to be a cap'tin, wid a honest, han'some face—somehow, we bof felt safe wid him, and Judy, she picked up her spirits, child-fashion, and smiled w'en he put mos' a whole br'iled chicken on her plate.

" He was out on deck mos' all day; but we had to stay in de cabin, for we darsn't show ourselves till we got out in de ocean; den Judy begun to be sick wid de rollin' of de vessel. You ought to see how dat great, strong man nussed her up, and brought her hot tea, and took car' of her as if she was a baby.

" She wasn't sick long; when she'd got over it, we rea'ly 'gan to enjoy ourselves.

" If it hadn't been for my chil'ren in de ole cabin at home, I should have been very happy; I was beginning to realize de hopes of fifteen years of toil and trouble.

"De capt'in was a very interesting man; he was a great talker, and he was so kind as to tell us all kind of stories to amuse us; den Judy, she sung for him, to please him. She sung sweeter dan all de birds in de world—she'd allers been called a wonderful singer; and de capt'in he never take his eyes from her face w'en she was singing.

"His name was Ephraim Slocum; 'fore we got to de end of our voyage he'd told us a good deal 'bout hisself; dat he had no parents living; dat his friends and relations live in State of Maine; dat he'd got his own education and made his own way, and he 'spected by end of anodder year to buy de vessel he was sailin', and be an undependent man. I liked his pride and sperit. It was different from ole Virginny pride; he wasn't 'shamed of work, and he liked to tell he'd made his own fortune. He use to study of evenings. He had maps and charts and 'rithmetics and hard books on his little table; but he didn't stick to 'em very close on dis voyage, 'cause he was too much taken up wid Judy.

"He gave up his own bed to us, and slep', like as not, on deck, hisself. Judy allers read her Bible and sung a hymn before she went to bed, and he use to stay to hear her. De chile was as gay as a lark; she liked de capt'in, and she showed it out so innocent, it pleased him dreffully. I could see he was wrapped up in her—dat he'd never seen anything in the world before, dat he t'ought so bright and so purty.

"He got me to tell him my story. I told it all to him: who Judy's father was, and why we came away, and how car'ful I'd brought her up, and w'at my hopes was about getting her settled 'mongst w'ite folks.

"'Yis, yis!' says he, 'she ought to be taken car' of, dat's sartain.'

"I 'fessed to him dat I had more money; for I had so much confidence in him, I wasn' afraid to let him know; I asked him to befriend me, w'en we got to de great city; to find us a safe, quiet place, whar we could stop, till I found a school for her.

"He promised; and he kept his word. He made us stay on his vessel 'till he'd found us rooms in a nice, plain house; dar was enough furniture in 'em for us to begin living, and we was to board ourselves—so we could be as retired as we wished. He kep' a sharp look-out, for fear massa had sent on officers to take us; and he took us off in de night, and brought us to our new home.

"Judy cried and sobbed w'en he shook hands wid us, and said good-bye; my own t'roat choked up so's I could hardly t'ank him for all his kindness.

"'Don't cry, little one,' says he, broad and hearty, 'I'm not going off forever. I shall be in New York several weeks, and shall come to see you most every day. If Miss Ginny t'inks she'll be in order to see company so soon, mebbe I'll drop in and take tea wid you to-morrow evening.'

"I had a mighty nice supper ready when he come. You know nobody can beat Ginny at cooking, and I did my best for him. He was in good spirits, and we had a nice time. I wasn' disturbed at all by his comin' to see us, and being so polite to my daughter; for he was so respectful, he seemed mos' 'fraid of her; and he never said rude things, nor jested before her. Fact is, Judy was so pure and purty, no decent-minded man could help being good to her.

"Woll, he kept coming, a'most every evening, long as he staid on shore.

"I saw how t'ings was going. I noticed Judy, w'at a change had come over her. She used to sit and never stir, day-times, thinking of something; and when I'd speak to her, she'd blush. And every time she heard *his* step come a flying up de stairs, I'd see her start, and her heart begin to beat, and her cheeks to get red, and she wouldn' hardly dure look up when he first come in. I see all de signs of de young girl's heart, when it first finds out w'at it's made for. t'ought he seen it too; for my chile was so artless, she couldn' put on no airs. I was a little oneasy; for I couldn' forget she had brack blood in her, and dat he knew it, dough nobody wouldn' have guessed it if dey hadn' been told.

"I felt anxious for him to speak out w'at he meant, or else to get Judy 'way, whar she'd have a chance to forget him.

"Woll, one day he come in, w'en Judy was out of an errand, and we got to talking 'bout w'at it was best to do wid her. He liked my idea of sending her to some boardin'-school; I had plenty of money to buy her clo'es and keep her dar a year; and as for myself, I could make my own livin', any time.

"He said he knew of a nice school up in Connecticut, whar a cousin of his had once gone; and whar de principal knew all 'bout him; he'd take her to dat school hisself, and tell 'em she was Southern girl, an orphan, who'd been sent up in his care from de South—and den he was silent little while, and I waited, feeling as if he'd more to say.

"'Mrs. Ginny,' he begun at last, 'you must have seen dat I love Judy. I do love her, wid all my heart and soul. I think she's too good for any man living. I mus' marry her —dat is, if she loves me, and will marry me. I can't help it. I'm a New-Englander; and I've my prejudices against black blood. I tell you candidly. I don't think it's right to mix it wid w'ite. But I'm so infatuated wid dat angel, I forget everything only dat I love her. I've made up my mind to ask her to be my wife. But, Mrs. Ginny, though I've overcome my prejudices, I never could dose of my relatives; I'd never like to tell 'em dat my wife had African blood in her —I'd never like 'em to know dat you was her mudder. I tell

you now, 'fore I speak to Judy, so you can decide for yourselves. If you're willing to keep it secret dat you're her
mudder, and only see her w'en we come to visit you, it'll be
all right. You shall be took good care of, and we'll both
love you and respect you, as we do now. Only I'm so
infernal proud, I don't want my relatives to know 'bout you.
You must speak as you feel. Dat chile needs a protector—
even you, her mudder, can't protect her as I could. She's so
beautiful, dar will be evil persons after her. I will make her
a good husband—she shall be as happy and as honored as
any daughter of de North. Speak, Mrs. Ginny; how shall
it be?'

   " ' It shall be jus' as you want it, for *her* sake, Mr. Slocum,'
says I, chokin' down de lump in my t'roat. 'I've allers
wanted her to have a w'ite man—she's worthy of de best—
and I believe you're among de best. I don' blame you for
not wanting a slave mudder. I've always 'spected to give
my chile up—I've been schooling myself to it for years, and
I'm only too glad and happy to see her in such honest hands,'
—here I broke down, crying, part with joy, and part wid
sorrow, for it *was* hard to disown my own sweet chile, to
give her up, as it were—but it was for Judy's good, and w'at
else did I live for but for *dat?*

   " ' You musn' feel bad,' he says, his own voice tremblin' a
little. 'I know it's a hard thing I ask, but I can't help it.
We're a proud family, Mrs. Ginny, if we have hewed out our
own way—and I'm one of de grittiest of de stock. But dat
chile of yours would melt a rock. Don' feel bad—I shall let
her love her mudder as much as she pleases. And if I can
fix it so's to settle in New York, we can see you a great deal;
you shan't be parted entirely.'.

   " ' Dat'll be enough for me,' says I, wiping my eyes.

   " ' Woll, now, let's finish up our plans; for I've got to sail

again next week. You want Judy to go to school, and so do
I. She's too young to be married yet, and I'm not quite
ready. A year will fix us out all right. Let Judy go to
school a year. She must learn music, sartain; she'll take to
it like a bee to honey; and dat voice of her's must be trained.
At de end of a year, I'll buy my vessel, and be an independent
man; I can keep a wife in clover; she shall come back here,
and we'll be married. Hurrah, it's glorious, isn't it? only so
little Judy herself consents!'—and he laughed, and walked
around de room, looking as bright as a dollar.

"Just den Judy come in, all sparkling and fresh from her
walk; she took off de veil which I allers made her wear in
de street, and she looked so lovely, de young man couldn'
contain hisself—he went up, and took her hands, and kissed
her on de cheeks, and says:

"'Your mudder says I may have you, Judy. Say, little
one, w'at you say to dat?'—she looked at him and at me, and
begun to color up. 'Will you love me, Judy, and be my wife
w'en you get a little older?'

"She look frightened for a minit, and den she blushed,
and said, softly:

"'I do love you, now, Mr. Slocum,'—and run to me and
hid her face.

"Well, we had a happy day, talking over matters and
arranging 'em. Judy dreaded to go 'way into a strange
school—she was timid, and had never left her maumy—but
she knew her lover wanted her to be educated, and she was
so proud, and so anxious to please him, dat it made her
willing to try. He could only spare us two days to get her
ready; he took her 'way to school, and left 'her dar. Heigho!
I felt lonesome 'nuff, all alone in dat big city; but I had de
comfort of feeling dat all was going right, and I set myself to
work, to cure myself of pining for my chil'ren.

"Capt'in Slocum got me place to cook in a restaurant; I had good wages, and got 'long nicely. All I was 'fraid of was dat somebody might spy me out, dat had known me in ole Virginny; but I didn' have to show myself out de kitchen; and if dey did get *me*, dey couldn' find Judy, and I knew de capt'in would take car' of her, if anything happened to me.

"I was so busy day-times, I hadn' much time to think; but nights I'd lie awake and please myself dreaming 'bout my chile. I laid up all my wages to buy her weddin'-clo'es. I's bound dey should be splendid, and dat she should have 'em from *me*, so's not to have to take 'em from her husband. Five, six times, during de year, Capt'in Slocum was in New York; he took his meals to dat restaurant, and I'd chances to talk wid him, and hear all 'bout how Judy was getting along. He'd read me her letters—dey was beautiful—I know dat. I got nice letters from her, too. I could read writing, handy enough, dough I couldn' write much myself, for want of practice. I'd send her messages in de capt'in's letters—he had special permission to write to her from de principal of de 'cademy.

"Woll, de year went by; it went as quick as any in my life. Sometimes it seemed long; but w'en 'twas rea'ly over, I was surprised, it was so short.

"I got a month's absence from my situation; for I wanted to go back to our ole rooms and help Judy make her wedding-clo'es, and 'joy her society while I could. After she was married, I 'spected to go back and keep my place—I had good wages, and I liked it well enough. Hush, chil'ren! w'at in de world was dat?"

"I hear nothing," said Hyperion.

"Only your heart beating, Maumy," said Rose.

"I thought I heard blood gurgling," resumed the story-teller, in a strange voice, which made Rose shiver and creep closer

to her lover—" but it mus' have been de water in dat lake out
dar—it never will keep still !

"Capt'in Slocum come ashore in time to go after Judy and
bring her home. Things had prospered wid him; he had
bought his vessel, and was in high heart. W'en I had Judy
in my sight and in my arms I was mos' wild wid delight. · I
t'ought she was *perfeck* before; but I saw how much she had
improved. She'd caught the best of everything she saw; de
capt'in said she'd been de pride and favorite of de school—
and I could see how proud of her he was hisself.

"'I'll give you t'ree weeks, Mrs. Ginny, to get her ready,'
said he, when we'd settled down, after the first excitement.
'I've got to take a little trip that'll keep me over a fortnight,
to arrange my affairs to suit; but I can't have any waiting
after I return. Be sure and be ready, little one; I've waited
a year, now. And take good care of my birdie, Mrs. Ginny.
Don't let her fly abroad—the hawks may pounce on her.
Do all the going out yourself. Keep shady, little one, till you
get a husband, and den we'll snap our fingers at the hull
world.'

"He made light of his own words; but somehow he felt
uneasy; I could see it; and when he'd kissed Judy over and
over, and shook hands wid me, and said ' Good-bye' de last
time, and de door shut on him, I felt oppressed, and wished
de t'ree weeks was over instead of jus' begun.

"One day, he'd been gone about a week, we went out to
do some shopping. We bof of us wore thick veils, and did
raise 'em at all in de street.

"'You shall have a white silk wedding-dress, my chile,'
says I. 'I've set my heart on dat, and we'll go to Stewart's
and get a good one.'

"I 'lowed Judy to pick out de pattern suited her best. I
was so happy seeing her so animated and happy—I paid for

de silk as proud as a queen, and we took home a bundle of beautiful things.

"Dat evening we was setting sewing in our room. Don' you speak to me, chil'ren—jus' let me talk as fast as I can, and get tru' wid dis—we was settin' sewing. We had a bright light to sew by; de table was covered wid lace and han'some things; Judy was running up de bread's of de white silk; it glistened like pearls all over her lap and de floor; I was making de boddice. I'd fitted it very nice—I was a good dress-maker. She didn' put her frock on, w'en I'd basted de new one, for I wanted to try it on again; she sot dar in her petticoat and corset, and I kep' noticing de dimples in her shoulders, jus' as soft and fair as dey was w'en she was little baby. She had taken off de gold beads missus gave her, which she allers wore, and laid 'em down on de table, till I was tru' a-fitting her dress. She was singing to herself, and stopping to 'mire de glittering of de silk every little while.

"We sot dar sewing, never thinking of nothing, only de wedding, w'en de door suddenly opened, widout nobody knocking; and w'en I looked up I saw Massa Raleigh standing dar, and two officers behind him. De needle jus' dropped out my hand, and I turned stone cold, but I couldn' move. Judy she knew him, right 'way, and she gave one scream went right tru' my heart.

"'So,' says he, 'my little bird,' (dat's just what Ephraim called her w'en he went away,) 'you flew off from me, didn't you? I've found your nest at last—just when I wasn't looking for it. If you hadn't put up your veil when you got interested in dat bit of dress-goods to-day, I shouldn't have tracked you. Are you ready to go home with your master, now?'

"We just stared at him—we could neider of us speak.

"'You live right snug here—lots of purty things! Hope

you haven't sold yourself to anybody e!se, my girl,' and he looked about suspiciously.

" 'No, she hasn't,' I spoke up, for I understood him. 'For God's sake, let us alone, Massa Raleigh. Judy's 'gaged to be married—dese are her wedding-clo'es. Her husband's well off, and he'll give you twice what you gave for my chile, if you'll only let us alone till he comes back.'

" ' I ought to have some interest, after lying out de use of my money a year,' he says, wid a wicked laugh. 'So, she's 'gaged to be married, is she? Woll, I pity de man dat's got took in. He ought to thank me for coming and claiming my own, before de knot was tied. Who is it?'

" ' It's a capt'in of a vessel—a nice young man,' says I, 'fore I thought.

" 'Aha! de same sloop dat helped you get 'way, I'll be bound. No, curse him! if it's that d—d capt'in, he shan't have her, if he offers twenty t'ousand dollars. I'll punish him for dat trick.'

" ' 'Twasn't dat one,' says I, but he was too sharp to believe me.

" ' Come, Judy,' says he, ' put your frock on, and come 'long. I'm in a hurry.'

" ' Oh, Massa Raleigh, let me stay till Ephraim comes back,' cries my chile. 'I'll give you my word and honor I won't try to run away. Only let me stay till I see him ; and if he can't buy me 'way from you, I'll go home wid you den.'

" ' Got to leave town to-morrow, and mus' take you 'long. No, no, Miss Judy, "a bird in de hand is worth two in de bush,"—you've played me one trick.'

" She threw herself down and clasped her hands about his knees.

" ' Please, please, Master Raleigh, let me stay wid my mudder till he comes !'

" I saw his wicked eyes gloating over her lovely head and shoulders; he stooped down and patted her on de neck:

" 'Not a single night,' says he; 'I've been kep' out my property long enough. Come, girl, get what duds you want, and come 'long.'

" 'May I go, too ?' I asked.

" 'No! you cussed, impertinent nigger—you made all de trouble in de first place. Massa Gregory may cotch you when he can—I shan't help him. Come, girl, get your bonnet. What you standing dar for ?'

" Her big eyes opened like a frightened deer's; she looked at him, but didn' stir. I prayed hard and fas' to de Lord, but he didn' 'pear to hear me. Oh! how I prayed dat Cap'n Slocum would come in and knock down all dose cruel men, and save my chile—but he was hundred miles 'way—dar was no help.

" 'Here, fellows, help her dress if she can't help herself,' says Massa Raleigh, and he picks up a bonnet and goes towards her.

" 'I'll be d—d if I do !' I heard one de men say—de oder one stepped forward; Judy ran to me and clung 'bout me wid her hull strength; dey tried to force her 'way, but we bof held out. Dey tore de clo'es half off my poor chile.

" 'For de Lord's sake, and sake your own chil'ren, don't give up my poor girl to dat bad man,' I pleaded wid de officers.

" 'Dey darsn't refuse to do der duty. She's mine; I paid roundly for her, and I'm going to have her; you jus' behave yourself, ole girl, or you'll get hurt.'

" Wid one strong wrench he pulled her 'way from me, and dragged her to de door.

" 'Save me, mudder !'

" 'I will, chile. Dat man shall never take you alive, Judy,

"'Shan't hey?' said he, wid a chuckle dat drove me raving mad.

"I sprung at him and tore her 'way ag'in; I was strong as a tiger; I got her 'way, and held bof his arms so he couldn' stir, dough he cussed and swore, and tried hard to get his pistol out his pocket.

"'You jes' run, Judy,' says I, 'and don't you stop for me. Run 'way, and hide, no matter whar—only don't you come back here.'

"'Take hold of her, fellows,' says Massa Raleigh, twisting and turning, but I held him like a constrictor.

"'Blast me if I do,' said de same man spoke before. 'If I'd known *dat* was de kind of slave you'd set me to cotch, you wouldn' have got me here,' and he looked at my poor, beautiful white chile. 'She's whiter dan I am, and a darn sight purtier. Come Jem, let's leave here.'

"'I'll have you fined and 'prisoned, you rascals,' shouted Massa Raleigh.

"'Cap'n Slocum pay all de fines, and reward you besides, says I. 'Judy, why don't you run?'

"'I don't like to leave *you*, mudder.'

"'Never mind me, chile. I can take car' myself. Like as not dey'll keep me, in hopes of catching you; but don't you show yourself roun' here. Mind!'

"She took up an ole shawl, and run like a cat out in de hall, and away. De men dey bof laughed.

"'Bully for her!' says one.

"'I'd as soon help cotch my own sister,' says de oder.

"'Hold on to him, ole girl. You're a tough one,' laughs t'odder.

"'Don' bite him.

"'Why don' you kiss her?'

"'She's a trump!'

"Woll, you better b'lieve Massa Raleigh get mad. Dar I was a-holding him, and dem officers laughing at him—down South, dey wouldn' dar' to laugh at an ole Virginny gentleman ; but dese fellers was independent—dey t'ought it very good joke. Judy hadn' much more'n time to fly down de stairs, 'fore I felt my strength giving out ; and de nex' thing I know I didn' know nothin'—he'd flung me down on de floor so hard dat I was stunned entirely.

"When I come to myself I was in de hospital—my arm was broke a-falling on it ; and I hadn' been dar but t'ree, four days, 'fore Massa Dudley come after me, and made me go back wid him. I don' believe he cared much dat Judy had got away from his cousin ; he let me go back to my rooms and see to things. De officers had locked it up, and took car' of things. I found Judy's gold beads on de table, and I took 'em to remember her by. I never 'spected to see her again. All I was 'fraid of was, dat Massa Raleigh would cotch her. I saw de officer dat was friendly to me dat night. I thanked him for letting my chile off ; and I begged him to keep watch, and if she come round to enquire for me, to tell her what had happened to me, and to warn her 'gainst Massa Raleigh—dat he was still in de city, watching 'round. And I told him 'bout Cap'n Slocum, and to tell de cap'n, for me, to take good car' my chile—I never 'spected to see her ag'in, and he mus' be good to her. 'Cap'n Slocum,' says I, ' will pay you for all your trouble, whatever you're mind to ask. You won't lose by being kind to my Judy till he comes back,' —and he promised to hunt up de capt'in, and let him know what had happened.

"So I just prayed de Lord to keep my white lamb from de wolf, till her husband dat was to be, should get back to take car' of her ; and I come away wid my Massa Dudley back to ole Virginny.

"My heart was sick and sore to leave New York widout knowing what was Judy's fate. If I could have seen her settled for life, wid a good man, I shouldn' have felt bad to come back a slave—for I wanted to see Jackson and my chil'ren. But I couldn' help fearin' w'at might befall her 'fore Cap'n Slocum got back; or thinking, p'raps, *he'd* get shipwrecked or·lost, and de poor chile never have any friends in dat great city. It was brooding ober all dese things, that made my heart as heavy as lead.

"Woll, I never knew, till I got clean back to de plantation, dat I had no husband and chil'ren for to see. Dey was sold down South—every chick I had, and Jackson too. Massa was so mad when me and Judy run away, dat he jus' sold Jackson right off, for helpin' us escape—sold him 'way down to de Florida Keys. Den Massa Gregory died ; and de young folks was eatin' up de plantation as if it would last forever—dey'd sold all my pickaninnies, every one.

"'Tain't an easy thing to go childless—'specially when your chil'ren ain't dead, but scattered all over, you don' know whar, nor what has happened to 'em. My poor heart has done nothing but ache—it done gone aching now, and is jus' dumb and cold—it don't car'. I never heard 'bout Judy. I don't know dis blessed day whedder she's safe and happy, or what become of her dar. I take out her gold beads, and look at dem, and pray for her—but what's de use ?

"Sometimes I think I'd like to see my youngest pickaninny—she was a little girl, too—but what's de use ? I don't even know what State she's sold to.

"When I wake up in de night, I hear my chil'ren hollerin' and cryin'—I hear de whip on der backs, or 'see em tired and hungry—oh, I has awful dreams.

"Woll, I went round so stupid-like, thinking of my Judy, and de rest of 'em, dat I wasn't much use. Missus got

dreadfully out of patience wid me; and finally, she got massa
to sell me down to New Orleans. I was such a splendid cook,
he got a good price for me. I was in New Orleans but a
little while, when Massa Fairfax bought me. I use to keep
a-looking out all de time on de street, to see if I could see
any my chil'ren, in New Orleans, and dat master said I was
lazy. Masters don' like der niggers to get de dumps.

"So I's dragged out life jus' any way I could. I t'ought
dar wasn' no more sap in de ole tree, sence it was struck;
but when I see you two chil'ren living my troubles over
again, dar put forth one little green branch. I couldn' help
taking to you and trying to help you.

"If I could only know what had happened to Judy! It
gnaws at my vitals all de time, de fear dat something has
gone wrong wid her.

"If we only get away from here, and make our way up
North, mebbe I shall find out about Judy—mebbe I shall see
her. Oh, Rose! what if I should see my chile again!"

"Cheer up, Maumy! maybe you will. Who knows? I
hope you will, Maumy."

"I'd walk dar all de way, on coals of fire, to hear from
Judy."

CHAPTER XII.

THE YANKEE CAPTAIN.

Why must we look so oft abaft?
  What is the charm we feel
When handsome Harry guides the **craft**,
  His hand upon the wheel?

His hand upon the wheel, his eye
  The swelling sail doth measure :
Were I the vessel he commands,
  I should obey with pleasure.

He would seem taller, were he not
  In such proportion made ;
He wears as frank and free a brow
  As golden curls can shade.

Fresh youth, and joyance, and kind heart,
  Gleam in his azure eye;
And though I scarcely know his voice,
  I think he cannot lie.—MRS. HOWE.

COLONEL FAIRFAX was walking up and down the portico
in front of his mansion, with that hasty step which sounded
as if he were endeavoring to walk off some mental irritability.
The crisp January air was having its desired effect; the
knitted brows gradually relaxed, the step grew more slow
and regular, and the planter's countenance toned down to its
usual placid tints. He had been excessively fretted by the
escape of two of his most valuable slaves, and by the result
of all the attempts which had been made to track them; he
thought he, of all men, ought to be spared such trials of his
patience, when he had always been considered one of the
kindest and most indulgent of masters. He sympathized
with his neighbor, Judge Bell, in the unpleasant predicament
in which he was placed, by the sudden disarrangement of the
business affair he was about to conclude with such satisfaction
to himself and his creditor.

"There's neither gratitude nor common sense in any of the race," soliloquized the Colonel. "What did they want to cut up such a freak for?—leave comfortable homes, protection and plenty, for cold, hardships and poverty—like as not, to starve in the swamps—or, what is worse, to go up North, and perish of cold and hard work. I did think that boy was a little above the average—but it seems what wit he's got has been used to his own ruin! A pretty piece of sentimentality between a couple of darkies—ha! ha! A runaway match! —took Maumy along to tie the knot, I suspect! Ridiculous! ridiculous!"

"I presume Hyperion caught his sentimentality from constant association with *me*, father," laughed Philip, coming out in time to hear the above. "You see, he apes my dress and my manners, and now he's going to imitate me in my love affairs."

"Why, you never eloped with any silly young lady, did you?" queried the Colonel, growing good-natured under the smile of his only son.

"No—I *haven't* done such a thing, so far. But I rather think I should be hurried into such a course, if I found somebody else about to step in and carry off my lady-love, against her consent and mine."

"Nonsense, Philip! The mistake you make is in applying the same rules to your servants as to yourself—as if the delicacy of their feelings was to be consulted in all our arrangements. Ignorant, thoughtless, brainless, indolent, troublesome children—I wonder how they'd fare, if we didn't look after their interests better than they know how themselves?"

"I'd trust Hyperion to take care of himself, anyhow—the rascal! I wish he'd come back and attend to my room—I haven't had anything decent since he went away."

"Well, I've lost two, and the Judge only one—but I guess

he feels his loss the more keenly,—it's upset his arrangements finely!"

"Good enough for him!—he'd no business to go and dispose of that girl to such a person as Mr. Talfierro. I'll say so, if he is Virginia's father. I don't believe *she* feels very badly about Rose's running off."

"Oh, of course not! You young people can afford to be very pretty in your sentiments, and very careless of your property, as long as you have us to take charge of you. But I think, by the time you've had charge of a plantation for twenty years, you'll look at these things in a business point of view. Talfierro is getting out of patience. The Judge was over this morning, to see if he could borrow money from me, towards making up the amount he owes him. I expect I shall have to let him have a part of what he wants. If we don't hear from the fugitives by to-morrow, I've promised to try and accommodate him. Blast 'em! don't I wish they all had a sound whipping for their tricks?"

Philip did not reply, his attention having been arrested by the sight of a horseman trotting leisurely along the level road; it was so seldom travellers passed by, they always excited more or less remark. This one, as he reached the avenue diverging from the road into the planter's private grounds, turned his horse's head towards the mansion, much to the excitement and arousal of a dozen negro children in "the quarters," and half as many men and women lounging about the yards and offices.

By the time he had reached the place of dismounting, he was surrounded by a small throng of curious spectators, who hardly among them all could manage to take the bridle of the animal for him, but who seemed to consider their chief duty to consist in the display of an astonishing quantity of glowing eyes and "ivories."

" Does Colonel Fairfax reside here ?"

" Oh, yis, massa !   Dis Colonel Fairfax's, suah."

" That's a Northerner, or I miss my guess," said Philip, aside to his father, as the stranger walked up to the porch.

With the courtesy native to him, the planter stepped forward to greet the new-comer, inviting him in before inquiring name or business.   He was sufficiently well-spoken and well-dressed to warrant the invitation to the library extended to him, and which he accepted, with an apology for intruding upon the time of the host.   Nevertheless, although he apologized for intruding, he did not immediately state what business brought him ; but showed himself an interested stranger to the country, inquiring with intelligent curiosity into the peculiarities of sugar-planting, climate, etc., of that part of Louisiana. The three were in the midst of an animated conversation, when they were summoned to dinner.

An invitation to partake of that meal was accepted as frankly as it was offered.   There was something about the stranger that amused and entertained his hosts, while it compelled their respect.   It was certain that Captain Slocum, from Maine, as he introduced himself, was not a gentleman after their own model ; he had no high-bred manners, no courtly polish—yet he committed no breaches of etiquette, was neither uncouth nor unrefined, but had an air of his own, frank, earnest, and—acquisitive !   Yes, it was acquisitive, no doubt, and faithful to his New-England parentage—not the acquisitiveness of the miser, but of the ardent mental strength and growth, reaching out all the time, and absorbing the elements about it.   His looks were in great contrast to those of the two Southern gentlemen, with their sallow complexions, and that air of languor, or at least, repose, peculiar to their climate.   His face was fresh and florid ; his eyes blue, bright and keen ; his features clear-cut and handsome. He talked incessantly, and his language was not always chosen for its elegance; though nothing coarse fell from his lips, since Mrs. Fairfax was at the table. No gentleman could have been more deferential, than seemed natural to him, when he addressed himself to her. It was difficult for the Colonel, accustomed to the exclusive *castes* of southern society, to judge where to place his guest, who certainly was not " poor white trash," and just as certainly was not a " first-family" born gentleman, laying his claims to their respect upon the ground that he had inherited wealth and indolence from the blood and toil of others. Captain Slocum had an air of courage and se.ℓ-reliance not born of bowie-knives and revolvers, but of innate strength of will, that was exhilarating to come in contact with—one could forgive him for a little roughness, as they could a winter wind for the vigor and healthful energy which it provoked. He came across others like a salt breeze of that ocean with which he was familiar.

Philip, who had not so much talking to do as his father, and consequently more leisure for observation, noticed that the stranger scanned with a searching eagerness the faces of the women who came in to wait on the table; and that his eyes glanced at every new-comer, and out of the windows and doors, as if looking for some one.

" Hope he has no designs on our property," thought the young man. " Can't afford to lose any more at present. But, pshaw! he isn't an abolitionist, I'll be bound! He talks too much common sense."

While the dessert was being brought in, Captain Slocum broached the subject which had evidently been on his mind, underneath all others.

" The business which brought me here to-day, Colonel Fairfax, was to inquire after a colored woman whom I have heard belongs to you—have you a slave, an elderly woman, called Maum Guinea?"

"I wish I could tell you something about her, sir. I've as much curiosity to hear from her as you have, I presume," was the answer, with a good deal of irritation in the tone.

"Then you no longer own her?"

There was so much disappointment in the tone of the question, that the family looked at him in surprise.

"Why do you wish to know?"

"Don't look at me so suspiciously," half-laughed the stranger. "I have no intention of stealing her, nor of inciting her to run away. But I should like to buy her, very much indeed. In fact, that was the principal object of my long journey to Louisiana; and I should be willing to give you all she is worth possibly to you—she's getting rather old, you know, and can hardly be called a first-class servant any longer,"—a touch of Yankee business carefulness suddenly dashing the eagerness of his manner. Now, the Captain would have given one of his little fingers for the property in question, if he could not have obtained it otherwise; but he did not choose to betray this willingness until necessary.

"Maum Guinea is good for her work many years yet—there's no better cook this side of New Orleans."

"She's a capital cook," responded the Captain; and his mind went back to certain exquisite suppers served up in a little room in a secluded corner of a great northern city, years ago — wonderful suppers, whose daintily-concocted dishes derived an inimitable flavor from the piquant sauces of sentiment and secrecy which no scientific Soyer ever combined—a face of marvellous beauty beamed upon him from the other side of the table, and Maum Guinea, dignified and stately as some antique Egyptian empress, in her richly-colored silken turban, dispensed elegant hospitality at his right hand. As this vision rose before him, like an enchanting mirage in the desert of memory, he forgot the present for a moment, and was aroused from a deep reverie by the planter remarking :

"If it's a first-rate cook you are after, I think I know a neighbor who would part with a woman I could recommend."

"I want Maum Guinea herself. Did I understand you that she was not with you now ? Could you give me any clue to her ?"

"I wish I could, Captain Slocum ! I wish I had some clue to her myself. The fact is, the wench, favored and petted by all of us though she was, up and run away about five days ago, and the devil of a trace can we get of her."

"I'm sorry, extremely sorry,"—and the stranger looked all he said.

"Not so sorry as I am, sir. I regarded her as a very valu-able servant. More mind and judgment than most of 'em— a great comfort to Mrs. Fairfax. Another of my best boys went with her. Fact is, our servants give us more trouble than they're worth. What with sickness and deaths, and accidents, and runaways, and improvidence, they keep us constantly in hot water. I wish they were all back in Guinea !"

"Have you given up all hopes of recovering the fugitives?"

"Why, no, not all hopes. We have officers on the watch at the different steamboat landings for twenty miles up and down the river ; if they should manage to reach the water, I doubt if they could get off. Where they are, I cannot guess. We've searched the woods and swamps thoroughly, and still keep a sharp look-out. They might possibly be concealed in some jungle yet, in the woods back of the plant-ation, if they could get enough to keep them from starvation, and could endure the cold. 'Twas a pretty brisk night, last night, for them to lodge out of doors. They're easily chilled, sir. There were three of them. One of my neighbor's girls

ran away with a boy of mine, and Maumy went along to see
that 'twas all right, I suppose."

"Aha! just so!" and again the Captain's mind recalled
certain circumstances of the past, which rendered it quite
probable to him that Maum Guinea might sympathize with
a pair of distressed lovers, and aid them in efforts to accom-
plish their hopes. "Well, Colonel Fairfax, I do not see as I
can take any farther steps in this business at present. I hope
that you will succeed in finding your servants; and in that
hope I shall remain in the village as long as there is the
slightest prospect. If you should find Maum Guinea, I stand
ready to purchase her at any reasonable price, and therefore
desire that she shall not be punished in any way."

"Oh, I never punish my people to hurt or disable them,
sir. If I do get her back, probably I shall be willing to
dispose of her; for if she's discontented and uneasy, we shall
not have so much confidence in her. Where are you stopping
in the village, Captain?"

"At the St. Charles Hotel, where I should be happy to
hear from you, if you have any news to communicate. I
will no longer trespass upon your hospitality, but with many
thanks for your kindness, will bid you good-day."

They had left the dining-room, in the course of their conversation, and the stranger now resumed his hat and gloves and
stepped on to the portico. The planter felt curious to know
the reason of his especial interest in Maum Guinea, but there
was nothing in the demeanor of his visitor which encouraged
him to inquire; and he allowed him to ride away, with his
curiosity ungratified.

That evening Philip paid his tri-weekly visit to his
betrothed. The light and laughter, the music and jesting of
the family-circle gathered in the parlor, were very pleasant for
a while; but it is surprising what a fondness the most

common-place lovers acquire for moonlight and solitude,
whispering breezes, starlit walks, and all the sympathetic
influences of out-door nature. So it was not long before the
young man was wrapping a shawl about Virginia, and the
two, arm-in-arm, slowly promenaded the pleasant verandah,
in the sweet whisperings and sweeter silences of "love's
young dream." A slender crescent of silver shone in the
dark-blue sky; a heavy dew, which was gradually congealing
into frost, sparkled over the lawn.

" You are not in earnest, Virginia, about making me wait
a year ?"

" Mother thinks I'm very young to be engaged, Philip."

" Well, you're not too young to be married, if you are to
be engaged," laughed the lover. " You half-promised me
you know, the last time we talked about it. As long as there's
nothing in the world to prevent or interfere, what's the use of
losing a whole year out of one little life of happiness ?"

The young girl wondered, too, " What was the use ?" but
it was not in her feminine nature to yield immediately to such
pleasant argument.

" Since Rose ran away, papa has felt troubled about his
affairs. I'm afraid my *trousseau* will not equal my wishes, if I
do not wait until he gets his business straightened out a little."

"*Trousseau!* nonsense! you just want to provoke me, little
one! I shouldn't know or care, if you had but one dress to
your name."

" Well, *I* should—and so would you! It's very pretty of
you to say so—but we must do as other people do, for all that."

" I suppose your father has not heard from the fugitives?"

" Of course not. And for my part, I'm glad of it—I really
am, Philip. I'd rather put the wedding off a year, than to
see Mr. Talfierro carrying my poor Rose off. Poor girl! I
hope she isn't cold or hungry."

Philip admired the bright tears which rushed into the young girl's eyes as she thought of the hardships which might imperil her pretty favorite.

"I think she really loved Hyperion; and any one could see his heart was bound up in her. He could not take his eyes off from her, when she was around. If papa had known just how the case stood, I do not believe he would have sold her. Wouldn't it have been nice, Philip, to have had them married when—when—we were, you know,"—very timidly—"they would have been such useful servants, and so happy together."

"It would have been charming," responded he, pressing the little soft hand. "If I could only find them, I would buy Talfierro's claim out, myself, and make you a wedding-present of your waiting-maid."

"Oh, *would* you? What a generous, kind-hearted man you are, dear Philip."

"Dear" Philip! She had never ventured to call him that before, and the lover was in ecstasies.

"If I had to dispose of my favorite riding-horse, and half my trinkets, to raise the money, I would do it gladly," he pursued, animated by her grateful admiration. "But the deuce of it is, Virginia, we can get not the least clue to them. That Maum Guinea is a terribly sharp woman! It's her doings, I feel sure, their getting off so cunningly. By the way, there was a person at our house to-day, who wished to buy her—came on purpose. A Northener, too, and opposed to slavery, as he did not hesitate to tell us. I liked his honesty. I'd trust him with my people, without fear; a man who had the courage to speak his mind as moderately and as frankly as he did. I am curious to know what in the world he wants to purchase Maumy for."

While he was speaking, a dark figure flitted out of the

negro-quarters, and took up a position at a corner of the
verandah which was buried in shadow, remaining there,
listening and motionless, while the young people continued
their conversation.

"I wish we could get track of them, Philip."

"I wish we could. The stranger was evidently so anxious
to secure Ginny, that he would have paid a good round price
for her."

"It's strange what a Northerner could want of a slave."

"Yes; and what he should have come down here for, to
look her up. He told us he had traced her from her old
home in Virginia, to her master in New Orleans, and from
there, here. He seemed much troubled to be disappointed at
last."

"What did he seem to be?"

"He gave his name as Captain Slocum; he's been captain
of a vessel some time, but not recently. He's got some
personal interest in her, I'm sure."

"I've always thought Maumy had some secret history·
She's a strange woman."

"It's a pity she took it into her head to run away just
now."

"Poor Rose! I can't help thinking of her, this chilly
night. I am afraid she is cold,"—and Virginia shivered inside
the warm folds of her shawl. "Every time I waken in the
night, I think of her. She's always taken care of me, since
we were children together, and I feel lonely without her."

Philip wrapped the shawl closer about his betrothed, and
they resumed their walk, forgetful soon of the unhappy fugitives, in their own consciousness of love and safety. The
dark figure which had skulked at the corner stole away, and
as it emerged into the moonlight of the open lane, it proved
to be that of Johnson. He had been driven to this resort in

his anxiety to learn the plans of his master with regard to
farther pursuit of the runaways.

"I mus' see 'em to-night," he muttered, "ef I can anyways
possibly get off. Dat overseer, he's 'spicious of me; he keeps
mighty sharp watch over me now-a-days. I mus' see 'em to-
night—'kase I'm sure Rose is hungry, and mos' worn out
a-waitin' for news. 'Sides, I mus' tell Maum Ginny what I
heerd 'bout *her*—'spect she'll know whedder it's good news
or bad."

But Johnson had no chance to get off that night. The
overseer came down the lane, and ordered him in pretty
sharply—it was past the hour at which slaves were allowed
to be out, and as he had some reason to suspect Johnson of
being in communication with the runaways, or proposing
to follow their example, he was keeping a stricter watch
than ordinary over his actions. Johnson knew that he must
be suspected, as he usually enjoyed privileges denied to the
common slaves.

The next day he contrived to get sent to the village on an
errand. He did not hurry himself, once there, but lingered
about the hotel, to catch a glimpse of the person who was
interested in Maum Guinea. Not having heard her story, he
had no clue to the link existing between her and this northern
sea-captain. He did not even know whether his purpose was
dangerous or friendly; but he resolved to find out, and to
allow this knowledge to control his actions. If this were a
friend of Maumy's, and a northern man, perhaps he might
aid the whole party of fugitives in making their escape. He
had a kind of confused idea that the whole northern race was
engaged in the benevolent pursuit of freeing colored people
from bondage.

After disposing of his master's errand, he proceeded to the
St. Charles with a basket of eggs, which he disposed of to the

steward for his own benefit, the eggs being a part of the
"lawful spoils" which occasionally fell to his portion, and
kept him in pocket-money. When he came up from the
kitchen, he lounged against a post in front of the house,
taking a survey of the various persons coming in and going
out, lingering in the bar-room or smoking cigars about the
doors. He was not long in determining that the light-com-
plexioned man, sitting on a chair in the verandah, tilted back
against the wall, reading a paper and casting occasional sharp
glances about him, was the person he was in search of·
Johnson hung around· for some time, not knowing how to
approach him; and finally went into the bar-room and purchased two or three papers of tobacco, and a bunch of cigars,
which he placed in his empty basket, and sauntered out along
the verandah.

"Buy a fus'-rate segah, massa?"

"I don't smoke."

"*Don't* you? Mos' gentleum does. Buy some 'baccy?"

"Don't use it, boy."

Seeing the fellow did not move on, the stranger looked up,
slightly annoyed; something in the manner of the mulatto
caused him to forbear ordering him off, and to glance at him
again.

"Massa from 'way up North?"

"Why, yes. I reckon I'm not one your yellow Southerns."
The Captain began to think this was some discontented slave,
who, perceiving him to be a Northerner, was trying to work
upon his sympathies. He had no idea of making trouble, or
mixing himself up with the business of others, and he
surveyed the intruder rather coldly.

"Massa wanted to buy a fus'-rate cook?"

"Not unless I find just the right one."

"I hearn somebody say you was 'quiring 'bout Maum Ginny."

" Well, what of that ?"

" Oh, nuffin'!"

Captain Slocum saw there was something behind the
assumed indifference of the man, who now picked up his
basket as if to walk away.

" Do you know anything about Maum Guinea, boy ?"

" I *use* to know 'bout her 'fore she run away."

" Do you know anything about her *now ?*" eagerly, but
lowering his voice.

" I's a berry pertikler friend of Ginny's, massa. I don'
want to see no harm happen to her. I's glad she's cl'ar'd
out."

" So am *I* a very particular friend of hers—the best she
ever had, or ever will have. I'm *sorry* she's cleared out.
Because I came here, hoping to do something good for her.
She would be glad to hear from me."

" Do you rea'ly t'ink she would, massa ?"

" I know she would. If I knew anybody that could give
me a clue to her whereabouts, they'd never regret it. Don't
look frightened, boy—I don't want to steal her—I mean to pay
for her handsomely."

" 'Twasn' *dat*, massa," answered Johnson, in evident trepida-
tion. " I mus' go now," and he glanced nervously at the parlor
window, close beside of which Captain Slocum was leaning,
and behind whose curtains he saw, as he followed. the startled
glance of the mulatto, the handsome but disagreeable . face of
an elegantly-dressed man. " I don' know nuffin' 'bout Ginny,
sence she run away, but I *use* to be great frien's wid her
Sorry she's gone off, jus' dis time," and as he stooped to pick
up his basket, he continued in a whisper : " Somebody a-lis-
tenin', massa ; but I's comin' round ag'in to-morrow," and he
was hurrying off across the square before the Captain had
time to realize what he had said. Johnson had been home

but a short time, before Mr. Talfierro rode up to Judge Bell's
in no very good humor; though he bowed with his usual
suavity to Miss Virginia as he passed her in the hall, on his
way to her father's library.

" I've just overheard your boy Johnson in confidential communication with that confounded Yankee who's hanging
about here, Judge," began the gentleman, as soon as the compliments of the day had been passed. " If you don't keep
your eyes open, you'll lose more of your property. It's my
belief, that he's nothing more nor less than a northern abolitionist. And further, I believe that Johnson knows, this
minute, all about the runaways, and where they are. I'm
tired of this fooling. I shall start for New Orleans to-morrow afternoon, if nothing is heard of the girl in the mean
time. Either the girl or the money, to-morrow, Judge. You
know I've been vexed about this, and kept waiting for a
week of very valuable time."

The Judge had no doubt, in his secret soul, that the time
of Mr. Talfierro was of immense value ; he acknowledged that
he had reason to feel irritated and out of patience ; said he
should take Johnson to task, in the hopes of getting some
satisfactory information, and that if none were obtained, the
gentleman's claim should be settled to enable him to get
away the following evening.

Talfierro then related the suspicious nature of the interview he had witnessed, and the two separated, mutually
inflamed against the innocent Northener for his kidnapping
propensities.

CHAPTER XIII.

A DANGEROUS KIDNAPPER.

"Sometimes a place of right,
  Sometimes a place of wrong,
Sometimes a place of rogues and thieves,
  With honest men among."

He deserves small trust,
Who is not privy councillor to himself.—Ford.

The holiday life of the negroes on Colonel Fairfax's plantation, was exchanged for the toil which was to occupy them
until Christmas came again.

The banjo and fiddle were hung upon the cabin wall, the
smell of roast pork and 'possum came to the ebon laborer
only in dreams.

It was upon a sparkling January morning that the field-
hands turned out to prepare the ground for the cane-planting

Captain Slocum, who had met Philip in the village, the
previous day, had been invited by him to ride out and
acquaint himself with the first steps in the process of making
sugar; he had accepted the invitation with pleasure, and it
was still early in the forenoon when the two rode forth and
joined the overseer, who was getting his gangs of men into
working order. The two chatted pleasantly together.

The sturdy Northerner took an especial fancy to the gay
and generous young man, whose character was written on his
expressive face. But while that congeniality of feeling was
springing up between them which comes of mutually generous
impulses, a storm was brooding at the house, of which they
perceived no symptoms.

Judge Bell, his usually agreeable mood ruffled by the fact of
his having a five-thousand-dollar note to pay in the afternoon,

had come over to communicate to his neighbor his well-
grounded suspicions that the plausibly-speaking stranger
was playing the base part of a kidnapper.

" Talfierro overheard the whole conversation between him
and my boy, Johnson ; and it proves his guilt conclusively.
I believe that he has not only been the agent in getting the
others away, but that Johnson and others of our most valuable
people are in the plot, and awaiting the first opportunity
for getting off," said the excited Judge.

Such news was of the most inflammatory character.
Worried and disappointed by their previous loss, neither of
them were in the mood to hear of farther depredations, nor
to be put to farther inconvenience, now, when a busy season
was about to begin ; their anger rose against the despicable
meddler who was even at that moment beguiling Philip into
betraying information to him which he was to use against them.

Having obtained the solicited loan from his friend, Judge
Bell rode back in all haste, to the village, in the first place
to settle his account with his New Orleans creditor, and in
the second place to get out a warrant for the arrest of Captain
Ephraim Slocum as a kidnapper, and procure the services of
the sheriff in carrying it into effect.

This latter step had been taken, and the two, going to the
hotel, expecting, perhaps, to find the person returned to his
dinner, did indeed meet him there under circumstances calculated to deepen their suspicions. Notwithstanding he had
been strictly forbidden to leave the plantation that day, they
saw, as they crossed the square, Johnson again in conversation with the stranger ; so absorbed was he in what he had to
say, that he did not perceive his master until his hand was
laid heavily upon his shoulder. His evident alarm and
agitation proved still further the consciousness of some guilty
secret.

Instead of eating the comfortable dinner which he had ordered at the hotel, Captain Slocum fasted that day, upon bread and water, in a little apartment of the square log house which served as the parish jail. There was not much satisfaction in kicking the wall, or tramping about the narrow oom, or using strong language, deep not loud—but such as it was, the Captain took the full benefit of it.

"I'd rather pay a hundred dollars an hour than be kept here, at this crisis," he muttered. "She may be starving, or they may get away! Confound the luck! I wish I could, at least, have finished my talk with that mulatto. He might have done something, in my place, while I was shut up in this hole. I suppose, though, that he is a prisoner too, and perhaps being punished. Jerusalem! what an institution!"— and he dashed his boot against the wall, making a wreck of the plaster in that part.

"I'll thrash 'em!" he continued, after his irritation had again risen, momentarily subdued by the satisfaction of shattering the plaster—"I'll thrash those two old fogies within an inch of their lives, when I get out of here. They may bring on their bowie-knives and revolvers—I won't condescend to use anything but a raw-hide on *them!*"

He was in no very courteous mood, when, just before twilight, the jailor unlocked the door, ushering a visitor into his apartment. It was Philip Fairfax.

"I come to tell you how mortified and grieved I am at the hasty step which my father has taken," said the young man. "I know that he is mistaken in his suspicions—I could swear to it, Captain Slocum—and I feel that no apology can atone for these unpleasant proceedings. Rest assured I shall use all my influence to get you out of this as quickly as possible."

"Thank you," was the dry response.

"I am indignant myself," continued Philip, "when I see how touchy and suspicious my own people are. They make themselves ridiculous by their fears and their extreme sensitiveness. If our institutions stand on a firm basis, they need not be so eager to defend them, nor so afraid of harm to them. I hope that I, for one, am free from such weakness. I despise a meddling abolitionist as heartily as any one; but I have no reason to suspect you of being one, and until I have, I give you my confidence and friendship freely. Do not visit your first displeasure at my father upon my head also; but allow me to ask if there is any way in which I can serve you. I am anxious to do so."

Captain Slocum was too ardent in his own feelings to resist the earnest manner in which Philip spoke; he shook hands with his visitor, and invited him to occupy the only chair of his apartment, while he seated himself on the little table where his bread and water still stood, vainly inviting him to partake of their luxurious refreshment.

"Is that the dinner that rascally jailor gave you?" suddenly inquired Philip, as his eye fell upon it.

"It's good enough for a kidnapper, isn't it?" queried the prisoner, smiling.

The young gentleman sprang hastily to his feet and knocked on the door with rather more than his usual indolent softness.

"Go to the St. Charles restaurant and order everything decent there is to be had. I'm going to take supper with this gentleman."

The peremptory tone of the order did not admit of argument; the jailor became suddenly very obliging; a clean cloth soon covered the table, and shortly thereafter the two sat down to it, carrying on their conversation during the pauses of an excellent repast.

"What have they done with the slave whose communication with me has furnished such evidence of a conspiracy?" asked the Captain.

"Judge Bell has confined him in the guard-house on his plantation for the present."

"He would allow *you* to see him, of course?"

"Oh, of course. No one suspects *me* of wanting to get rid of my own property, or my father-in-law's," laughed Philip

This was the beginning of a long interview, at the close of which the two separated, feeling still more confidence in each other.

CHAPTER XIV.

HOW THE FLIGHT ENDED.

My heart grows sick with weary waiting.
BAYARD TAYLOR.

Oh ! they listened, looked and waited,
  Till their hope became despair ;
And the sobs of low bewailing
  Filled the pauses of their prayer.—WHITTIER.

Sweet, as the desert fountain's wave,
  To lips just cooled in time to save.—BYRON.

"Oh, Maumy, I's so tired, and so hungry, and so cold!"

"Poor chile! you'll perish, sure enough, if we don't get out of dis, mighty quick. 'Perion ! what you settin' dar for, wid yer face in yer hands? Can't you cheer up dis poor baby? Jes' rub her hands—dey'r cold as ice ! See here, honey here's a few drops more of brandy. It'll warm you up."

"You need it yerself, Maumy. You give me de last piece o' bread—you've eat nothin' for two days, I know. Drink it yerself, Maumy."

"I shan't do nothin' of de kind. I's strong, and got

courage. You's a chile, Rose—poor girl, you haven't much sperit—no wonder! 'Perion! it's for *you* to be brave, and help her bar' her troubles. It don' look well to see a man settin' wid his face on his knees—givin' up, while thar's anything to be done."

" What *is* to be done, Ginny ?" asked Hyperion, looking up, showing a face worn and gaunt. " If dar was anything to be *done*, I'd do it. Its jus' setting here, waiting, dat uses me up. I can't bar' to see *her* a-sufferin'—dat's what takes de sperit out of me. I could starve to death myself, and willing, rudder dan go back—but I can't stand to see *her* so hungry and mis'able."

" Dar's no use waitin' any longer to hear from Johnson. If we hadn't waited on his advice we might have been far 'way while our stren'th lasted. Now we've got to start off wid empty stomachs. You must try and kill a coon, or cotch a fish, or somethin' 'fore we start to-night, or I fear Rose'll give out de very first night's tramp. She's weak as a chicken, now."

" Poor Rose !"—the half-despairing, altogether devoted look the lover gave the girl showed that all his anxiety was for her

He made no complaint of his own sufferings. Although he had not touched food for forty-eight hours, he cared not for himself, if only *she* were comfortable; they had cheated her into partaking of the last morsel, the day previous, and had themselves gone fasting.

" Yis, we must get off to-night," continued Maum Guinea. " If you don't get anything to eat in de woods, I mus' travel back to de plantation, and trust to luck to get something dar."

" Oh, how dare you, Maumy ?"

" I'll jes' keep a sharp eye out, and I'll get in some cabin, or de corn-bin, or I'll cotch a chicken—see if I don't, with-out getting caught, too. So, you jus' cheer up, chil'ren."

"It 'll take all one night to do dat."

"Dat's so. I'll have to get 'nuff to las' more'n one day 'cause we shan't make out to start till next evening."

"Maybe I'll cotch a fish," said Hyperion. "I's got a big pin dat I's made a good hook out of, and I's got a bit of string."

"It's bin such a long, long day," moaned Rose, "and it ain't getting dark yet. 'Pears to me de sun'll never set."

"'Pears to me de Sun of Righteousness will never rise," muttered Maum Guinea.

"Dar's no light for colored folks dis side of Jordan."

"Let's all go out and drown ourselves in de lake," whispered Hyperion.

"Don' talk about it, 'Perion," answered Maum Guinea, with startling energy, "don' talk about it! Do you know, dat's what dat water been a-sayin' to me ever sence we come here! Night and day—night and day, it jus' calls me and calls me to come rest from my troubles."

"Oh, don't say so, eider of you," shuddered Rose. "I ain't ready to die, yet,"—and she turned and pressed her lover's hand to her lips with a passionate gesture, full of the hope and warmth of youth and life.

And he—how could he feel ready to die, with that loving face before him, and those clinging arms reaching out towards him? He did not. It was only the passing impulse of a momentary despair. His resolve to do and dare, and only to perish in defence of what was dearer to him than life, rose up higher than ever in the midst of surrounding difficulties. His eye kindled, his lip compressed, the fire of a desperate will flashed out from his thin, haggard face.

"You shan't die, honey; you shall live and be free and happy," he said.

She tried to believe him; she crept closer to him,

and laid her head on his breast, trying to forget that she was famished and weary—that her bones ached and her flesh was sore and her heart faint.

So they sat a little while in silence and thought, that dark group, in the dim and dew-dripping cavern, waiting for night.

While they sat thus, they heard a long hoped-for sound. Johnson parted the screen, and stood before them once more.

"Have you brought us food?"

"Laws! I forgot all 'bout you must be starved!" he exclaimed, glancing almost in terror at their haggard faces. "But never you mind dat, now. Jus' come out dis ugly place, now and forevermore. Come!"

"'Tisn't dark yet. S'posin' somebody sees us," hesitated the *valet*.

"Never you mind dat! Don't s'pose Johnson would get you into danger, do you? Dar's nobody 'round dat'll hurt you. Come out!"

They did not stop to guess what he was so anxious to get them outside for; obeying him by impulse, they emerged from the low passage, and stood on the bank of the lake. As they turned to look toward the setting sun, they discovered a party of whites surrounding them—Colonel Fairfax, his son, Judge Bell, and several others.

"Betrayed!" cried Hyperion, with a fierce glance at Johnson.

Rose gave a dreadful scream, and threw herself against his breast.

One arm he placed about her; with the disengaged hand he drew out the revolver from his pocket. Maum Guinea pulled from her belt the keen knife which glittered there. Motionless, desperate, threatening — resolve and despair pictured upon the sickly yellow of their faces, their black eyes flashing, the miserable fugitives awaited the attack.

"Hyperion, my boy, put up that weapon," called out

Philip, in a hearty, cheerful tone; "it's mine, you rascal, and you musn't take liberties with it."

"Don't shoot," exclaimed Johnson, who was by the *valet's* side. "It's all right. Dey's your friends, and you mus' give up."

"Never!" responded Hyperion, tightening his hold on Rose, his eyes·turning in search of the man who had come between him and happiness. If Mr. Talfierro had been present then, it would have gone hard with him—but he was not of the party."

"Not if I tell you that we've come especially to publish the banns of marriage between you and Rose?" asked Philip.

Hyperion looked incredulously into his master's smiling face; surely, there was no anger there, no threat of punishment, nor in any of the faces to which his glance now quickly wandered.

"What you say, massa?" he stammered, slightly lowering the threatening revolver. Rose had heard and comprehended with the rapid instinct of her nature; she lifted her head, and gave a startled glance like that of a fawn.

"Where's Massa Talfierro?" was her first question.

"Gone back to New Orleans, where he belongs," answered Philip. You're mine, now, Rose. I bought you of that gentleman on purpose to make you a wedding-present to my wife, when I'm so happy as to have one."

"God bless you, Massa Philip," cried the girl, dropping on her knees and bursting out crying.

"It's a poor time to cry, Rose," spoke Judge Bell. "Dry up your tears, and come back to Miss Virginia. She can't get along without you."

"And you, Maumy, put up that knife, and take it home to cut bread with," added Colonel Fairfax.

"I don't car' for myself, massa, w'edder I ever go back or not. I'd as lief jump in dat lake as any thing else—but if it's all right, wid my chil'ren here—if dey are satisfied to go back and get married, I don't car' what becomes of me."

"Maybe there's good news for you, too, Maumy."

"No! no! never no good news for Maum Ginny dis side of Jordan."

"Just look about you, and see if you can't brighten up a little."

Something in the planter's tone warned Maum Guinea. that he was not jesting; she threw a suspicious glance about her, which suddenly turned to one of amazement and delight. One of the party, whom she had not previously observed, had stepped forward, and lifted his broad-brimmed hat, which he had purposely kept slouched over his face.

"Capt'in Slocum!"

"Yes, Guinea, the very same. Jerusalem! didn't expect to see *me*, did you?"—and the fresh, sea-ruddy face twinkled all over. "How d'ye do, Mrs. Guinea? I've come a good ways to see you, and I was plaguy near to not making out, after all. Tricky as ever, I see!"

She did not stop to take his extended hand—she did not hear half his remark—she just dropped the knife, ran towards him, and held up her arms:

"Judy! Judy! Tell me 'bout my chile, Capt'in."

"Mrs. Slocum is well and hearty, I thank you—a good wife, and the mother of three of the—*purtiest* babies."

"De Lord bless you—de Lord forever bless you, Capt'in! Be you speakin' the trute?" cried the woman, convulsively. And what with fasting, and the rapid change from one terrible tumult of feeling to another, her strong frame gave way, and she fainted as she spoke.

"It's hunger," said Johnson, tersely; "dey're all starving."

"Oh, ho!" cried Philip; "then we won't pause here for explanations."

One of the company had a flask of whiskey, and all three of the fugitives were obliged to take a portion, before they could rally sufficiently to attempt the return to the plantation.

When Maum Guinea came to herself, Captain Slocum lifted her on to his own horse, and walked back by her side. By the time they reached the forsaken cabin, she had heard and understood all her happiness.

"The first hour after I got back from that voyage," told the Captain to her, "I flew to the nest of my bird. I comprehended in a moment that something had happened; how dreadful, I could only conjecture; and you'd better believe the frame of mind wasn't enviable in which I set about making inquiries. That police-officer was true to his promise; I met him the next morning, and he told me the whole story. He said that he had seen Judy, and had been the means of getting her off to a safe place, when she ventured back to find out about her mother; he had told her that it was no use for her to risk her own freedom, since her parent was already carried off beyond reach. He persuaded her to keep quiet, and await the return of her lover in a private house, where he found her board with a respectable person.

"Here," cried the Captain, "I found my birdie, her eyes red with much weeping; and I made it my business to cheer her up and take her into my own particular care. We were married the very next day. Judy got her dress made, and wore it—the very one you bought her. I rewarded the officer handsomely, and made him my friend for life; and I made the good widow who'd taken my birdie in, a present of such a splendid shawl and dress that she opened her eyes in mute astonishment. I tell you, Judy made a lovely bride. I took her up to my friends in Maine; they loved her and admired her, and were so proud of her, I could never rake up courage to confess that she was an octoroon. It wore on

my wife's mind. She wanted me to go and buy her Maumy
and bring her home. I saw that she felt even more then she
said. So, after our first baby was born, she held up the pretty
creature, and pleaded with me to bring her Maumy to her.
I couldn't stand it; so I wrote to her owner, Mr. Gregory,
offering any price for her he might see fit to ask. I got an
answer that he had sold her, and had no clue to her present
whereabouts. Poor Judy cried and grieved. I promised her,
as soon as I could find time and means, to hunt you up, if
you were anywhere on this western continent. Years
slipped by, and there was always something to prevent; till
finally, I saw it wore on Judy's mind and health, and I just
told her, one evening, about six weeks ago, that I was going
down South after her mother, and I shouldn't come back
without her, or news of her death. So the next morning I
kissed her and the babies, and started. I went to Mr.
Gregory's—found out all I could about the master who purchased you and took you to New Orleans—got trace of you,
and thought I had actually laid my hands on you at last,
when—blast it, there was more trouble than ever. They had
me in jail for a kidnapper—and all kind of times. However,
upon an intimate acquaintance with Mr. Philip, there, I found
that he was not a bad-hearted young man, and that he would
do the right thing by the rest of the fugitives, if they could
be found—he'd made up his mind to purchase the girl, himself, and thus secure the smiles and gratitude of his lady-love,
as well as a nice attendant for his future wife. So he did it,
and sent Mr. Talfierro—confound his selfish skin!—adrift,
mourning. And I came down handsomely, to the Colonel,
with a pocket full of gold, and you're my Maumy, now,
Guinea. I've got the deed for you in my vest, here—all
right. You see, Johnson found out I was your friend, and
he took me into his confidence. The poor fellow was in

www.ingramcontent.com/pod-product-compliance
Lightning Source LLC
Chambersburg PA
CBHW032257280326
41932CB00009B/601